A Kingdom
without a
King

A Kingdom without a King

The Journal of the Provisional
Government in the Revolution of 1688

Robert Beddard

Phaidon · Oxford

In memory of my parents,
John Ernest and Ellen Louisa Beddard

Phaidon Press Limited
Littlegate House
St Ebbe's Street
Oxford OX1 1SQ

© 1988 by Phaidon Press Limited

British Library Cataloguing in Publication Data

A Kingdom without a king: the journal of
the provisional government in the revolution
of 1688.
1. Great Britain. Political events, 1688–
1689. Readings from contemporary sources
I. Beddard, Robert
941.06'7

ISBN 0–7148–2500–X

Typeset, printed and bound in England by Butler &
Tanner Ltd, Frome

Frontispiece illustrations: p. 1. James II's Great Seal.
Engraving from A. van Loon, *Histoire metallique des
XVII Provinces des Pays-Bas* (The Hague, 1732).
Frontispiece: James II. Oil painting by Nicolas de
Largillière. Greenwich, National Maritime Museum.

Photographic Acknowledgements

14, 25 Studio 85, Bob Thorogood Photography,
Burnham-on-Sea; 9, 46 by permission of the Master
and Fellows of Magdalene College, Cambridge; 6
courtesy of the Board of Trustees of the Royal
Armouries; 5, 7, 27, 28, 32, 48, 50 reproduced by
courtesy of the Trustees of the British Museum; 44
Conway Library, Courtauld Institute of Art; 13,19, 20,
21, 22 Guildhall Library, London (Godfrey New
Photographics, Sidcup); 17 Mansell Collection, London;
Frontispiece, 4 National Maritime Museum; 10, 36, 37
reproduced by gracious permission of Her Majesty the
Queen; 40, 41 reproduced by kind permission of the
Rt. Hon. the Earl of Clarendon; 26 Dean and Chapter
of St Peter's, Westminster; 3, 8, 11, 12, 48 Sutherland
Collection, Ashmolean Museum, Oxford; 16, 23, 34, 35,
49 Bodleian Library, Oxford; 30 the Curators of the
Examination Schools, University of Oxford; 2 courtesy
of the Revd. the Rector of Stonyhurst College; 39 by
permission of Geoffrey Taylor, Esquire.

CONTENTS

PREFACE

The Revolution of 1688, unlike most controversial episodes in England's past, has not been allowed to fall into oblivion, but has been continuously studied and debated ever since it occurred three centuries ago. Linked to long-living political ideologies and to longer-living religious faiths, it has never lost its power to fascinate successive generations, or to divide Williamites from Jacobites, Whigs from Tories, and Protestants from Catholics. Such was its acknowledged importance in the internal ordering of English government and society and in the transformation of England into a major European power, that, before the impact of Marxism in the 1930s led to the misappropriation of the term to the Great Rebellion and its abortive republican sequel, it was simply referred to as 'the English Revolution'.

From Gilbert Burnet, the first begetter of the Protestant Whig interpretation of English history in the late seventeenth century, to G. M. Trevelyan, the last confident exponent of that interpretation in the early twentieth century, it continued to attract a sequence of historians. So assured was their command of the evidence, and so commanding their literary prowess, that more recent historians of the 1688 Revolution have devoted very few pages of their accounts to reconsidering the events of the revolutionary period. Indeed, Maurice Ashley in 1966, John Carswell in 1969, and J. R. Jones in 1972, to name only the most notable of these, preferred to enquire into the background of the Revolution, to concentrate on William of Orange's invasion and assess the factors impelling him to make his 'descent on England', with the consequence that the Revolution seems little more than a tail-piece to the invasion, with no claim to a historical life and importance of its own.

Here, I have essayed a different and more detailed approach, one which adheres to chronology, and, in so doing, seeks to unravel the domestic complexities of the story. After dealing with the threat to the Protestant Ascendancy under James II, in order to establish the social, political, and religious context of the Revolution, I have focused attention on what actually happened in England during November and December 1688 in an attempt to understand how events fell out the way that they did, and why William's expedition resulted in usurpation, even though he had repeatedly disclaimed any such intention in coming into his father-in-law's Kingdom. An important distinction is drawn between the steady progress of a welcome invasion and the sudden onset of divisive revolution: a point on which the contemporary record is very clear.

For all that it sprang out of a foreign invasion, the logic, timing, and organization of which depended primarily on European considerations, the Revolution took place on English soil and in response to English circumstances, local and national. It was not the product of a minutely conceived and carefully executed master plan on William's part. Fast-moving events in London and the South (not, I hasten to add, in Nottingham and the North), over which neither he, nor James, had any control, played an essential role in the unfolding drama, and none more so than the formation of a provisional government in the capital. The City of London and the metropolis at large were the scene of decisive action. It was there, on 11 December, that James was first panicked into flight by the menace of violent Anti-Popery, and the approach of William's army; there, on the 13th, that the loyalist peers of the provisional government decided to rescue James from Kent, and bring him back to Whitehall on the 16th; there, that the returned King subsequently failed to re-establish his authority through the opposition of the City Whigs; and there, too, that the Prince's emissaries were forced to go to expel him on the 18th. Finally, it was in the City of London that William's rule found political recognition and the vital funding which sustained it until the Convention voted supplies.

But, if the Englishness of the English Revolution is not in doubt, neither is its revolutionary character, *pace* the advent of petulant revisionism. By specifically showing how it was that the Kingdom came to lose its lawful, God-given King in 1688, not by abdication, nor by desertion, but by forcible deposition on 18 December, well before the so-called transfer of the crown in the Convention of 1689, I wish to emphasize the most revolutionary phase, and, I submit, the most revolutionary aspect of the 1688 Revolution. I mean, of course, the dynastic revolution, which was effectively over, if not entirely done with, before December was out, and which a hastily summoned Convention was called upon to ratify in the new year. For the first time since 1485 the legitimate reigning monarch was overthrown, and with him the rightful House of Stuart. His son and heir, the Prince of Wales, was callously cast aside, and the claims of legitimacy spurned by the triumphant usuper. Little wonder that Archbishop Sancroft saw 'no difference' between Lord Protector Cromwell and the Prince of Orange, 'but that the one's name was Oliver, and the other William'. The sole concession wrested from the Prince by the votes of the House of Lords and the lobbyings of the politicians in 1689 was a grudging admission of his wife, Mary, to a share in the title, but not in the exercise, of his newly seized sovereignty. That violent means had accomplished a 'totall change of persons' on the throne of a hereditary monarchy was, in itself, sufficient to constitute a revolution in the eyes of contemporaries, whether they gloried in it or not.

The genesis of this book began with the discovery of the official Journal, or minute book, of the little-known provisional government formed by the peers of the realm during James's absence from London between 11 and 16 December 1688. I was alerted to its existence by casual references contained in the Earl of Clarendon's *Diary* and the Marquess of Halifax's autograph memoranda on the Peers' meetings. An investigation of the Rawlinson MSS in the Bodleian Library turned up a draft Nonjuring tract, corrected by Bishop Turner, in which there were quotations from the Journal. After years of searching through the aristocratic papers of the period I eventually found it in the collection of Richard Temple-Nugent-Brydges-Chandos-Grenville, 1st Duke of Buckingham and Chandos, which, since 1883, has been housed in that great repository of unread manuscripts—the British Library. My discovery, it must be said, was not of the original, but of a clerical fair copy: MS Stowe 370. I am grateful for pemission from the Trustees of the British Library to publish my edition of the document.

Its authenticity is vouched for by the subsequent locating of a dozen or more of the Peers' scattered original orders, with which it has been collated. These, plus the extracts included in Turner's tract and Halifax's memoranda, substantiate the reliability of the copy, the texts being identical, save for a number of minor scribal variations. In editing the Journal I have retained the original spelling, modernized the punctuation and capitalization, extended abreviations, omitted duplications, and altered the layout to fit into fewer printed pages. Editorial additions appear in pointed brackets (as in all other quotations from original sources), and connecting narrative in square brackets. Slips of the pen have been silently corrected.

I acknowledge with gratitude the help and encouragement I have received from my colleagues at Oriel, Mr. Walter Mitchel, Dr. Jeremy Catto, and Dr. Mark Whittow; also from Dr. Gerald Aylmer, Master of St. Peter's; Dr. Jeremy Black, of Durham University; Dr. Peter Barber and Miss Frances Harris, of the British Library; Mr. John Creasey and Mrs. Janet Barnes, of Dr. Williams's Library, the Trustees of which I also thank for permission to publish portions of Roger Morrice's Entering Book; Mrs. V. E. Aldous and Mrs. J. M. Bankes, of the Corporation of London Records Office; Fr. M. K. O'Halloran, S.J., the Revd. Rector of Stonyhurst College; Mr. Jeremy Smith of the Guildhall Library; Mr. R. C. Dean, Vicar of St. Andrew's, Burnham-on-Sea; Dr. Pieter van der Merwe, of the National Maritime Museum; Dr. Malcolm Rogers, of the National Portrait Gallery; and my former pupils, Dr. Kenneth Fincham, Dr. Andrew O'Shaughnessy, Dr. Paul Seaward, Mr. Henry James, and Mr. Colin Harrison, who have endured innumerable accounts of my disturbing what Charles Lamb delighted to call 'the elder repose of the manuscripts', and have helped to clarify my findings. Finally, I thank Miss Jane Higgins and Mrs. Valerie Kemp for their warmly appreciated secretarial services.

Oriel College, Oxford,   R.A.P.J.B.
The Feast of SS. Peter and Paul, 1988.

1 William of Orange on horseback, with the fleet anchored in Tor Bay. Oil painting by Jan van Wyck. Greenwich, National Maritime Museum.

THE DYNASTIC REVOLUTION

When, in 1660, a fiercely Protestant English nation recalled the exiled Stuarts to the throne of their royal ancestors, it never for one moment dreamt that within the compass of a few short years James, Duke of York, the second son of the Anglican martyr, Charles I, and heir presumptive to his brother, King Charles II, would turn his back on the Protestant Church of England and embrace the forbidden rites of the Roman Catholic Church. On the eve of the Stuart Restoration it was not the least of their assets that all three sons of the murdered Charles I had remained Protestant. Having endured impoverishment and withstood the temptations of exile in Catholic Europe, there was no reason to suspect their fidelity to the Church of England, which, after 1660, resumed its accustomed place alongside the hereditary monarchy, as one of the bastions of a revitalized Protestant Ascendancy.

So determined was the Protestant ruling class to safeguard the religious orthodoxy of the restored monarchy, that in 1661 Parliament passed a new law incapacitating from public office all who dared to defame the King by affirming him 'to be an heretick, or a Papist', or by accusing him of endeavouring 'to introduce Popery'. It knew from bitter experience that there was no more effective way 'to incite or stir up the people to hatred or dislike of the person of His Majestie or the established government'. Such charges, which belonged to the stock-in-trade of faction-mongers, had contributed to those 'great and deplorable confusions', which had engulfed church and state in the Great Rebellion, and brought on the country 'the miseries and calamities of well nigh twenty yeares'.[1] Without its impeccably Protestant record it is to be doubted whether the House of Stuart would ever have been restored at the invitation of repentant Protestant rebels and staunch Protestant Royalists in 1660.

It was, therefore, with amazement and alarm that the Protestant Royalist, John Evelyn, noted James's abstaining from communion in the Chapel Royal on Easter Day 1673. He confided his inner sense of foreboding to the secret pages of his diary: 'What the Consequence of this will be God onely knows, and Wise men dread'.[2] Later, in the same year, the Duke resigned all his offices rather than offend his conscience by taking the anti-Catholic oaths and declarations required by the newly enacted Test Act.[3] Three more years passed before he finally forsook Protestant worship, and 'appeared no more in the Chappell' at Whitehall, 'to the infinite griefe' and, Evelyn believed, the 'threat⟨e⟩ned ruine of this poore Nation'.[4] His fears for the safety of church and state, for the Church of England and the hereditary Stuart monarchy, were widely shared, not just by ordinary folk, but by the entire governing class.

Looking back from the political calm of Charles II's last years, the eminent parliament man, Sir Edward Dering, identified James's conversion as the turning-point in the growth of unrest and faction among his fellow Protestants, for, he maintained, it 'gave no unreasonable foundacion to feare that, the King having no children, when the Duke should come to the crowne, the protestant religion would be at least opprest, if not extirpated'. For the first twelve years of Charles II's reign, from 1660 to 1672, the English 'lived in peace, plentie, and happinesse above all nacions of the world. But this blessing was too great to be continued long to those who deserved it so ill as we, and then the nacion began to thinke that the court enclined to favour poperie and France'.[5]

In a Europe which largely adhered to the Augsburg principle of 1555, that the religion of the prince determined the religion of his people, the religious 'apostasy' of the heir of the Ruling House presented Englishmen with a terrifying prospect. The exaggerated fear of Popery which four generations of Protestantism had bred in the nation meant that there was bound to be a violent reaction to any Stuart who went 'awhoring after foreign gods'. Overnight, the conversion to Rome of James, Duke of York, was seen to confer on Catholicism an influence at Court and in the counsels of the realm, which was not only unwarranted by the number, status, and ability of its adherents, but was also in violation of the laws of the land. After more than a century of unremitting Protestant hostility the Catholics constituted less than one per cent of the population of England and Wales.[6] Though they were better represented in the aristocracy and gentry, they had lost their hold on the greatest families, and years of official denial had robbed them of political and administrative experience. Prohibited from worshipping in public, excluded from university education, debarred from government office, and forbidden entry to the royal presence without special licence, they were treated as political and social outcasts. Some measure of the enmity and dread with which the nation regarded Popery can be seen in the brutal, but eloquent fact, that for a Protestant to turn Catholic was, in the eyes of the law, to commit a treasonable act—an act of disloyalty against the Protestant crown of England.

Today it may seem odd to many that the question of religious profession was a matter for public, indeed for political concern, given the modern separation of politics from religion and the dilution of religious conviction within the community. But, if we are to make sense of James II's England, it is imperative to realize that it was, first and foremost, a credal society, in which religious beliefs were expected to play, and often did play, a decisive part in the shaping of political conduct. Despite fashionable thesis-mongering on the decline of religion in the century and a half following the Reformation, seventeenth-century England was officially, by law, and effectively, in practice, a deeply Protestant country, whose people liked to regard themselves and their rulers as the chief patrons of the Protestant interest in Europe. The English Reformation, carried out under the auspices of the Tudor monarchy, had refashioned the medieval unity of church and state as twin aspects of a single *respublica Christiana*. In place of the universal authority of the Papacy it had set the national authority of the crown. By this unique arrangement, made in parliament and guaranteed by parliamentary statute, the kings of England became the Supreme Governors of the Reformed Church of England. As Defenders of the Faith—the Protestant faith—they were rendered an unqualified obedience by their subjects.

After the sectarian challenges of the Cromwellian Interregnum, which had turned 'the world upside down', the Stuart Restoration saw an emphatic return to the pre-civil war concept of the unity of church and state, as a means of first setting, and then keeping, the world the right way up. By 1660 the governing class was less, not more, tolerant of religious nonconformity. In a spate of parliamentary legislation, much of it highly penal in character, it reduced those Protestants who separated from the national Church to the rank of second-class citizens, by denying them the right of public worship and refusing them access to office in the state and preferment in the church. So it came about that newfangled Protestant Dissenters were forced to join that older breed of nonconformist, denominated 'Popish recusants', that is Catholics who refused to attend their parish church. Religious privileges and civil liberties were reserved for communicant Protestants of the Church of England 'as by law establisht', and denied Catholics and Dissenters. Profoundly conservative in their social and political outlook, the landowning families of the Protestant Ascendancy looked askance at the least appearance of subversive Popery or 'trouble-church' fanaticism. They cherished their Church, and the laws that safeguarded it, as a bulwark against religious unrest, arbitrary rule, and civil commotion. Any action taken against their Church was perceived as a threat to their own highly privileged position in society: a position which, like that of the Church of England, was based on the rights of property and the laws of parliament.[7]

If confessional allegiance loomed large in the life of the subject, it tended to dominate the life of the prince in the era of 'sacred majesty'. With the exception of the *politique* Charles II, who set little personal store by religion, the strongly held beliefs of successive Stuart monarchs, from Mary, Queen of Scots, in the late sixteenth century, to Queen Anne in the early eighteenth century, coloured their view of life and affected their conduct of government. With Mary of Scotland, whose Tudor descent brought the Scottish Stuarts to the throne of England in 1603, it was Roman Catholicism which shaped her life and sealed her death. With James VI and I, the first of the Protestant Stuarts, it was Calvinism which predominated; with Charles I, Arminianism; and with James II, Catholicism again. Of James II's post-revolutionary successors, Mary II favoured latitudinarian Anglicanism; William III, strict Calvinism; and Anne, the last of the Protestant Stuarts, pietistic high churchery. For the most part, these royal preferences reflected changing emphases inside a basic, national, Protestant tradition, and were, as such, more or less compatible with the creed of the country and its people. Only in the case of downright 'Popery'—to give Catholicism its contemporary and correct English name—was Stuart preference anathema; though it has to be admitted that, in popular estimate at least, Charles I's ritualistic brand of Arminianism smacked of Rome. It is no coincidence that, once the Reformation had taken firm root in Britain, those Stuarts who were Catholic, or were thought to be sympathetic to Catholicism, came to grief: in 1587 Mary, Queen of Scots, was executed for treason by her Protestant cousin, Elizabeth I; in 1649 Charles I was beheaded after a bogus trial conducted in the name of his Protestant subjects; and in 1688 James II was dethroned by his Protestant nephew and son-in-law, William of Orange.

I The Dynastic Context

Modern historians are reluctant to admit the peculiarly unmodern character of the Revolution of 1688. Yet, like so much of Stuart 'politics', it is best understood in dynastic and confessional terms: in terms of a family—albeit a Royal Family—dispute, in which the senior Catholic and junior Protestant branches of the House of Stuart took different sides. For the Catholic King James the Revolution, which cost him his throne, was more than a political disaster, it was a personal tragedy of crippling proportions, the emotional impact of which goes a long way towards explaining his unexpected failure of nerve in the crisis. In the course of November and December 1688 he saw his family torn apart by the deepening consequences of William's invasion of England. At first, he had been unable to believe that 'a Person so nearly Related' could embark on 'so Unchristian and Unnatural an Undertaking' against an uncle and father-in-law.[1] But, incredible as it seemed to a fond and loving father, his two daughters, the Protestant Princesses, Mary of Orange and Anne of Denmark, children of his first, Protestant marriage to Anne Hyde, and his Protestant nephew, William of Orange, had turned against him and his second wife, the Catholic Queen Mary Beatrice of Modena, and their infant son, James Francis Edward, the Catholic Prince of Wales. Worse was to follow, when, following his and his family's flight to Catholic France, William and Mary accepted the formal offer of his throne from the Convention on 13 February 1689. The Revolution of 1688-9 was essentially a confessional and dynastic revolution.

For William of Orange, champion of the beleaguered Protestant interest in Europe, the decision to invade England had not been an easy one. He came not as a political adventurer seeking to usurp his uncle's throne, still less as the head of a hostile power, but as the Protestant representative of the ruling House of Stuart—as the husband of James's elder daughter, Mary, who for the past eleven years had been her father's heir, and as Charles I's grandson, who, after Princess Anne, was himself third in the line of succession. If, as he was assured, many English Protestants believed the newly born Prince of Wales was an impostor, a changeling foisted by a Catholic King and Queen on a Protestant Kingdom, in order to perpetuate Catholic rule by defrauding the rightful Protestant heirs of their inheritance, it was his duty to investigate the truth of the matter.

Dynastic considerations aside, William had powerful political and religious motives compelling him to intervene in English affairs. His position inside the complex federal constitution of the United Provinces was that of *Stadhouder*, an officer of state, not a hereditary monarch. Though the House of Orange had prestige and wealth, it derived its sovereign status from the petty principality of Orange in Southern France. Only in times of war was this limited constitutional office capable of quasi-monarchical powers, when the state's need for military leadership became uppermost. As a minor prince and a convinced Protestant, William was alarmed by the overtly expansionist policies of the Catholic King of France, Louis XIV, who, he believed, desired not only to dominate Europe, but to eradicate Protestantism.

His ability to oppose French ambition had long been hampered by the pro-French sentiments of the *regenten*, the burgher patricians of Amsterdam, who, as practising republicans, distrusted Orangist dynastic aspirations. By 1688 their views had changed. Louis's occupation of Orange in 1682, his revocation of the Edict of Nantes in 1685 (which sent a flood of French Protestants into Holland), and his pursuit of a trade war against the Republic in 1687 considerably strengthened William's position. Alarmed by the might of Catholic France, the Protestant Dutch began to fear that James II's diplomatic neutrality cloaked secret French sympathies. His growing estrangement from his Protestant subjects, and the cordiality with which Louis XIV greeted the birth of a Catholic heir in England, seemed to confirm their suspicions of a Catholic league between the two crowns.

William took advantage of this revised Dutch perception of Anglo-French relations and sought the support of the States General for his plan for armed intervention in English affairs. He rested his case, not on private dynastic concerns, but on public national policy. Only by rescuing the English Protestants by vindicating the existing legal establishment, and persuading James to hold a free parliament, could the Dutch hope for a firm English commitment to opposing Louis XIV's European designs.[2]

William's intentions in undertaking his expedition—too long the subject of historical dispute—are clear. The evidence for them is full, consistent, and convincing. His letter of 6 October to his Catholic ally, the Emperor Leopold I, spoke of 'the misunderstandings' between James and his subjects, which had 'come to so great extremities', that they were 'on the point of breaking out into a formal rupture'. It was, to say the least, a dubious reading of English politics: one which he owed to his adherents in England and to the Whig exiles in Holland, neither of whom were capable of an unbiased view. Encouraged 'by many peers' and other men of substance, he felt obliged to intervene. His objectives, though backed by military force, were political and legal. He assured the Emperor that he had 'not the least intention to do any hurt to His Britannic Majesty, or to those who have a right to pretend to the succession of his Kingdoms, and still less to make an attempt upon the crown, or desire to appropriate it' to himself. He wished to redress illegalities by securing the clergy, nobility, and people in their religion, liberties, and rights 'in a parliament lawfully assembled and composed of persons duly qualified according to the laws of the nation'. He hoped from this 'that there will follow a good union and sincere confidence between the King and his subjects, that they may be in a condition of being able to contribute powerfully to the common good'—that is, to the peace of Europe, in which both he and Leopold were immediately concerned as opponents of French aggression. He re-iterated his aversion to religious persecution and promised liberty of conscience to Catholics.[3] Three days later he wrote to the Marquis de Gastagaña, Governor of the Spanish Netherlands, in identical vein.[4] In the United Provinces the States General were similarly assured that in going to England he 'had no intention of removing the King from the throne'.[5]

All of these statements agree exactly with what William said in his all-important *Declaration*, issued from The Hague on 30 September, which formally announced to the English nation 'the reasons inducing him to appear in arms in the Kingdom of England'. Overlong and cumbersome though it was in its expression, it nevertheless made plain that the Prince's purpose in coming to England was threefold: first, to support the laws, liberties, and religion of the people, which he did at the invitation of 'a great many Lords, both spiritual and temporal, and by many gentlemen and other subjects of all ranks'; secondly, to investigate the birth of the 'pretended' Prince of Wales, in which he and his wife had 'so great an interest ... and such a right, as all the world knows, to the succession of the crown'; and thirdly, to bolster the Protestant interest in Europe by gaining an influence over England's foreign policy, particularly in the disposal of its military and naval resources. The instrument chosen for realizing his aims was 'a free parliament', which, in itself, showed that he wanted a peaceful solution to the problems posed by a Catholic monarch ruling a Protestant Kingdom. In itemizing the 'great and unsufferable oppressions', under which English Protestants groaned, care was taken to cast the blame not on King James, but on his 'evil counsellors', who, William claimed, had attempted 'to alienate the King more and more' from himself and the Princess of Orange. By their persistent advocacy of Popish counsels they had driven a wedge between James and his children.[6]

II Royal Catholicism

The strength of the monarchy and the policies of the monarch together account for the spectacular re-emergence of the fear of Popery in the life of the nation after 1685. Had James II not been a powerful monarch, he could not have attempted what he did, let alone have defied the wishes of the bulk of his subjects for so long. A marked improvement in the yield from crown revenues gave him a degree of financial, and therefore of political, independence unknown to Charles II before the last years of his reign.[1] After the suppression of Monmouth's rebellion in the West, and that of Argyll in Scotland, in 1685, there were no threats to internal peace. The creation of a large standing army saw to that. By November 1688 it stood at around 40,000.[2] It also

2 The sumptuously decorated cover of James II's Holy Week Book, containing the rites and ceremonies of the Catholic Church for the sacred paschal season. Stonyhurst College, Lancashire.

permitted a policy of armed neutrality abroad, the least time-consuming of foreign policies, which suited the King's preference for domestic politics. He had, then, the opportunity to frame more ambitious policies at home than any of his Stuart predecessors, and the capacity to pursue them. Paradoxically, it was from this position of unaccustomed monarchical strength that his fatal weakness sprang. An ardent Catholic, free to rule as he pleased, he chose to indulge his personal religious ambitions. In contrast to Charles II, who abominated even the 'talke of conscience in busines‹s›',[3] James allowed his private conscience to dictate his public policy. In this he resembled his father.

Though James spoke, rather misleadingly, of his desire to 'establish' Catholicism in England, he meant only to ensure its survival by putting his co-religionists on an equal footing with members of the Church of England. His infamous design to enslave English Protestantism, when looked at dispassionately, amounted to little more than allowing Catholics to worship in public, educate their sons at Oxford and Cambridge, and seek employment in the state and armed forces. The trouble was that none of these modest objectives could be obtained without his appearing, at best, to challenge, and, at worst, to undermine the Protestant Ascendancy and its respected role in society as the guardian of 'the religion, laws, liberties, and properties' of the governing class. Such were the legal privileges of the Church of England, with its statutory monopoly of worship, education, and office, that James could not give to Catholics without being seen to take away from Protestants, and that at the expense of flouting the laws of his Protestant predecessors. From an antagonized Protestant viewpoint, the King appeared to be the aggressor, the real revolutionary, not his conservative subjects who strove to uphold the laws of the land. It was from this genuine contemporary perception of his Catholicizing policies that the classic Whig interpretation of his reign, as a 'Popish tyranny', bent on 'subvert‹ing› the constitution of the Kingdom', derives;[4] it cannot be explained solely, or even principally, by reference to the retrospective partisanship of nineteenth-century Whig historians.

Already turned fifty, and with only Protestants to succeed him, James came to the throne late in life. If succour was to be given to the dwindling Catholic community, he had to act swiftly. But the urgency with which he pursued his religious objective cannot be explained merely in terms of his being an ageing monarch in a hurry. The explanation lies deeper than that. For the past thirty-six years he had taken second place to his elder brother, whom he had obeyed, even to the extent of not announcing his conversion: a denial which greatly rankled with him. He felt ashamed that he had been forced, as he put it, to 'lackey' his conscience to Charles's convenience.[5] Before 1685 his letters to the Pope had declared his 'unalterable desire' to 'advance the Church and the Catholic religion',[6] but while Charles lived he had been unable to do anything, except check the levying of recusancy fines.[7] At last, as King, he was in a position to own his faith, and make amends for what he regarded as his shameful public neglect of it.[8] Few that knew him questioned the sincerity of his convictions, or his determination to promote the Catholic cause, once he was able. The Duke of Lauderdale, who had ample opportunity to study him, summed him up with prophetic skill. He was 'as very a Papist as the Pope himself, which', he said, would 'be his ruine', for, had he 'the empire of the whole world, he would venture the loss of it, for his ambition is to shine in a red letter after he is dead'.[9] The truth was James had the restless, high-minded, over-optimistic zeal of the convert, which in a solidly Protestant country could only spell disaster, as Charles II had recognized: hence his remark to Sir Robert Howard, 'that his brother, the Duke, longed impatiently for a crown, and, if he had it, he would lose it within three yeares'.[10] His prediction was not far wide of the mark; it took him nearer four.

James's efforts to improve the lot of his Catholic subjects undeniably strained the allegiance of his people, and lost him their affection. Yet, the assertion made in the Bill of Rights of 1689, that he had endeavoured 'to subvert and extirpate the Protestant religion', is false.[11] An examination of his ecclesiastical policies shows that they were directed towards advancing Catholicism, not attacking Protestantism. He was utterly opposed to the forcing of conscience, which, he believed, was 'under the dominion of God alone'. That his 'judgment' was 'much against persecution for conscience sake, or matters of meer religion', was shown by his criticism of the Church of England for its persecution of Dissenters,[12] and by his dislike of Louis XIV's forcible conversion of the Huguenots, for whose escaped brethren he authorized charitable collections in England.[13] Equally false is the notion, affirmed by the Convention in 1689, that everything he did proceeded from 'the Advice of Jesuits'.[14] True enough, he did favour the Society of Jesus, and Fr. Edward Petre, Clerk of the Closet, and Fr. John Warner, his Confessor, were prominent at Court; but the Jesuits were the servants, not the masters of the King. As a Catholic prince James naturally consulted, patronized, and promoted Catholic priests, but, like his Protestant father and grandfather before him, he was the maker of his own policies.[15] In this respect his reign does not differ from the overall pattern of sacred monarchy in the Stuart century. It is a myth, which dies hard, that Catholics do only what their priests tell them.

The 'very handsom‹e› speech' made by James to his Privy Council on 6 February 1685, 'promising to maintain the laws and religion' of the nation 'as they were then established', re-assured his Anglican Tory supporters—though not for long.[16] Within the week he went publicly to Mass, and, a portent of things to come, gave instructions that the doors of the Queen's oratory were to be 'set wide open' during the times of service.[17] After four generations of repression and concealment he believed that the Church of Rome should be visible, and her sacramental ministry available to all. With him this was a point of honour no less than of policy, though he fully appreciated that, if he was to succeed in replenishing the depleted ranks of the Catholic laity, there was a need to win converts from the ranks of influential Church of England men.[18]

Had he been worldly wise, content to exercise his religion in private, and sacrifice 'the true service of God' by disregarding the plight of ordinary Catholics, as he had been forced to do under Charles II, matters might have gone differently for him. His German cousin, Philipp Wilhelm, the Catholic Elector Palatine, managed to do just that, and, in consequence, kept the loyalty of his Protestant subjects. But James was both a divinely ordained prince and a *dévot*. Having waited a long time for the crown, he rejoiced in being a Catholic King, and refused to deny himself and his co-religionists the freedom to worship God in public—a privilege which the meanest of his Protestant subjects took for granted.[19] He insisted that Catholicism, as the royal religion, should be given a high profile at Court and in the capital. He opened the royal chapels to the public. He commissioned Wren to build a sumptuous Catholic Chapel at Whitehall, and lent personal and financial support to the establishment of 'mass-houses' and schools in London. In 1685 he welcomed Bishop Leyburn as Vicar Apostolic of England, paid his salary, and gave him lodgings in Whitehall;[20] in 1686 he sent the Earl of Castlemaine on an embassy of obedience to Rome;[21] and in 1687 he granted the Papal Nuncio, Archbishop Ferdinando D'Adda, a public reception at Court.[22]

In the brief flowering of Jacobean Catholicism the year 1688 saw a distinct step forward. Two new 'mass-houses' were opened in the heart of fashionable London in Lincoln's Inn Fields; one by the Franciscans, the other by the Dominicans, thus adding to the opportunities for Catholic worship.[23] At Easter the Imperial Ambassador reported to Vienna that Catholics could visit eight or nine altars of repose in the capital, not counting those in the Catholic embassy chapels.[24] Following Pope Innocent XI's decision in January, effective episcopal authority was restored in England for the first time since Mary Tudor had sat on the throne. The Kingdom was divided into four pastoral Districts, each with its own Vicar Apostolic, the prelate appropriate to a missionary field, such as Protestant England was deemed to be by Rome. The King paid the stipends of the four bishops, which were set at £1,000 *per annum*: a clear mark of the value he put upon their sacred office and ministrations.[25]

By mid-May the last of the papal nominees had been consecrated in the Queen Dowager's Chapel at Somerset House,[26] and the four Catholic bishops—Dr. John Leyburn, Bishop of Adrumetum, Dr. Bonaventure Giffard, Bishop of Madaura, Philip Ellis, Bishop of Aureliopolis, and Dr. James Smith, Bishop of Calliopolis—prepared to go down to their Districts. Before doing so they published a *Pastoral Letter*, summoning the faithful to the work of Catholic evangelization. Whereas, in the past, before James had lifted the penal laws and granted them 'a share of the Government', the exercise of their religion had been 'private and precarious, tending rather towards the Preservation of it' among themselves, 'than a Propagation of it in others', they were now to make public profession of their faith and win converts to the Church by their shining lives and good deeds. They were exhorted to improve the opportunity James had given them, and, for inspiration, the royal example was held up to them: 'You live under a Prince of your own Religion, to whom, next unto God, you owe this Felicity. You have his Power to protect you in the free Exercise of your Religion, and his Example to encourage your discharge of this Duty in a most edifying manner'.[27]

Such open avowal of the King's espousal of 'the conversion of England' enraged Protestants. The bishops of the Church of England—'gli pseudo-vescovi', false bishops, as the Papal Nuncio D'Adda called them[28]—were outraged at the establishment of what they saw as a rival episcopal jurisdiction, and disgusted that royal authority, once their own greatest political possession, could be turned against the Protestant faith it was, by law, supposed to defend. Thereafter, the Protestant clergy, especially in London, took every opportunity to denounce the Church of Rome and 'all its detestable enormities' in a sustained attack from the pulpit and the press. Their alarmist preaching did much to arouse the Anti-Popery of the metropolis, in which low churchmen and Dissenters abounded.[29]

III The Tories' King

James's accession, in spite of its peaceful appearance, had not been automatic; quite the reverse. It was the outcome of the most intense political campaign ever waged by the hereditary monarchy on behalf of a legitimate successor—a successor whose Catholicism made him personally and politically unacceptable to a large body of English Protestants, particularly to low church Anglicans and Dissenters. As these ultra-Protestant 'Whigs', with their policy of excluding 'a Popish successor', came to dominate the House of Commons between 1679 and 1681, the Stuart Princes had formed a powerful alliance with the high church 'Tories' of the Church of England, led by James's Protestant brothers-in-law, Henry Hyde, 2nd Earl of Clarendon, and Lawrence Hyde, 1st Earl of Rochester, and Dr. William Sancroft, Archbishop of Canterbury. It was to the success of this high church Tory alliance that James owed his crown; it had not only defeated, but routed, the Whig advocates of Exclusion.[1] He was in every sense the Tories' King. They and the Church of England, to which they belonged, were the sheet anchor and strength of his monarchy. Of their attachment to Protestantism there was no doubt. They resented Charles II's dying a Catholic as a 'great cheat' put upon them[2], and viewed any relaxation of the penal laws as tantamount to disestablishing their Church.

In persistently furthering the cause of Catholicism James gradually eroded Tory affection, and with it the basis of consent on which the authority of his government rested. In effect, he committed political suicide. Having failed to obtain even a modicum of Catholic relief from the 'Loyal Parliament' of 1685—a parliament composed of high church Tories, he progressively abandoned his 'old friends'. In desperation he cast about for an alternative 'King's party', to act as a counterweight to the unyielding Tories. In 1687 he turned to a policy of outright religious toleration, such as Charles II had repeatedly and unsuccessfully tried before him. By cultivating Catholics, Dissenters, and compliant churchmen he hoped to compass the impossible: a parliament of nonconformists and nonconformist sympathizers, who would give him what he wanted. Thus, during 1687 and 1688, the last years of James's reign, there was much motion, but precious little movement, towards his desired goal of a statutory enactment of Catholic emancipation, which alone could permanently improve the status of his co-religionists.

Yet, conspicuous as was the King's failure to win either religious or political converts to his way of thinking, his unflagging zeal and heavy-handed methods of persuasion produced results as unexpected as they were disastrous for his hold on power. They stimulated the growth of virulent Anti-Catholicism inside the Church of England, which, confronted by the Catholic

3 *'Sala Reggia'*: the birth of the Prince of Wales, the Catholic heir to James II's throne, 10 June 1688.
Italian engraving, Rome, 1688.

claims of the Church of Rome, began to renew its Reformation roots. They also enhanced the attractions of the Protestant reversionary interest, centred on William and Mary, to such an extent that not one in twenty Englishmen was prepared to accept the prospect of another 'Popish successor' in the birth of a Catholic heir to James's throne. The mere announcement of Queen Mary Beatrice's pregnancy, late in 1687, was resented as tending 'to give a rebuke to the Prince of Orange' and his setting himself up as the patron of the Protestant interest in England.[3] It was this Protestant predisposition to refuse recognition to a Catholic heir, not any irregularities in the birth of Prince James Francis Edward on 10 June 1688, which occasioned the convenient, though palpably crude and preposterous fiction, that the infant was 'a suppose child' smuggled into the Queen's bed in a warming-pan.[4] The fabrication is as clear an instance of Protestant superstition as history affords. By April 1688 William had decided to invade England, on condition that he was 'invited by some men of the best interest' to come over and 'rescue the nation'.[5] Before July was out he had received such an invitation from seven political and religious malcontents: the Earls of Danby, Shrewsbury, and Devonshire, Lord Lumley, Bishop Compton of London, Edward Russell, and Henry Sidney—the 'Immortal Seven' of Whig hagiography, who, unable to oppose James's policies unaided, appealed to the Prince for outside help.[6]

IV The Dutch Invasion

By 6 October the Dutch fleet was under orders. Shore leave was cancelled, and final stores taken on board. It comprised over 200 assorted transports and a fighting escort of 49 men-of-war and 10 fireships.[1] On the 19th the Prince embarked, making *The Brill* frigate his headquarters.

All was ready to set sail on his long-awaited mission 'to maintain the Protestant religion and freedom of the Kingdom of Great Britain'.[2] His strategy was to avoid a sea–battle, which, irrespective of its outcome, would antagonize English patriotism—the very force which his skilful propaganda campaign had sought to annex to his cause. In line with the argument of his *Declaration* he continued to appeal for the support of the nation. His appointment of the English Protestant, Arthur Herbert, one of James's dismissed Tory officers,[3] as Lieutenant-Admiral-General of his fleet, was more than the reward of a partisan. It was a deliberate move to underline the domestic status of his expeditionary force and advertise the peaceful purpose behind his coming. There was no declaration of war either on England, or on England's King, and Herbert's orders were drawn accordingly. He was to convey William's army to England, not engage James's fleet under Lord Dartmouth.[4] The difficult logistics of transporting an army across the Narrow Seas, within range of a hostile fleet, were made more hazardous by the unpredictability of winter weather, as was immediately seen at its first putting to sea on the 20th, when a ferocious gale scattered the fleet, driving it back to Hellevoetsluys. By the 23rd it had re-assembled. Structural damage was less than had been feared. The chief loss was of time and horses. On 1 November the fleet again put to sea.[5] In the interval, a period in which morale plummeted, the Whig exiles completely panicked, and tried to push William into launching an attack on the English fleet, but he held fast to his strategy.[6]

Given the reported concentration of the royal army in and about London, and the need for his troops and horses to recover from the crossing, the landing place had to be well away from the capital, but not too remote to challenge the King's 'evil counsellors' and their plans to oppose him. William's options were, therefore, limited. He could aim either for the North, or the

4 William of Orange's fleet, 1 November 1688. Dutch engraving by Adriaan Schoonebeeck, Amsterdam.

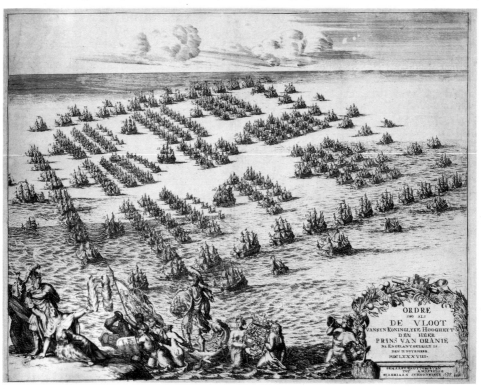

South-West, for he was against dividing his forces. The North was favoured by his supporters in England, particularly by Danby, who had a better base for concerting a rising there, and, according to Burnet, by William himself.[7] The Prince's instructions to Herbert, calling for subsequent diversionary operations in Scotland and the West of England, confirm this.[8] In the end it was the arrival of a strong east wind—the celebrated 'Protestant wind' of Whig epic—that decided the direction he took,[9] not advance planning, and certainly not any last minute attempt to ditch Danby and the northern lords for fear of incurring unwanted obligations.[10] William's fleet in 1688, like Philip II's Armada in 1588, was at the disposal of providence: *Deus flavit*. After striking a northerly course from Holland, the fleet veered south-west with the wind on 2 November, slipped past the English fleet stationed on the Gunfleet, off Harwich, and entered the Straits of Dover. With wind and tide against him there was little that Dartmouth could do to catch the Dutch; and the near-mutinous state of his captains, who had already addressed the King for a free parliament, ruled out the mounting of punitive raids once the invaders had landed.[11]

The vast variegated flotilla, stretching for many miles, presented 'a brave sight' to onlookers crowded on both sides of the Channel to watch it pass by.[12] In daylight it was 'like a thick forest' of masts and sails;[13] at night like a glittering constellation of stars twinkling in the dark. As if to advertise his mission, William's guns saluted both Calais and Dover Castle, while martial music sounded from the decks of his warships. An eye-witness on board ship noted approvingly: 'France trembled at the sight and England, seeing her deliverer coming in full sail to her aid, trembled with joy'.[14] From the mast of *The Brill* streamed the English colours, bearing the legend: 'The Liberty of England and the Protestant Religion'; beneath them those of the House of Orange with its defiant motto: '*Je maintiendrai*'—'I will maintain'.[15] Carefully avoiding Portsmouth, where James's illegitimate son, the Catholic Duke of Berwick, commanded an Irish garrison, William made for Tor Bay,[16] the most convenient anchorage between Southampton and Plymouth. The fleet, having overshot its destination, was yet again obligingly wafted into Tor Bay by a sudden shift of the wind to the west. There it dropped anchor. After the return of a reconnaissance party William landed at Brixham, a small fishing village to the south of Tor Bay. It was the afternoon of 5 November: the anniversary of that earlier Protestant delivery from Popish gunpowder, treason, and plot, which had spared the life of his great-grandfather, James I, and of Parliament in 1605.

The landing was unopposed. Protected by Herbert's warships and the prevailing westerly wind, the disembarkation was completed inside two days.[17] On the 9th William entered Exeter, the local capital, with detachments of infantry and cavalry. Though received with 'great acclaim' by the populace, the gentry, clergy, and mayor declined to visit him.[18] They had been set a compelling example of loyalty by their diocesan, Bishop Lamplugh, who fled to the King's Court in London, where he was instantly rewarded with the vacant Archbishopric of York.[19] Lamplugh's withdrawal prompted the Prince to remark that in leaving 'his flock' the Bishop had 'committed the care of it to him'.[20] Far from being downcast at his reception, and contemplating a return to Holland, as has sometimes been alleged, he ordered Herbert to arrange for a convoy to take the transports home and to mount guard against French aggression.[21] His own attention he gave to establishing an effective military and civil administration.

William's army numbered around 15,000—12,000 foot, 3,000 horse. It was composed mainly of foreign mercenaries, many of them Catholic, drawn from a variety of sources, Dutch, German, Swiss, and Scandinavian, besides those belonging to the House of Orange. There was a substantial Huguenot presence in his Guards and in the cavalry,[22] and, more unusually, '200 Blacks brought from the Plantations of the Neitherlands in America'.[23] Conspicuous among the infantry were the six battalions, under Hugh Mackay, of the Anglo-Dutch Brigade, a British formation on loan to the Republic, which James had unsuccessfully tried to repatriate earlier in the year.[24] Yet, for all its polyglot character and religious diversity, William's army constituted a disciplined force, well officered, and well equipped to do battle. Its commanders, headed by the veteran Protestant ex-Marshal of France, Friedrich Hermann von Schomberg, had no say in formulating the political objectives of the expedition. They remained firmly in William's hands. Indeed, if his supporters in England had the courage of their convictions, he hoped to spare his soldiers the rigours of fighting, for he saw the function of the army primarily in defensive terms. It was there to protect him, not attack the King.[25] Only if he were 'obliged' to fight, would he do so:[26] hence his landing far from James's army, and the slow pace of his advance towards the capital, once he had established a bridgehead at Exeter. He was content to play a waiting game, to give time to his hidden allies to rally to him and to the clandestine conspirators in James's army to desert. He had no wish to open hostilities. Having provided himself with three months' pay for his troops,[27] he could afford a leisurely approach to the problems before him.

Why, then, did he bring so large an army with him, if he was aiming at a peaceful settlement from the start? The answer is simple. He required two things of his army: protection and power. First, he had to be sure that he could defend himself against superior odds in the field, should the necessity arise; and secondly, he relied on military might to put political pressure on King James and his Catholic Court. A smaller task force might well have fulfilled the former requirement without meeting the latter.[28] Contradictory as it may seem, William needed a powerful army for his pacific policy to work. He intended to use his military muscle to prize the Catholic priests and 'evil counsellors' away from the King's side—preferably by frightening them away!

V William's Supporters

There was one section of the expeditionary force whose political and religious views mattered to William, namely the large contingent of discontented English and Scottish exiles, who served as volunteers in his army, or chose to accompany him on his mission. They included in their

5 The landing at Tor Bay, 5 November 1688. Dutch engraving, 1688.

ranks enough disreputable types to disturb any decently run kingdom that did not happen to agree with them—disgruntled peers, redundant MPs, proclaimed traitors, escaped spies, fugitive rebels, suspected republicans, renegade officers, and mischievous divines: casualties, in the main, of the defeat of Exclusion in England and of the continuation of Lauderdale's iron rule in Scotland.[1] Among the English were Lords Macclesfield, Wiltshire, Mordaunt, Coote, Shrewsbury, and Savile, and well-connected gentlemen, such as Sir Robert Peyton, Sir John Guise, Sir Rowland Gwynne, Sir John Hotham, Sir William Waller, Sir Richard Buckley, Sir Edward Villiers, Henry Sidney, Edward Russell, William Harbord, Henry Herbert, John Locke, Dr John Hutton, Colonel Thomas Tollemache, and Captain John Cutts. The prominent Scots were Lords Leven, Melville, Sutherland, Cardross, Forfar, Colville, and Elphinstone, Sir James Dalrymple of Stair, James Johnston of Warristoun, Andrew Fletcher of Saltoun, and James Stewart. Among the Protestant ministers of religion three were of note: the maverick episcopalian, Gilbert Burnet, the canting Presbyterian William Carstares, and the nonconformist Robert Ferguson—suggesting the embryonic pan-Protestant alliance which the Prince, an old-fashioned predestinarian Calvinist, personally favoured. For good measure the ex-Leveller, Major John Wildman, and the murderer of Archbishop Sharp of St. Andrews, John Balfour of Kinlock, were of the party. There were many lesser figures: mostly survivors from Monmouth's rebellion, 'many Scotch', and an 'abundance of officers turned out of Ireland' by Lord Deputy Tyrconnell's Catholicizing policies.[2]

To begin with, the more able of them were given regimental or administrative posts in the expedition, but their real value to William was political and propagandist. Together with the 3,000-strong Anglo-Dutch Brigade, their presence lent colour to his claim to have come as a Stuart Prince on national business and at the invitation of James's subjects. As the army marched eastwards, and as he began to make decisions that affected the outcome of his enterprise, they sought to influence him by their advice. Solidly Whig in their politics and uncompromisingly Protestant, even anti-episcopal, in their religious outlook, they knew what political defeat and royal disfavour meant. Their lives, and in some cases their fortunes, had been broken by them. Though disappointed by the conciliatory tone of William's *Declaration*, they had joined the expedition as a chance to return home and reverse the policies which they had always opposed in church and state.[3] They hated not only King James and his Catholic régime, but their old political adversaries, the high church Tories, whom they identified as the true authors of the present ills and their inexorable enemies. Exile had not cooled their passionate Whiggery, but had enflamed it. In December 1686 one Tory, writing to another from The Hague, reported of the Whig *emigrés*: 'They still talke for the Bill of Exclusion, and jeere the Church ‹of England›, saying this is *our* King'.[4] In having rejected the policy of Exclusion, the Tories had a lot to answer for in Whig eyes.

As the King's most implacable enemies, these embittered Whigs were to play a more significant role than William could possibly have imagined when he admitted them to his service before leaving Holland. They were to provide him with a brand of radical thinking and a range of political and ecclesiastical contacts beyond what his own, rather limited, and largely Tory, political experience gave him. Only after the arrival at Exeter of Clarendon's heir, Lord Cornbury, and the Earl of Abingdon on the 14th,[5] followed by Sir Edward Seymour and Sir William Portman on the 17th,[6] did his camp begin to acquire a Tory dimension; and, even then, the Tories were outnumbered by such Whig recruits as Lord Colchester, Lord Edward Russell, Thomas Wharton, William Jephson, and Colonel Charles Godfrey, who brought with them 'the go‹o›d news that all p‹e›opell are of our side, and the ffleatt espetial‹l›y'.[7] The arrival of the first three—the sons and heirs of the Whig peers, Earl Rivers, the Earl of Bedford, and Lord Wharton—was deeply gratifying to William, who welcomed them as an earnest of the aristocratic support which would be his as he moved towards London.

During his stay in Devon the Prince made the fullest possible use of his English supporters, the Whig *emigrés* especially. His first night ashore he was found a lodging by Sir William Waller, who got his grudging brother-in-law, Sir William Courtenay, to lend him Forde Abbey, near

Newton Abbot.[8] In the days which followed Edward Russell and Lord Leven were sent to the Earl of Bath to negotiate the surrender of the royal citadel of Plymouth;[9] the Earl of Shrewsbury and Sir John Guise with '700 horse' were ordered to secure Bristol;[10] Lord Wiltshire and William Harbord, with Anthony Rowe, were appointed his commissioners for collecting crown revenues in the West.[11] With William's connivance, Burnet took over prayers in Exeter Cathedral,[12] while Ferguson commandeered the Dissenters' meeting-house.[13] Both were strenuous advocates of his cause in pulpit, prayer, and propaganda. Perhaps no service was more extraordinary than that performed by Admiral Herbert from on board his flagship, *The Leyden*, riding in Tor Bay. He was required to engage in an unusual form of naval bombardment. Having landed in a remote corner of England, so far from the mainstream of politics as to be, in William's telling phrase, 'out of the world',[14] it was necessary to announce the Prince's arrival and stimulate local response to his enterprise. Herbert was authorized to send individual written appeals to neighbouring gentlemen, inviting them, 'as trew Englishmen', to join forces with the Prince in his bid to rescue Protestantism and the rule of law. He enclosed copies of the Prince's *Declaration*.[15] In this fashion William and his allies worked to knit the West Country to his cause.

On occasion, Tory services were no less acceptable. Sir Edward Seymour, Speaker of the House of Commons in 1678, was quickly caught up in William's affairs. He was appointed to his Council,[16] and, when the army moved on, was left behind as Governor of Exeter.[17] He it was who proposed the key Association,[18] without which, he maintained, the Prince's supporters 'were as a rope of sand', lacking formal identity, so that 'men might leave us as they pleased', being 'under no tie' either to the Prince, or to each other.[19] In the coming weeks the signing of the Association—a promise to defend William's life and cause against all comers—became the test of goodwill towards him and his mission.[20] It was to be of considerable importance, for it helped to focus Protestant hopes directly on the person of the Prince.

While at Exeter the printing presses, including one imported from Holland, were set to work.[21] They produced some notable pieces of Orangist propaganda, including an impressive account of William's *Publick Entrance into Exeter*,[22] his stirring *Speech to the Army*,[23] and his spirited *Second Declaration*, which encouraged (erroneous) belief in the 'private league' between James and Louis XIV.[24] Other items were his *Speech to the Gentlemen of Somerset and Dorset*,[25] Burnet's *Form of Prayer* for a blessing on the expedition,[26] and copies of the influential *Memorial from the English Protestants to Their Highnesses*.[27] William's determination to carry out his declared aims was attested by a government informer, who reported to Whitehall that 'two impeachments of high treason', one against Lord Chancellor Jeffreys, and the other against Lord Chief Justice Wright, were printed 'by the Prince's command': the former framed as a 'manifesto', denunciatory of 'arbitrary' policies; the latter as 'articles', ready to be placed before parliament, when it assembled. 'Design'd to be dispersed when the Prince comes near London', they formed part of his campaign to rid the Court of 'evil counsellors', among whom James's ultra-Tory lawyers were reckoned some of the worst.[28]

Again, in pursuit of his *Declaration*, William discouraged respect from being shown to the title and person of the Prince of Wales. Though the Cathedral clergy were allowed to 'continue their prayers for the King', indicating that William did not regard his occupation of Exeter as constituting a conquest, they 'received severe command not to mention the Prince of Wales' in the prayers for the Royal Family.[29] This, in itself, demonstrated a difference in his attitude towards the King, with whom he wished to strike an accord, and the King's 'pretended' son, whom he rejected as 'supposititious'.[30] He also promoted the local call for a free parliament, the demand for which was fast becoming the *Leitmotiv* of Protestant protest throughout England.[31] By the time he left Exeter, on 21 November, William had 'a mighty full splendid court', which grew more so by the day. A letter of the 21st illustrates the way in which his presence had galvanized the West: 'For some dayes none of our gentry appeared, but now most of the gentry of the country have made visits to the Prince, and ... have resolved to defend the establisht laws and religion. Severall noblemen and gentry are also come from other counties, and also many of the King's soldiers dayly repair hither. The soldiers are marcht eastward. Here is a petition to the King for a free parliament promoting in this county, and . . . the gentry will also associate for their common defence'.[32] It was a remarkable achievement, one which was to be repeated at each stage of his advance towards London. To William and those who had ventured with him across the perilous sea the growing welcome must have been as music to their ears.

VI James's Advance and Retreat

James was caught in a dilemma. Now that William had broken through his naval defences and was advancing from Exeter unopposed, he could either stay in London and force the enemy to continue to march towards him, or he could go out to meet him and fight. Neither alternative was ideal, but on balance he favoured seizing the military initiative. He decided to try to confine William to the south-west peninsula. Despatching troops to Salisbury to establish a forward position, he ordered the Tory Duke of Beaufort to hold Bristol and sent a detachment to break Keynsham bridge.[1] Though anti-Catholic rioting continued in London, with some loss of life,[2] he prepared to march westwards, brushing aside the objections of his French military adviser, the Comte du Roye. On the morning of 17 November, just before he set out, nineteen peers, led by Archbishop Sancroft, presented a petition to him, calling for a free parliament as 'the only visible way' to settle grievances and prevent bloodshed.[3] 'At the reading of it His Majesty made exception to the word, *free*, but promised to call a regular parliament (such as they should think so) as soon as he hath beaten his enemies; also *grievances*, he said, was a harsh word'. Though he denied their petition, 'he dismissed them fairly, and desired their prayers for his safety and success'.[4]

Despite reports of defections to William, including that of his nephew, Lord Cornbury,[5] he set out leaving a 'strong guard' behind him to keep 'the rabble in some awe' and preserve 'the threaten'd chappels'.[6] His departure, which raised the spectre of civil war, with Englishmen ranged against Englishmen, saddened loyal observers: 'it made my heart ake to see him. God preserve him, and send us peace upon a good foundation'.[7] None doubted his 'full resolution to give the enemy battle' and 'give them no quarter'.[8]

Besides his warlike proclamations, which were everywhere in print,[9] James repeated 'the promise he had before made, that, if it should please God to blesse his arms with successe in this enterprize, he would divide the estates of as many as should be found abettors to the invasion amongst such of the soldiery as should signalize themselves in the action'.[10] Before leaving London the King made his will in favour of 'our most dear son, Prince James': the infant whose birth had triggered the invasion. In the event of his death, he directed that Queen Mary Beatrice was to have 'the sole gouvernance, tuition, and guardianship' of the Prince of Wales, until the age of fourteen, and the power to make and remove Privy Councillors at will,[11] thus ensuring a Catholic Regency for his Catholic heir.

The King reached Salisbury on the 19th. There everything went wrong for him. The winter rains bogged down his cavalry and disrupted supplies. A crippled postal service, aggravated by popular sympathy for William's cause, denied him reliable intelligence. Protestant unrest among officers and men, compounded by talk of further desertions, sapped the morale of his army,[12] while the news of Lord Delamer's revolt in Cheshire added to his anxieties.[13] Having driven himself into the ground with work and worry, his health gave way. For three days he suffered from persistent nose bleeding and a debilitating lack of sleep.[14] Yet, at this wretchedly late stage of the crisis, his military officers, Tories to a man, tried to pull him from the abyss. Led by his nephew, the Duke of Grafton, who had signed the peers' petition of the 17th, and was deep in the army officers' conspiracy to desert to William, they argued strongly against fighting. Grafton 'faithfully and plainly dealt with the King, telling him severall times he could not fight the enemy, neither by sea, nor land, whilst his army was under such great dissatisfactions, and how they would be removed now he knew not; therefore he humbly advised him . . . to send to the Prince to know his desires, and to come to terms with him, which would certainly be better now, while his army was entire and strong, then when it was weakened or broaken'. James did

6 James II's suit of armour by Richard Hoden, of London, 1686. The faceguard is pierced and engraved with the royal arms and the King's personal initials. This is the last surviving armour of an English King. HM Tower of London, Royal Armouries.

not take kindly to his advice. Shortly afterwards his second-in-command, Lord Churchill, backed by Colonels Kirke and Oglethorpe, 'confirmed what the Duke had said', though 'in more courtly language'; and, after them, the Earls of Feversham and Dumbarton, his staunchest commanders, 'told him they had the same sense, and humbly offered him the same advice as before', but 'it had as ill entertainment from them, as it had from those that went before them'.[15]

Surrounded by growing signs of disaffection in an army he had created, and in which he 'knew not whom to trust',[16] he accepted the military advice of his generals to retreat. At a council of war, on the 22nd, there was one dissentient[17]—the perfidious Churchill, who was for advancing only to make his desertion easier.

On the 23rd the retreat began. It was the signal for another and more wounding bout of desertions. 'Villany upon villany, the last still greater than the first':[18] James's nephew, Grafton; his favourite, Churchill; his son-in-law, Prince George of Denmark, with a train of noblemen— all went over to William. Such was the 'hurly-burly' of the retreat, with every man 'thinking of himself', that 'nobody minded the King', who was again plagued with nose bleeds.[19] News of collusive rebellions in Yorkshire and Nottinghamshire, instigated by the Earls of Danby and Devonshire, came through.[20] On the 26th James arrived back at Whitehall a broken man. There he learned of the unnatural defection of his daughter, Princess Anne, who, 'pretending that the King, her father, did persecute and use her ill for her religion, shee being a Protestant and he a Papist', had fled the Palace.[21] Accompanied by her bosom friend, Sarah Churchill, and her old mentor, Bishop Compton of London, she joined the rebels at Nottingham.[22] 'God help me', exclaimed James, 'my own children have forsaken me'.[23] At Court the Catholics reckoned 'the loss of the Princess as great as that of the army'.[24] All thoughts of resistance were over. In despair the King turned to the peers in London to save him.

VII The Hungerford Negotiations

At a hastily summoned 'Great Council' at Whitehall on the 27th, attended by 'about forty peers', James asked for advice. Rochester began by defending the petition of 17 November. He advocated the summoning of parliament and 'sending to the Prince of Orange'.[1] After 'long and learned debates', in which there was much plain speaking, and no little heartburn, the King was advised to call a free parliament, to grant a general pardon to those in arms against him, to name commissioners 'to goe to the Prince to know his intentions and to adjust a cessation of arms', to adhere to the Treaty of Nijmegen, and to dismiss Catholics from office: 'all which His Majesty received very favorably', granting the first three proposals, and referring the rest 'to the discretion of a parliament'.[2] The next day Lord Chancellor Jeffreys announced in Westminster Hall that the King 'would call a parliament' to meet on 15 January 1689, 'and that writts should pass the Seale on Thursday'.[3] Three Commissioners were appointed to go to the Prince— Halifax, Nottingham, and Godolphin.[4] They received their instructions on 1 December.[5] Besides acquainting William that a parliament had been called, 'in order to the composing of the present distractions', their commission was 'to adjust with him all such things as shall be necessary in order to the freedome of elections, and that the parliament may sitt without fear of disturbance to consult of … the peace of the nation'. As a step towards peace, they were to propose that William's army 'shall be immediately obliged not to advance nearer to London than the distance of fourty miles'. If that proved unacceptable, then they were to desire from him what 'preliminaries' he thought were 'necessary to that end', and to notify them to the King.[6] As an afterthought James issued an 'additional instruction', offering to remove his forces from London 'some reasonable time before the sitting of the parliament', so that it might deliberate freely.[7]

In response to a request from Lord General Feversham, William issued passports for the Commissioners on the 3rd, and took the occasion to ask for one in return.[8] For him the march had turned into a virtual triumph, and he showed no hurry to get down to business. From Hindon he moved to Berwick St. Leonard, then on to Salisbury, taking time off to visit the 'house and gardens' at Wilton and admire the Earl of Pembroke's van Dijks.[9] On the 6th he left Salisbury for Collingbourne, and, though the Commissioners were at Ramsbury that night, spent the next day riding about the countryside and viewing the Earl of Craven's mansion at Hampstead Marshall. He reached Hungerford 'just before it was dark'.[10] It is difficult to interpret William's behaviour as anything other than the deliberate pursuit of delaying tactics—part of the continuing war of nerves to which he subjected his adversary at every turn. On being met at Andover on the 5th by St. Leger, an officer of William's Guards, who had been detailed to conduct them to Ramsbury, the Commissioners 'asked him when the Prince intended to be there'. To this, 'he could not answer us positively, but said he had heard the Prince intended to go 20 miles tomorrow, and supposed he might be there as soon as we'.[11] For the King, impatient for re-assuring signs of progress, it was not an auspicious start to the negotiations.

It was not until 10 a.m., on the 8th, that the Prince received the Commissioners at Hungerford. They met in his bed-chamber at The Bear Inn. At his express 'desire' he was attended by the Lords and gentlemen who had joined him. He wished to impress the Commissioners with the strength of his support, and at the same time involve his supporters in the negotiating process. Their presence also served to prevent petty jealousies from breaking out among them. Halifax was the Commissioners' spokesman. Having delivered the King's letter and credentials to the Prince, he began by asking whether he 'should say to him what we had in command there, or if he would hear us elsewhere'. He replied that they should speak to him there. So the Marquess delivered 'their errand by word of mouth' to him, as he stood apart from the company at the window. 'The Prince said, he did not doubt but we had seen his *Declaration*, and he had little more to say, than what was therein expressed, touching the grounds and reasons of his coming into England, which was to maintaine the Protestant religion and to preserve the lawes and liberties of the people; but that those Lords, who had joined with him, being concern'd in the matter, he would send some of them to speak with us further about it'.[12] The Commissioners then withdrew to another room.

William next read the King's letter aloud to the company, observing, Clarendon thought 'with tenderness', that it was 'the first letter he ever had from the King in French', and not written 'in his own hand'.[13] The display of emotion was momentary, perhaps caused by James's still addressing him as his 'son and nephew'. The letter, which was brief, stated the purpose of the embassy. It was 'to settle' with him 'the necessary points regarding the meeting of parliament ... and to remove all obstacles which may hinder an accommodation'. The letter ended on a more cordial note with an assurance of the King's 'sincere disposition towards establishing a firm and lasting peace'.[14] Not trusting to his memory to repeat what Halifax had said to him by the window, William asked the Commissioners to put what they had said in writing, so 'that the Lords might consider of it', and named Schomberg, Oxford, and Clarendon to see to it, which they did.[15]

Surprised to find that Clarendon had got to the Prince before him, Halifax took the occasion to ask that Burnet should be sent to him. But William 'had no mind' that any of his attendants should communicate with the Commissioners. He knew that if the wily Marquess and talkative Doctor got together 'there would be fine tattling'.[16] A disappointed Halifax reported back to Middleton: 'we observed that there was particular care taken, that none of the English should speake to us, the reason for it being given us, that it was to avoyd giving any cause of jealousy to any of the Lords who might be disposed to it; and it was hinted to us, that many of the Lords were very suspicious, least an accommodation should be made, which might not provide so largely for their security as they expected'.[17] Evidently, some of William's Whig followers were distrustful that an agreement between him and the King might yet be to their disadvantage. Being proclaimed outlaws and rebels, they had need for caution, suspecting that neither Stuart wished to be caught fast in the snares of politicians. As yet uncertain of their hold on the Prince, they wished for nothing 'so much' as to encourage James 'to go away'. They had no desire to make him their prisoner; they simply wished him gone, out of their and the Prince's way.[18] After dining the Commissioners at The Bear, William used the 'unquietness' of the inn as an excuse to retire to Littlecote. Before he went he requested 'all the Lords and gentlemen, who were with him', to meet in the afternoon, 'and prepare an answer' to the Commissioners' paper.[19] He was not going to allow them to shirk their responsibilities. They had freely joined him, so now they must serve him, and help him to find a basis on which to accomplish the aims of his *Declaration*.

At noon 'all the persons of any quality, except those of the Scotch and Irish nation', who were not allowed a say in English domestic affairs, met, according to the Prince's nomination of them, 'in the biggest room in the inn'. That William was right to insist on his supporters' taking an active part in the negotiations was shown by the difficulty they found in appointing a chairman, for 'nobody had a mind to the office'. Eventually the Earl of Oxford, a peer of impressive lineage, but of less impressive abilities, 'was persuaded to take the chair'. The Prince's English secretary, William Jephson, next produced the Commissioners' paper calling for agreement 'upon such methods as might make the meeting of the Parliament', summoned by James for 15 January, 'free and safe'. A number of proposals were considered, but at length discussion was terminated by a motion, 'that the writs for calling a Parliament should be superseded'. Clarendon tells us that this was 'with great vehemency urged and seconded' by Sir Henry Capel, Sir John Hotham, William Harbord, and others. The reason which they gave for laying aside James's writs was their fear 'that they could not get into the House of Commons' by dint of their long absence from their countries. Others present, most notably Lords Shrewsbury, Abingdon, Colchester, and Clarendon, opposed the motion. But, 'being put to the vote, after a long and warm debate, it was resolved, that the repealing the writs for the calling a Parliament should be one proposal to the King in order to a treaty'. Thus the ground was cut from beneath the Commissioners' feet. 'It was urged, that now we had nothing further to do; for, the whole errand of the commissioners being to consider of methods to make the meeting of the Parliament free and safe, if it were resolved that the writs should be superseded, what could we do else?' The answer was that 'the resolution was taken'. On that the meeting broke up.[20]

Clarendon's explanation of so radical a motion—derived from the electoral convenience of three would-be MPs—is scarcely convincing. Whatever superficial reasons may have been adduced, it was intended to be a wreaking motion, that would break the present truce and prevent immediate steps from being taken in the direction indicated by William's *Declaration*. The ulterior motive of Capel, Hotham, and Harbord is obvious. All three had been parliament men. More to the point, all three had been, and at heart remained, avid Exclusionists. Capel, son of the Royalist commander executed at Colchester in 1649, and Clarendon's brother-in-law, had more recent political links with his Whig brother, the Earl of Essex, who had committed suicide in the Tower in 1683 while awaiting trial for treason. Though he had made his peace with James, he had lived in semi-retirement since 1681. During the Exclusion contest he had solemnly predicted that 'the English are of a quiet nature, but should we be so unfortunate as to have a Popish King, it would bring us all into confusion and blood'.[21] Hotham, a choleric Yorkshire baronet, and William Harbord, a moderately gifted administrator, had been much more violent in their Whig professions, and, in consequence, had fled to Holland in the course of James's reign, only to return with the Prince.[22] Both had shown overt hostility to the Stuarts, particularly on the score of their Catholic marriages: Hotham opposing the Modenese marriage in 1673,[23] and Harbord accusing the deceased Queen Mother, Henrietta Maria, in 1680, of having 'perverted' James to Popery.[24] All three hoped to re-enter politics; hence their concern for a parliamentary seat. Harbord was already Commissary-General in the present expedition. His irreconcilability to James was attested by his boasting to Clarendon that 'he had drawn his sword against the King; that he had no need of his pardon; but they', the Whigs, 'would bring the King to ask pardon of them, for the wrongs he had done'.[25]

Clearly, the Whigs' game was as audacious as it was resolute. They aimed at wreaking the Tory-inspired treaty and, by refusing to come to terms with James, strove to push William on to the throne. The Tory Earl of Abingdon, who had already acquainted Clarendon with his misgivings 'that no good was intended', now observed to him: 'Here are people with the Prince ‹who› will bring all into confusion if they can'. Neither Earl was re-assured by the presence in William's camp of the republican Major Wildman and the fanatic Ferguson. They began to have doubts that, despite the mild tone of William's *Declaration*, there were more unpleasant things afoot.

The answer of the meeting was carried to the Prince at Littlecote, who straightway said 'he did not like the clause for superseding the writs for the Parliament': a firm admission that he was for continuing to negotiate with the King. Capel twice argued against its deletion. The second time the Prince cut him short, saying: 'By your favour, Sir Harry: we may drive away the King; but, perhaps, we may not know how easily to come by a Parliament'. He ordered the offending clause 'to be struck out'. But this was not the end of the matter. There was too much at stake for the Whigs. The next day, the 9th, when Jephson reported the amended draft to the company at Hungerford, 'there grew a very warm debate about superseding the writs', in which Hotham and Harbord denounced those who had advised the alteration, not knowing that it had been 'purely' the Prince's doing. After 'much wrangling' it was again voted on, and 'carried by a majority'. The clause was re-inserted, and carried back to Littlecote. Once again William voiced his dissatisfaction, yet was prevailed on 'to hear it debated', which was 'done with great warmth'. Unmoved by their argument, the Prince overruled his opponents. 'God be thanked!', remarked Clarendon, 'the Parliament is to meet, there being, in all probability, no other way to reconcile matters'.[26]

The tussle over the King's writs demonstrated two things: first, that William's Whig followers, who had been joined by Delamer and Stamford from the rebellious North, harboured more revolutionary sentiments than did the Prince, who stuck by his *Declaration* and still desired a negotiated settlement; and secondly, that for all their numerical strength, when it came to a political disagreement, it was William's decision that counted. He knew that they could not do without him; he could therefore please himself, and did.

Why was it that the Whigs carried their opposition to the uncivil extreme that they did? Halifax's report to Middleton, written on the previous evening, provides a clue. In recounting what little he had been able to glean from chance exchanges since his arrival at Ramsbury, he noted: 'It is ... sayd by some that though they could bee secure in coming to Parli)ament, yet if the King should bee perswaded to dissolve it, before their grievances bee redressed and their libertyes secured, it would be a certaine delay, and very much hazzard their dessein for the good of the publick, which by the methods they are now in', meaning their march on London, 'they think they shall quickly obtaine'.[27] The reluctance of William's followers to embrace the royal offer of a parliament was sufficiently well-known to be reported in the newsletters of early December: 'small regard is given by the King's enemies to the intended calling of a Parliament, such imagining the greate busines(s) will be over in halfe forty dayes'.[28] They felt that with James still King, and a parliament in being, summoned on his writs, and in all likelihood dominated by the Tories, the political future would remain uncertain, and, with it, their own political prospects.

The Whig plan was to resist any attempt by James to halt the march forward by concluding a treaty. In this, as we shall see, they were not alone. They had allies elsewhere in the Prince's camp, and in London. Dr. Burnet was one such. On the 5th he had poured scorn on the idea of a treaty, exclaiming: 'How can there be a treaty? The sword is drawn: there is a supposititious child; which must be inquired into'.[29] Again, elated at the news of James's retreat, the Dutch soldiers became infected by the loose talk of the English Whigs, who congratulated themselves that 'now the businesse is done'.[30] They spoke of 'the great difficulties' there would be in coming to an agreement, especially over the claims of the Prince of Wales. Such idle chatter was not relished by their superiors. Their master's Dutch favourite, Hans Willem Bentinck, silenced their speculation by stating that the Prince must abide by his *Declaration* and refer outstanding problems to a free parliament.[31] It was for the English nation, not the Dutch, to decide what should be done.

At 9 o'clock on Monday morning, the 10th, the Commissioners met the Prince's representatives, Oxford, Shrewsbury, and Bentinck, at Littlecote to receive the preliminaries to a treaty. They read more like the demands of a victor than the proposals of a kinsman. The curt economical style, in which they were couched, reflected the dramatic shift in military advantage away from the King to the Prince.[32] William demanded the disarming and dismissal from civil and military posts of 'all Papists and such persons as are not qualified by law'; the recall of royal proclamations censuring him or his supporters as rebels; the release from custody of any that had assisted him; the handing over to the City of London of the Tower and Tilbury, and the securing of Portsmouth 'to prevent the landing of French or other forreign troops'. In the event of James's wishing to stay in London for the meeting of parliament, William wished to be present 'with an equall number' of guards; alternatively, they should both withdraw from the capital to an equal distance to be appointed by the King. Their armies should remove thirty miles outside London, and 'no more foreign forces' (meaning Scots or Irish) were to be brought into England. Finally, he demanded that he and his army should be maintained out of the public revenue until parliament met.[33]

In the circumstances of a near collapse of regal authority William's terms, though intended to be 'terrible' enough to James,[34] were not unduly severe. They had for the most part been anticipated in the peers' discussions on 27 November, and fell short of the Commissioners' worst prognostications two days before. They left James's title as King intact. They did not abridge his parliamentary prerogatives, and made no move to discountenance the claims of the Prince of Wales. To all appearances they furnished grounds for a settlement.[35]

Finding that certain of the demands exceeded their powers to agree, the Commissioners felt it necessary to recur to the King in accordance with their instructions. However, they made a mistake in not taking 'the most expeditious way of knowing his mind', which was, of course, by return of express. Instead, they decided to wait on him in person with the demands, conceiving 'it may be more effectuall for us to lay them before him ourselves'. Seeing that this would unavoidably retard the concluding of a treaty, and well knowing the importance which James attached to the halting of William's march, they made a counter-proposal: that the Prince should not 'advance nearer to London than the distance of 30 miles ... till after Thursday night', the 13th, 'which', they explained, 'by our computation is the soonest that an answer can be return‹e›d'. It remains unclear whether William gave this undertaking. If he did, it was not entered in the official record of the embassy kept by Owen Wynne, the Commissioners' clerk, and can, therefore, have formed no part of what was forwarded to James. Either way, it was not until noon of the 10th that the Prince's demands and the Commissioners' counter-proposal were despatched to Whitehall, 'that His Majestie may have as much time as is possible to consider of it before my Lords do arrive', which, they expected, would be by 'tomorrow evening'. Wynne begged Secretary Middleton to excuse the Commissioners to the King for not writing 'in forme, there being not time for it'.[36] The result was that, when the despatch arrived at Whitehall late on the 10th, William's demands were unaccompanied by any assessment of the negotiations in general, or of the Prince's intentions in particular. It was a calamitous omission.

VIII The Third Declaration

Events in London had not stood still since the Commissioners' departure on 2 December. James had continued to sustain the routines of government, and had taken pains to please the Tories at Court by preferring two of his Protestant chaplains to vacancies in the Church. He nominated Knightley Chetwood to the see of Bristol in succession to Bishop Trelawny, translated to Exeter in November;[1] and Benjamin Woodroffe to the deanery of Christ Church, Oxford, vacated by the flight of John Massey, the Catholic Dean.[2] There was even a flicker of Stuart family feeling. At their request the King granted passports on the 3rd to William 'to send into Holland to the Princesse',[3] and on the 6th to George of Denmark to receive his servants and horses.[4] Anne, holding court among the insurgents at Nottingham, also sensed an improvement, and wrote to have 'the back stairs at the Cockpitt' painted against her coming home.[5] Men took heart again and began to hope that 'this stupendious crisis' was 'exceeding likely to pass over without shed‹d›ing of bloud'.[6] But these faint and fleeting signs of a return to normality were utterly extinguished by the panic spread by the publication in London, on the 4th, of William's so-called *Third Declaration*—an ultimatum 'which', it was remarked, 'thunders judgment against all Papists' who dared to serve the King in contempt of the law.[7]

Masterly in its timing, and exactly calculated to shatter at one blow the precarious peace of a rumour-laden capital, the effect of the *Third Declaration* over the next few days was psychologically devastating on Catholics, the City, and the King himself. It raised the sense of communal distrust between Catholics and Protestants, dissolving the last vestige of respect between the local population and the disintegrating Catholic Court, and fed the gathering forces of Anti-Popery, exposing the Lord Mayor to Whig pressure to act against the Catholics. The *Declaration* asserted (for no proof was offered) that there had been a recent build-up of 'armed Papists' in London and Westminster, in order 'to make some desperate Attempt upon the said Cities, and the Inhabitants, by Fire or a sudden Massacre, or both'. Should that diabolical design miscarry, then they were ready to join 'a Body of French Troops', who were hourly expected 'to land in England' to execute Louis XIV's plans to extirpate the Protestant religion. Catholics were given a clear warning. If they resigned from office and surrendered their arms, they would be spared. But if they were found 'in open Arms, or with Arms in their Houses, or about their Persons, or in any Office Civil or Military ... contrary to the known Laws of the Land', they would be treated as robbers and bandits, 'incapable of Quarter, and intirely deliver'd up to the Discretion' of William's advancing army. All who aided and abetted them would be adjudged 'partakers of their Crimes', and punished accordingly. Besides issuing these dire warnings, it called on magistrates to disarm Catholics and dispossess them of office.[8] Cried on the streets and posted in public places about the town, its message of Protestant retribution struck terror into the Catholic community.

What no one knew at the time was that the Prince's *Third Declaration* was spurious, the invention of some anonymous 'bold man',[9] forward to do William's work for him. Dated 28 November from Sherborne Castle, in Dorset, where William had been the guest of the Earl of Bristol, it bore the hallmarks of authenticity: the Prince was given his full Christian names, William Henry; it was countersigned by his Dutch secretary, Constantijn Huygens; and its sentiments were known to accord with William's own. Only the ferocious language marked it out from its two predecessors. Though the Prince later repudiated it as a forgery, its impact contributed in no small measure to the triumph of the Protestant cause.[10]

'The *Third Declaration* has frighted the Papist‹s› most wonderfully', commented one observer.[11] The outcome of their 'most cruel anguish' was everywhere apparent.[12] It was with evident satisfaction that Evelyn noted the results: 'The Popists in offices lay down their Commissions & flie: Universal Consternation amongst them: it lookes like a Revolution'.[13] Even Protestant soldiers serving under Catholic officers were intimidated, and deserted in droves from James's army. The confessional and political polarization of London society was complete: 'It is already a scandal to be neuter passive, as it will be accounted a crime hereafter . . . There is no such thing as treason now, so we have lost a word'.[14] Such an authoritative communication, seemingly coming from the Prince, considerably emboldened Protestant vigilantes to assert themselves. They turned to the law courts for help in prosecuting the common enemy. A number of anti-Catholic presentments were made to the grand juries of London and Westminster. They denounced eminent converts, such as the Earls of Sunderland, Salisbury, and Peterborough, who, by being 'reconciled to the Church of Rome', had incurred the penalties of 'high treason'.[15] Their action displayed a new determination to confront the patrons and leaders of the Catholic mission in London. They even attempted to indict Lord Craven and a section of the King's Guards on a factious charge of 'wilful murder', or 'treason', for killing a number of Protestant youths during an assault on an illegal Catholic chapel in Clerkenwell in mid-November.[16]

Nor were lesser folk immune from their attention when they deliberately offended Protestant sensibilities. One Catholic citizen was presented 'for saying all persons of different persuasions' from his own 'were hereticks', and 'that he hoped in a short time to see their gutts ript up'; and Catholic soldiers were presented 'for forcing persons to drink health to the confusion of the Protestant religion'.[17] Alarmed at the increasing violence of the attacks on their chapels and convents, which James seemed unable to prevent, the Catholic clergy removed their valuables, forsook their premises, and made for the safety of the continent.[18] At Court, too, the *Declaration* took its toll, hastening the break-up of the Catholic camarilla, and encouraging Anglican collaborators with the King's policies, especially the prerogative-minded judges, to go into hiding or flee abroad.[19] There was much 'scampering'. The Catholic régime was dismantling itself, which was just what William wanted; that way he could avoid upsetting his friends in Catholic Europe. 'Now cunning men are gone, if fooles play on the game, they will play it very foolishly'.[20]

Not all Catholics chose to sit still in the crisis. As Catholic Lord Lieutenants were dismissed, and Protestants took over, and as they, in turn, were authorized 'to displace all Roman catholicks' and 'putt in church men', the forces of Anti-Popery grew visibly bolder. With the gentry in several counties independently declaring a 'resolution not to act under popish officers',[21] the populace embarked on spontaneous acts of violence in the provinces. In Bristol, Bury St. Edmunds, Hereford, York, Cambridge, and parts of Shropshire the rabble rose against the 'popish chappells, and proceeded so far as to pull down the houses of several Roman Catholicks'.[22] Too scattered to resist, and fearing for their safety 'in most counties', Catholics of rank and fortune left their homes and fled 'into the City for security'.[23] Given the heightened sense of Protestant unrest in London, their arrival there during late November and early December gave rise to fresh alarms, as if they were come to bolster the King's will, and, by attempting a last-ditch stand against William's approaching army, to dispute the universal desire for a parliamentary settlement of Protestant grievances. Individual and innocent as, no doubt, were their motives in removing to the capital, their mere physical presence, close to the seat of government and within call of loyal Catholic troops, was seen as provocative in the extreme.

For a time the Tory Lord Mayor, Sir John Chapman, held out against the demand to take action. Over the course of three or four days he was presented with no fewer than nine copies of the Prince's *Third Declaration*, 'and urged to execute it'.[24] He was also petitioned in print by 'divers Trades-men, Apprentices, and others', who, while protesting their resolve 'to defend the King and the Protestant Religion, as by Law established', begged him to save the City from 'the horrid Contrivances' of the Catholics by giving them 'leave to search all Papists Houses' for arms and ammunition, and by commanding the Trained Bands to garrison the town.[25] By the 7th public concern was sufficiently aroused for a deputation of '12 citizens'—led by the ultra-Protestant Whigs, Lucy Knightley, James and John Houblon, Jarvis Byfield, and Edmond Harrison—to lodge a formal complaint with him of 'the town being very full' of Catholics.[26] They informed Chapman 'that the inhabitants of this City are much allarmed at the great resort of Papists and suspected persons to this place', and emphasized 'that there are apprehensions of some sudden attempt by them intended to be made upon this City'.

Once again Protestant fear, compounded by partisan suspicion, worked to the disadvantage of the King's co-religionists. Anxious 'to allay those fears', the Lord Mayor responded firmly, but in a way which seemed to give credence to the allegedly sinister designs of Popery. He issued a precept requiring the Aldermen to send 'immediately' for the deputies and Common Councilmen of their wards to make 'a generall and careful search in their severall precincts'. With the assistance of the parish constables they were empowered to compile 'a full and exact account of all inhabitants and lodgers', and return 'an account of all Papists and suspicious persons' to him, so 'that such further care may thereupon be taken as shall be requisite for the security and peace' of the City. This was to be done, as the mayoral precept stated, for the 'satisfaction and quieting of people's minds and preventing any such danger' as was generally imagined.[27] Within hours the searches were under way in the City and westward along the Strand. The searchers appear to have taken it upon themselves to confiscate the arms of all Catholics, as they were urged to do by William's *Third Declaration*.[28] In the highly charged, over-emotional, volatile atmosphere of the metropolis the systematic search for Catholics, parish by parish, served not to calm, but magnify, Protestant passions. Soon the entire population of the City was made aware of the threat of Catholic aggression—a threat that was not prospective, but actual; not remote, but immediate. The reaction was electrifying. It is against this background of abnormal activity by the civic authorities, concerned to discover the extent of Catholic infiltration of the City, and motivated by fear of an imminent Catholic *coup*, that the massive eruption of Protestant mob violence occurred in London.

IX *James's First Flight*

Over the weekend of the 7th to the 9th the King's mood turned from despair to alarm, as events seemed to close in on him. Having still not heard a word from his Commissioners, from whom he clearly hoped to have good news,[1] he was caught completely off balance by the uncompromising tone of the Prince's *Third Declaration*, which appeared to preclude the possibility of an accommodation, and by the massive flare-up of Anti-Catholicism in the City, which he was unable to control. He fell 'under such a consternation, that he neither knew what to resolve on, nor whom to trust'.[2] With Fr. Petre, the Scottish Secretary Lord Melfort, Attorney General Powys, and Lord Chief Justice Herbert fled, and other of his courtiers on the wing, James felt dangerously isolated. His Court had shrunk to a mere handful of devoted Catholic servants and minor Italian diplomatists.[3] On the 8th, after several delays and much paternal anxiety, his son arrived back at Whitehall under guard from Portsmouth, from which port Admiral Dartmouth had declined to carry him to France. The continued safety of his heir forced the King to act. Convinced that his enemies had all along 'aime‹d› at' his son, he threw what little energy he had left into finalizing his contingency plans to remove, first the Queen and infant Prince, and then himself, from the Kingdom.[4] Later that day he took the Great Seal from Lord Chancellor Jeffreys, and demanded the parliamentary writs which had not been sent out. They were duly delivered to him sealed up 'in a bag'. Having decided to quit the government, but not daring to appoint 'a Commission of Regency', for he knew not in whom to confide, he deliberately burned them. His intention was to create political chaos by making it impossible for William and his supporters to obtain a parliament without recourse to him. He hoped also to gain time in which 'to adopt a convenient posture'—presumably in France, and in concert with his Catholic cousin, Louis XIV.[5] Neither Jeffreys, nor the English Secretaries of State, Middleton and Preston, were made privy to his intended withdrawal. They were Protestants, and not to be trusted.

On the 9th, a day of black despair, James received more bad news. A report came in that Dover Castle, of which the Catholic Sir Edward Hales was Governor, had been seized on the 8th by a Protestant rabble, thereby depriving him and his family of an obvious escape route.[6] At long last he heard from his Commissioners. Their letter, written at Ramsbury on the 8th, at the outset of the negotiations, when they could do no more than 'conjecture' what his enemies intended, gave a quite misleading impression. They told him that in their opinion William's army was unstoppable. More alarmingly, for it revived memories of the fatal Long Parliament of 1641, they hinted that some of the Prince's supporters were unwilling to sit in a parliament which James could dissolve at will. To a monarch whose mind was pre-occupied with the fates of Edward II, Richard II, and his father, Charles I, all of whom had fallen victims to regicide at the hands of their rebellious subjects, it was a spine-chilling thought; and one which appeared more sinister still in the light of Halifax's postscript, informing him 'that the Association, which was begun in Devonshire, is signed by all noblemen and gentlemen whatsoever that come in to the Prince as he marcheth'.[7] It is uncertain whether James knew the precise contents of the Association, but his long-standing dislike of such combinations is well known.

The unrelieved pessimism of the Commissioners' letter served but to confirm James's worst fears. On top of this 'an expresse' arrived from Reading with the frightening news, that, in a skirmish with the Prince's vanguard, his English and Scottish forces had refused to fight alongside loyal Irish soldiers, and that the local population, similarly animated by Protestant hatred of the Catholic Irish, had sided with the enemy.[8] James could hesitate no longer. He gave leave to the Papal Nuncio, Archbishop D'Adda, to withdraw, and 'ordered the queen to be gone with the prince of Wales'. In the middle of the night she and their son left for France in the company of the Comte de Lauzun, 'an old disgrac'd favourite of the French King'.[9]

The exact sequence of events at Whitehall on the 10th is difficult to establish. But one thing is clear, the King wrote two letters to Dartmouth late that day: a day spent in giving audiences, in negotiating for money, in delivering his papers and a large capital sum to the Florentine Envoy Terriesi, and in taking leave of his sister-in-law, the Dowager Queen Catherine.[10] In the first letter he announced that 'things having so very bad a prospect', he could 'no longer defer securing the Queene and my sonne', which he had already done by sending them 'out of the reach of my enemys'. Having done so, he felt 'at ease'. He went on to say: 'I have not heard this day, as I expected, from my Commissioners with the Prince of Orange, who, I beldieve, will hardly be prevailed with to stop his march', which was what Halifax had told him, 'so that I am in no good condition, nay, in as bad a one as is possible'. He ended the letter by promising to write again, giving Dartmouth his 'resolution concerning the fleett'.[11] A note made by Owen Wynne on his copy of the Commissioners' negotiations at Hungerford states that William Trevers, the messenger, 'arrived at Whitehall about 9 that night', evidently after James had written this letter.[12] The King did, therefore, receive William's proposals, but only *after* he had sent his family away, and too late, it seemed to him, to risk altering his plan to follow them, which he was intending to do within a matter of hours.[13]

Everything was prepared for flight. Sir Edward Hales had 'early in the evening' hired a boat to ferry James to Vauxhall on the first stage of his journey to the Kentish coast.[14] Thus, when James came to write his second letter to Dartmouth, he had received the proposals, which,

7 King James II burns the parliamentary writs before fleeing the Palace of Whitehall on 11 December 1688. Dutch propaganda print.

lacking an up-to-date assessment from his Commissioners, he construed in the pessimistic vein of their earlier, ill-informed letter of the 8th. Taking what can only have been a short time to consider them (for Ailesbury tells us he retired to bed after midnight and Secretary Middleton 'made his report' after that),[15] he resolved, whatever became of him, 'to ventur‹e› all rather then consent to anything in the least prejuditial to the crowne or my con‹s›cience'. He was particularly offended at the rebels' outright refusal of his proffered pardon, they maintaining all along that they had no need of one, not having committed any crime. Having been 'basely deserted' by many of his forces, he confessed he 'could no longer resolve to expose myself, to no purpose, to what I might expect from the ambitious Prince of Orange and the associated rebellious lords, and therefore have resolved to withdraw till this violent storme is over, which will be in God's good tyme, and hope that there will still remaine in this land seven thousand men which will not bow downe the knee to Baal, and keep themselv‹e›s free from assosiations and such rebellious practices'. As for the fleet, if any ships were free to follow his commands, they were to make for Ireland, 'where there are still some that will stick to me', and 'follow such orders as they shall rece‹i›ve from Lord Tyrconnel', his Viceroy. 'If they will not, there is no remedy, and this I may say, never any Prince took more care of his sea and land men as I have done, and been so very ill repayd by them'. As for William's demands of him, 'he saw plainly what was aim'd at', and 'he was too well acquainted with the ambitious views of that Prince to immagin‹e› (as many did) that all this undertakeing was out of pangs of conscience for the religion and liberties of the people; that in those ar‹r›ogant demands he assumed in a manner already the royal authority'.[16]

Yet, as he retired for the night, James managed to keep up appearances, saying 'that he intended to go tomorrow to see three of his regiments muster at Uxbridge, and they were brave regiments indeed'.[17] His faithful servant, the Earl of Ailesbury, knew better. He had learnt of the King's intended flight, and implored him not to go; or, if he must, to put himself 'at the head' of his loyal troops and march to Princess Anne and the lords at Nottingham. 'The door must either be shut or open: your daughter will receive you, or she will not. If the latter, and that she retires perhaps towards Oxford, all will cry out on her; if she doth stay to receive your Majesty, you will be able to treat honourably with the Prince of Orange'. But, should this family strategem not succeed, then he urged the King to press northwards, and summon York, where the Earl of Danby was 'with his broomsticks and whishtail militia', who, being no match for professional soldiers, would, he prophesied, 'all run away'. From thence he might 'secure Berwick, and march into Scotland', which Kingdom, he avowed on the word of a Bruce, 'will be entirely yours'.

Ailesbury's advice was more than the extemporary vapourizings of a one-off loyalist. He spoke for others as well as himself. Earlier in the day he had been approached by Charles Bertie, brother of the Tory magnate, the Earl of Lindsey, in the name of 'several chief officers of the army that stuck to the King', begging him to assure their master 'that they would have ready at twenty-four hours warning' between three and four thousand horse 'to march with him wherever he would command them'.[18] But it was no use. James was deaf to their entreaties. He had made up his mind to go. He had promised the Queen that he would follow her to France. As a loving husband and affectionate father, he 'perhaps indulged his uneasy thoughts, with reflecting, that he now abandon'd three Kingdoms, not so much to save himself, as to follow a Wife and only Son'.[19] He preferred to 'reserve himselfe safe for a better juncture, which he might hope for, partly because the Prince possibly may not be the person he is thought to be, and, if he be so, it is impossible for him to satisfie the expectations of the generality of those that fall in with him'.[20]

Having sent orders to the Earl of Feversham, the commander-in-chief of his forces, instructing him not to resist 'a foreign army and poisoned nation', the King surreptitiously left Whitehall in the small hours of the 11th.[21] Before withdrawing 'by a back way out of the bed-chamber', he commanded the Duke of Northumberland, his Gentleman in Waiting, not to open the door of the Royal Apartments before the usual time of his rising, to give him chance to get away.[22] Accompanied by Hales and a couple of Catholic servants, he went by coach from Whitehall Gate to Westminster Stairs, crossed the river to Vauxhall, took horse, and rode eastwards to pick up the boat which had been ordered to take him to France from the Isle of Elmley.[23] As he was rowed across the Thames he jettisoned the Great Seal of England in a final bid to perplex any attempt by William to establish a legal government in the wake of his departure.[24]

X William's Regal Ambition

James's flight opened up the prospects for revolutionary change, of the kind which William had hitherto refused to contemplate. Ever since landing at Tor Bay, five weeks before, he had stuck to his *Declaration* in the belief that lawful aims, publicly stated and politically pursued, would win him the support necessary to effect a change of policies. Moreover, like all Stuarts, he attached an exaggerated value to his word, once it had been pledged. 'The Prince', Bentinck assured Clarendon, 'preferred his word before all other things in the world'. Although he had been unable to stop wild talk among his Whig followers, some of whom did not hesitate to give out 'that the Prince aspires at the crown',[1] he had resolutely rejected their advice when it endangered negotiations with the King and threatened to encroach upon the settled prerogatives of the crown. He had not come to England in support of established laws and institutions, only to let them fall foul of radical demands, raised inside his own camp, after he had arrived. His kinship with the King, the promise he had made to Mary not to harm him, the need not to offend his allies in Catholic Europe, and, underlying all other considerations, the sheer uncertainty as to how the bulk of the nation would react to more aggressive measures, reinforced his natural disposition to caution. His none too happy experience of English politics and politicians had taught him to tread warily.

But the King's voluntary withdrawal from government changed everything. It made his advancement to the throne physically possible, and in circumstances which could scarcely attract the stigma of usurpation. Whatever else James's going signified, it demonstrated his rejection of a negotiated settlement. With the King out of the way, and presumed well on the way to France, and no regent deputed to rule in his stead, the throne *appeared* to be vacant—his, it seemed, for the taking. Such a 'totall change of persons' had previously been canvassed only by the most outspoken of his Whig adherents, who judged 'it the greatest folly to graft anythinge upon the old stocke', being 'taught by too sad experience that the difference of religion makes it irreconcilable to trust, though but the name of power' to a Catholic King.[2] William had always wanted a total change of policies. Now these two separate objectives became one in his mind: dynastic change would both produce the desired about-turn in the direction of government, and guarantee its permanence, by placing him on the throne. At some time between the afternoon of the 11th and the morning of the 12th he decided to take the crown, not doubting that a free parliament—a parliament free, that is, from royal influence—would help him to it. The expedition, as originally conceived and undertaken by him, was at an end. It had yielded to the *force majeure* of dynastic revolution.

The news of James's flight reached William at Abingdon, four miles south of Oxford, where it was brought to him on the morning of the 11th by Lord Griffin.[3] At first he was so 'surprised', that 'he knew not well how to believe' it—scarcely the reaction of a would-be usurper intent on plotting, in true Machiavellian fashion, to force his uncle into flight! At two o'clock the news was confirmed by courier from the King's Commissioners, who, on reaching the verge of London, had been overtaken by the astonishing fact of James's disappearance.[4] William instantly recognized the opportunity which chance had given him, and took it. A practised opportunist, he required no goading from his Whig attendants. He accepted the King's going from Whitehall as providential, for it solved the very considerable difficulty of what he was to do as he approached the capital. He immediately changed his plans. He cancelled his visit to the University, where he was expected the next day, to receive the acclaim of the sychophantic dons, eager to worship the rising sun, and to rendezvous with his sister-in-law, Princess Anne, and the rebel lords from Nottingham. Instead, he turned south to resume his march to London.

Initially, William thought it 'absolutely necessary' to hasten to London 'to settle matters there and to prevent the effusion of blood',[5] but was dissuaded from advancing faster than his troops could afford him protection. The London road was strewn with soldiers, stragglers from James's retreating army, and the fear of assassination was very real: 'any resolute officer might have seized or killed him'. The advice not to hasten to London, warranted though it may have been by concern for the Prince's safety, was to have momentous repercussions, which were to rob him of the initiative he had so boldly seized. Burnet correctly observed that 'if it had not been for that danger, a great deal of mischief, that followed, would have been prevented by his speedy advance: for now began that turn, to which all the difficulties, that did afterwards disorder our affairs, may be justly imputed'.[6] The mischief he alluded to was that caused by the counter-revolutionary activities of the King's 'old friends', who, even at this late stage of the crisis, were reluctant to abandon him, though he had abandoned them.

Thwarted in his desire to press on, William found time to answer the accumulating letters of his foremost English ally, the Earl of Danby, leader of the Yorkshire uprising. The letter which he wrote to him from Abingdon reveals, better than anything else, his belief that the invasion was over, and that nothing stood between him and the throne. 'Affaires being now altered by the King's retirement', he told Danby to disband his forces, and advised the gentlemen with him to go back to their homes, 'and stand for to be chosen parliament men in their counties'. Understandably, since his mind was set on the crown, he urged them to keep 'their inclinations' for him.[7] This was as near as he ever came to canvassing votes for his kingship. Having sent off the letter, there seemed little left for him to do, but pack up the expedition and its local amateur side-shows, hold a general election, and meet parliament to work out a settlement. Later that day, back on the London road, at Wallingford, Clarendon found the Prince in great spirits, dining in Marshal Schomberg's quarters: 'he was very cheerful, and could not conceal his satisfaction at the King's being gone'.[8] As yet neither the loyal Earl, nor his nephew, the disloyal Prince, knew anything of the remarkable transactions which were taking place in the capital.

XI James's 'Old Friends'

James's withdrawal was a possibility which his supporters had been unable to ignore since he had talked openly of fleeing 'beyond seas' before the peers at Whitehall on 27 November. His 'old friends', the high church Tories, feared that his departure would inevitably jeopardize whatever chances they had of influencing the outcome of the crisis. For the past two months they had painstakingly applied to him in the hope of settling 'all things upon the foot they were at his coming to the crown' in 1685. They wanted a return to Anglican Tory ministers with Anglican Tory policies of the sort that had defeated Exclusion in the early 1680s. Though they had been 'somewhat severely used of late', their position was that of a loyal opposition, opposed to the King's evil counsellors, not to the King. They still regarded James, in spite of his Popery, as their lawful, God-given sovereign. As decent episcopalians, they had no wish to exchange him for a Dutch Calvinist. When approached by James in September, Clarendon had undertaken that they would 'behave themselves like honest men' and heartily serve the King.[1] His undertaking was not one of disinterested loyalty. He and his brother, the Earl of Rochester, expected to return to office, just as their clients, the Protestant bishops, expected to regain Court favour. As of old, in the turmoil of Exclusion, so now, in the turbulence of revolution, they stood ready to do battle for the King and the loyal principles of the Church of England.[2] Their efforts, afforced by the impact of William's invasion, had won notable concessions from James during the autumn: sufficient, in their eyes at least, to convince them that their bid for office depended on his survival as King.[3] The progressive collapse of his authority, coupled with the suddenness of his flight, threatened to undermine their long-term measures to reconcile the King to his Protestant subjects, and put them upon seeking more desperate remedies.

Alerted by the sense of despondency at Court, Rochester and his confidant, Bishop Turner of Ely, drew up an emergency plan of action for use in the event of the King's leaving London without appointing a regent. They proposed nothing less that the formation of a provisional government, recruited from the peers in and about the town, many of whom had shown themselves willing to back the Earl's earlier initiative in opening negotiations between James and William. In making their proposal they had two purposes: to provide a focus for law and order, and to uphold James's kingship. They, therefore, 'drew a declaration ready' to put before the peers, 'then went together privately to Lambeth and engaged the Archbishop; then writt a great many billetts (to send forth as soone as His Majesty should withdraw) to entreat the Lords, as *consiliarii nati*, that they would convene at Guildhall, and take uppon them the gover‹n›ment for the preservation of the Kingdome and this great Citty'. This they did without James's knowledge or consent, believing that he would neither 'dislike', nor 'dissent' from their way of proceeding, 'since, for his owne sake, hee must needs bee content to have a Kingdome preserv‹e›d for him'.

Albeit 'perfectly a stranger' to James's intentions 'to the last moment of his going away', Rochester acted swiftly on receiving the news that he was 'secretly withdrawn', sending summonses to the lords spiritual and temporal to meet at the Guildhall.[4] So it was that he and Turner were 'the sole contrivers' of the provisional government, which not only sat, but also governed, in London during the most critical week of the Revolution of 1688. The discovery of the official Journal, or minute book, of the Peers' provisional government has made possible for the first time an accurate chronological reconstruction of this important missing link in the chain of events between James's flight on 11 December and his return to London on 16 December.[5]

XII The Provisional Government

Ignored by an older generation of Whig historians, keen to portray the 'Glorious Revolution' as a national event, and omitted by present-day historians, reluctant to abandon the undue telescoping of events which remains the most damaging legacy of the Whig interpretation of 1688, the successful establishment of the provisional government demonstrated two things: first and foremost, the determination of the peerage not to let slip the reins of government, even at the cost of minimizing irreconcilable political differences among themselves; and secondly, the existence of a sizeable body of King's friends, who, at this eleventh hour, regarded James's political preservation as vital to the future prosperity of Anglican Toryism—a form of government which had crystallized around the defence of hereditary monarchy in the late 1670s and early '80s. The former is important for appreciating the social and political cohesion of the pre-eminent section of the governing class—the aristocracy; the latter for understanding the visceral origins of that most potent, if erratic, of post-revolutionary political phenomena—Jacobitism.

On arriving at the Guildhall the peers found the Lord Mayor and Court of Aldermen waiting for them. 'In the name of all the rest' Lord Rochester assured the City fathers of 'their affection and care for the publick safety'. He explained their purpose in coming into the City was 'that they might with better security consult and take the best meanes for the publique weale'. Mulgrave noted that the civic authorities were 'under such a consternation, that they all entirely submitted to the conduct of those few Peers, who were almost in as much apprehension themselves'.[1] The Peers did not, however, sit or consult with them. Conscious that their claim

8 James II's first flight from London, 11 December 1688. Dutch engraving by Pieter Pickaert and Adriaan Schoonebeeck.

to govern in the absence of the King rested on their right as peers of the realm, they retired to 'the Gallery adjoyning to the Councell Chamber'. There they 'continued together untill towards the evening'. Their first act was to appoint a secretary to take minutes of their proceedings and write out their orders. They chose an experienced civil servant, Francis Gwyn, who had served under Rochester at the Treasury in the earlier part of James's reign.[2]

Twenty-seven Peers attended the meeting: the Archbishops of Canterbury and York, ten earls, two viscounts, four bishops, and nine barons. Bishop Lloyd of Peterborough arrived late, and the Earl of Craven, the hard-pressed Lord Lieutenant of Middlesex, put in a brief appearance. Politically, they were of 'a most mixed constitution'. Although James's 'old friends', led by Rochester and the Protestant bishops, could rely on the support of two-thirds of those present, they encountered opposition from 'a strong party of Lords', who were covert 'Williamites'. The presence of 'violent' Whigs, such as Wharton and Montagu, and of 'angry' displaced courtiers, such as Newport, Culpepper, and Dorset, caused Archbishop Sancroft to fear that 'violent things would be in agitation'. By virtue of his primatial office he should have presided, but, pleading age and deafness, he 'proposed' Rochester, 'and he accordingly presided'.[3] By 11 o'clock they got down to business, having spent the better part of an hour settling themselves.

The most urgent concern was to secure the Tower of London, for the citizens were 'extreamly apprehensive ... imagining all their houses would tumble down at the first gun that should be shot from thence'.[4] Though James had replaced the hated Catholic Lieutenant, Sir Edward Hales, who had suggested mounting mortars on the battlements to quell anti-Catholic rioting, his appointment of the Protestant Bevill Skelton, on 27 November, had not allayed their fears. Neither Skelton's pro-French sympathies, nor the meanness of his estate, endeared him to the citizenry. He was, moreover, known to be in William's disfavour, as a result of his earlier mischief-making at The Hague, where he had tried to make trouble between the Prince and Princess on the grounds of William's marital neglect of Mary.[5] On Newport's proposal Skelton was sent for, but he was found to be absent from his post.[6]

There the business of the Tower rested unsatisfactorily, the Peers being compelled to turn their attention to a greater emergency. Complaint was made to them that mobs were rampaging through the suburbs. Hearing this, they authorized the Lord Lieutenant of Middlesex to raise the militia 'for preventing any disorders which might happen' within his jurisdiction, which included Westminster, where many of their lordships resided, and Southwark, a recognized breeding-ground for mobs. But, already apprized of the situation, Craven had anticipated their order. Coming in soon after, he informed them of the actions he had taken. As it transpired, these proved to be woefully inadequate.

Local demands subsiding, the Peers broached those of national peace-keeping. Their most important task was to prevent hostilities between the opposing forces of the King and Prince. Ignorant of the orders which James had given to the commanders of his land and sea forces on the 10th, they despatched at noon an order to Lord General Feversham. Knowing that it was William's intention 'to lead his army' into London, and that detachments of the royal forces were 'in his way hither', they required Feversham to remove them 'to some distant quarters'. Similar orders 'to prevent acts of hostility between the two fleets' were sent to Admiral Dartmouth, and another, instructing him 'to remove all Popish officers out of their respective commands'. In each case the Secretaries of War and of the Admiralty undertook to deliver their orders. Other motions of a strategic nature were entertained, such as the disarming of Catholics in the garrison at Tilbury, but rejected out of hand. Another proposal, to send orders to the forts on the Thames estuary to stop passengers going down river, was aimed at preventing fugitives fleeing the country: a motion which, though again let fall, articulated the Whigs' desire to bring James's 'accomplices' to trial.

Probably in an effort to discourage further Whig demands, the Peers sent for the Secretaries of State. No sooner had they done so, than they were taken off by an alarm that Catholic soldiers were gathering in arms about Hounslow, the scene of James's summer encampments. Another order was hastily got off to Lord General Feversham, telling him 'to disarm all Roman

Catholicks'.[7] The Earl was much blamed for his disbanding the King's forces without first disarming and paying them. National integrity was also a matter for concern. Having presumed that James had withdrawn to France, the meeting showed its fear of French aggression by taking special note of the government of the Channel Islands, where the absence of the Protestant Governor of Guernsey, Viscount Hatton, and the presence of Catholic officers in the garrison there, gave grave cause for anxiety.[8]

The arrival from the Tower of Lord Lucas, a Protestant officer, who happened to be 'quarter'd there with his company of foot', allowed them to deal with the unresolved problem of the custody of the Tower. They straightway appointed him 'Chief Governour of the Tower', for which they received the 'approbation' and effusive thanks of the Lord Mayor. 'At his entrance he disarmed and cashiered all the Papists he found there'.[9] The tension existing between the more conservative peers, loyal to James, and those who were 'angry' with him, and wished to savage what remained of his authority, was shown by the treatment meted out to Skelton. When he appeared 'some hours after he was summoned', and 'offered to excuse himself for coming no sooner', Ailesbury, seeing that the King's Lieutenant would be removed, 'desired he might not be called in', so 'that he might fall gently'. But Newport would not hear of it. 'No, I will see his face, and how he behaves himself in adversity, and for to humble him that was so proud in prosperity'.[10] As an old Cavalier, who had been humiliated by James's turning him out of the Treasurership of the Royal Household and the Lieutenancy of Shropshire, in 1687, for not countenancing royal policies, Newport wished to revenge himself on one of the King's jumped-up creatures. As the sting of personal rejection and official unemployment had led over the past two years to a hardening of political opposition to James and his synthetic régime of Catholics, Dissenters, and compliant churchmen, so now it propelled some of 'the adverse lords' into taking aggressive measures against both. The royal flight had created the opportunity to deserve well of a new master. What James had taken away William could restore, as Newport agreeably discovered.[11]

Only after ascertaining that James had left no orders with the Secretaries of State did the Peers decide to publicize their assumption of authority in the capital by issuing 'a declaration of the cause of their meeting'. They nominated Rochester and Turner, together with Viscount Weymouth and Bishop Sprat, to draft a statement. The loyalists were quick off the mark with their prepared draft. They proposed 'treating with the Prince on the foot of his *Declaration*', a conservative document, which, as we have seen, maintained that his object in coming to England was to uphold the established laws in a free parliament. They emphasized their identity of purpose with the Prince, and, in calling for 'effectuall securitys for our religion and laws in a free parliament', stipulated that it should be in a parliament 'of His Majesty's calling'. For them a parliamentary settlement was but a step towards bringing 'the King home againe with honor and safety': a phrase which signified an unqualified resumption of government by the absent monarch. In short, James's friends in seeking 'an accord, if possible, betweene the King and the Prince', were reviving the policy of the Hungerford embassy, with the additional requirement, made necessary by the flight, of James's restoration.

The counter-revolutionary objective of the draft attracted 'strong' opposition from William's partisans, who 'had even then a secrett purpose, if they could, to depose the King'. Led by Wharton, Montagu, Newport, and Culpepper, 'the violent party' managed to delete the clauses most favourable to the King, particularly that calling for his return 'with honor and safety'. Although the loyalist majority was greatly perturbed at this, they were forced 'to agree upon other inoffensive, but less and shorter expressions', in order to assert political unanimity in the face of rising anarchy on the streets of London.[12] After 'some pretty warm debates', in which one of their opponents accused the Protestant bishops of 'returning to their vomitt of Popery', they signed the watered-down version of their manifesto 'with a heavy heart'.[13] It was this reversal which persuaded Archbishop Sancroft to absent himself the next day. The resolute intervention of the Whig peers and their allies not only prolonged, but improved, the opportunity for dynastic revolution created by James's leaving the capital.

Nevertheless, the Guildhall Declaration, as published on the 12th, betrayed sins of omission, not of commission, with respect to the King. It cannot be seen as the 'equivalent to a renunciation' of James's kingship. It contained no invitation 'desiring' William 'to come and take the government of the nation into his hands', as Burnet falsely claimed.[14] The Peers deliberately refrained from bidding him to Whitehall, or Windsor, 'or any of the King's houses', and did so 'upon prudentiall considerations'. They did not care to encroach unnecessarily on a royal preserve.[15] In praising the Prince's expedition to rescue them 'from the imminent dangers of Popery and slavery', and pledging their assistance in calling a free parliament, they did no more than testify their desire to promote his 'generous intentions for the publick good'. In traditional fashion they blamed misgovernment, not on the misguided monarch, but on his misguiding ministers. A newsletter neatly depicted the loyalists' state of mind: 'The most zealous Protestants' of the Church of England 'relent for the King, but all exclaim against his wicked, pernicious, and Jesuitical course'.[16] Even his withdrawal was imputed to 'the pernicious counsels' of the Papists, who were characterized as 'persons ill affected to our nation and religion'. Nor were the Peers unmindful of James's latter-day efforts to set things right by issuing his proclamation for a parliament, in which resolution, they confessed, 'we did reasonably hope ... we might have rested secure'. Yet the loyalists among them felt decidedly uncomfortable. In trusting to William's 'generous intentions', they had 'very misgiving thoughts by this time that His Highness would not bee a slave to his word, nor bate the great advantage success had given him'.[17] Time and events were to substantiate their misgivings.

The unanimous approval of the Declaration was the most important act of the Guildhall meeting, for it established the authority of the provisional government in the difficult days ahead. After appointing four peers, one 'of each rank', to carry it to William the next morning, a copy was communicated to the Lord Mayor and Aldermen, who, having acknowledged 'their Lordshipps' great favour' to the City, summoned a Common Council to advise them on what to do 'in this conjuncture'. For their assistance they called on the services of three lawyers, Holt, Treby, and Pollexfen, all of whom were antipathetic to the King's cause. They also ordered the shutting of the City gates and the hanging of chains 'crosse all the streets' between ten at night and six in the morning 'untill further order'.

That evening the Common Council met, and, following the Peers' lead, resolved to apply to the Prince by way of an address. The text produced by a drafting committee, in which Treby and the Whigs predominated, was 'very well liked', and ordered to be carried to Henley by the members of the committee.[18] Though in wording comparable to that of the Peers, it in fact went much further. It invited William to London. Having implored his protection, they besought him 'in the name of this Capitall City' to repair to them, promising him that he would be 'received with universall joy and satisfaction'.[19]

Their enthusiastic response was, in turn, exceeded by the Lieutenancy of London, which was one of the first institutions in the City to rid itself of Catholics,[20] and, under the direction of Sir Robert Clayton, to display overt Orangist sentiment. Its address urged William to make 'what convenient speed' he could to town 'for the perfecting the greate worke', which he had 'soe happily begun, to the generall joy and satisfaction of us all'. Meantime the Lieutenancy undertook to put itself in 'such a posture', that it would be 'capable to prevent all ill designes, and to preserve this Citty in peace and safety'.[21]

Compared with the open-handed welcome extended by the City, the Guildhall Declaration sounded distinctly stand-offish when read to the Prince at Henley on the 13th. Clarendon noted the difference in his reception of the three addresses: 'he seemed much pleased with those that came from the City, but not at all with that from the Lords'.[22] William showed his appreciation by returning 'the City his most gratefull acknowledgement', and by accepting their invitation, 'which he would readily close with as soon as ever his methods would admitt him'. Having thanked the Peers for the Guildhall Declaration, he pointedly informed them 'that he intended to be in town within a few days, *the City having invited him thither*.'[23] When Bishop Turner, one of the Peers' deputies, came from his audience, he was met by Clarendon, who privately told him 'all was nought, the Prince affected the crown, and nothing less would content his followers, whatever else was pretended'.[24]

Meanwhile, in London, the provisional government remained in being for the rest of the week. By prior agreement the Peers removed on the 12th from the Guildhall to the Council Chamber in Whitehall. They had not found the Lord Mayor to be, as some had thought, 'the best man' to preserve the peace 'in the King's absence', but a broken reed. Sir John Chapman had little spirit. He preferred to obey, rather than command.[25] More conveniently located and better provided with messengers and officials for the communication of their orders, Whitehall had the added advantage that the 'policing' agencies of the capital and Kingdom were accustomed to receiving instructions from the Council Chamber. In the confusion following James's withdrawal from government any appearance of normality, however slight, was to be welcomed. There they continued to meet, morning and afternoon, for the next four days.

On the morning of the 12th the Peers decided to summon James's Privy Councillors to join them, probably in a move to strengthen their authority after the breakdown of law and order on the 11th, and to improve the loyalists' hold on proceedings after the tussle over the wording of the Guildhall Declaration. Six Privy Councillors attended,[26] of whom three were peers: the Duke of Hamilton and the two Principal Secretaries of State, the Earl of Middleton and Viscount Preston. Without a specific summons to attend, their Scottish peerages did not qualify them to sit and act with the Peers of England, any more than they entitled them to a seat in the English House of Lords.

From the 12th to the 15th the attendance of Peers and Privy Councillors in the Council Chamber fluctuated between 22 and 38, according to the day and hour. The Earl of Carbery, an Irish peer, usually referred to by the title of his English barony as Lord Vaughan, was the sole peer to attend all sessions of the provisional government, though Rochester and Halifax missed but one meeting each. Only at the emergency session, held in the early hours of the 13th, did numbers drop to a mere 10, but with no perceptible lessening of their authority. On the 12th also the Marquess of Halifax, the senior of the Commissioners sent by James to the Prince, was voted into the chair on Mulgrave's motion. He it was who presided over the nine remaining sessions. Cynically, Mulgrave believed he would 'serve any turn'.[27] His appointment seems, however, to have been a formality, for at the time of his election he was outranked only by the Archbishop of York, and, as Lamplugh belonged to the Spirituality and had been in office less than a month, he lacked the weight and experience to make an effective chairman.

The deliberations, decisions, and directives of the provisional government—hitherto unknown to historians and published here for the first time from the official Journal—made a timely and crucial contribution to the stabilizing of government in the tumultuous interval between the King's flight on the 11th and his return to Whitehall on the 16th. Its achievement may be summarized under three heads: peace-keeping, military supervision, and political initiative. In all three areas its decisions materially affected the outcome of the Revolution of 1688.

XIII The Eruption of Anti-Popery

The enforcement of law and order dominated the early sessions of the provisional government, which was faced with mob violence on an unprecedented scale in and around London. The like had not been seen even in the darkest days of the Great Rebellion. The night of the 11th was one of uninterrupted riot, arson, and terror, as the long gathering storm of Anti-Catholicism finally broke over the capital with devastating ferocity. 'No sooner was the King's withdrawing known', wrote one newspaper reporter, 'but the mobile consulted to wreak their vengeance on Papists and Popery'.[1] Catholics rose from their beds to find their royal protector vanished, and themselves at the mercy of enraged Protestants. Totally demoralized, they spent the day 'running into all holes to hide themselves, weepeing and crying for fear of their lives and all their temporall interest, carrying their good‹s› away in bundles to one Protestant's house, and then to another, and very few durst receive them'. Their plight evoked little sympathy, for their fate was no

9 G. Bower's design for a medal commemorating the destruction of the Catholic Chapel in Lincoln's Inn Fields, 11 December 1688. Cambridge, Magdalene College, Pepys Library.

different from that which, a short time before, Londoners had thought 'was likely to have been the case of all Protestants', so well had the Prince's *Third Declaration* done its job.[2]

The universal chaos, caused by 'People flying, Goods removing, Hangings pulling down, and all things portending a Dissolution',[3] was worse confounded by the arrival of the postboy from Rochester with 'news that that Ancient City was on Fire, and most part consumed'.[4] Confident of the Prince's near approach and excited by the sight of the magistracy's disarming Catholics, the London populace fell with terrible force on the Catholic chapels—the public symbols of 'Popish idolatry' and the propagandizing power-houses of the hated Catholic mission.[5] Throughout the day neither the local magistrates, nor the militia men, showed the least concern at the steady build-up of the rabble, but seemed genuinely to derive comfort from their presence. As the ultra-Protestantism of the people was well attested by their long and distinguished record of hostility to the 'mass-houses', they knew they had nothing to fear: 'they were all of one side, soldiers and mobile, so that there seemed to be no danger at all to the Protestants' of a massacre or fires.[6] Unchecked by their superiors, 'they entered into the Romish Convents and Chappels' and made light work of their arduous task of destruction. They were in their element breaking, pillaging, and burning. That there was no bloodshed owed more to the fact, that 'all the Moncks, Fryers and Priests were fled', than to any superior sense of restraint on their part. As darkness fell early on the longest night of the year (it was the winter solstice) the streets from Whitechapel to Westminster, and from Kentish Town to London Bridge, were awash with 'very great concourses of people', intent on mischief.[7]

In Lincoln's Inn Fields 'a prodigious Number' of the rabble met, 'and gradually from top to bottom pulled down the large new Mass-house', which the Franciscans had built 'near the Arch'. They 'took out the Timber and all that was combustible, and burnt it in the Fields'.[8] 'This night', wrote one Londoner to a friend in Dublin, 'I was frighten'd with the wonderfull light in the sky, and it was the rabble ‹which› had gotten the wainscote and seates of a Popish chaple in Lincoln's In‹n› Feilds, and sett it on fire . . . till wee knew what it was, wee guest it to be a great fire'. Not since the Great Fire of 1666 had the sky above London been so red from the glare of conflagration—'the whole Town seem'd in a Flame'.[9] The rabble did not stay its hand until the building was 'perfectly gutted': the episode introduced an unpleasant metaphor into the language, one that was well suited to this novel piece of barbarism! 'They did the like to the chappels of St. John's, Clerkenwell, and Lime Street; but, not easily breaking into the latter, cryed they would down with it, were it as strong as Portsmouth. And accordingly, having levelled them, they carried all the trumpery in mock procession and tryumph, with oranges on the tops of swords and staves, with great lighted candles in guilt candlesticks, thus victoriously passing by the guards that were drawn up', who did nothing to stop them. Such 'mock processions' had not been seen in London since the extravagant 'pope-burnings' which had been so marked a feature of the Exclusion movement.

'Having bequeath'd these trinquats to the flames, they visited Harry Hills's printing house', in Blackfriars, 'which they served in like manner'.[10] Hills was the King's Printer, the foremost publisher of Catholic propaganda, and himself a convert to Catholicism. He having already fled the country, there was no one to stop the wanton destruction of 'six good presses with all the stamps and perquisit‹e›s thereof', which, with 'two or more cartloads of bookes of very great value', were 'tumulteously carried out of his house and burnt ... neare Fleet bridge'.[11] But what was 'most ungratefull' was 'their execution reaching to the Spanish Ambassador's', at Weld House, off Great Queen Street, they not only defaced the buildings, but also plundered it of 'all its rich furniture, plate, money, and 3 coaches, to the value, as is computed, of 20,000£'.[12] It did not matter to the rabble that Don Pedro de Ronquillo's master, Carlos II of Spain, was one of William's allies. It was sufficient for them that he was a prominent Catholic, had taken into his custody the valuables of English Catholics (including the altar plate from the King's Chapel at Whitehall),[13] and had countenanced the spread of Catholic influence in the City. Such was the abruptness of the attack on his residence that it was only with difficulty that the Sacred Host was rescued from the tabernacle of his chapel, and he himself escaped unharmed.[14] It is hard not to conclude that this spate of iconoclasm was connived at, if not encouraged, by practically all Protestants, including those in immediate authority. The mobs, often 'a great many thousands in number', were not to be restrained: 'they are uncapable of hearing advice or counsell of their friends, for enemies they have none in appearance, nor none in seacret like to give them any opposition or affront'.[15] Few pitied the Catholics, and many applauded what was looked on as a just act of communal revenge: 'confounded be all they that worship graven images and boast themselves of idols'.[16]

The full extent of the damage was apparent on the morning of the 12th. The Peers were appalled, particularly at the attacks on foreign embassies. Those of Venice, Tuscany, Cologne, and the Palatinate had also been assaulted. Indeed, 'all sober people' were 'extraordinarily concerned at this horrid violation of the law of nations', which involved England's international standing. The Peers sent the King's Master of Ceremonies to apologize to the Catholic Ambassadors for the 'insolencies that were offered to them last night by the rabble', and to promise them 'satisfaction' for the damage which had been done. He was instructed to begin his round with Ronquillo, 'he having suffered most'.[17] Evidently, the provisional government was taken unawares by the violent behaviour of the *mobile vulgus*, which, as a result of its infamous career of destruction, was already being shortened to the monosyllabic, and now more familiar, 'mob'.

Conscious of the gross dereliction of duty which at the local level had allowed the outrages to occur, the Peers issued a severe order 'to the civil magistrate to preserve the peace'. They threatened all who attacked buildings, especially embassies, with imprisonment and 'the utmost rigour of law'. They commanded Protestant officials, from County Sheriffs to Parish Constables, 'to execute their respective offices', and 'take effectual care' to prevent similar disturbances. If they could not cope, then the Deputy Lieutenants were empowered to call out the Militia and

Sheriffs the *posse comitatus*. Lastly, they were to apprehend 'obstinate offenders'. Their order was immediately sent to Edward Jones, a printer in the Savoy, for speedy duplication. Its publication steadied the magisterial class and did much over the next few days to restore order in the metropolis.[18]

In the mean time the Peers had to deal with emergencies as they arose. They were soon presented with an opportunity to show their determination to crush mob violence. Towards midday on the 12th they were informed 'that the rabble are grown to an ungovernable height' on the perimeter of Whitehall. They instantly signed two orders, authorizing Colonels Selwyn and Bagot, of the Foot Guards, to use their 'utmost endeavours to quell and disperse the said rabble, and in case of necessity to use force and fire upon them with bullett'. It was an order which was repeatedly re-issued in the course of the next twenty-four hours of unrest, as the mobs, deflected and dispersed from one target, re-formed and went in search of another.

The Peers recognized the social dangers implicit in uncontrolled Anti-Catholicism. As members of a conservative, law-abiding, propertied aristocracy, they had nothing to gain, and everything to lose, from mindlessly giving way to 'a state of bandit‹b›i', in which the entire capital would 'certainly ‹have› bin the spoyle of the rabble'.[19] In such dangerous circumstances they did not hesitate to authorize the armed suppression of popular disturbance. Unlike the London lower orders, they feared social subversion even more than they detested Catholicism. With them the protection of property mattered more than the savaging of Popery.

Before the close of the afternoon session on the 12th the Peers were informed 'that the rabble threatened St. James's', and 'that, if great care was not taken, there would be great disorders upon pretence of pulling down the Chapel there'. The sacking of Weld House had revealed the presence in the mob of hardened criminals, thieves and looters, so that the Peers had good grounds for suspecting that popular Protestant ardour was being exploited for reasons of sordid profit. Fearing that the royal palaces would make easy plunder, they called up the regular forces to defend them. Having been briefed by the officers of the Guard on the strength and disposition of the available Household troops (Selwyn and Bagot commanded 400 men each), they required Sir Harry Shere, who had just returned with the Train of Artillery from Salisbury, to send six gunners to Whitehall. Next they deployed the Horse Guards, 80 at St. James's, and 80 at Whitehall; and a further 300 foot were 'drawn up in the broad place before Whitehall, and 3 pieces of cannon before the Gate'. The Second Troop of Guards was put on alert, and army officers were sent to assist the civil magistrates in the environs of the palaces. At St. James's the troops arrived in the nick of time. They found the rabble already inside the Palace, 'where they were clambering up to pull down the Organs, and deface the Chappell'. After a brisk confrontation they 'were forcibly repelled' by the Guards.[20]

Something of the general state of alarm can be gauged from the request sent to the Lords by the Queen Dowager, Catherine of Braganza, for reinforcements of cavalry 'to disperse the rabble' outside Somerset House. She was so terrified, that she refused to shelter the Spanish Ambassador, who had fled in terror from his embassy, and would not let Lord Feversham, her Chamberlain, leave her, to make arrangements with the Peers for her defence.[21] That night the precautions taken by the provisional government foiled a premeditated assault on the royal palaces. In fact, they proved such a success, that the Peers repeated them the following night with equal success.[22]

Elsewhere in the metropolis the marauding mobs proved more truculent, 'they crying out the Fire should not go out till the Prince of Orange came to Town'. The Orangist sentiment of the Protestant rabble was frequently apparent in their loud 'acclamations of *An Orange, An Orange!*' and in the parading of 'Oranges upon their Sticks' as they marched purposefully to and fro. As was to be expected, the residences of Catholics still bore the brunt of demotic displeasure, though, increasingly, the armed forces managed to beat the rabble off before too much damage was done. Powis House in Lincoln's Inn Fields, the Florentine Embassy in the Haymarket, the Nuncio's lodgings in St. James's Square, the 'mass-house' and presbytery in Southwark, and a number of private dwellings and business premises in the City—all came under attack.[23] But the combination of cavalry charges and the Peers' ordering the soldiery 'to fire with ball' gave 'a check to those disorders', though the rabble, it was observed, 'seem still resolved to go through-stitch' with the downing of Popery.[24]

XIV The Irish Fear

Feeling uneasy at the persistence of mob violence, the Peers agreed before they left the Council Chamber on the 12th, that, 'if any tumult should happen' in the night, they would 'meet wholly in Whitehall' to take concerted measures. In an emergency they did not wish to be at cross purposes with each other. Events showed that they were prudent to act on their premonition. After midnight, in the early hours of the 13th, 'a report was spread all over the town that a great number of Irish' were 'got together, that they had burnt Uxbridge and put all to the sword, and were marching up directly to London'.[1] Aroused from slumber by the strident 'noise of drums, trumpets, and kettle drums', the entire population got out of bed to cries of 'Rise, arme, arme, the Irish are cutting throats'. After the astonishing ups and downs of the past few weeks the 'allarme' was instantly credited, 'insomuch that in half an houre's time there was an appearance of above 100,000 men' ready to make 'head against any enterprise of that nature'. To shed light on the pitch-black scene, and the imagined atrocities, 'all the windowes of the houses' were lit 'with candles from top to bottome', and outside those houses which were 'not illuminated' there was such a 'bawling' that their inhabitants were forced to follow suit. The 'panick feares of an Irish massacre' rapidly raised 'the greatest uproare that ever perhaps was knowne in London'.[2]

Amid the clamour and confusion ten Peers met at Whitehall. While the rest of the town ran hither and thither, to no effect, they authorized the only action that was necessary. They took steps to verify the report. They 'sent out horsemen to bring intelligence, who returned with an account that there were no persons stirring'. It was 'a false alarm'. Notwithstanding, 'to prevent the rabble's gathering together upon this pretence', they ordered the Regiment of Fusiliers 'to stand at arms', and, 'to quiet the apprehensions of the City', despatched a re-assuring message to the Lord Mayor, telling him to do nothing 'extraordinary' unless he heard further from them.

After a night of 'strange consternation', in which many citizens stood armed at their front doors 'in expectation of nobody knows whom, that were coming to cut their throats',[3] they 'began to be undeceiv'd' round 'about 4' o'clock in the morning, and returned 'to bed again, leaving one or two in a house up' in case of trouble.[4] There was none. Though later that day the Lieutenancy of London officiously planted field-pieces around the City, it never had cause to use them.[5]

The nervous and physical exhaustion induced by the long restless night of the so-called 'Irish Fear' had one beneficial result. It took the zest and energy out of anti-Catholic rioting. Perhaps it was that the young apprentices, who formed a significant element in the mobs, simply could not take more than three nights in a row without sleep. Certainly life was much quieter on the 14th, and almost back to normal on the 15th, by which time 'the mindes of the mobile seem‹e›d quieted'. On the 17th the Trained Bands, who had stood guard over the City by night, were cut from three regiments to one. By the 24th only half a regiment was required for duty.[6] There can be no doubt that, without the Peers' 'care and vigilance' in the forty-eight hours between the 12th and 14th, London would have been 'in ashes', for on the 11th 'the rabble were the masters' of the capital, 'if the beasts had known their own strength'.[7]

XV Military and Civilian Administration

The provisional government inevitably found itself drawn more and more into the exercise of military authority. Though a civilian body, it functioned in the aftermath of an abortive military campaign, which had ended in a retreat on London. It was surrounded by large numbers of the

King's forces, many of whom were uncertain how to act following James's flight. For all that the abandoned officers of the King's army had, with Lord Rochester's encouragement, lost no time in submitting to William, they scrupled going over to him in a body, and in many cases preferred to remain in town. They held it their duty 'to preserve good order' in the capital by doing 'everything which might contribute to it'.[1]

The Peers soon let it be known that they disapproved of Lord General Feversham's giving the order to disband, albeit on James's authority. Having prevented hostilities between the opposing armies, their policy was to try to keep together the Protestant officers and soldiers of the King's army. A beginning was made on the 12th, when they directed the officers of the First Regiment of Foot Guards, who had laid down their arms 'upon a mistake that they were disbanded by the Earl Feversham', to 'keep together all the Protestant soldiers under their respective commands, and to be aiding and assisting to the civil magistrate when thereunto required'.[2] Thereafter they issued a sequence of orders calling on various regiments, including Scottish and Irish ones, 'to repair to their colours'.[3] From their peace-keeping activities they knew that disbanded soldiers and outright deserters had joined the Protestant mobs in pillaging and looting the Catholic chapels and embassies of the metropolis. To ensure that their policy was more than empty words they consulted the Earl of Ranelagh, Paymaster of the Forces, on the 13th. Having ascertained that army pay ran out on 14 December, they made a general order for the payment of 'one week's subsistence to such of the forces as are together in town'.[4] They also signed individual orders for the payment of named regiments, when and where circumstances warranted them.[5]

Appreciating that the Irish Catholic troops brought in by James to swell the opposition to William constituted a special problem, particularly following the night of the 'Irish Fear', they drew up an order requiring them to return to their old quarters and to behave 'peaceably'. They offered them subsistence 'untill they shall be otherwise provided for', but insisted that they deliver their arms to the officers of the Ordnance, to be stored in the Tower. Those Irish who refused to comply with their order were to be seized by the civil magistrate. They had their order printed, and instructed the Postmaster General to despatch copies 'to be put up in all towns within 20 miles of London'.[6] Often the friendless Irish were grateful to the Peers for their care of them. Lt.-Colonel Tuite actually sought their 'Lordships' protection' for those detachments of Lord Forbes's Regiment who had come to London. Despite 'their civil deportment', they were 'in continual danger of being massacred by the rabble'. In issuing a printed order for their removal to Barnet, in Hertfordshire, the Peers rescued them from an invidious situation.[7] They did a comparable service for Colonel Slingsby's forces, quartered in Smithfield, where 'every night' they went 'in danger of the rabble and the Trained Bands for lodging within the City'. They ordered them to remove to the safety of nearby Holborn.[8] In a multiplicity of acts—some purely military, such as authorizing the issue of arms and ammunition from the Tower or the assigning of quarters to newly arrived battalions from Uxbridge, and others bordering on the political, such as enquiring into an attempt on the Duke of Grafton's life or ordering the detention of Lt.-Colonel Dorrington, as 'a dangerous person'—the provisional government successfully regulated the presence in the capital of a huge number of military personnel at a time of acute communal tension and widespread civilian unrest. Its efforts helped to preserve, not only the peace, but whole sections of the royal army intact, an object which was already receiving the independent attention of the Prince.[9]

Among its last acts on the 15th it took care that none of the broken Irish soldiers 'should go into Ireland, nor that any intelligence should go thither', lest the King's Viceroy, the Catholic Earl of Tyrconnell, 'might prepare himself to make a disturbance in that Kingdom'. Advised by Samuel Pepys, Secretary to the Admiralty, on the most effective means of achieving that end, it imposed an embargo on all ports: Dover, Plymouth, King's Lynn, Portsmouth, Harwich, Gravesend, Chester, Falmouth, Carlisle, Dartmouth, Berwick, Yarmouth, and Holyhead. It also commanded the Postmaster General 'to put a stop to all foreign posts out of England, not only to all foreign parts, but to Ireland and Scotland'. The intention was to give the Kingdom a breathing space in which to set its own affairs in order, before turning its attention to the dependent realms of Scotland and Ireland.[10]

The political activity of 'the Lords, who now direct the great affairs of the Nation',[11] was by no means confined to the sealing of ports and the suspension of foreign mails: actions which, in themselves, inauspiciously recalled the measures taken by the Privy Council on the eve of Charles II's death.[12] Besides ordering the disarming of all Catholics, they addressed the problem of the fugitives, Catholic and Protestant. On the 11th they sent to Sir John Knatchbull in Kent, and to Sir William Thomas and Sir Thomas Dyke in Sussex, 'to use all manner of diligence' in arresting 'Jesuits, Popish priests, and other eminent offenders' against the law, who were attempting 'to fly from justice' by going abroad.[13] The order into Kent was remarkably productive. In that precociously metropolitanized county, where events in town were closely watched, the populace was extraordinarily busy in apprehending 'criminals'. On the look out for easy pickings, it tended to anticipate the Peers' instructions, and, when apprized of them, was inclined to exceed them, for even before 11 December parts of the county were in the throes of the 'Irish Fear'.

On the coast the poor seamen, or 'owlers' as they were locally called, were no less keen to try their hand at 'sailing for priests and plunder', as the King found to his cost.[14] By the end of the week there had been an impressive string of arrests, including King James, the Catholic Earls of Salisbury and Peterborough, Bishops Leyburn and Giffard, Sir Edward Hales, Dr. Obadiah Walker, the converted Master of University College, Oxford, and the Protestant collaborator Sir Thomas Jenner, Baron of the Exchequer.

In London the policing of the River presented special difficulties, not least because it was reported to be stiff 'night and day' with boats and lighters.[15] At their first meeting the Peers had been reluctant to give order for the stopping of 'all passengers' on the Thames. On the 12th they changed their minds, and ordered Samuel Pepys, at the Admiralty, to examine river traffic 'below Gravesend', and let none pass without a passport 'under the hands and seals of 5 Peers, or from the Lord Mayor of London'. Subsequently, they signed a number of passes, mostly to peers and their servants.[16] They denied passports to those they thought dangerous. One such was James Stanford, the English-born Envoy of the Elector Palatine, who had opened the highly controversial Catholic Chapel in Lime Street in the City. On the 15th he was refused a pass to go into Catholic Lancashire.[17]

On the 12th the Peers were informed that Lord Jeffreys, the former Lord Chancellor and one of the most detested of James's ministers, was lurking on board a ship 'lying near Shadwell Dock', preparatory to making a get-away. They ordered the authorities to search the ship and seize him, which they did. Not daring to carry Jeffreys as far as Whitehall for fear of the mob, which pressed menacingly about them with cries of 'the King of the West' and 'Remember Cornish' (allusions to his savage punishment of Monmouth's Protestant rebels in the 'Bloody Assize', and the execution of the London Alderman, Henry Cornish, the Whig conspirator, in 1685), his captors had to be content with hauling him before the Lord Mayor at Grocers' Hall. He was later removed to the Tower at his own 'desire', being terrified that, unless Lord Lucas took charge of him, he would be torn to pieces by the irate mob. Such was Sir John Chapman's shock at seeing his old patron brought before him as a common criminal, that he suffered a stroke, from which he never fully recovered.[18] Three days later the Peers were constrained to put off bringing Jeffreys to Whitehall for interrogation, because they feared provoking renewed unrest in the City. Mercifully for him, he died in the Tower, in April 1689, before the more vindictive of the Whigs were able to make an example of him. A similar information regarding the whereabouts of Fr. Edward Petre, given to the Peers on the 14th, and instantly authorized by them to be pursued, led nowhere. The scent had gone cold.[19]

In keeping with their Guildhall undertaking to assist the Prince 'as occasion shall require',[20] the Peers did all they could to co-operate with him. Early on the 14th the Duke of Grafton arrived at Whitehall, and acquainted them that he had William's orders to occupy the Fort at Tilbury. He required transport for 'two battalions of his Regiment'. They straightway ordered the City to provide him with four barges. Previously, on the 11th, they had declined to command the Governor of Tilbury 'to disarm the Papists', probably because they realized that he was in no position to comply, given the large Irish contingent in his garrison. However, since then, some '700 Irish soldiers', not knowing what unkind fate awaited them, had on the 12th 'run from Gravesend and Tilbury', 'seiz‹e›d a ship in the river bound for the East Indies, richly laden, and endeavoured to carry her off', only to 'run her aground'. On complaint from the Turkey Company of London, proprietors of the *Asia* and her valuable cargo, the Peers had ordered *H.M.S. Kent* to secure the striken vessel. After a 'scuffle', in which 'some persons were killed', the potential danger was defused, and Tilbury Fort returned to safe Protestant hands.[21] The Company's impromptu offer to give the Irish 'something to keep them from starving' no doubt helped the settlement. All too often the zeal with which the Protestant authorities tackled the congenial task of disarming Catholic troops had stripped 'the miserable, poor, distressed Irish' of their uniforms and supplies 'only for the satisfaction of the mobile', leaving them cold, hungry, and mutinous.[22]

The surrender of Portsmouth provided another instance of the Peers' collaboration with the Prince. On the 15th they were appealed to by Secretary Preston. In the absence of his senior colleague, Middleton, he had received a letter from the King's son, the Duke of Berwick, Governor of Portsmouth, who, like his father, was anxious to prevent unnecessary bloodshed. Taking note of the King's 'being gone, and the nation being desirous that all Roman Catholicks should lay down their arms', the Duke offered to resign his post to the Prince, provided that he would give 'passes and safe conduct' to the officers and men under his command 'to go to their respective countreys and elsewhere'. Preston communicated his letter to the Peers, who despatched it to the Prince, and ordered the Duke's messenger, Lt.-Colonel Sir George Berkeley, to accompany their own bearer to Windsor to make the arrangements for the surrender. At the same time they forwarded a letter which Lord Weymouth had received from Sir John Knatchbull, 'giving an account' of the fugitives taken in Kent. Gwyn enclosed the originals in a cover and addressed them to Bentinck.[23]

Having promised their 'utmost endeavours' to assist William in obtaining a parliament 'with all speed',[24] the Peers also felt it their duty to investigate what had become of the Great Seal, the instrument for authenticating documents of state, together with the writs authorizing elections for the parliament which James had called for 15 January. As yet they made no question that this parliament would provide the necessary forum for working out a lawful and lasting settlement. On the 13th Lord Lucas reported on the 'discourse' he had had with the former Lord Chancellor in the Tower, which made it clear that he had 'delivered the Seal to the King in Will Chiffinch's lodgings in Whitehall'. Chiffinch was summoned and examined, but could throw no more light on the matter. The Peers, therefore, ordered that the King's Closet should be sealed. As for the parliamentary writs, the situation seemed less bleak. Jeffreys maintained that he had sent out 'all the writts where there were Protestant Sheriffs, but had returned the writts of those counties, that had Popish Sheriffs, to the King'. Though the Earl of Thanet, himself a Protestant Sheriff, pointed out that he had not received a writ, the Privy Councillor, Sir John Ernle, was able to tell their lordships that 'there were 16 writts delivered out and 36 not'. While much of the 15th was spent in taking sworn depositions from Chiffinch and his servant, Joseph Hough, and in sending three Lords to interrogate Jeffreys in the Tower, the Peers made no further headway. It was plain that none but the King could give them a satisfactory answer.[25]

XVI Bringing the King Back

Apart from his disappointment at the 'lankness' of the Guildhall Declaration and the Peers' refusal to invite him 'forward',[1] William found fault with only one action taken by the provisional government in London: its unexpected decision to rescue King James, who, unfortunate even in flight, had been arrested by a Protestant mob at Faversham, in Kent.[2] Yet again, the Journal allows us to follow in detail this most important, and, for William, vexatious development, which threatened to deny him the crown he now coveted for himself. On the morning of the 13th the Peers' deliberations were momentarily interrupted by the arrival of a letter brought from Lambeth by a servant of the Archbishop of Canterbury. The letter, written from Canterbury the previous night, served to introduce and vouch for its bearer, Thomas Liniall, a Canterbury joiner, who, 'it was whispered' about the Council Chamber, 'had brought news of the King being stopt in Kent'. At first the letter was not communicated to the Peers, presumably because Halifax, the chairman, was disinclined to countenance the report. Liniall was ordered 'to withdraw alone' and 'not discourse with any'.

For a while nothing further was done. But, growing impatient, two of the loyalist peers— Bishop Mews of Winchester, the only bishop present, and the Earl of Berkeley—went out, and, in defiance of the order, cross-questioned Liniall 'concerning the King'. He told them all he knew.[3] Public silence on the matter was eventually broken by another peer, who came in late. Earlier that morning the Earl of Mulgrave had been 'advertised privately' of the King's arrest, and that 'a poor countryman' had been sent 'with the news, in order to procure his rescue: which was like to come too late, since the messenger had waited long at the Council-door, without any body's being willing to take notice of him'. He boldly acquainted the Peers with what he had heard, and told them that he thought it 'his duty to move the Lords to take off any restraint'. Taken aback by this outburst, Halifax 'hastily' tried to adjourn the meeting, but Mulgrave would not be shut up. Ignoring the chairman, he went on with his disclosure, 'so that meer shame obliged them to suspend their Politicks a-while'.[4]

Liniall was 'thereupon called in', and produced the pass which had been given to him by five JPs of Kent, who, out of loyalty to the King, had authorized his 'urgent' journey to the capital. Though the pass did not mention James's detention, for the signatories 'knew that many different parties were upon the road, and some of them might perhaps have stopt him in case they had met with anything they had not liked', Liniall was able to give a full account of the capture of the King; not from personal knowledge, but from 'the gentlemen who signed the pass', who 'had seen the King', and sent him to the Archbishop. He told the Peers 'that the King was in the hands of the rabble at Feversham', and that James had sent to the former, Protestant Lord Lieutenant of Kent, the Earl of Winchilsea, to come to his aid. He was fairly certain that he had passed the Earl's coach-and-six on the road into Faversham.[5]

Liniall's news burst like a bombshell on the assembled Peers, afflicting loyalists and 'Williamites' alike, though for diametrically opposed reasons. The major concern of the loyalists was for the King's safety; that of the 'Williamites' was for themselves. Mulgrave, seconded by Berkeley, immediately moved that 'a party of horse' be sent 'to secure His Majesty from the rabble'. The motion struck terror into the hearts of 'the adverse lords', who, until then, had seemed likely, with William's slow, but unimpeded advance towards London, to be 'the prevailing party'. Ailesbury noticed that 'their looks were enough for to betray their hearts'.[6] Bowled over by this latest development, they badly 'wanted time for concerting enough together about so nice, and so very important a matter, as saving or losing a King's life'. All were 'under some difficulty' as to what to do for the best: 'For, as there was danger of displeasing' the Prince, 'by doing their duty, so there was no less, by omitting it; since the Law makes it highly criminal to be only passive in such an extremity: besides that, most of them, unacquainted as yet with the Prince of Orange, imagin'd him prudent, and consequently capable of punishing so base a desertion, either out of generosity or policy. These found afterwards their caution needless'.[7] The Journal shows that Halifax again intervened, this time to better effect. A secret well-wisher, of long standing, to William's espousal of the Protestant interest, he had increasingly taken his side after James's flight had broken off the Hungerford embassy, which had left him exposed to Whig accusations of conducting fraudulent negotiations with the Prince. He used the influence of the chair to give the 'Williamites' a chance to take stock of events. Objecting that Liniall's 'information may not be true', it being unsupported hearsay, he moved from the chair that 'nothing' should 'be done at present', but that they 'meet again in the afternoon'. Though Mulgrave spiritedly resisted his motion by desiring that Liniall should testify to the truth of what he said 'on oath', the chairman's adroit intervention swayed the meeting, which agreed to adjourn till 'four of the clock'.[8]

To the afternoon session 'all the peers in the town', and 'likewise the Privy Council', were summoned. In recognition of the importance of the business before them attendance shot up from 28 in the morning to 38 in the afternoon, the highest attendance at any session of the provisional government. With the exception of the Earl of Essex, all the newcomers were loyalists: the two Archbishops (Sancroft came out of his self-imposed retirement at Lambeth House);[9] the Duke of Grafton; the Earls of Litchfield, Burlington, Yarmouth, Nottingham, and Middleton; Lord Delawarr and Bishop Sprat. After dealing with fresh outbreaks of rioting in Southwark and Charing Cross, the Peers were about to turn their attention to Liniall again, when the Sword-Bearer of the City arrived from the Lord Mayor. He brought with him 'a seaman', Robert Clinton, who had brought Chapman 'an account of His Majesty'. Clinton was promptly introduced, and gave 'a clear, unmasked, and full answer' to the Peers' questions, 'which were very many'.[10] He confirmed Liniall's report of the King's captivity, and added so many compelling circumstances, that Bishop Mews pronounced himself 'sufficiently satisfyed' that James was at Faversham. Halifax's feeble attempt to delay proceedings further, by observing that neither informant said he knew the King, was brushed aside by Rochester and Middleton. The Secretary of State desired that 'if any there doubts the truth of this matter, he would demand an oath, but, for his part, he was satisfyed of it this morning, and that such a number of Guards should be sent to him as would secure him from the rabble, but that he should be left at entire liberty to go where he pleases, and that some Lords should attend him, and give him their advice'. Bishop Mews loyally declared his belief, albeit mistakenly, that, if the King 'had staid untill the proposals came back from the Prince of Orange, he might not have gone at all'.[11] The signs were that the loyalists were confidently hoping to induce James to return to them. In this they were amply supported. It was noted that Clinton's account moved 'great pitty and compassion, and the greatest in those that are the most serious Protestants and the most inflexibly set for securing the Protestant religion, our lawes, properties, and liberties, and leaves the deepest impression upon them'.[12]

The Journal reports the debates which ensued, and again shows that Halifax was strongly opposed to sending any 'message or advice' from the meeting, arguing that 'it would look like restraint', particularly if accompanied by troops. In conclusion, the Peers appointed Feversham, as Colonel of the Life Guards, Middleton, as Secretary of State, Yarmouth, as Treasurer of the Household, and Ailesbury, as Gentleman of the Bedchamber, to attend the King. Feversham, who owned himself desirous 'to see His Majesty's return', refused to act without the Peers' explicit order. Having already felt their displeasure in carrying out James's order to disband the army, he wished to know precisely where he stood and by what authority he was called upon to act. Even when he got his order to draw out a detachment of guards and grenadiers, and to 'march with all speed with them to attend His Majesty', he had it altered to include an express authorization 'to receive his commands and protect his person from insolence'.

Halifax appears to have gained his point 'that no advice should be sent'. Instead, it was left that 'the Lords that went might say what they thought fit for themselves, but nothing from them'.[13] The fact that all four Lords sent to wait on James were unwavering loyalists ensured that their advice would be unanimously in favour of his returning to Whitehall. Ailesbury, who had openly 'told their lordships that ... the only step' they 'could take was humbly to desire of his majesty to return to his Court',[14] volunteered to ride ahead of the Guards and other Lords, in order, on Rochester's suggestion, to give the King 'convenient' notice of their coming to him. There can be little doubt that he gave the King a strong lead to return to London. He left that night, armed with the Peers' passport.

After a traumatic journey through towns and villages in the grip of the 'Irish Fear' (with the usual rumours of Catholic arson and butchery, tailored to local circumstance, such as 'that all Dartford was on fire, and the streets ran with blood') Ailesbury arrived at Faversham on the 14th, exhausted, but none the worse for 'the great dangers' he had encountered along the way.

Conducted by Winchilsea to the Mayor's house, he found the King 'sitting in a great chair, his hat on, and his beard being much grown', so that he 'resembled the picture of his royal father at the pretended High Court of Justice' painted by Edward Bower. On the 15th the King left Faversham. He stayed over night at Sir Richard Head's house in Rochester. From Rochester the King sent the Earl of Feversham with 'a polite and friendly compliment' to the Prince, telling him 'he would be glad to see him at London' on the 17th, where he proposed 'a personall conference to settle the distracted Nation'.

On the 16th James resumed his journey to London. At Blackheath he was assured of a warm welcome in the City, which was indeed the case. 'From St. George's, Southwark, to Whitehall . . . there was scarce room for the coaches to pass through and the balconies and windowes were thronged, with loud acclamations beyond whatever was heard of'. Before his coach 'some of the common people ran bareheaded'. James was 'hugely surprized' and touched by 'the unexpected testimonys of the peoples affection', and saw that the popular anger, which had prompted his withdrawal from the capital, 'was not at his person, but at his religion'. Before going to Whitehall he stopped at Somerset House to give the Queen Dowager 'a short vissitt'.[15] On arriving at Whitehall he was reported to be 'in very good Health', better than he had been in for sometime.[16]

XVII William and the City of London

William received James's letter at Windsor on the 16th. The intimation that he intended to return to Whitehall visibly shook him. Dismayed at the threat to his new-found ambition, the Prince vented his displeasure on the messenger. Already 'very angry' with Feversham for disbanding the King's forces, without either consulting him or disarming them, he ordered his arrest on the trumped up charge of entering the enemy camp without a passport.[1] Yet, even in this rare display of passion, he sought to reverse the wheel of fortune. Besides putting a public slight on James's resumption of authority, his action was calculated to alarm the King personally, by reminding him that a state of hostility still existed between them, and to warn opponents that he had reached the limits of his patience.[2] The truth was he was extremely annoyed with James, and with the meddlesome Lords in London for daring to send to the King after having, as he thought, submitted their authority to his.

So far as William was concerned, the goodwill that had informed the Hungerford negotiations only days before was at an end. The compassing of the crown alone mattered to him. Sensing a challenge to his mastery of events, he decided to show the King and the Peers in town that he was not to be trifled with. He despatched Count Zuylestein, one of his most trusted servants, to James, bluntly requesting him 'to stay at Rochester'.[3] As for the unwelcome invitation to come to St. James's and re-open talks, he studiedly ignored it. Uncertain whether Zuylestein could reach Rochester in time to prevent James from returning to London, or, even if he did, whether the King, surrounded by Lords and troops who remained loyal to him, would comply with his request, William made sure that his return would avail him nothing. This he did by calling on the support of his surreptitious well-wishers in the capital.

Clarendon, who missed little of significance in the Prince's court, noted the presence at Windsor on the 16th of Sir Robert Howard, Auditor of the Receipt in the Exchequer, and Henry Powle, a well-connected, well-to-do parliamentary figure.[4] Both men had a record at Westminster of opposition to 'the growth of Popery', and had been fearless critics of James since the time of his second, Catholic marriage in 1673.[5] What he cannot have known was that Howard, an unrepentant Exclusionist, had already urged on William the necessity of deposing the King and taking his place, and that Powle, a widely respected moderate, had been in touch with The Hague before the invasion. Their arrival 'together' at Windsor, and being 'a long time in private with the Prince', more than warranted any suspicions Clarendon may have had of them.

Howard, who had recently written to William, was, on his own admission, acting 'by the advise of some considerable persons' in London, 'whose interest in the Citty and parliament', he assured him, 'will be very great'.[6] Evidently encouraged by James's restoration of the charter on 6 October,[7] and the first election for five years of a Common Council on 28 November,[8] the City Whigs—those who had survived the Tory take-over in 1683—were beginning to reckon up their strength in readiness for staging a political come-back: a development which would inevitably operate in favour of a Williamite settlement in the state and a pan-Protestant review of policy in the church. Though Howard took care to name no names, it is clear that his Whig backers included such City stalwarts as the two ex-Lord Mayors, Sir Robert Clayton and Sir Patience Ward; the former Sheriff, Thomas Pilkington; Dissenters of the calibre of Sir William Ashurst, Master of the Merchant Taylors' Company, and William Love, an old Cromwellian Councillor of State; merchants of Huguenot descent, like the Houblons and Lethieulliers; and 'opposition' lawyers of the stature of Sir George Treby, Sir John Maynard, Sir John Holt, and Henry Pollexfen—all of whom were to sponsor William's claim to the throne. Powle's presence at Windsor was particularly revealing, for it indicated that the Prince's adherents in London embraced genuine moderates, not just vengeful Whigs bent on settling old scores. Unlike Howard, a contractualist Whig, Powle had opposed Exclusion in 1679 and 1681.

Anticipating James's return to Whitehall, Howard and Powle had come from London on purpose to encourage William to act resolutely in his own, and their, best interest, and to see whether they could serve him. As a result of their representations, which must have convinced him that his support in the City was substantial, the Prince wrote a forthright letter to the Lord Mayor and Corporation, telling them in no uncertain fashion that James's coming back was 'done without my approbation; nor doe I thinke it proper at this time, not knowing what it may produce, considering the present circumstances of affaires'. He informed them of Zuylestein's mission, required them to secure the City, and promised to be with them within two days. He entrusted the letter's safe delivery to Howard and Powle, whom he also authorized to act as his emissaries to the City fathers: 'You may give full creditt to what these two gentlemen shall further tell you upon this occasion'.[9]

While this was taking place at Windsor, another Whig was busying himself in London on William's behalf. At an adjourned meeting of the Court of Aldermen on the afternoon of the 16th, a Tory motion to go and congratulate James's 'gracious returne' to Whitehall[10] was defeated

10 Dutch infantrymen, 1680s. Drawing attributed to Allaert van Everdingen. Royal Collection.

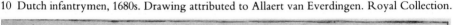

by the single-handed efforts of Sir George Treby, the restored Recorder of the City. After several denials he had been persuaded only the day before to resume the Recordership,[11] which had been his before the *quo warranto* proceedings that had swept the Whigs from office in 1683.[12] Using his considerable forensic skill, he showed 'how utterly inconsistent' such a course would be with their invitation to the Prince, for, he argued, James 'must necessarily be come with a designe to oppose the Prince', so that their congratulating him would be tantamount 'to the maintaining of a war against him'. More convincing than this rather fanciful scenario was his overt allusion to the power of the London mob. If 'the King had legall authority', and 'the Prince ‹whom› they had invited had power', they had also to take notice of 'another power, though it were very unwar‹r›antable, that the mobile had, and contradicting the invitation they had given the Prince' to come to town, 'which quieted the rabble, they might give them a provocation to commit such forceable rapes upon their houses, as they had done upon others'.[13]

Treby's argument, which conjured up the menace of renewed mob violence, was intended to intimidate. Ostensibly drawn from political prudence, and directed towards preserving the peace of the City, it really expressed his secret design to serve the Prince's cause. His aim was to prevent an automatic resumption of normal courtesies between the City and the King. In this he was wholly successful.[14] The Aldermen, as magistrates and men of property, had no desire to run the risk of being labelled by the Whigs as 'favourers of Popery'. They remembered the terrible accuracy with which the Protestant mobs had targeted their destruction; not just on 'mass-houses' and Catholic embassies, but on the private mansions and business premises of eminent Catholics. The debate thus fell, and with it Sir Thomas Rawlinson's loyal motion which had occasioned it; 'and so they did not go to congratulate the King, nor order publick bonfires, nor ringing of bells, as they had thought to have done'.[15] Had the City Tories felt the ties of loyalty more keenly, had they feared popular unrest less, had they understood the extent of Treby's enmity to the King, and responded to James's return by adding the weight of official civic recognition to his resumption of authority, he might not have fallen so easy a prey to William's ambition. But, stunned by the eruption of mob violence, and lacking an effective Lord Mayor, they were not prepared as a corporate body to discount Treby's partisan advice. Believing that to act in haste, might yet be to repent at leisure, they did nothing.

James was barely back at Whitehall when again the scene began to change with Zuylestein's belated arrival. Since his errand had been 'to forbid the King's approaching to London',[16] there was not much that he could do. James, however, repeated his hope that William 'would come the next day' to confer with him, only to be told 'planely' that he certainly would not come until all the royal troops 'were sent out of Town'. Seeing it was useless to argue, James wrote yet another letter to William re-iterating his invitation. He had just handed it over, when the Comte du Roye informed him of Feversham's arrest. Against this he protested most vehemently, and with reason, it being 'against the Law of Nations and the universall practice to detain a publick minister'. Zuylestein answered, he knew nothing of it.[17] Whether this was true, or not, Feversham's arrest had the desired effect. It completely unsettled the King, whose fears for his own safety returned with increased force. It was perhaps at this point that he made his penultimate attempt to avoid what again seemed to him to be his only alternatives—flight to the safety of France, or, if he stayed, falling into· William's clutches. Anxious to avoid either trap, he cast about for a means of staying safely in the Kingdom.

Unaware of resurgent Exclusionist sentiment in the City, but recollecting the 'two eminent merchants' who had besought him at Blackheath 'to pass through the City' on his return from Kent, and the enthusiastic reception the Londoners had given him, the King made an approach to two wealthy citizens of his acquaintance: Thomas Lewes, a Turkey merchant, and Sir Thomas Stampe, Alderman of Cripplegate. 'Whig collaborators', with nonconformist sympathies, they were, like the King, strongly averse to religious persecution.[18] James offered to remain in their hands until he had given 'full satisfaction to his people in all things relateing to Religion, libertie, etc.' He asked only one thing from them, that 'they would undertake to secure his person'. He believed he could give no greater proof of his sincerity than by making 'the people in a manner

Master of their own terms, by being so of him': clear evidence that he did not go in fear and dread of his subjects, as has often been alleged.

Lewes and Stampe were responsive and responsible enough to put the proposition to the Common Council of the City, but, there, progress was blocked by the intervention of another committed Exclusionist, Sir Robert Clayton, the King's sworn enemy and the very man who, on the 11th, had rushed to William with the Lieutenancy's invitation to come to London.[19] Neither William at Windsor, nor his well-placed allies in the City, wanted 'an accommodation'. This was shown by the alacrity with which 'many that had ventured for the Prince' left London for Windsor, shortly before James's arrival back in town, 'for fear of being apprehended' on charges of treason. They included Halifax, the chairman of the provisional government, and Montagu, one of the leading 'Williamites' at the Guildhall meeting. As yet 'no men were sure which way the current would run'.[20]

XVIII James's Return

James's return to London on the 16th radicalized political options by demonstrating, even to those who, until the day before, had preferred to ignore the legal fact, that there was yet a King in Israel. His unchallenged resumption of authority made nonsense of the Whigs' notion of 'a cession' in government, which was shown to be no more than wishful thinking, and, in the process, false footed the Prince's advance towards the throne: a throne which was not vacant, as he and they claimed, but was still occupied by his uncle and father-in-law. Now it was the turn of the self-proclaimed 'Williamites' to flee the capital in terror. As yet they did not dare to withstand the King to his face. As for James, he had never thought of himself as having abdicated; nor was he prepared to concede that his flight had in any degree impaired his title as King. When, on 27 November, he told the peers at Whitehall of his conviction that William 'came for the crown', he had emphatically stated 'that he would not see himself deposed; that he had read the story of King Richard II'.[1] The whole point of his withdrawing was to elude the wretched fate of that medieval monarch. By avoiding captivity he hoped to safeguard the prerogatives of the crown, no less than save his person from harm.

Though his regal status and bearing had been temporarily eclipsed by the 'rudeness' of the mob during his detention at Faversham,[2] he recovered both as soon as he was set at liberty. He commanded that he be served 'with ceremony' on bended knee, he oversaw the disposition of his guards, made the Earl of Winchilsea Lord Lieutenant of Kent and appointed him Governor of Dover Castle in place of Sir Edward Hales. Back at Whitehall, he 'appeared more cheerful than before his withdrawing', dined in state, received the congratulations of peers and bishops on his safe return, and gave audience to foreign ambassadors. The Protestant bishops were particularly pleased 'to see the Head of the Church of England come home again'.[3] James summoned the Privy Council, which met on the evening of the 16th. Eight Councillors attended, all of them Protestants. They included both Secretaries of State and the Master of the Rolls, none of whom scrupled to act with him. Two orders-in-Council were drawn up, signed, and gazetted: one authorizing local officials to suppress continuing popular unrest, the other lifting the peers' embargo on the ports.[4] The machinery of royal government began to revive. Treasury business, having ceased on the 11th, resumed on the 17th, when a warrant was issued to the Commissioners of the Excise ordering them to direct their Cashier, Charles Duncombe, to pay immediately into the Exchequer all the excise money remaining in his hands for the King's use.[5] Only in the sphere of military affairs was the King hesitant to act.

More remarkable than the routine functioning of government was the rapid reconstitution of the royal Court. To hostile spectators it seemed that distressingly little had altered as a result of the King's five-day absence, for others, besides James, behaved as though he had never been away. The Catholics came out of hiding and made straight for Whitehall. Having survived the Protestant onslaught, they again looked to the King to protect them. Understandably, they could hardly bear to let him out of their sight. Their presence in the Palace, numerous 'even to the filling of the Court', was adversely commented on. On Sunday evening, the 16th, amid 'a throng of Papists' James went to Mass in the Chapel, Ronquillo's priests officiating at the altar.[6] On the 17th it was reported that '30 or 40' Catholics were 'at His Majestie's dinner, and no other priest, but a Jesuit, to say grace', which made some Protestants harbour retrograde thoughts, that the Papists 'have not done with him yet'. It was feared that 'their power is like to be so much the greater, because he looks upon them as his sufferers, though, in truth, he is theirs'.[7] At Windsor William was quick to seize on this rallying of Catholics to Whitehall as a pretext for getting the King out of London.[8] But, before he had time to do so, James's 'old friends' made yet another bid to reach an agreement with him, as the foundation on which to re-stabilize government by asserting his kingship against the revolutionary policy of William and his supporters.

In loyalist negotiations on the 17th, perhaps conducted by Secretary of State Preston, it was put to James that he and 'the hierarchy' of the Church of England 'might yet save one another, and they could neither of them be saved by any other meanes, and they had endangered the utter destruction of one another by misapprehensions'. The King, in reply, 'confessed it was his fatall errour, that he had made use of the Papists' in government, 'and deserted the hierarchy, and that, upon his royall word, he would never attempt the like again'. Following this promising *éclaircissement* four Protestant bishops—Archbishop Lamplugh of York, Turner of Ely, White of Peterborough, and Sprat of Rochester—waited on James 'in the forenoone', and 'he and they gave one another the most full and reciprocall satisfaction, and parted with great complacency'.[9] Inevitably, Bishop Turner led the discussion. He was the most politically adept of the bishops and a former domestic chaplain of the King, whom Sancroft was grooming to succeed him at Canterbury.[10] He told James 'he could not expect' that William 'would accept of any lesse concessions, then such as should put it out of his power to do such things, as he had done heretofore against the laws'.[11]

After the audience, in which the bishops drove a hard bargain for the Protestant interest, Turner was convinced that a basis existed for reconciling the King and Prince. He informed the Bishop of St. Asaph, who favoured William's dynastic pretensions, that James 'was willing to do all that could be required of him', even to being 'reduced to the state of a Duke of Venice, committing all the power of war and peace, and of making all officers, ecclesiastic and civill, to the Prince for his lifetime; and that he would consent to bills in parliament for the purpose', including those 'offer'd for the security of religion and civill rights'. Such a condescension he particularly welcomed as being 'most agreeable to His Highnesse's *Declaration*'—the ground on which so many loyal Church of England men, including the loyalist peers at the Guildhall, had countenanced William's endeavours to rescue them from the 'dangers of Popery and slavery'.[12] With their dual loyalties to a Catholic King and a Protestant Church the loyalists wanted the best of both worlds. They wished to obtain a permanent guarantee for the Protestant Ascendancy, without breaking their sacred oaths of allegiance to James II, as the Lord's Anointed. What neither they, nor James, yet knew was that no concessions would satisfy the Prince and his partisans, for whom the much vaunted *Declaration* was fast becoming irrelevant.

On Monday the 17th, the morning after James's return, the Court of Aldermen and Common Council of the City assembled at 9 a.m., when the Common Serjeant acquainted them that the deputation which they had sent to the Prince on the 11th had been 'kindly received'. Then Sir Robert Howard and Henry Powle were introduced, who brought the all-important letter from William to the City. Having received his 'gracious letter', informing them of his disapproval of the King's coming back, the City responded quickly and firmly to the 'assurance' of his kindness and protection. They re-affirmed their gratitude for his 'great and glorious undertaking' to preserve their 'religion, lawes, and liberties', and, by way of return, assured him that they would 'not spare to expose' their lives and estates (an obsequious phrase usually reserved for the sovereign) in helping him to obtain 'those ends'. They also undertook to prevent 'all dangers from those restlesse spirits that have now appeared'—meaning, of course, the Papists that flocked to Whitehall to pay court to a Popish Prince, who by his ignominious flight had, the Whigs maintained, ceased to be the effective ruler of England.[13]

What Howard and Powle had to say to the City in William's name is not known. But in all probability they used the large appearance of Catholics at Whitehall on the 16th as proof that James had undergone no change of heart as a result of his ordeal in Kent, and remained as 'very a Papist' as ever he had been. The presence at Court of the French Ambassador Barillon, the Prince's principal enemy in England, was both disconcerting and provocative.[14] Already it was credibly reported in the City that 'the Papists cryed they had another day for it'.[15] They, too, it seemed, had not learnt the lesson of Protestant chastizement.

The speed with which the Aldermen acted on William's cue to keep the City secure—when there was no danger, apart from that fictitiously posed by the 'great concourse of Papists' about the King's person—strongly suggests that it was the familiar and persistent fear of Catholic reprisal which drove them deeper and deeper into 'Williamite' measures. There can be no doubt of their alarm, for they promptly ordered 'an extraordinary guard' to be mounted, calling on the pro-Orangist Commissioners of the Lieutenancy to increase the Trained Bands 'to the number of three regiments'.[16] To attest their growing attachment to William, and the Protestant interest which he personified, in contrast to their declining allegiance to James, who personified Popery, they offered to appoint a 'convenient' residence for the Prince in the City, 'free', as they told him, 'from the resort of persons disaffected to your great self and glorious designe'.[17]

XIX The Windsor Consultations

While William's allies worked to tighten their grip on the capital, at Windsor he had been contemplating his next move. Since he had committed himself to be in London on the following day, the 18th, time was short. All round him his supporters continued to argue that James's return had altered nothing, and that his 'going away' on the 11th was 'a cession of his right to the crowne'. Burnet, who was present, has recorded the state of feeling at Windsor. 'The prince heard the opinions, not only of those who had come along with him, but of such of the nobility as were now come to him, among whom the marquis of Hallifax was one. All agreed, that it was not convenient that the king should stay at Whitehall. Neither the king, nor the prince, nor the city, could have been safe, if they had been both near one another. Tumults would probably have arisen out of it. The guards, and the officious flatterers, of the two courts, would have been unquiet neighbours. It was thought necessary to stick to the point of the king's deserting his people, and not to give up that by entering upon any treaty with him'.[1] That William agreed with this line of reasoning was demonstrated by his spurning the King's repeated invitations to St. James's, even though that brought to him by Zuylestein permitted him 'to send what forces he pleased to town'.[2]

Whatever action he took now needed to be decisive and collaborative. It was imperative to involve his English adherents in what he did. Having listened to the views of individuals, he knew that there was support for bold measures. As before, at Hungerford, he summoned a meeting of the English with him, only this time he confined his summons to the peers—perhaps in tacit acknowledgement of their prominence in the crisis, but very probably because their views had become more important to him, as a result of the undiminished respect shown to the King by certain of the Lords in London. He had to face the fact that they would sit in any parliament, however free, not by election, but by hereditary right. By asking them 'what was fit to be done upon the King's being come to Whitehall', he intended to get as many of them as he could to commit themselves to an agreed course of action, and, he hoped, to his claim to the throne.

Eleven peers answered the summons, though another, Clarendon, arrived late at the meeting, and after 'the resolution' had been taken. As Lord Chandos, a peer known to be devoted to King James, was 'in the outward room', but not 'suffered' to go into 'the inner room' where they met, it would seem that those who attended had been carefully selected by the Prince. Indeed, Clarendon's attendance may have been more by accident than design. Halifax presided. He it was who recounted to Clarendon 'what they had resolved upon' before he came.[3]

Predominantly Orangist in sentiment, they were not of a single mind, reflecting the diversity of their backgrounds. Four had come over from Holland with the Prince (Shrewsbury, Mordaunt, Macclesfield, and Wiltshire); two were rebels from the North (Delamer and Stamford); two were revolted Generals from the King's army (Grafton and Churchill); and two had been pro-Orangist members of the provisional government in London (North and Carbery). Of these only the first six, along with Halifax, can at this stage be accounted committed Williamites.

Delamer, supported by Macclesfield and Stamford, showed his revolutionary fervour by proposing that James be sent to the Tower. They argued that his flight on the 11th amounted to a 'dissolution of the government', with the corollary that he was no longer King of England. They were opposed by Grafton and Churchill, though, according to Halifax's testimony, 'all spoke against his going to any of his own houses', or doing 'anything that might look like treating him as King'. In conclusion, it was agreed that he 'should be advised to leave Whitehall, and to go to Ham', the Duchess of Lauderdale's villa on the Thames.[4] For all that William had ostentatiously absented himself from their meeting, the appearance of aristocratic independence was a sham. Prior discussions had left little doubt as to the outcome. On Clarendon's asking why the King had to leave his own Palace, Halifax revealingly replied that 'the Prince did not believe he could be safe there',[5] showing that he, for one, had been primed by William. Why it was unsafe for the King to stay at Whitehall, protected by his guards and attended by his servants, and in the midst of a capital city which had greeted his return with enthusiasm eighteen hours before,[6] was wisely not explained. There was no explanation, save William's soaring ambition and the exorbitant expectations of his partisans.

At the close of their deliberations the Prince was invited in. Halifax informed him of their decision. It cannot have surprised him. Clarendon, disturbed at the recommendation of the meeting, took advantage of his nephew William's arrival to say, that 'it seemed strange ... that the King should be, as it were, directed to go to Ham; that if it were not safe for His Majesty to be at London, why might he not be at liberty to go where he pleased? or be desired to go to some of his own houses, Hampton-Court, or Windsor, and to have his own guards about him?' Such persistent questioning, combined with his undisguised concern for James's physical welfare, was too much for the brittle temper of Lord Delamer—'a little thing puts him into a passion'. He snapped back 'very angrily', that, unlike Clarendon, 'he did not look upon him as his King, and would never more pay him obedience'.

At last the truth was out, though it took a puritanical, ill-tempered, Whig Exclusionist to shame the devil by telling it. From the time that he had entered the House of Commons in 1678, as Knight of the Shire for Cheshire, until a month ago, when he had raised that county against 'Popery and slavery', he had distinguished himself as one of James's bitterest opponents. Believing that James's title had been extinguished, and that 'he ought not to be like a King' housed and cosseted in a royal palace, he 'earnestly pressed that he might be directed to Ham'. His choice of word evinced his wish to take a tougher line towards James. Whereas the peers, acting collectively, thought he 'should be *advised* to leave Whitehall', Delamer thought 'he might be *directed*' to go to Ham House.

It is noteworthy that Delamer's Whig outburst was the only reply that Clarendon got to his questions. William simply 'approved of what the Lords had done', and cut short further exchanges. Cautious as always, Halifax wished to cover the tracks of treason. He told the Prince that 'there had been very free debates, which would not be very fit to be talked of; whereupon his Highness enjoined secresy'. His injunction to all present did not stop the Windsor meeting of peers from attracting wide notice and wilder speculation as to what had been discussed by them.

William next raised the manner of delivering the message to the King. Needless to say, there were no volunteers for this ungrateful task. Keen to stay in the background, while others shouldered the responsibility for implementing the peers' decision, Halifax was the first to speak. He thought it best that 'some of the Prince's officers' should carry it, and named Count von Solms-Braunfels, Captain of William's personal bodyguard, the Blue Guards. But the Prince was against that. He was fully prepared to supply military backing for the recommended plan of action, but insisted that his English followers should play their part in executing it: 'By your favour, my Lord, it is the advice of the peers here, and some of yourselves shall carry it', and, so saying, he named Halifax, Shrewsbury, and Delamer 'in the same breath'.[7] His nomination of the politically slippery Halifax, famed in his day as 'the Trimmer', was rightly seen as making a 'tryal' of his newly discovered loyalty to himself. It has to be remembered that he had declined to join in the invitation of the 'Immortal Seven', and had subsequently accepted the King's commission to lead the Hungerford negotiations, much to William's surprise. Shrewsbury and Delamer could be expected to undertake 'this extraordinary embassy' to the King; but, in placing Halifax at the head of it, William 'could not help smiling (as he own'd afterwards) to see him, who came a Commissioner to him from the other side, accept to act so low a part so very willingly'.[8] His name having been spoken, the Marquess could do no other than accept with as good a grace as he could muster. In one masterly move William had 'fixed' him to his interest for life.

Before the meeting broke up it considered the military requirements of the plan. William decided to employ his own Guards, and gave order for them to march to London. He commanded Solms to follow them and 'take possession of the posts at Whitehall'. He intended to make the King his prisoner before attempting to deliver the message directing him to vacate Whitehall. Not wishing to leave any part of the operation to the vagaries of chance, he also raised the question of 'what guard' should 'attend upon the King' at Ham House. One of the peers said that 'it would be fit to instruct the officer, that should be appointed to command it, what to do, in case the King should endeavour to make his escape from Ham'. His interjection, which clearly envisaged James's remaining a close prisoner of the Prince, gave rise to 'some debate'; enough for the moderate Shrewsbury to move that it might be made 'the subject of another consultation'—perhaps without the loyal Clarendon present.[9] It was instantly agreed.

Having outstayed his welcome, Lord Clarendon quitted the Castle in sombre mood, and took coach for London. His 'designe' in going in to the Prince had not been to desert the King's interest, as was commonly supposed, but an attempt to save his 'poor master', whom he was convinced was 'just upon the point to be sacrificed, if it were not prevented'.[10] Animated by his high church principles of loyalty, his mistrust of Halifax, and his desire to regain office, he had hoped to strengthen William's resolve to stick to his *Declaration*—the basis on which so many loyal Tories had joined his expedition on its march through Southern England. Yet, his good intentions had been overwhelmed by the flood-tide of Whig ambition and the Prince's sudden conversion to the revolutionary Whig notion of 'a cession' in government. Denied the opportunity to mediate between his nephew and brother-in-law, he foresaw political disaster for the King, himself, and the high church Tories. Late on the 17th—the day on which the fate of the unsuspecting King had been settled at Windsor—he recorded his feelings in his diary: 'I thought it the most melancholy day I had ever seen in my whole life'.[11]

XX William the King-Breaker

Soon after Clarendon's departure from Windsor the three Lords deputed to carry the message to James were given their formal instructions in writing by the Prince, who also signed them. As the document which authorized the essential act of deposition, leading to the King's second, and enforced, removal from London, I quote it in full:

> We doe desire you, the Lord Marquis of Hallifax, the E‹a›rle of Shrewsbury, and the Lord Delamer, to tell the King that it is thought convenient, for the greater quiet of the City and for the greater safety of his person, that he doe remove to Ham, where he shall be attended by guards, who will be ready to preserve him from any disturbance. Given att Windsor, the 17‹th› day of December 1688.
>
> G. Prince d'Orange.[1]

Concise and matter of fact though it is, the message is highly instructive. Besides emphasizing that the King was in some unspecified physical danger, which was bound to alarm him, concern for the peace of the City of London was again made use of as the overriding argument to justify taking quite unjustifiable measures against him. Indeed, in William's mind, the security of the City took precedence over concern for the King's safety, as well it might, since there was absolutely no danger to his well-being beyond what might have come from himself and his adherents.

The Dutch troops—three batallions of the Foot Guards and some cavalry—entered London about ten o'clock at night. Having secured the posts at St. James's Palace, they marched on Whitehall in battle formation, their matches lit for action. Around eleven, as the King was going to bed, he was advertised of their presence in the Park. He said he 'could not believe it, because he had heard nothing of it ... from the Prince'. He thought there must be some mistake. Supposing they had come to occupy St. James's, ready for the Prince's coming the next day, he sent for the Dutch commander. When told by the King that he was 'mistaken' in his instructions, Solms was 'positive' that he was not, and produced his orders. Having vainly 'argued the matter with him for some time', James ordered the Earl of Craven, who commanded at Whitehall, to withdraw his men—but not before the gallant Craven, who was in his eighties, protested his resolution 'to be rather cut in pieces, than resign his post ... to the Prince's guards'. Their places were taken by William's troops 'to prevent the possibility of a disturbance from guards belonging to several masters'.[2]

That night the King retired to bed surrounded by Dutch soldiers, a prisoner in his own Palace. After midnight Halifax, Shrewsbury, and Delamer arrived at the Palace, and demanded to 'bee immediately admitted' to the King. Though Secretary Middleton, who was currently Gentleman in Waiting and 'lay by the King', would have had them stay till morning, 'they answer'd that their business would admit of no delay'.[3] Middleton woke the King, who was fast asleep, and admitted the Lords 'to his bed-side at that unseasonable hour'. It was turned one o'clock. James did not get up.[4] What followed is best related in Halifax's own words in his hitherto unpublished letter to the Prince:

> May it please Your Highnesse,
> It was so late before Your Highnesse's guards were placed in Whitehall, that the King was in bed before wee could bee admitted to him. When wee came to him, wee shewed him the paper signed by Your Highnesse, with which hee said hee would comply; and wee desired him, that hee would remoove tomorrow morning, so as to bee at Ham before 12 of clock. Hee said hee would endeavour to do it by going by water to Putney, and from thence to Ham in his coach. Hee asked whither hee might chuse the servants hee was to carry with him, to which wee answered hee might, having understood it to bee Your Highnesse's pleasure that it should bee so. Wee took our leave of him, and by that time wee had gone the length of 3 or 4 rooms wee were called back, and then hee told us, that hee ... desire‹d› hee might goe to Rochester, it being the place where Your Highnesse would have had him stay, and hee still desireth that hee may raither go to Rochester, than to any other place, and wished that wee would represent it to Your Highnesse, which wee promised him to do. Wee hope an answer may be sent with Your Highnesse's resolution before 8 of clock tomorrow morning, which is as soon as the King can with any convenience set out. Wee hasten away the messenger, that no time may bee lost, being desirous to acquit ourselves in every particular of the commands wee have receaved from Your Highnesse, as becometh, etc.[5]

James was not the only prince to be abruptly awakened that night.

Having received Halifax's letter at Syon House, Bentinck woke William to obtain fresh instructions. At 5 o'clock, on the morning of the 18th, Bentinck wrote to Halifax that the Prince found 'no difficulty in agreeing to what the King asks, being indifferent if he is in one place or the other'. He was, therefore, to let him go to Rochester in place of Ham. It is impossible to believe that William, any more than James, was not aware of the advantages of Rochester, over Ham, as a place from which to escape to France. One thing was made perfectly plain. James was to go to Rochester 'under the same guard' that had been ordered to escort him to Ham.[6] There was to be no escape until William decided to let go of him.

After sending 'so generous an invitation' to his son-in-law to come and confer with him on measures to secure the peace of the nation, William's peremptory message, delivered in the dead of night, 'when he was weary and fast asleepe', and 'in such a manner as might seem almost to pronounce his doom', was 'heinously' taken by the King.[7] Alarmed as he was for his personal safety, he protested against the Prince's high-handed treatment of him, telling Solms that 'this was a force upon him, and he was driven hereby from London'. The Count, whose behaviour throughout was 'very disrespectful' to the King, did not deny the charge. Rather, he attempted to justify it. He retorted that 'force must be opposed by force', and that James had 'raised the first force for the destroying of the subject', together with 'the religion, lawes, liberties, and lives' of his people.[8] In saying this Solms, who was no mere instrument of the Prince's will, but his near kinsman and ally of long standing, spoke William's sentiments exactly. Ever since the meeting of the peers at Windsor, on the 17th, William had acknowledged himself 'so well satisfyed in the cause' he had espoused, 'that he could act against the King in the way of a fair warr'.[9] As the victor in a bloodless campaign, he felt free to dispose of the vanquished King as he chose. James had ceased to be his opponent. He had become the defeated enemy and his defenceless prisoner. 'The King', we are told, 'understood the message, as well as his danger in being refractory'.[10] Powerless to resist, he bowed to the command to be gone. Right had, perforce, to yield to might.

However, abject as his position undeniably was, James was not finished yet. He took refuge in the divinity that 'doth hedge a King'. Like his father before him, he sensed his proximity to a martyr's crown just as the imperial crown was slipping irretrievably from his grasp. The next morning, when the Protestant bishops, 'the loyal nobility', and foreign ambassadors 'came to pay their last respects' to him, he went out of his way to stress the fact that he was not leaving the capital of his own volition, but under duress. He made a particular point of telling Archbishop Lamplugh of York, the senior ecclesiastic present, that 'hee was chased away from his owne house by the Prince of Orange'. As the injured party, he 'desired him to pray for him'. The royal request struck a deeply sympathetic chord. Lamplugh 'prayed God to bless His Majesty, saying that hee was an old man, and that, if hee saw His Majestye's face no more, hee hoped that they should meet together in heaven'. After tearful farewells James stepped into his barge 'about ll a clock', attended by 'three Lords of the Bedchamber', the Earls of Ailesbury, Arran, and Dumbarton.[11] Under an armed Dutch guard he was conveyed down river, never to return.

For those who, helplessly, watched the enforced removal of the King they loved it was a terrible emotional wrench. Barillon reported to Louis XIV that 'the English who saw him leave were very sad, most of them having tears in their eyes', and that 'the same sadness appeared in the consternation of the people when they knew that the King was leaving surrounded by Dutch guards'. Such was the overpowering melancholy of the occasion, that one onlooker, John Evelyn, himself on the point of tears, actually feared that there was 'something more dismal by boading'.[12] Even the unflinching Halifax was agitated. Afraid that the sight of the King's equipage 'might cause disorder and move compassion', he opposed its being sent 'through the Citie'; as, indeed, he had earlier insisted that James should go to Gravesend 'by water', not over land, for fear that his being seen to be a prisoner would provoke 'an insurrection' in his behalf.[13] In the end, after a 'hideous' shooting of London Bridge, always a dangerous exercise when the River was at low tide, James's dismissal passed off quietly. The decent-minded Anglican, Ailesbury, terrified by the hazardous negotiation of the bridge, consoled himself with the loyal thought that, if he perished, 'it was in a righteous cause' in 'not forsaking my King and Sovereign in his bitter afflictions'.[14] The King reached Gravesend after nightfall, and was lodged discreetly, under 'very strict watch', in the house of a common attorney. The following day he was escorted to Rochester by armed Dutch guards.

11 The reception of William of Orange in London, 18 December 1688. Dutch engraving by Romeyn de Hooge.

XXI William's Arrival

Only hours after James's removal William came to town with Marshal Schomberg. His calash was 'preceded and guarded by a numerous company of his army', led by four regiments of foot under Major-General Mackay. He was 'accompanied by multitudes of all ranks on horseback'. On the outskirts of St. James's Park he was met by the Sheriffs of London and Middlesex, who had been sent by the City to welcome him. In time-honoured ceremony they 'surrend‹e›red their white staves to His Highness', and received them back in token of the trust that existed between him and the City fathers. Already the Prince was assuming the mantle of monarchy. With the King removed, and Catholics once more at the mercy of Protestant laws and Protestant officialdom, William did not need to take up residence in the City. Instead, he proceeded directly to St. James's Palace, which had been prepared for him by royal command. He arrived at three o'clock 'in extraordinary great grandieur'.[1] His troops entered immediately upon guard duty.

The same day a Londoner wrote to his correspondent in the country: 'You may imagin‹e› it was no unsurprizing spectacle to see (if I may so phrase it) a forraign enemy in an hostile manner march through the metropolis of the Kingdom with no other diversion than the repeated huszas and loud acclamations of the inhabitants, who shewed no other concern for this revolution, but what might express their satisfaction and approbation. In a word, all things conspired to testifie their joy on this occasion'.[2] Despite 'the excessive rain', which fell all day, there was a vast turn-out of citizens to greet the Prince's troops marching to their quarters. As they passed along Fleet Street the womenfolk 'shooke his soldiers by the hand', shouting 'welcome, welcome. God blesse you, you come to redeeme our religion, lawes, liberties, and lives. God reward you'.[3]

That evening at St. James's 'the crowd was so great' that Clarendon could not get to see his nephew. Having been artificially parochialized by James's pro-Catholic policies, which had excluded them from the Royal Household as well as from government office, the Protestant nobility and gentry instinctively flocked back to Court. Their numbers were such that 'the like' had 'not been seen in England these many yeares'. One cause of the unusual press of clients was the conspicuous return to Court of the Whig lords and gentlemen, eager to congratulate 'the hero', who, in addition to rescuing the nation from 'Popery and slavery', would, they hoped, deliver them from the wilderness of a decade of royal disfavour. Returned to Protestant safe-keeping, the Court promptly recovered its power to attract the support and service of the entire ruling class. Seeing 'the ambitious and the covetous' canvassing 'for places of honour and rich employments', Evelyn concluded that 'those who seeke employments, before the grandees are served, may suspend their solicitation'.[4] William was recognized by all, Whigs and Tories alike, as the central figure on whom everything now depended. Whatever difficulties remained in the way of obtaining a settlement, his views would be decisive. It was as Halifax told him: 'he might be what he pleased ... for as nobody knew what to do with him, so nobody knew what to do without him'.[5]

The mood of the capital, so exultant at the prospect of a lasting return to law and order with William's arrival, was much chastened as the news of James's dismissal gained currency. On the 19th Clarendon noted: 'It is not to be imagined what a damp there was upon all sorts of men throughout the town. The treatment the King had met with from the Prince of Orange, and the manner of his being driven ... from Whitehall, with such circumstances, moved compassion in those who were not very fond of him'.[6] It offended against the norms of family decency and political propriety, for it showed that 'the person of the king was now struck at, as well as his government'.[7] It occasioned deep resentment among the Tories, the clergy and soldiery especially, who held 'that it was a gross violation' of the Prince's *Declaration* 'to send the King away, and utterly against their sense'.[8] Some of William's supporters were troubled at 'the poor King's misfortunes'. When writing to Admiral Herbert, at sea with the Dutch fleet, Burnet accepted that Herbert, a Tory, could not 'have acted as some others have done' towards James, but roundly told him 'whatever one may think of that, wee must now shut our mouths, for there is discontent enough already, and the army seem generally out of humour and uneasy at what they have done'. Burnet was right to think that 'the foolish men of Feversham' had, by stopping the King's flight, thrown William 'into an uneasy after-game',[9] yet it must be emphasized that the Prince's own resolve to be rid of the King cost him 'the universal applause of the whole nation',[10] which had been his since he landed at Tor Bay. His dramatic intervention from Windsor had completely shattered Protestant unanimity. William the liberator was welcomed by all, but William the usurper was not.

In the heated controversy which ensued the Tories, who adhered to the doctrines of passive obedience and non-resistance, forgot the ignominy of James's earlier flight. They concentrated their attention instead on William's having driven the King from Whitehall against his will and by force of arms. Perturbed at the favour he bestowed on Whigs and Dissenters, they began to believe what James had claimed all along, that 'this specious undertaking would now appear to be only a disguised and designed usurpation'.[11] Although William had in fact had no such design, and had only moved towards the throne in response to the King's first flight, in retrospect it seemed to many of them that they had been duped. Having accepted at face value the limited political aims contained in his *Declaration*, they 'were startled' and shocked to discover 'that the Prince aimed at something else'. Sir Edward Seymour, who like 'all the West went in to the Prince of Orange upon his declaration', announced, on coming to town, that 'it would be impossible for honest men to serve him'.[12] Looking back at the encouraging state of Tory negotiations with James on the eve of the invasion, and aware of the understanding reached with him on the 17th, some concluded that foreign intervention had not only been otiose, but deleterious. Believing that they had been 'in a sure way to deliverance before the Prince came in with his army', they felt that they had been 'deluded with artificiall contrivances' and that 'the dangers of Popery' had been 'magnified when they were in no danger at all'.[13] The events of recent days in and about the capital certainly warranted their feeling as they did. Even before Dutch William set foot in his uncle's palace the seeds of Tory disillusionment were germinating.

For two days William hesitated at St. James's, uncertain what to do. He had clearly rejected the advice of 'the greatest lawyers and those that came in with' him to declare himself king, by right of conquest, after the example of the victorious Henry VII, and issue writs for parliament in his own name.[14] Wishing to recapture the unanimity which had greeted his original expedition, he fell back on his *Declaration*. On the 20th he convened yet another assembly of peers. On the 21st sixty-five peers met in the Queen's Presence Chamber at St. James's to give their advice on 'the best manner' of pursuing his declared objectives. The meeting proved worse than useless. There was chronic disagreement on every issue that was raised: on the urgency of proceeding, the wording of an address of thanks to the Prince, the signing of the Association, the choice of learned counsel to assist their deliberations, and even the venue for further meetings. Though the Williamites made the running in the debates on the 21st and 22nd, when, having adjourned to the House of Lords, Halifax was again put into the chair, the outcome of both meetings was disappointing to William: an address of thanks and an embarrassing order banishing Catholics from London, which he was hard put to to explain to his Catholic allies in Europe. His supporters, worried at the growing rift between themselves and the loyalists, contented themselves with an order restraining the number of visitors to Lord Jeffreys in the Tower, who was naively regarded as the source of disaffection.[15] As for considering how to obtain a parliament, the purpose for which they had been called together, they did absolutely nothing. They were completely inhibited by the knowledge that King James was still in the Kingdom. Without his co-operation there could be no parliament.

XXII James's Second Flight

From the 19th to the 23rd James remained at Rochester. There he received daily accounts 'how matters went in Town'. Though informed of the Archbishop of Canterbury's refusal to wait on William because of his being kept 'under restraint', James was more impressed by the all but 'universal running into the invader', and again thought of withdrawing. The Tories, 'who wished him well', as they had every reason to after the bargain they had struck with him on the 17th, argued against his going, advising him to 'keep himself private in the Town or Country'.[1] As long as he remained in the Kingdom he could not be denied a voice in the making of a settlement. Bishop Turner sent Dr. Robert Brady, a royal physician and leading Tory polemicist, to Rochester 'with reasons in writing' against withdrawing, 'which he press'd very earnestly'.[2] Clarendon deputed an 'honest Roman Catholic' to tell him that 'his enemies wished that he would be gone and his friends feared it'.[3] Bishop Mews of Winchester actually went to him to drive home the point.[4] But time and again James reverted to the same topic—his personal safety. Though the bishops could not credit that William would 'attempt anything against his Majestys life', they could not guarantee it. In discoursing with Secretary Middleton the pros and cons of staying he received scant re-assurance. Middleton confessed that he found it 'hard' to counsel him, saying 'that to advise him to stay was extream hazardous, considering how his Father had been used, tho‹ugh› it began not much so violently against him'. Of one thing the loyalists were 'very confident', which was 'that if his Majesty went out of the Kingdom, the door would immediately be shut upon him'.[5]

James therefore made one last effort to avoid flight, probably in response to the loyalists' attempt to get both him and Archbishop Sancroft to attend the meeting of peers appointed for Christmas Eve.[6] As before, at Whitehall, he had approached the City of London to secure his person until he had satisfied the nation, so now, at Rochester, he made 'the same offer' to the bishops of the Church of England, and particularly to Bishop Mews, an old Cavalier, who had fought as a soldier for his father, his brother, and, most recently, for himself in 1685, when he had cast aside his rochet to direct the cannon against Monmouth's rebels at Sedgemoor. Sadly, he received 'the Same answer, that they could not promis‹e› him security', whereupon he 'thought it madness not to get away as fast as he could'.[7]

The Prince did everything he could to speed him on his way. He ordered the Dutch guards under Colonel Wijck to relax their vigilance, especially at the back of Sir Richard Head's house, which faced the Medway, and even furnished the Duke of Berwick with blank passports to carry to his father.[8] More in keeping with his former strategy of intimidation, William wrote to the City of London to omit tendering 'the usual oaths to the King', including the Oath of Allegiance, following the election of a new Common Council on St. Thomas's Day:[9] news of which was rapidly transmitted to James by 'one of the lords that was admitted into Councils that the Prince of Orange held', with the additional advice that he 'would not be safe if he stayed in the realm'. It seems that James had also learnt something of the Windsor discussions on the 17th, for he told Ailesbury that, if he stayed, he would be sent to the Tower, and 'no King ever went out of that place but to his grave'. Alongside these discouraging intimations, on the one hand, and the encouraging letters which he received from 'the Court of France', on the other, telling him of the safe arrival of the Queen and Prince of Wales, and bringing a 'kindly' invitation from Louis xiv to join them, the blandishments of the loyalist peers paled into insignificance. On the 22nd he made up his mind to go. Having taken leave of the ever faithful Ailesbury, to whom he affirmed he would 'always be in a readiness to return', once his subjects' eyes were opened, he retired for the night.[10] Before daybreak on the 23rd he 'silently' left the sleeping house. Attended by Berwick, he took ship, and sailed for France. The news of his 'being again withdrawn' reached London by the afternoon of the same day. To Clarendon, Bishop Turner, and the loyalists it was 'like an earthquake', destroying their hopes and shattering their measures.[11] England was, at last, what William and the Whigs wanted it to be—a Kingdom without a King.

James's flight removed the sole obstacle to William's compassing the throne. Seeing that the

12 The final flight of James II from England, Rochester, 23 December 1688. Dutch engraving.

Peers were profoundly divided,[12] he consulted his Whig advisers, and, on their advice, summoned an irregular assembly of commoners, which, by its very composition, ensured that it would be hostile to James. He called a meeting for the 26th of the surviving MPs of Charles II's reign, the Lord Mayor and Court of Aldermen, and fifty representatives of the Common Council of London.[13] By deliberately ignoring the Tory members of James's 'Loyal Parliament' of 1685 he obtained a predominantly Whig assembly.[14] In the past the Whigs had demanded Exclusion from Charles II, but had been refused it. William was now in a position to give it to them, especially as James's going emancipated his enemies in the peerage. This was seen in the Peers' meeting on Christmas Eve. For the first time there was open talk of 'a demise' in government. Though the loyalists fought a valiant rearguard action, they were unable to stem the advance of Williamite sentiments. Berkeley, Rochester, and Bishop Turner demanded an enquiry into the circumstances of the King's withdrawing, particularly whether it was done 'freely or by constraint'; Pembroke raised the independent claims of the infant Prince of Wales; Abingdon and Craven moved to hold a parliament on the King's remaining writs; Clarendon called on William to receive 'a legate' from the King, and Nottingham was for offering the King 'proposals'—but none of their motions commended themselves to a majority, any more than did their opponents' more precipitate demands.[15] After protracted debate, from nine in the morning to five in the afternoon, the meeting concluded that 'the government of the Kingdome was extinct in a manner' by James's going.[16] It adopted two addresses, requesting William to issue his circular letters to the constituencies for electing a Convention (which obviated the intractable problem of how to come by a parliament), and asking him to assume the direction of government until the Convention met on 22 January (which sidestepped the difficulty of defining the status of the departed monarch).[17] On Boxing Day 1688 the assembly of commoners presented a similar petition, in which 'the poore King' was 'not considered or mentioned', and 'the do‹o›re shutt upon him as if he had never bin'.[18] On the 28th William accepted the responsibilities of government.[19]

By the end of December 1688 the dynastic revolution was essentially complete. William was, in all but name, regent of the realm. Temporary though his position yet was, it was inconceivable that he should be asked to settle for less. It is one of the myths of the Revolution of 1688 that it was a parliamentary revolution. It was no such thing. The Convention—a body unknown to the laws of the land—was called to settle public affairs in the wake of a successful dynastic revolution. The proceedings of the Convention of 1689, which engrossed the attention of politicians and political commentators at the time, just as they have continued to mesmerize historians ever since, were of secondary, not primary, political importance. The decisions that mattered had been taken before it met. They were made by William and James, acting either alone or in concert with their supporters. It was the actions of the dynasts, not the ruminations of the Convention, which were politically decisive.

In the end, whatever the conflicting interests and opposed principles of its members, the Convention had to come to terms with dynastic and confessional realities over which it had little or no control. England was emphatically a Protestant Kingdom which needed a King, but could not stomach a Catholic King. The Catholic James II and his Catholic son were in any case absent from the Kingdom. Worse still, they were in Catholic France, pensioners of the nation's foremost enemy, Louis XIV, and increasingly surrounded by the relics of a fugitive Catholic Court. James's Protestant nephew and son-in-law was present in the Kingdom, but already, by 30 December 1688, threatening not to stay, 'if King James came again', and equally determined to go, 'if they went about to make him Regent', an office he utterly disdained.[20] As the tide of political opinion intermittently ebbed and flowed, first one way, then another, over the ensuing six weeks of the interregnum, it repeatedly struck and finally halted before one adamantine fact: whether the English liked it, or not, William was politically indispensable to Protestant England. The effect of James's Popery had been to stand the Augsburg principle on its head. Henceforth the religion of the English people was to determine the religion of their princes. Protestantism, in alliance with William of Orange's ambition, had triumphed over primogeniture.

The Proceedings of
the Lords Spiritual and Temporal
from their first meeting at Guildhall, London,
from the 11th of December to the 28th following,
1688.

[Conscious of possessing 'an inexpressible authority and jurisdiction kneaded (next to that invested into the imperiall crown of England) into the very essence and fundamentall constitution of our lawes in such extraordinary junctures as this is', the Peers of the Realm formed themselves into a provisional government in the absence of the King. Without reference to either James or William of Orange they assumed power in the emergency. By virtue of their right as Peers they issued orders in the name of 'the Lords Spiritual and Temporal': orders which from the start were intended to be 'legal commands', carrying the force of law.

Day one. The Peers' first concern was for the security of the City of London, signified by their efforts to ensure that the Tower was in safe hands. After that they turned their attention to preserving the peace by authorizing the raising of the Militia of Middlesex, Westminster, and Southwark. They were alarmed at the build-up of the rabble, or mob, in the West End and in the more fashionable suburbs, outside the boundaries of the City, where the chapels of the Catholic mission were concentrated.]

13 South prospect of the Guildhall, London, the meeting place of the provisional government on 11 December 1688. Engraving, *c.* 1689.

AT GUILDHALL, LONDON
DECEMBER 11TH, 1688

The Lords Spiritual and Temporal in and about the Cities of London and Westminster met at the Gallery at Guildhall. They called in Mr. Gwyn, and commanded him to attend them as Secretary.

PRESENT

His Grace the Archbishop of Canterbury; His Grace the Archbishop of York; Earl of Pembroke; Earl of Dorset; Earl of Mulgrave; Earl of Thanet; Earl of Carlisle; Earl of Ailesbury; Earl of Burlington; Earl of Sussex; Earl of Rochester; Earl of Berkeley; Lord Viscount Newport; Lord Viscount Weymouth; Lord Bishop of Winchester; Lord Bishop of Ely; Lord Bishop of Rochester; Lord Bishop of St. Asaph; Lord Wharton; Lord North and Grey; Lord Chandois; Lord Mountague; Lord Culpepper; Lord Vaughan of Cherbury; Lord Jermin; Lord Crew; Lord Ossulstone.

Mr. Skelton,[1] Lieutenant of the Tower, sent for to attend the Lords.

Their Lordships signed an order first for Mr. Skelton, Lieutenant of the Tower, to attend them, and sent to the Lord Mayor of London[2] to dispatch a trusty messenger therewith immediately, who thereupon sent the Sword-Bearer of the City[3] to serve him with the order; who returned that Mr. Skelton was not at the Tower, and that he had followed him to Whitehall, but could not find him.

> Whereas His Majesty hath privately this morning withdrawn himself, we, the Lords Spiritual and Temporal, whose names are subscribed, do require you immediately to attend us, now assembled at Guildhall, London, to receive such orders as shall be necessary in the present juncture for the peace and security of the Kingdom. Tuesday, 11th December 1688, at 11 o'clock.
>
> W. Cant.; Thomas Ebor.; Pembroke; Dorset; Carlisle; Mulgrave; Thanet; Aylesbury; Burlington; Berkeley; Rochester; Sussex; Newport; Weymouth; P. Winton.; Francis Ely; Thomas Roffen.; Thomas Petriburg.; William Asaph; North and Grey; Chandois; R. Mountague; T. Culpepper; Cherbury Vaughan; Jermin; Crew; Ossulstone.
>
> To Bevill Skelton, Esquire, Lieutenant of the Tower.

Earl of Craven to raise the Militia.

Their Lordships gave directions, that an order should be drawn to the Earl of Craven, Lord Lieutenant of Middlesex, Liberty of Westminster, etc., to call together the Militia of Middlesex,

Liberty of Westminster, and Southwark, for preventing any disorders which might happen in the suburbs of London; and the Earl of Craven, coming in some time after, acquainted their Lordships, that he had already given directions to the purpose, whereupon no order was signed.

[Anxious to prevent hostilities between the opposing forces of the King and Prince, the Peers despatched orders to James's General, the Earl of Feversham, at Uxbridge, and his Admiral, the Earl of Dartmouth, on board *H.M.S. Resolution*, stationed at Spithead.]

Earl ⟨of⟩ Feversham to remove the Forces to distant quarters to prevent hostilities.

Their Lordships dispatched an order to the Earl of Feversham to give all manner of necessary orders, either by removing the Forces under his command to distant quarters, or by any other ways his Lordship should think most fit for preventing hostilities; which order was immediately signed and delivered to Mr. Blathwaite,[4] who undertook to give it into my Lord Feversham's own hand with all speed.

Whereas His Majesty has this morning privately withdrawn himself, we, the Lords Spiritual and Temporal, whose names are subscribed, considering the Prince of Orange has declared his intention to lead his Army into this City of London, and that several of the Forces under your command are in his way hither, whereby the effusion of blood may ensue; we do, therefore, require you to give such necessary order, either for the removal of the said troops to some distant quarters, or otherwise, as your Lordship shall think fit for preventing any hostility in this juncture. Tuesday, the 11th of December 1688, at 12 of the clock, Guildhall, London.

W. Cant.; Thomas Ebor.; Dorset; Burlington; Mulgrave; Aylesbury; Sussex; Rochester; North and Grey; Weymouth; P. Winchester; F. Ely; Berkeley; Pembroke; Carlisle; Thomas Roffen.; W. Asaph; Wharton; Mountague; Culpepper; Jermin; Crew; Ossulstone.

To the right honourable the Earl of Feversham, Lieutenant-General of the Forces, or to the Commander-in-Chief in his absence.

Lord Dartmouth to prevent acts of hostility between the two Fleets, and to remove all Popish Officers.

Their Lordships sent orders unto my Lord Dartmouth to prevent any acts of hostility between the Prince of Orange's Fleet and that under his command, and likewise to remove all Popish Officers out of their respective commands. Delivered to Mr. Pepys[5] to transmit the same.

Whereas His Majesty hath privately this morning withdrawn himself, we, the Lords Spiritual and Temporal, whose names are subscribed, being desirous to prevent the effusion of blood in this juncture, and considering the Prince of Orange's Fleet, now on the English coast, and possibly may meet with that under your Lordship's command; we do, therefore, require you to give such necessary order, as you shall think fit, for the prevention of all acts of hostility. And that no inconveniencies may happen in the Fleet, we do likewise require you forthwith to remove all Popish Officers out of their respective commands. Dated this 11th day of December 1688, at the Guildhall, London.

W. Cant.; Thomas Ebor.; Berkeley; Carlisle; Aylesbury; Burlington; Rochester; Mulgrave; Pembroke; Thanet; Weymouth; P. Winchester; Thomas Petriburg.;

Thomas Roffen.; North and Grey; Chandois; Dorset; Sussex; Culpepper; Vaughan of Cherbury; Jermin; Crew; Ossulstone.

To the right honourable Lord Dartmouth, Admiral of the Fleet.

It was moved, that orders be sent to the Forts on the River to stop all passengers, but nothing was done in it.

Likewise to the Governour of Tilbury[6] to disarm the Papists, but nothing was done in it.

The 2 Secretaries of State to attend.

Letters were sent to the Earl of Middleton and Lord Preston, the two Secretaries of State, to attend their Lordships.

[Much of the Peers' business was dictated by the need to respond to outside events as they occurred. They were dependent upon private informations and official complaints for their knowledge of what was going on in London, Westminster, and the suburbs. The fear that the Catholics would strike a blow against the reviving fortunes of Protestantism was remarkably persistent, as this and subsequent orders for disarming them show.]

Lord General to disarm all Roman Catholicks.

The Earl of Rochester acquaints the Lords that Sir Robert Sawyer[7] informs him, that Catholicks are got together in arms about Hounslow. Orders were sent to the Lord General of the Army to disarm all Roman Catholicks.

14 The centrepiece from the high altar of the Catholic Chapel Royal in Whitehall, carved by Grinling Gibbons and Arnoldus Quellin, and removed after the Revolution of 1688. The Catholic image of an irradiated dove, symbolic of the Holy Spirit, has been erased by Protestant ardour, and replaced by the biblical motif of the sacred tetragrammaton in Hebrew. Burnham-on-Sea, Somerset, Parish Church.

[Assuming that the King had fled to his cousin, Louis XIV of France, the Peers feared the possibility of French aggression against the vulnerably located Channel Islands.]

Ordered, that a note should be taken concerning the Government of Jersey and Guernsey.

Lord Lucas made Chief Governor of the Tower.

Their Lordships, with the approbation of the Lord Mayor, sent orders to the Lord Lucas to be Commander-in-Chief of the Tower of London, and his Lordship took care therein accordingly.

> Whereas His Majesty hath privately this morning withdrawn himself, we, the Lords Spiritual and Temporal, whose names are subscribed, considering of what great consequence the safe custody the Tower of London is at this juncture, and reposing great trust in your Lordship, have thought fit to constitute you Cheif Governour of the Tower of London, requiring you forthwith to take into your hand‹s› the charge and government thereof, untill further orders. And we likewise require your Lordship to disarm all Papists whatsoever within the said Tower. Dated the 11th of December 1688, at the Guildhall, London.
>
> W. Cant.; Thomas Ebor.; Dorset; Mulgrave; Thanet; Carlisle; Aylesbury; Burlington; Pembroke; Sussex; Rochester; Newport; Weymouth; P. Winchester; Thomas Roffen.; W. Asaph; Thomas Petriburgh.; North and Grey; Mountague; Culpepper; Vaughan of Cherbury; Jermin; Crew; Ossulstone.
>
> To the right honourable the Lord Lucas.

Lords appointed to draw up a Declaration.

Their Lordships, judging it necessary to make a Declaration of the cause of their meeting, appointed the Earl of Rochester, the Lord Weymouth, Lord Bishop of Ely, and Lord Bishop of Rochester to prepare such a Declaration; and their Lordships withdrew in order thereunto.

Lord Preston examined about the King's departure.

Lord Preston attended, and was asked by their Lordships, if the King had left any orders with him before his going away. His Lordship answered, he had not seen His Majesty since seven o'clock the night before. Being asked concerning the Great Seal, ‹he› answered, he knew nothing of it.
  The Earl of Middleton was not at home.

[A Catholic convert, who had announced his conversion while visiting Rome, the Earl of Salisbury became at his return, in 1687, one of the most active patrons of the Catholic mission in London. As such he was loathed and feared by the citizenry. A militant Catholic, he had openly blamed Admiral Dartmouth for his failure to stop the invasion fleet, and in November had accepted a commission to raise a regiment of horse for the King.]

Orders to seize arms at the Lord Salisbury's house.

One Mr. Cooper[8] acquainting their Lordships, that he saw several backs and breasts putt on board a lighter from the Earl of Salisbury's house,[9] the Sheriff of London[10] was desired to seize them.

Lord Mayor returns thanks to the Lords for making the Lord Lucas Governor of the Tower.

The Common Sergeant[11] returns their Lordships thanks from the Lord Mayor and Court of Aldermen for their appointing Lord Lucas Governour of the Tower.

[Designed to publicize their assumption of authority, the Guildhall Declaration (which was printed on the 12th) demonstrated the Peers' willingness to make common cause with the Prince in obtaining a free parliament, as the best means of securing the Protestant interest at home and abroad. However, a dispute over its precise wording revealed the presence of a small, but vociferous, revolutionary faction of 'Williamite' peers in a body which was predominantly loyal to the absent King. As yet, these political divisions were unknown to the general public.]

Earl of Rochester and Lords Committees appointed to draw up the Declaration returned, and the draught first read all together, afterwards paragraph by paragraph. Lord Wharton moves it may again be read all together, which was done, and afterwards paragraph by paragraph. The first paragraph agreed to. The paragraph concerning the King read; Lord Wharton, Lord Mountague, Lord Newport, and Lord Culpepper moved ‹it› might be left out quite. Ordered to be left out. The words, *the established government*, added in the paragraph before. And, after those and some other amendments, ordered to be writt fair for their Lordships' signing, which was done, and signed.

The Declaration of the Lords Spiritual and Temporal in and about the Cities of London and Westminster, assembled at Guildhall, the 11th of December 1688.

THE DECLARATION.

We doubt not but the world believes that, in this great and dangerous conjuncture, we are heartily and zealously concerned for the Protestant religion, the laws of the land, and the liberties and properties of the subject; and we did reasonably hope that, the King having issued his proclamation and writts for a free parliament, we might have rested secure under the expectation of that meeting; but, His Majesty having withdrawn himself, and, as we apprehend, in order to his departure out of this Kingdom, by the pernicious counsels of persons ill-affected to our nation and religion, we cannot, without being wanting to our duty, be silent under these calamities, wherein the Popish counsels, which so long prevailed, have miserably involved these Realms.

We do, therefore, unanimously resolve to apply ourselves to His Highness, the Prince of Orange, who, with so great kindness to these Kingdoms, so vast expence, and so much hazard to his own person, hath undertaken by endeavouring to procure a free parliament to rescue us, with as little effusion of Christian blood as possible, from the imminent dangers of Popery and slavery.

And we do hereby declare that we will with our utmost endeavours assist His Highness in the obtaining such a parliament with all speed, wherein our laws, our liberties and properties may be secured, the Church of England in particular, with a due liberty to Protestant Dissenters, and in general the Protestant religion and interest over the whole world may be supported and encouraged to the glory of God, the happiness of the established government in these Kingdoms, and the advantage of all princes and states in Christendom, that may be herein concerned.

In the mean time we will endeavour to preserve, as much as in us lies, the peace and security of these great and populous Cities of London and Westminster, and the parts adjacent, by taking care to disarm all Papists, and secure all Jesuits and Romish priests, who are in or about the same.

And if there be anything more to be performed by us for promoting His Highness's generous intentions for the publick good, we shall be ready to do it, as occasion shall require.[12]

W. Cant.; Thomas Ebor.; Pembroke; Dorset; Mulgrave; Thanet; Carlisle; Craven; Aylesbury; Burlington; Sussex; Berkeley; Rochester; Newport; Weymouth; P. Winchester; W. Asaph; F. Ely; Thomas Roffen.; Thomas Petriburg.; P. Wharton; North and Grey; Chandois; Mountague; T. Jermin; Vaughan Cherbury; Culpepper; Crew; Ossulstone.

The Earl of Craven desired to sign the Declaration at 7 of the clock the next morning, and went to the Earl of Pembroke's lodgings, and afterwards called on Mr. Gwyn, and told him he had done it.

Lords to carry the Declaration to the Prince of Orange.

It was moved that the Earl of Rochester, with some other Lords, should attend the Prince of Orange with the Declaration; but his Lordship excusing himself, and desiring some of the elder Earls might be employed, with some others, their Lordships ordered the Earl of Pembroke, Viscount Weymouth, Lord Bishop of Ely, and Lord Culpepper to wait upon His Highness therewith, and acquaint him with what was further done at that meeting by their Lordships, and sign an order accordingly.

Whereas His Majesty hath privately this morning withdrawn himself, we, the Lords Spiritual and Temporal, whose names are subscribed, being assembled at Guildhall, in London, having agreed upon and signed a Declaration, intitled *The Declaration of the Lords Spiritual and Temporal in and about the Cities of London and Westminster, assembled at Guildhall, 11th of December 1688*, do desire the right honourable the Earl of Pembroke, the right honourable the Lord Viscount Weymouth, the right reverend Father in God, the Lord Bishop of Ely, and the right honourable the Lord Culpepper forthwith to attend His Highness, the Prince of Orange, with the said Declaration, and at the same time acquaint His Highness with what we have further done at that meeting. Dated at Guildhall, 11th December 1688.

Thomas Ebor.; Dorset; Aylesbury; Thanet; Sussex; Berkeley; Newport; Vaughan Cherbury; Mountague; North and Grey; Chandois; W. Asaph; Thomas Roffen.; Thomas Petriburg.; Crew.

Which Declaration, together with an account of their proceedings,[13] was delivered to their Lordships the same night at eleven of the clock by Mr. Gwyn.

[Aware that fugitives from 'justice' were attempting to leave the country, the Peers alerted trustworthy Protestant gentlemen in the neighbouring maritime counties of Kent and Sussex, and empowered them to stop 'suspected persons'—chiefly Catholic clergy, Catholic courtiers, and their Protestant collaborators.]

Letters to Kent and Sussex to stop all priests and suspected persons.

Their Lordships sent letters to Sir John Knatchbull[14] for Kent, Sir William Thomas[15] and Sir Thomas Dyke[16] for Sussex, to seize all Jesuits, priests, and other suspected persons in any of their ports in their respective Counties.

Whereas His Majesty hath privately this morning withdrawn himself, we, the Lords Spiritual and Temporal, whose names are subscribed, taking into consideration that

15 *HMS Resolution*, flagship of the English Fleet under Lord Dartmouth. Oil painting by Willem van der Velde. Greenwich, National Maritime Museum.

many Jesuits and Popish priests, and other eminent offenders, may endeavour to fly from justice by going to parts beyond the seas, do hereby require you forthwith to use all manner of diligence for apprehending all such persons, or suspected persons, as shall be found in your County; and that you likewise take all possible care to stop all such persons from passing out of any the ports in your County, and secure them. Dated this 11th day of December 1688.

Thomas Ebor.; Dorset; Thanet; Aylesbury; Sussex; Newport; W. Asaph; Thomas Roffen.; Thomas Petriburg.; North and Grey; Chandois; Weymouth; Culpepper; Crew.

Directed to Sir John Knatchbull, at his house, in Kent.

The like letter was written to Sir William Thomas and Sir Thomas Dyke.

Both which letters were sent by Herne, the Messenger,[17] inclosed in a letter to Mr. Frowde,[18] to be sent forward.

The Lords that prepared the draught of the Declaration ‹were› ordered to carry it to my Lord Mayor. They returned with orders, that a copy thereof should be forthwith delivered to his Lordship.

The Lords appointed to meet in the Council Chamber, at Whitehall, tomorrow morning at ten of the clock. Sir Robert Sawyer and Mr. Heneage Finch[19] desired to meet their Lordships there.

[Day two. The Peers summoned James's Privy Councillors, who were not already of their number, to attend their meetings. This led to a change in the formula for issuing their orders, which henceforth ran in the name of 'the Peers of the Realm, with some of the Lords of the Privy Council'. The major concern of the morning and afternoon sessions was to remedy the widespread breakdown of law and order in the capital, the result of anti-Catholic rioting, to which the municipal magistrates had initially turned a blind eye, and which had been made worse by the disbanding of the King's soldiers by Lord General Feversham, acting on the orders of the absent King.]

WEDNESDAY MORNING, DECEMBER 12TH, 1688
AT THE COUNCIL CHAMBER, AT WHITEHALL

PRESENT

His Grace the Archbishop of York; Marquess of Hallifax; Earl of Dorset; Earl of Mulgrave; Earl of Thanet; Earl of Berkeley; Earl of Craven; Earl of Anglesey; Earl of Nottingham; Earl of Aylesbury; Earl of Sussex; Earl of Rochester; Earl of Feversham; Earl of Carbery; Lord Viscount Newport; Lord Bishop of Duresme; Lord Bishop of Winchester; Lord Bishop of Rochester; Lord Bishop of Peterborough; Lord Mountague; Lord Lucas; Lord Chandois; Lord Godolphin; Lord Jermin; Lord Crew; Lord Ossulstone.

The Marquess of Hallifax took the Chair and the rest of the Lords and others of the Privy Council were summoned, and met the Peers there.

Duke ‹of› Hamilton; Earl of Middleton; Lord Viscount Preston; Sir John Ernley;[20] Sir John Trevor;[21] Collonel Titus.[22]

16 The Tower of London in 1688–9, the custody of which the Peers entrusted to Lord Lucas. Engraving from Leonard Knyff and Jan Kip, *Britannia Illustrata* (London, 1707).

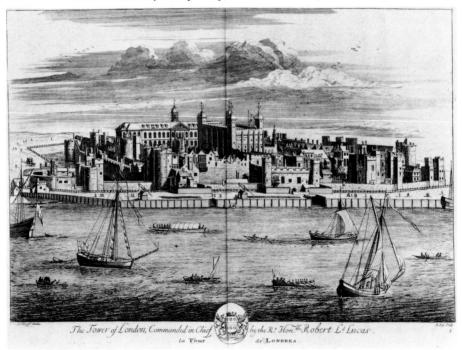

The Tower of London, Commanded in Chief by the R.t Hon.ble Robert L.d Lucas.
la Tour de Londres.

Sir Robert Sawyer and Mr. Finch attended by the desire of their Lordships.

Sir Charles Cotterell[23] attended. He is desired to wait upon all the Foreign Ministers from their Lordships, and on the Spanish Ambassador[24] first, he having suffered most last night;[25] that he is to acquaint them, that they are very sorry for those insolencies that were offered to them last night by the rabble, and they would endeavour to procure them satisfaction.

The Lord Lucas desired their Lordships, that he may have Captain Thomas King[26] for his Deputy in the Tower, he being a person that he could entirely depend upon. Whereupon their Lordships made the following order.

Captain King to be Deputy in the Tower to the Lord Lucas.

> We, the Peers of the Realm, with some of the Lords of the Privy Council, do hereby authorize and impower you to take under your care the Tower of London, as Deputy to the right honourable the Lord Lucas, Chief Governour of the same. Given at the Council Chamber, at Whitehall, the 12th day of December 1688.
>
> Hallifax; Kent; Mulgrave; Carlisle; Berkeley; Nottingham; Jermin; North and Grey; P. Winchester; Thomas Roffen.; Crew; Chandois.
>
> To Captain Thomas King.

There being a complaint made, that several Officers of the First Regiment of Foot Guards, formerly under the command of the Duke of Grafton, had laid down their arms, and disbanded their Companies, upon a mistake that they were disbanded by the Earl of Feversham, their Lordships made the following order.

Officers of the 1st Regiment of Guards to keep the Protestant Officers and soldiers together.

> We, the Lords of the Realm, with some of the Lords of the Privy Council, now assembled in the Council Chamber, do hereby order and direct, that Lieutenant-Colonel Hastings,[27] Major of the First Regiment of Guards, and Lieutenant-Colonel Hare[28] and others, the Protestant Officers of the said Regiment of Guards, and all the Protestant Colonels and Officers of any other Regiment, do keep together all the Protestant soldiers under their respective commands, and to be aiding and assisting to the civil magistrate, when thereunto required. From the Council Chamber, at Whitehall, the 12th day of December 1688.
>
> Hallifax; Kent; Aylesbury; Nottingham; Craven; P. Winchester; Thomas Roffen.; Thomas Petriburg.; North and Grey; Chandois.

The Lord Mountague moved, that Oates[29] and Johnson[30] might be discharged from prison, but nothing was done.

Order to the civil magistrate to preserve the peace. Printed.

> We, the Peers of the Realm, being assembled with some of the Lords of the Privy Council, do hereby require all persons whatsoever to keep and preserve the peace, and to forbear pulling down or defacing any house or building whatsoever, especially

those of Foreign Ministers, upon pain of imprisonment and of being further proceeded against to the utmost rigour of law. And we do hereby require the Sheriffs of the City of London, and likewise of the Counties of Middlesex and Surrey,[31] and all Justices of the Peace, Deputy Lieutenants, and Constables, who are Protestants, to proceed to execute their respective offices untill further order, and to take effectual care to prevent any disturbances of that nature. And in case they cannot by the assistance of the civil officers suppress the routs and riots, which shall happen, that the Deputy Lieutenant‹s› do make use of the Militia, and the Sheriffs raise the *Posse Comitatus*, for the suppressing thereof, and for apprehending all such obstinate offenders, that shall be found disturbing the publick peace. At the Council Chamber, in Whitehall, the 12th day of December 1688.

Thomas Ebor.; Hallifax; Kent; Mulgrave; Sussex; Aylesbury; Berkeley; Rochester; Carlisle; Nottingham; N. Duresme; P. Winchester; Thomas Roffen.; Chandois; Lucas; Vaughan Cherbury; T. Jermin; Ossulstone.

Jones to print the Declaration.

We, the Peers of this Realm, being assembled with some of the Lords of the Privy Council, do hereby order and require you forthwith to print and publish the Declaration herewith sent unto you. At the Council Chamber, in Whitehall, the 12th of December 1688.

Thomas Ebor.; Hallifax; Kent; Anglesey; Berkeley; Carlisle; Nottingham; P. Winchester; Sussex; Thomas Petriburg.; Ossulstone; Chandois; Aylesbury; Thomas Roffen.; T. Jermin; Crew.

To Edward Jones, Printer, at the Savoy.[32]

Order to search all vessells going down the River.

We, the Peers of this Realm, with some of the Lords of the Privy Council, now assembled in the Council Chamber, do order and direct, that all ships, boats, and vessells, that shall go down the River Thames below Gravesend, be examined; and no person be suffered to pass, that does not produce a passport under the hands and seals of 5 Peers, or from the Lord Mayor of London. From the Council Chamber, in Whitehall, December the 12th, 1688.

Hallifax; Kent; Aylesbury; Sussex; Berkeley; Anglesey; Nottingham; Newport; Ossulstone.

To Samuel Pepys, Esquire, at the Admiralty Office.

[The military's seizure of the arch-Quaker, William Penn ('Father Penn', as his Anglican detractors sarcastically styled him), embarrassed the Peers. He had been arrested on common fame as one who had endeavoured to further the King's policy of religious toleration. His attempt to influence William and Mary in favour of repealing the penal laws, and his interference in the case of Magdalen College, Oxford, made him suspect in Anglican eyes. There being no specific criminal charge against him, the Peers discharged him on bail, which was put up by two peers of dissenting sympathies.][33]

William Pen[34] being seized on by the Officers of the Guard in Scotland Yard, the Lords made the following order.

> Our very good Lord,
>
> Whereas we are informed, that William Pen, Esquire, is taken into custody, we do hereby pray and authorize your Lordship to discharge and dismiss the said William Pen upon his ent‹e›ring into 5,000£ bail, with two sureties for his appearance in the Court of King's Bench the 5th day of the next Term. From the Council Chamber, at Whitehall, the 12th day of December 1688.
>
> Your Lordship's very affectionate friends,
>
> Hallifax; Kent; Dorset; Sussex; Berkeley; Aylesbury; Anglesey; Mulgrave; Carlisle; Newport; North and Grey; Vaughan Cherbury; Nottingham; P. Wharton; T. Jermin; P. Winchester; N. Duresme; Thomas Roffen.; Chandois; Thomas Petriburg.
>
> To our very good Lord, the Earl of Craven.

[Sir Henry Shere was returning from Salisbury to London with the Train of Artillery following James's abortive campaign:[35] a reminder that the King's army was still in the process of retreating to its quarters in and about the capital. The unusual amount of troop movements was an additional factor fostering alarm in the civilian population of London.]

Mr. Musgrave[36] read a letter from Sir Harry Shears, which the Lords agree with, and make the following order.

Order to bring the Train of Artillery to St. James's Park.

> Whereas we, the Peers of the Realm, with some of the Lords of the Privy Council, have received a letter from you, dated this day, giving us an account that you are marching up with the Train of Artillery under your care, guarded by the Regiment of Fuziliers, towards St. James's Park; we have thought fit to signify unto you, that we approve thereof, and accordingly we do hereby direct you to bring the said Train of Artillery to St. James's Park, where you are to expect such further orders, as shall be sent unto you. From the Council Chamber, in Whitehall, the 12th day of December 1688.
>
> Hallifax; Kent; Mulgrave; Aylesbury; P. Winchester; Thomas Roffen.; Thomas Petriburg.; North and Grey; Carlisle; Anglesey; Berkeley; Nottingham; Newport; T. Jermin; Vaughan Cherbury; Crew.
>
> To Sir Henry Shears, Knight, Lieutenant-General of the Train of Artillery.

There being intimation given, that the Lord Jeffreys was on board the ship, *Hopewell*, an order was given to search her.

Order to seize the ship Hope, alias Hopewell.[38]

> We, the Peers of this Realm, being assembled with some of the Lords of the Privy Council, do hereby order and require you forthwith to seize and secure the ship, *Hope*, alias *Hopewell*, of London (James Porter, Master),[39] lying near Shadwell Dock;

and to apprehend, and bring before us, all suspicious persons on board the said ship. And we do hereby require all Officers, both civil and military, to be aiding and assisting to you in the execution hereof. And for so doing this shall be to you, and to them, a sufficient warrant. From the Council Chamber, in Whitehall, the 12th day of December 1688.

Hallifax; Kent; Carlisle; Berkeley; Anglesey; North and Grey: N. Duresme; Chandois; Craven; Jermin; P. Winchester; Ossulstone.

To Sir Henry Johnson[40] and Sir John Friend,[41] Knights, Champion Ashby,[42] and Thomas Cook, Esquires, or to any two of them.

Lady Baltimore[43] and her daughter discharged.

We, the Peers of the Realm, with some of the Lords of the Privy Council, now assembled in the Council Chamber, do hereby order and direct you to discharge the Lady Baltimore and her daughter, but to secure the priest, whom you have already[44] seized, till further order. Dated 12th December 1688.

Thomas Ebor.; Hallifax; Kent; Dorset; N. Duresme; Mulgrave; Aylesbury; Anglesey; Newport; Thomas Petriburg.; North and Grey; Wharton; P. Winchester; Vaughan Cherbury; Thomas Roffen.; Crew; Ossulstone.

We, the Peers of the Realm, assembled with some of the Lords of the Privy Council, being informed that the arms and ammunition of a Company of Foot, under the command of Captain John Reddish,[45] and by you seized and detained, do hereby authorize and require you forthwith to deliver the said arms and ammunition to the said Captain Reddish. Given at the Council Chamber, in Whitehall, December the 12th, 1688.

Hallifax; Kent; Sussex; Mulgrave; North and Grey; Vaughan Cherbury.

To the Constables of the Town of Bromley, in the County of Kent.

[Anti-Catholic rioting continuing unabated in the capital, and the ordinary means of keeping the peace proving wholly inadequate in the face of rampaging mobs, the Peers showed their determination to crush popular violence by making full use of the military forces at their disposal. Where necessary they authorized, as in these two orders, the troops to fire on the mob.]

Whereas the rabble are grown to an ungovernable height, we, the Peers of the Realm, being assembled with some of the Privy Council, do hereby direct and require you to use your utmost endeavours to quell and disperse the said rabble; and, in case of necessity, to use force, and fire upon them with bullett. And for so doing, this shall be your warrant. Given at the Council Chamber, in Whitehall, 12th day of December 1688.

Hallifax; Kent; North and Grey; Aylesbury; Mulgrave; Anglesey; Berkeley.

To Colonel Selwyn,[46] or the Officer-in-Chief commanding the Foot Guards.

The like to Colonel Richard Baggott,[47] or the Officer-in-Chief with Prince George, Hereditary Prince of Denmark's Regiment of Foot, signed by: Hallifax; North and Grey; Kent; Mulgrave; Aylesbury; Anglesey; Carlisle; Berkeley; Sussex; Rochester.

WEDNESDAY AFTERNOON, DECEMBER 12TH, 1688 AT THE COUNCIL CHAMBER, IN WHITEHALL, FOUR OF THE CLOCK IN THE AFTERNOON

PRESENT
His Grace ‹the› Archbishop of York; Duke ‹of› Hamilton; Marquess of Hallifax; Earl of Kent; Earl of Thanet; Earl of Craven; Earl of Anglesey; Earl of Berkeley; Earl of Carlisle; Earl of Nottingham; Earl of Rochester; Earl of Middleton; Lord Viscount Say and Seale; Lord ‹Viscount› Preston; Lord Bishop of Winchester; Lord Bishop of Petriburg.; Lord Mountague; Lord North and Grey; Lord Chandois; Lord Vaughan Cherbury; Lord Godolphin; Lord Bishop of Duresme.

[Although the Peers had ordered the arrest of the erstwhile Lord Chancellor, Lord Jeffreys, and were in this warrant prepared to commit him a prisoner to the Tower, they noticeably refrained from specifying any cause for his committal. It was an omission which was to worry the legalistically minded Earl of Nottingham, who was to raise the point on several subsequent occasions. General warrants were regarded as being of questionable legality, infringing the subject's right to know the charge on which he was committed to gaol.]

Sir Henry Johnson acquainted the Board, that the Lord Jeffreys was seized.

Whereas the Lord Jeffreys was seized, and brought to the house of the Lord Mayor, and was there in great danger by the insult of the people; to secure him from the said violence, and at his desire to the Lord Lucas to move him to the Tower, this following order was made.

We, the Peers of the Realm, being assembled with some of the Privy Council, do hereby will and require you to take into your custody the body of George, Lord Jeffreys (herewith sent unto you), and him to keep safe prisoner untill further order; for which this shall be your warrant. Given at the Council Chamber, in Whitehall, the 12th of December 1688.

Hallifax; Kent; Vaughan Cherbury; Aylesbury; North and Grey; Anglesey; Rochester; Mulgrave; Carlisle; Berkeley; Sussex; Nottingham; Crew; P. Winchester.

To the right honourable Robert, Lord Lucas, Chief Governor of the Tower of London.

The Lords appointed to examine the Lord Jeffreys were desired by the Lord Jeffreys to return to the Lords his humble thanks for their care in preserving him from violence.

[Warned that the mob threatened to assault St. James's Palace that night, on pretext of demolishing the Catholic Chapel there, the Peers made careful arrangements to protect the royal residences in the capital (all of which had Catholic chapels) by re-inforcing the guards, deploying artillery, and stiffening the civil magistrates by giving them military backing.]

The Lords were acquainted, that the rabble threatened St. James's tonight, and that, if great care

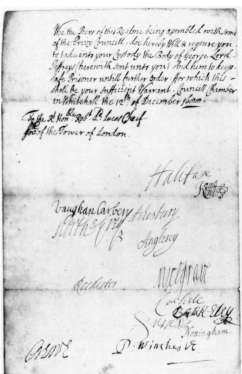

17 (*left*) The arrest of Lord Jeffreys, at Wapping, 12 December 1688. Contemporary engraving.

18 (*right*) The original warrant, signed by the Peers of the Provisional Government, committing Lord Jeffreys to the Tower of London (see p. 79). Kew, Public Record Office, War Office 94/2, fo. 137.

was not taken, there would be great disorders, upon pretence of pulling down the Chapel there. Whereupon the Officers of the Guard were called in, and were asked what numbers of men they had ready in arms. Colonel Selwyn, that commanded the Duke of Grafton's Regiment of Foot in-Chief, saith he hath 400; Colonel Baggott, Lieutenant-Colonel to Prince George's Regiment, saith he hath 400.

Sir Harry Shears ‹saith›, that these 12 Companies of the Fuziliers, of 6 in a Company, no Papists amongst them, ‹are› ready to obey their Lordships' order.

Sir Harry was asked, why he did not observe their Lordships' directions in bringing the Train of Artillery to St. James's Park. He said, he was marching up, above half way to the Tower, when he received their letter, and therefore went on, the carriage horses performing better than he expected.

He was ordered to send six gunners to attend at Whitehall, which he undertook to see done.

Captain Symms,[48] Brigadier of the Horse Guards, acquaints their Lordships there were 80 horse: half, mounted at St. James's; the other half, at Whitehall.

Their Lordships ordered him, as more horse came in, that there should be 80 at St. James's, and 80 at Whitehall; and that 300 Foot should be drawn up in the broad place before Whitehall, and 3 pieces of cannon before the Gate.

The Second Troop of Guards to be drawn up, as many as could be got together in St. James's, there to remain untill further order.

Their Lordships made an order, that the several Officers and soldiers should join and assist the Deputy Lieutenants, Justices of the Peace, and civil magistrates in the preservation of the peace.

> We, the Peers of the Realm, being assembled with some of the Lords of the Privy Council, do hereby authorize and require you to join and assist the Deputy Lieutenants, Justices of the Peace, and Constables, as occasion shall be, in preserving the peace, and suppressing all tumults and riots. Given at the Council Chamber, in Whitehall, the 12th day of December 1688.
>
> Hallifax; Kent; Carlisle; Anglesey; Aylesbury; Berkeley; Sussex; Litchfield; Rochester; North and Grey; Crew.
>
> To the honourable Colonel Villers,[49] at the Horse Guards.

The like order to Colonel Richard Baggott, at St. James's.

> [The Catholic Queen Dowager, Catherine of Braganza, also sent to Lord Mayor Chapman 'to desire him to send a Regiment of the City Militia to stand just without the Temple Bar that night for her security, but to march no nearer Summerset House; unlesse she had neede and sent for them, which he readily granted'.[50] Her Catholic chapel had been put at the disposal of the Catholic mission in London, so it was well known to the mob.]

The Queen Dowager[51] sent to desire 30 Horse to be drawn up before Somerset House, to disperse the rabble. Their Lordships thereupon sent to desire the Earl of Feversham to meet with them; and his Lordship sent an excuse, the Queen Dowager desiring him to stay to defend her from the rabble in case of danger.

The Turk⟨e⟩y Company complained, that 700 Irish soldiers, which were run from Gravesend and Tilbury, had seized one of their ships, richly laden and outwards bound, and that they had run her on ground, and would not quitt her. The Company promised their Lordships they would give them something to keep them from starving. Whereupon the following order was made, ⟨and⟩ delivered to Mr. Pepys.

> We, the Peers of the Realm, assembled with the Lords of the Privy Council, do hereby authorize and require you to stop and secure the ship, *Asia* (Captain Hazlewood, Commander), belonging to the Levant Company, with the men on board her, giving an account thereof to us; and to deliver the said ship and men to the order of the said Company. At the Council Chamber, in Whitehall, December 12th, 1688.
>
> Berkeley; Mulgrave; Aylesbury; Chandois; Middleton.
>
> To Francis Wheeler,[52] Commander of the ship, *Kent*.

> [The mob attempted several times to assault the Catholic Marquess of Powis's[53] 'great House', but eventually desisted on finding 'a Bill upon the Door', stating '*This House is appointed for the Lord Delameer's Quarters*; and some of the Company crying, let it alone, the Lord Powis was against the Bishops going to the Tower, they offered no Violence to it'.[54] The mob was also 'harangued by a Person from the House', telling them that Lord Powis, 'though a Papist', was 'a Friend to the Protestants ... and was ever averse to any violent proceedings against them'.[55]]

Lord Chandois informs, that the Marquess of Powis's house, in Lincoln's Inn Fields,[56] was pulling down.

Sir Thomas Row[57] comes in a little time after, and acquaints them the rabble in Lincoln's Inn

19 (*left*) This 'Knave', which belongs to a pack of playing cards commemorating the Revolution of 1688, shows an entirely fictional scene of Catholic clergy triumphantly singing Mass in the belief that French troops had landed in England to support James II's tottering Catholic régime. It is a good, if blatant, example of popular Protestant propaganda. London, Guildhall Library, reproduced by permission of the Worshipful Company of Playing Card Makers.

20 (*right*) From the same set of playing cards. The Protestants' destruction of the Jesuit Chapel in Lime Street, in the City of London, and the burning of the apparatus of Catholic worship.

Fields were dispersed, and no harm done to the Lord Powis's house, though they threatened at first.

The Constables of Lambeth acquaint the Lords, that they had seized arms of several Papists, soldiers disbanded. They are encouraged to keep them, and do the like.

They say they have 46 pounds in their hands, that belonged to a Captain, a Lancashire gentleman, whose name they have forgot.

If any tumult should happen, the Lords will meet wholly in Whitehall in the night.

[Day three. This emergency meeting of the Peers held in the middle of the night highlights one of the most extraordinary episodes of the entire revolutionary period: that of the 'Irish Fear', which anticipated by a century the better-known and better-understood 'Grande Peur' of the French Revolution of 1789. Never satisfactorily explained, either at the time, or since, the 'Irish Fear' demonstrated the extent to which Protestant London was in the grip of recurrent rumours of Catholic aggression, which had risen spectacularly to the surface with the publication (itself as yet unexplained) of the Prince's so-called *Third Declaration*. The night watch called every one up, shortly after midnight, telling them 'that the Irish were near, and at Knightsbridge had killed

21 (*left*) From the same set of playing cards. The attack on the Catholic Chapel at St John's, Clerkenwell, as depicted here, reflects the widespread, but false, rumour that the Catholic clergy were stockpiling 'instruments of torture' ready for the imagined forcible conversion of English Protestants: hence the gridiron prominently displayed in the foreground.

22 (*right*) From the same set of playing cards. The Protestant mob wreaks vengeance on the Franciscan Chapel (seen through the archway) in fashionable Lincoln's Inn Fields, 11 December 1688.

man, woman, and child', and were resolved to put all 'to fire and mas‹s›acre'.[58] The Protestant citizens were so terrified, that they were reluctant to stir from their homes, holding themselves in readiness to protect their wives and children as best they could. The night of the 'Irish Fear' did not, therefore, spark off a renewal of anti-Catholic violence in the capital. The incredulous reaction of at least two peers, Ailesbury and Sancroft, is worth recording. Though summoned to attend the Peers in the Council Chamber at one o'clock, both preferred their rest 'before anything else', for, as Ailesbury recalled, 'we knew too well for to be gulled by a pack of knaves that invented, and fools that gave in' to the alarm.[59] Yet, unfounded as the rumour proved to be, the forthright action of the few Peers who did respond to the emergency calmed popular fears throughout the metropolis.]

WHITEHALL, COUNCIL CHAMBER
DECEMBER 13TH, 1688
AT THREE OF THE CLOCK IN THE MORNING

PRESENT

Marquess of Hallifax; Earl of Mulgrave; Earl of Craven; Earl of Dorset; Earl of Rochester; Earl of Sussex; Lord Godolphin; Lord North and Grey; Lord Vaughan Cherbury.

A report was spread all over town, that a great number of Irish are got together; that they had burnt Uxbridge, and put all to the sword, and were marching up directly to London; which alarmed all the town, so that they all rose. Their Lordships sent out horsemen to bring intelligence, who returned with an account that there were no persons stirring. But, notwithstanding, the Lords to prevent the rabble's gathering together, upon this pretence, writt the following letter to Sir Harry Shears.

Fuziliers to be at their arms.

> We think fit to desire you, that the Regiment of Fuziliers be ordered to stand to their arms, untill further order from us.
>
> Hallifax; Mulgrave; Dorset; Rochester; Sussex; Newport; North and Grey; Vaughan Cherbury.

And afterwards, to quiet the apprehensions of the City, the Lords writt to the Lord Mayor, as follows.

> We think fit to acquaint your Lordship that, information being given us that there hath been some disorder at Uxbridge by some of the Irish Foot, lately disbanded (who cannot be any considerable number), we have taken all the precautions necessary to prevent a surprize, by sending out parties of horse, and by securing the town with the forces that are here. As there is further occasion, your Lordship shall hear from us. In the mean time, as your Lordship will, no doubt, take all reasonable care to secure the City in all events, so I (*sic*) believe your Lordship needs do nothing extraordinary, till further information from us. From the Council Chamber, in Whitehall, December 13th, 1688, at 3 of the clock in the morning.
>
> Hallifax; Sussex; Mulgrave; Dorset; Rochester; Vaughan of Cherbury; North and Grey.
>
> To the right honourable Sir John Chapman, Lord Mayor of the City of London.

Which being sent away by a Serjeant of the Foot Guards, the Lords adjourned untill ten of the clock in the morning.

WHITEHALL, COUNCIL CHAMBER
THURSDAY MORNING, TEN OF THE CLOCK
DECEMBER 13TH, 1688

PRESENT

Duke ‹of› Hamilton; Marquess of Hallifax; Earl of Kent; Earl of Dorset; Earl of Thanet; Earl of Craven; Earl of Berkeley; Earl of Feversham; Earl of Aylesbury; Earl of Carlisle; Earl of Rochester; Earl of Anglesey; Lord Viscount Newport; Lord Bishop ‹of› Winchester; Lord Wharton; Lord North and Grey; Lord Vaughan Cherbury; Lord Chandois; Lord Jermin; Lord Mountague; Lord Lucas; Lord Preston; Lord Godolphin; Lord Crew; Lord Ossulstone; Sir John Ernley; Sir John Trevor; Colonel Titus.

Sir Robert Sawyer and Mr. Finch attend, according to order.

It being reported the Earl of Feversham intended to speak to his Troop that morning in a mourning cloak, the Marquess of Hallifax desired him not to appear at the head of his Troop, or to speak to them; which, after some pressing, he promised not to do, and added he hath now nothing to do, and will not meddle any more.

[The following order, perhaps more than any other, checked the disintegration of the King's Army in and about London following Feversham's command to disband. In order to qualify for regular pay the troops had to remain together and be placed on the muster roll. The following orders, assigning proper quarters and instructing 'broken' soldiers to repair to their colours, ensured that a measure of military discipline endured in the wake of James's flight.]

The Earl of Ranelagh,[60] being called in, was desired to give an account in what state the Army was, in relation to their pay; and he acquaints their Lordships they were paid untill tomorrow, being Friday. Whereupon this following order was made.

Forces in town to have a week's subsistence.

We, the Peers of the Realm, assembled with some of the Lords of the Privy Council, do hereby authorize and require you to pay one week's subsistence to such of the Forces as are together in town. Dated at the Council Chamber, in Whitehall, December 13th, 1688.

Hallifax; Kent; Aylesbury; Rochester; Mountague; Preston; T. Jermin; Lucas; P. Winchester; North and Grey; J. Trevor; T. Titus.

To the Earl of Ranelagh, Paymaster of the Forces.

Sir Harry Shears and Major Soper[61] called in; and, having given an account in what condition the Fuziliers were, an order was made for their quartering, as follows.

The Fuziliers to be quartered in the Tower Hamlets.

We, the Peers of this Realm, being assembled with some of the Privy Council, do hereby direct and require you to cause the Royal Regiment of the Fuziliers to march into the Hamlets of the Tower of London, where they are to remain, untill further order from us; and the Officers are to take care, that the soldiers be kept together and behave themselves civilly in their quarters; and all Justices of the Peace, Constables, and other officers, whom it may concern, are hereby required to be assisting in providing quarters, as there shall be occasion. Given at the Council Chamber, this 13th day of December 1688.

Hallifax; Kent; Dorset; Thanet; Rochester; P. Winchester; North and Grey; Mountague; T. Jermin; Lucas; Godolphin; Ossulstone.

To Major Thomas Soper, or the Officers-in-Chief with the Royal Regiment of Fuziliers.

Lieutenant-General Douglas,[62] being called in, acquaints their Lordships, that there was at least 400 men of his Regiment, with most of his Officers, at Colnbrooke;[63] and that he could likewise gather together many of the soldiers belonging to Wachop[64] and Bochan's[65] Regiment, if he had order, especially if no passes were granted to any of them to go away. Whereupon the following order and letter to my Lord Mayor was dispatched.

Officers and soldiers of the Scotts Regiment to repair to their colours.

We, the Peers of the Realm, assembled with some of the Privy Council, being informed that many Officers within the Regiment of Scotch Guards, Colonel Wachop

23 Somerset House, the Dowager Queen Catherine of Braganza's residence, from the River Thames. Engraving from Leonard Knyff and Jan Kip, *Britannia Illustrata* (London, 1707).

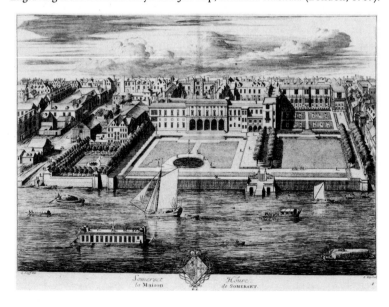

and Colonel Bochan's Regiment of Foot, have dismissed their soldiers under their commands, do hereby direct and require you to get all the Protestant Officers, so dismissed, together again, and to keep them in good order; to which end the Earl of Ranelagh, Paymaster-General of the Army, hath directions to see them duly and constantly paid their subsistence money, upon certificate from the Commissary General of the Musters, his Deputy, or Deputies, of their being returned to their respective Companies. Whereof all the Protestant Officers and soldiers of the said Regiment are required to take notice, and to conform themselves by returning accordingly; and all Justices of the Peace, Constables, and others concerned are required to take notice thereof, and to be assisting in providing quarters, and otherwise, as there shall be occasion. Given at the Council Chamber, this 13th day of December 1688.

Hallifax; Dorset; Aylesbury; Anglesey; Carlisle; Newport; North and Grey; T. Jermin; T. Titus.

To Lieutenant-General Douglas, and the Officers-in-Chief with the Regiments above-mentioned.

My Lord,

After our very hearty commendations, we desire your Lordship will not grant any pass to any Officer or soldier belonging to the Scots Regiments, lately commanded by Lieutenant-Colonel Douglas, Colonel Bochan, and Colonel Wachop, but to direct such of the said Officers and soldiers, as shall repair to your Lordship for passes, to go to Lieutenant-General Douglas, and receive his commands. We bid your Lordship very heartily farewell. Given in the Council Chamber, in Whitehall, the 13th day of December 1688.

Dorset; Aylesbury; Hallifax; Anglesey; Kent; Rochester; Carlisle; Newport; North and Grey; T. Jermin; Crew.

To the right honourable Sir John Chapman, Knight, Lord Mayor of the City of London.

[The Peers, who had already questioned Secretary Preston on the 11th concerning the Great Seal, which was missing (unbeknown to them James had thrown it into the Thames as he made his escape from Whitehall),[66] continued their enquiries on and off until the 15th, when, having traced it into the King's possession, they admitted defeat in the matter. Eager to co-operate with William in the holding of a parliament, they were also anxious to ascertain the whereabouts of the writs issued by the King following his announcement of a parliament summoned to meet him at Westminster on 15 January (again unbeknown to them the writs which Lord Chancellor Jeffreys had not sent out had been delivered to James, who had burnt them before leaving Whitehall).]

The Lord Lucas acquaints the Lords, that Lord Jeffreys told him in discourse he was sent for to the King on Saturday to Mr. Chiffing's lodgings, and that he there delivered the Seal to the King. Whereupon Mr. Chiffings[67] was sent for; and, appearing, told their Lordships that Lord Jeffreys sent to him, that he desired to speak to the King. It was Saturday, or Sunday night, he doth not well recollect which, about eight of the clock; that he thereupon spake to the King, who came to his lodgings, and met my Lord Jeffreys there. But whether Lord Jeffreys did then deliver the Great Seal, or the writts, or what became of them, he knows not, the King and Lord Jeffreys being alone together.

Their Lordships ordered, that three of their number should go to the King's Closet, and seal it; and the Earl of Kent, Earl of Mulgrave, and Lord Mountague went accordingly; and acquainted the Lords that they had each of them put their respective seals.

24 Impressions of James II's Great Seal. The Royal Mint.

The Lord Lucas likewise saith, that the Lord Jeffreys told him he had delivered out all the writts, where there were Protestant Sheriffs, but had returned the writts of those Counties that had Popish Sheriffs to the King.

Sir John Ernley acquaints the Lords there were 16 writts delivered out, and 36 not.

And ‹the› Earl of Thanet saith, he was a Protestant Sheriff, and sent 3 or 4 times for the writts, but they were denyed him.

> [Since the destruction of Weld House Ronquillo had been homeless. He and his staff (including his Catholic chaplains) had been furnished by the Peers with grace and favour lodgings in the Palace of Whitehall.][68]

The Spanish Ambassador being invited to lodge in Whitehall, upon the great violence that was offered to his house, the Lords desired that Sir Stephen Fox[69] might be spoke‹n› to, that the Green Cloth[70] would provide diet, with all other things convenient for his person. The Lord Godolphin undertakes to give orders therein to the Green Cloth accordingly.

Colonel Slingsby,[71] desiring to be admitted, acquaints their Lordship‹s› that his Regiment was quartered in Smithfield, but that they were every night in danger of the rabble and Trained Bands for lodging within the City, and not intending to fire bullett; that many of his Regiment, being Catholiques, are gone away, but that he had enough to make a good squadron out of the whole Regiment.

Earl of Craven called his Quartermaster to give an account where the quarters were empty, and the Lords made the order following.

Three Troops of Colonel Slingsby's Regiment to be quartered in Holbourn.

Sir,

You are to quarter three Troops of your Regiment in the inns from St. Giles's Pound to Holbourn Barrs, and you are to see that your soldiers behave themselves civilly, and pay their landlords; and all magistrates, Justices of the Peace, High Constables, Petty Constables, and others whom it may concern, are required to be assisting to you, as there may be occasion. Given under our hands, this 13th day of December 1688.

Hallifax; Kent; Mulgrave; Anglesey; Newport.

To Colonel Henry Slingsby, or Officer-in-Chief with the Regiment.

An Officer came in from Uxbridge, and acquainted the Lords, that there were two Battalions of the Foot Guards there, which were ordered to march to town.

The 2 Battalions of the First Regiment of Guards to be brought from Uxbridge.

We, the Peers of this Realm, being assembled with some of the Privy Council, do hereby direct and require you to cause the two Battalions of the First Regiment of Foot Guards at Uxbridge to march forthwith from thence to their former quarters about London, where they are to remain untill further order; and the Officers are to take care that the soldiers be kept together, and behave themselves civilly. And all magistrates, Justices of the Peace, Constables, and all other officers whom it may concern, are hereby required to be assisting to them in providing quarters and otherwise, as there shall be occasion. Given at the Council Chamber, the 13th day of December 1688.

Hallifax; Kent; Dorset; Anglesey; Aylesbury; Berkeley.

To the Officer-in-Chief with the 2 Battalions of the First Regiment of Foot Guards at Uxbridge.

[The killing of Captain Douglas, of the Middlesex Trained Bands, was variously reported. He seems to have been shot by one of his own men (not killed by the rabble), but whether by accident, or because, on his own authority, he commanded his forces to fire on the mob, then 'goeing to pull downe a Papist's house in the Haymarket', is uncertain.][72]

Their Lordships being informed that an Officer of the Trained Bands was killed by the rabble in the Haymarket, and that it was impossible to disperse them without the Trained Bands have leave to fire bullett, they made the following order accordingly.

Whereas the rabble are grown to an ungovernable height, we, the Peers of this Realm, being assembled with some of the Privy Council, do hereby direct and require you to use your best endeavours to quell and disperse the said rabble; and, in case of necessity, to use force, and to fire upon them with bullett. And for so doing, this shall be your warrant. Given at the Council Chamber, the 13th December 1688.

Hallifax; Anglesey; Carlisle; Thanet; Aylesbury; North and Grey; Mountague.

To Major Arnold, or the Officer-in-Chief with the respective Companies of the Trained Bands of the City and Liberty of Westminster and County of Middlesex.

[What follows constitutes one of the most unexpected turning-points of the revolutionary period—the discovery that King James had not made good his escape to France, but had been arrested by the seamen of Faversham, in Kent. The news first reached the Peers through a messenger, Thomas Liniall, sent to Archbishop Sancroft at Lambeth. His letter of credence from John Whitfield of Canterbury, his pass to travel to London signed by 5 Kentish JPs, and Liniall's *viva voce* report follow. The loyalists, Mulgrave and Berkeley, wanted the Peers to take prompt action to rescue the King, fearing that he was detained against his will, and that his life might be in danger; whereas Halifax, their chairman, who already favoured William's cause, prevaricated.]

A servant of the Archbishop of Canterbury's attends, and brought a letter, signed by John Whitfield,[74] to His Grace.

My Lord,

This bearer comes to give your Lordship a verbal account of our actions at Canterbury, which, being too long, I have only time to say I am,

Your Lordship's humble servant,

Canterbury,   John Whitfield.
12th December 1688, 7 at night.

25 This kneeling angel, carved by Grinling Gibbons and Arnoldus Quellin, has survived from the altarpiece of James II's Catholic Chapel Royal in Whitehall. Burnham-on-Sea, Somerset, Parish Church.

The bearer mentioned therein was one Liniall, of Canterbury; and it was whispered, that he had brought news of the King being stopt in Kent. Whereupon he was ordered to withdraw alone, and that he might not discourse with any in the mean time.

Earl of Mulgrave some time afterwards acquaints the Lords that there was a rumour, that the King was at Feversham, and he thinks it is his duty to move the Lords to take off any restraint, if there is any upon him.

Thomas Liniall, of Canterbury, was thereupon called in, and he first tells the Lords, that being ordered to hold no discourse with any person, yet two persons, which he pointed out to be the Bishop of Winchester and the Earl of Berkeley, came into the room, where he was, and asked him concerning the King; and he had told them what he knew of it, they being, as he was informed, part of their number. He produced the pass following, signed and sealed by the gentlemen underwritten.

Canterbury, Kent.

To all, whom these may concern, greeting.

The bearer hereof, Thomas Liniall, of the City of Canterbury, joyner, having urgent occasion to travel to London, you are desired to let him go, and return freely, without lett or molestation. Given under our hands and seals, this 12th day of December 1688.

Henry Palmer;[75] William Honywood;[76] Anthony Aucher;[77] J. Lee;[78] H. Gibbs, junior.[79]

Thomas Liniall, after his pass was read, saith that the gentlemen, who signed it, did not put anything particular in it, because they knew that many different parties were upon the road, and some of them might perhaps have stopt him, in case they had met with anything they had not liked. He saith he came from the Isle of Thanet at 3 of the clock in the afternoon yesterday, and came through Canterbury at six of the clock in the evening; that the King was in the hands of the rabble at Feversham (for the Militia without officers were no better than rabble); that the King was embarked from the Isle of Emley with Sir Edward Hales[79] and another gentleman, and some seamen, hearing Sir Edward Hales and two Jesuits, or priests, were with him, went out in a boat, and brought in the small smack, where the King was, with the rest, into Feversham; that the gentlemen, who signed the pass, had seen the King, but he had not; that the gentlemen had told him, that the King had sent for the Earl of Winchelsea;[80] and that, as he came by, within a little of Feversham, where the road lies, he met a coach and six horses, and he asked who was in it, and he was told it was the Earl of Winchelsea; that he did not call at Feversham, as he came by, being sent by the gentlemen, and therefore made haste.

He saith further, that in the Island of Thanet the Earl of Peterborough[81] was a prisoner, and he saw him; that there was a small boat went out, and endeavoured to board a dogger boat, but she, being stronger, shot at them, so they were forced to return, and manned out a stronger with blunderbusses; and he believes, by this time, they had taken her, and that the common discourse of the country people was, that the Queen's Majesty was on board of her, by reason of the resistance that was made; but the dogger was not taken before he came away, so that he only speaks their guess.

The Earl of Mulgrave moves, that a party of Horse may be sent to secure His Majesty from the rabble.

The Earl of Berkeley seconds it, and desires some persons of quality may be added to attend his person.

The Marquess of Hallifax moves, that there may be many reasons to doubt that this information may not be true; that, therefore, nothing may be done at present, but that they meet again in the afternoon.

The Earl of Mulgrave desired, that Liniall may have his oath. But it was ordered to meet at four of the clock in the afternoon.

AT THE COUNCIL CHAMBER
DECEMBER 13TH, 1688, IN THE AFTERNOON

His Grace of Canterbury; His Grace of York; Duke of Grafton; Duke of Hamilton; Earl of Kent; Earl of Dorset; Earl of Anglesey; Earl of Essex; Earl of Carlisle; Earl of Craven; Earl of Litchfield; Earl of Burlington; Earl of Berkeley; Earl of Yarmouth; Earl of Nottingham; Earl of Feversham; Earl of Rochester; Earl of Middleton; Lord Viscount Newport; Lord Viscount Preston; Lord Delawarr; Lord North and Grey; Lord Chandois; Lord Bishop of Winton.; Lord Bishop of Rochester; Lord Mountague; Lord Jermin; Lord Vaughan Cherbury; Lord Lucas; Lord Crew; Lord Ossulstone; Lord Godolphin; Sir John Trevor; Colonel Titus.

All the Peers in the town were summoned to be present, and likewise the Privy Council; notwithstanding the Earl of Mulgrave was absent all that afternoon.

The Lord Lucas acquaints their Lordships, that the rabble in Southwark were like to do great mischief, without speedy care. Thereupon the following order was made.

Order for Trained Bands to fire with bullett in Southwark.

> Whereas the rabble are grown to an ungovernable height, we, the Peers of this Realm, being assembled with some of the Privy Council, hereby direct and require you to use your best endeavours to quell, and disperse the said rabble; and, in case of necessity, to use, seize, and to fire upon them with bullett. And for so doing, this shall be your warrant. Given at the Council Chamber, the 13th day of December 1688.
>
> Hallifax; Thanet; Hamilton; North and Grey; Rochester; T. Jermin.
>
> To Mr. Nicholas Chounce, Major of the Regiment of Trained Bands of the Burrough of Southwark, and the parts adjacent.

Several complained that the rabble in great numbers were got together before Charing Cross. Whereupon orders were given, that the Horse should be drawn out before Whitehall and St. James's, as last night; and Colonel Villers received their Lordships' commands himself.

[Liniall's report of James's detention at Faversham was confirmed by a second messenger out of Kent, Robert Clinton, a seaman, who had brought similar tidings to Lord Mayor Chapman. His oral report encouraged the loyalists—Bishop Mews and Lords Berkeley, Rochester, Middleton, and Ailesbury—to press the Peers into mounting a rescue operation to free the King from the rabble.]

The Sword-Bearer of the City attended their Lordships, and acquainted them, that, my Lord Mayor at present being ill, he had brought with him a seaman, who came to my Lord Mayor, and could give an account of His Majesty.[83] His name was Robert Clinton, who, being called in, said that on Monday there were great numbers of the country up in Kent to apprehend Jesuits, priests, and others, that were flying from justice.

That on Tuesday night they had notice, that there were some Jesuits like to go away. Whereupon twenty or thirty went on board a little vessel, and seized a small smack, wherein was Sir Edward Hales and two gentlemen more, one whereof had a patch on his lip,[84] which they thought to be Jesuits when they saw them on shore on Wednesday at Chesne.

But when they came to *The Queen's Arms*, at Feversham, one Mr. Marsh[85] first knew one of the two with Sir Edward Hales to be the King, and, kneeling down, proffered to kiss his hand; which at first the King refused, pretending Marsh was mistaken, but afterwards, he persisting in it, the King gave him leave, and owned himself. Several other gentlemen kissed his hand likewise, the King telling them he hoped he was with honest gentlemen, and that they would do his person no hurt, which all assured him should not be. They got him some meat and oysters, and all was quiet untill night, when they were alarmed that there was a design of rescuing the King out of their hands. But they soon found there was no force, only one Maidston‹e› had hired a vessel to carry him away, which the gentlemen consented to, but the seamen would not permit him to go without the consent of the City, and had thereupon sent him up to know their resolutions. He added that, as soon as the King came to Feversham, he writt to the Earl of Winchelsea to come to him, who, he supposes, is there, but he was not when he came away.

The Bishop of Winchester moves, that since they are sufficiently satisfyed the King is there, that some of the Lords and other servants may be sent to attend him.

The Earl of Berkeley adds, that he thinks the King's person in danger, and therefore he desires a guard may be sent to secure him from the rabble, but by no means to restrain him, but that he may go where he pleases.

Earl of Rochester desires, that what was said might be upon oath.

Marquess of Hallifax. That neither of them says he knows the King.

But the Earl of Rochester takes notice, that the last described him with a patch on his lip, and said he had seen him before.

Earl of Middleton desires, if any there doubts of the truth of this matter, he would demand an oath; but, for his part, he was satisfyed of it this morning, and therefore he moves, that all respects should be shewn the King, and that such a number of Guards should be sent to him, as would secure him from the rabble, but that he should be left at entire liberty to go where he pleases, and that some Lords should attend him, and give him their advice.

Bishop of Winchester believes, if he had staid untill the proposals came back from the Prince of Orange, he might not have gone at all.[86]

Earl of Feversham desires some of the Peers and Guards might be sent, leaving His Majesty at liberty to do as he pleases, but that what was done ought to be done immediately.

Lord Mountague concurrs.

Lord Godolphin. That, since all agree, the order may be forthwith made.

Earl of Carlisle desires they would consider of making all things agreeable to what they had done before; and that therefore, since they had grounded their Declaration, which they had presented the Prince of Orange upon His Majesty's withdrawing himself, they ought to acquaint His Highness with their intelligence, and what they had done upon it.

Earl of Rochester. That the Prince might be forthwith acquainted with it.

Marquess of Hallifax agrees with sending some Horse to the King, though no great number, the last man seeming to say there was great respect paid to the King; that the Prince of Orange should be made acquainted with it, but no message or advice sent to the King by the Lords with the Guards, for it would look like restraint.

Earl ‹of› Middleton. That, notwithstanding the Guards, the King may be at entire liberty, which all agree to.

Earl of Aylesbury. That the First Troop of Guards and some Lords be sent forthwith.

Lord Mountague. That two Lords, Gentlemen of the Bedchamber, may go with the Troop, and that they may represent the present posture of affairs.

Earl of Feversham would as much desire to see His Majesty's return, and would do as much towards it, but nothing would induce him to it, but a request of the Lords.

Earl of Middleton. That the Privy Purse and other servants, belonging to his person, might go.

[The Peers did not relish sending to James the Catholic Earl of Dumbarton, Commander-in-Chief of the Scottish Army, who had previously suppressed Argyll's Rising in 1685, and had seen service under Louis XIV. As patriots they resented the Scottish military presence in England, and had not forgotten the unfortunate consequences of the Scots' invasion of 1640. They feared that the loyal Dumbarton might yet encourage the King to make armed resistance against William.]

Earl of Carlisle desires a pass for the Earl of Dunbarton[87] to wait on the King, which all deny.

Marquess of Hallifax. That no advice should be sent. The Lords that went might say what they thought fit themselves, but nothing from them.

Earl of Rochester. That sending the Guards, with advice, would look like a force on His Majesty, and therefore against the advice. But if some persons would go post immediately, and give notice that the Lords were coming to attend the King, with some of the Guards, it would be convenient.

Which the Earl of Aylesbury proffers to do, and had thereupon the following pass.

[The loyal Earl of Ailesbury, eager to serve the Tory cause by persuading his royal master to return to London, took his cue from Lord Rochester, and immediately volunteered to go ahead of the rest of the Peers deputed to wait on James. He, however, was less than satisfied with the lame wording of his passport. An earlier version he had thrown 'on the table with passion', declaring he 'would go without one'. This, the redrawn version, he accepted 'in a very slighting way', upbraiding those peers, whose loyalty was suspect, 'that God Almighty would protect those that did their duty'.][88]

Lord Aylesbury's pass.

We, the Peers of the Realm, assembled with some of the Lords of the Privy Council, do hereby require all Officers, civil and military, and other His Majesty's subjects, whom it may concern, to permit the right honourable the Earl of Aylesbury to repair forthwith to Feversham, in Kent, or wherever His Majesty is at present, without any lett, hindrance, or molestation whatsoever. From the Council Chamber, at Whitehall, 13th day of December 1688.

Thomas Ebor.; Hallifax; North and Grey; T. Jermin; Dorset; Anglesey; Mountague; Thomas Roffen.; Sussex; Berkeley; ⟨P.⟩Winchester.

Mr. Grahme's pass.

The like for Colonel Grahme[89] and his servants.

The Lord Preston desires, that the coaches and equipage might be sent down with the Guards; which Lord Godolphin thinks improper, for the coaches (unless His Majesty sent for them), with the Guards, would be like a restraint and forcing him back again.

The Guards were thereupon sent with the Lord Feversham by the following order.

We, Peers of the Realm, with others of the Lords of the Privy Council, assembled in the Council Chamber, do hereby pray and authorize your Lordship to draw 40 men out of each Troop of the Guards, and also 50 Grenadiers, and march with all speed with them to attend His Majesty, to receive his commands, and protect his person from insolence. From the Council Chamber, in Whitehall, December 13th, 1688.

Hallifax; Kent; Dorset; Craven; Berkeley; Nottingham; Yarmouth; Lawarr; Newport; P. Winton.; Thomas Roffen.; R. Mountague; T. Jermin.

To the right honourable the Earl of Feversham.

[Having been much criticized for obeying the King's order, of the 10th, to disband the royal army, and having been forbidden that very morning to address his Troop of Guards, wearing 'a mourning cloak' (in token of his regret at James's withdrawing), Feversham insisted that the Peers should be explicit in stating what they expected from him on reaching the King; hence the additional clause now inserted in his order.]

The last words of the order, *to receive his commands, and protect his person from insolence*, was (*sic*) put in after the first order was signed, by the Earl of Feversham's desire, and the order was writt and signed again.

An order was likewise made, that the Earl of Feversham, Earl of Yarmouth, and Earl of Middleton should forthwith attend His Majesty, with such of his Protestant servants, as they thought fit, and a pass was given accordingly to Mr. Grahme, Privy Purse, and several others.

A pass to Mr. Heywood,[90] Mr. Thompson, Mr. Frazier,[91] and John Rumsey, to go to the King.

A pass for Thomas Heywood, Page of His Majesty's Bedchamber; John Thompson, Yeoman of His Majesty's Robes; Thomas Frazier, His Majesty's Barber; and John Rumsey, Servant to the Backstairs, to repair to the King. Dated the 13th day of December 1688.

Hallifax; Wharton; Nottingham; Godolphin; Newport; Vaughan Cherbury.

[The Peers' letter to William had two purposes. First, it informed him that King James was still in the Kingdom; secondly, it was an attempt to keep on good terms with him. Having initially 'applied' to the Prince, they could scarcely do less than inform him of the latest developments, as Lord Carlisle had pointed out. They were, of course, wildly over-optimistic in expecting William's 'approbation' of their decision to send to the King. They also took care to inform Lord Mayor Chapman of what they had done, which suggests that they expected the King to return to the capital.]

Their Lordships thereupon writt the following letter to the Prince.

May it please Your Highness,

We think it our duty to acquaint Your Highness, that upon an information this day brought to us, that His Majesty is at Feversham, in the ‹County of› Kent, we have ordered four Lords to attend him, as also several of his other menial servants. And we think it necessary at the same time to send six score of the Guards and 50 Grenadiers to attend His Majesty's person, and to secure it from the insolence of the numbers of people, who may press to come near him upon this occasion. We hope this, that we have done, will have Your Highness's approbation. We remain, may it please Your Highness,

Council Chamber, Whitehall,   Your Highness's most obedient servants,
December 13th, 1688.

Thomas Ebor.; Hamilton; Hallifax; Kent; Dorset; Mountague; Rochester; Nottingham; Sussex; Berkeley; P. Winchester; Thomas Roffen.; Newport; Lawarr; Ossulstone; North and Grey; Wharton; Chandois; Vaughan of Cherbury.

Directed to His Highness the Prince of Orange.

Which letter was inclosed in a letter from Mr. Gwyn to Monsieur Benting[92] by their Lordships' order.

Monsieur,

Les Seigneurs, qui sont assemblez cey, inordonent de vous envoyer la lettre jointe pour Monseigneur le Prince d'Orange, laquelle ils vous prient de donner a Son Altesse. Plustost je suis, avec respect, Monsieur,

Votres humble et tres obessant serviteur,

Directed: A Monsieur, Monsieur Benting.   F. Gwyn.

The said letter was delivered to Mr. Repley, Serjeant-at-Arms attending the Treasury, between 7 and 8 o'clock at night, to be carried to him.

And the Lords called in the Sword-Bearer, and desired him to acquaint the Lord Mayor with what was done.

[This next letter, from the Prince to James's Secretary at War, written earlier in the day from Wallingford, on the London Road, shows the rapidity with which he sought to assume control of James's 'abandoned' Realm. Having come to England to gain control over her armed forces, it is not surprising that military and naval affairs claimed the Prince's earliest attention (especially as France had already declared war on the United Provinces). It is noteworthy that Secretary Blathwait had already left London to go to the Prince, without consulting the Peers, whose agreement he took for granted. He had presumably received an 'intimation' to do so, such as Paymaster-General Ranelagh received from William on the 14th.]

The Prince of Orange having writt a letter to Mr. Blathwaite, and sent it by express, it was this day brought to the Lords by Mr. Wroth.[93]

Prince of Orange's letter to Mr. Blathwaite.

Mr. Blathwaite,

I am informed that you have been for some time Secretary at War to the King; and to the end I may know the exact number of troops now on foot in this Kingdom, I desire you to bring me to Windsor on Friday next in the evening a perfect list of the same, that so I may give such order therein, as shall be best for the security and ease of the Kingdom.

Wallingford,   ⟨G. H.⟩ Prince ⟨d'⟩ Orange.
13th December 1688.

The Lords, being informed that Mr. Blathwaite was gone out of town towards the Prince, took no further care in it.

Captain Fowler[94] and John Robins, Esquire, giving their Lordships information, that several goods were privately set on board a vessel near Pickle Herring, in St. Catherine's, and that several persons were seen to go privately on board, had the following order directed to them.

To search ships at St. Catherine's.

We do hereby authorize and require you to go on board, and search all such ships and vessels, as you shall think requisite, which are now riding before the Precinct of St. Catherine's; and to secure and seize all such boxes and other things, as you shall think necessary; and all His Majesty's Officers, both civil and military, are to be aiding and assisting to you in the due execution hereof. And for so doing, this shall be to you and them a sufficient warrant. Given at the Council Chamber, in Whitehall, 13th December 1688.

Hallifax; Ossulstone; Sussex; R. Mountague; North and Grey; T. Jermin.

To Richard Fowler and John Robins, Esquire.

Several passes signed: one to Thomas Liniall to return to Kent, ‹one› to John Dumbleton to Gravesend, etc.

[Day four. The mob violence dying down in the metropolis, the Peers spent much of their time dealing with fugitives. Lord Feversham, on the point of going to the King, communicated a letter he had received from James, which showed that he was still under restraint, and without either clean linen or money. The Peers sent a request to the Lords deputed to attend the King to enquire of him regarding the fate of the Great Seal and the missing parliamentary writs. They ordered the securing of Sir Edward Hales, granted a pass to the Earl of Peterborough's servants to go to him at Ramsgate, authorized a search for Fr. Edward Petre, and signed a warrant for the committal of Fr. John Warner, the King's Confessor. In their hatred of Popery they were no respecters of persons.]

26 Portrait medallion of George Saville, 1st Marquess of Halifax. London, Westminster Abbey, Halifax Monument.

WHITEHALL, COUNCIL CHAMBER
FRIDAY MORNING, DECEMBER 14TH, 1688

His Grace of York; Duke of Grafton; Duke ‹of› Hamilton; Marquess of Hallifax; Earl of Anglesey; Earl of Sussex; Earl of Carlisle; Earl of Craven; Earl of Nottingham; Earl of Feversham; Earl of Rochester; Lord Viscount Newport; Lord Viscount Preston; Lord Bishop of Durham; Lord Bishop of Winchester; Lord Bishop of Rochester; Lord Delawarr; Lord Wharton; Lord North and Grey; Lord Vaughan Cherbury; Lord Lucas; Lord Jermin; Lord Crew; Lord Godolphin; Lord Ossulstone; Sir John Ernley; Sir John Trevor; Colonel Titus.

The Lords met at nine of the clock.

   The Duke of Grafton, arrived from the Prince, told their Lordships he had orders to go to Tilbury with two Battalions of his Regiment, and had occasion for barges to carry them thither. Whereupon their Lordships writt the following letter.

My Lord,

   Your Lordship is desired to cause to be provided four of the City barges, and to receive the orders from His Grace, the Duke of Grafton, to transport from hence certain troops to Tilbury, being of the Guards.

Council Chamber, Whitehall,
December 14th, 1688.

Thomas Ebor.; Hallifax; Craven; Vaughan Cherbury; Thomas Roffen.; North and Grey; P. Winchester; T. Jermin.

Directed to the right honourable Sir John Chapman, Lord Mayor of the City of London.

The Earl of Feversham having received a letter from His Majesty of the 12th, with a postscript of the 13th, from Feversham, acquainted the Lords with it, as follows.

King's letter.

Feversham, December 12, 1688.

   I had the misfortune to be stopped at Sheerness, and brought in here this day by a rabble of seamen, fishermen, and others, who still detain me here, though they know me. Lord Winchelsea came to me here,[95] but so late, that if those, who detain me, would let me go to Canterbury, I would not have stirred. I must see if that Lord can perswade them to permit it me tomorrow. However, speak to some of my most necessary servants to come to me, and bring with them some linnen and cloaths; and, if Frazier be in the way, let him be one. Direct them to come by Sittingbourne, and so, by this place, on to Canterbury, if I be not here. I know ⟨not⟩ if this letter will get to you safe, and so say no more.

J.R.

Let James Graham know I shall want some moneys. If he could, and bring some himself, or send some, it would be but necessary; those, who seized me, having taken all the little I had about me, when they laid hands on me.

J.R.

December 13th.

This letter should have come last night, but the person, that was to carry it, was so frighted, that he durst not stir out of the town, being stopt and frighted by the rabble. I hope he, that carries it now, will get through to you, though all the whole country are up, and have plundered most of the Catholicks' houses.

The Lords, upon reading the letter, ordered the original to be kept, and a copy thereof to be delivered to the Earl of Feversham, who, not being yet gone, had the following order, made by the Lords, delivered to him.

Sir Edward Hales to be secured.

We, Peers of the Realm, with other the Lords of the Privy Council, do hereby pray and require your Lordship to seize upon the person of Sir Edward Hales, and deliver him to the Sheriff of the County of Kent,[96] or to the Mayor of Rochester, so as the said Sir Edward Hales may be secured. Given at the Council Chamber, in Whitehall, the 14th day of December 1688.

27 The seizure of James II at Faversham on 11 December 1688. Dutch engraving by Romeyn de Hooge.

Thomas Ebor.; Newport; Thomas Roffen.; Hamilton; North and Grey; P. Winchester; Jermin; Crew.

To the right honourable the Earl of Feversham.

After his departure the Lords, having some discourse concerning the Lord Jeffreys, writt the following letter to the four Lords, who were to go to attend the King, which they sent by Bromwich, the Messenger.[97]

Lords with the King to enquire concerning the Great Seal and the writts for Parliament.

Our very good Lords,

Being informed that the Lord Jeffreys, now in the Tower, has declared that he delivered to His Majesty the Great Seal of England and those writts for the meeting of the Parliament, which were not delivered out before; we, Peers of the Realm, assembled with some of the Privy Council, do hereby pray your Lordships to inform yourselves of the truth of this matter, and to give us an account where the Great Seal and writts are now deposited. Given at the Council Chamber, in Whitehall, December 14th, 1688.

Thomas Ebor.; Hamilton; Hallifax; Mulgrave; Anglesey; Craven; Nottingham; Vaughan of Cherbury; Rochester; Newport; North and Grey; P. Winton.; Jermin; Ossulstone; Godolphin.

To the right honourable the Earls of Feversham, Aylesbury, Yarmouth, and Middleton.

The Duke of Grafton acquainting the Lords that some of the Irish Guards, who had lain down their arms, were in so ill a condition, that they were ready to starve, they directed the Lord Ranelagh, as follows.

80£ to the Irish Guards.

We, the Peers of the Realm, being assembled with some of the Lords of the Privy Council, do hereby authorize and require you to pay the summ of 80£ subsistence to His Grace the Duke of Grafton, or his assistant, for the use of the Battalion of Irish Guards in England. Given at the Council Chamber, 14th December 1688.

Hallifax; North and Grey; P. Winchester; T. Titus; Hamilton; Ossulstone; Godolphin; Newport; Jermin; J. Trevor.

To the right honourable the Lord Ranelagh, Paymaster-General of the Forces.

And likewise the following order ‹was› made concerning the Irish, which was printed.

Order concerning the Irish Officers and soldiers.

We, the Peers of the Realm, and others the Lords of the Privy Council, do hereby require all Irish Officers and soldiers to repair forthwith to their respective bodies, to which they do, or did lately belong; and we do hereby declare that, behaving themselves peaceably, they shall have subsistence paid them, untill they shall be otherwise provided for, or employed. And the said Officers and soldiers are to deliver up their arms to such of the Officers of the Ordnance, who are to deposit the same in the Stores of the Tower of London. And we do hereby require and command all Justices of the Peace, Constables, and other officers, whom it may concern, to seize all such soldiers, as shall not repair to their respective bodies, and that they be dealt with as vagabonds. Given at the Council Chamber, the 14th of December 1688.

Thomas Ebor.; Hallifax; Carlisle; Dorset; Nottingham; Rochester; Craven; N. Duresme; P. Winchester; North and Grey; J. Trevor; T. Titus.

Several of these orders were sent to Mr. Frowde to be put up in all towns within 20 miles of London.

Ordered to be printed.

Sir Henry Johnson acquainting the Lords, that having taken the Lord Chancellor on board the *Hope*, alias *Hopewell*, she might be permitted to proceed on her voyage, the Lords made the following order.

The ship, Hopewell, to be discharged.

We, Peers of the Realm, being assembled with some of the Privy Council, having by our order, bearing date the 12th instant, directed to you to seize and secure the ship, *Hope*, alias *Hopewell*, of London (James Porter, Master), these are to authorize and require you to set free and discharge the said ship and master. And for so doing, this shall be your warrant. Given at the Council Chamber, in Whitehall, 13th (*sic*) day of December 1688.

Hallifax; Kent; Sussex; Mountague; North and Grey.

To Sir Henry Johnson and Sir John Friend, Knights; Champion Ashby and Thomas Cross, Esquires; or to any two of them.

The following order was made for subsistence to Colonel Carney's Regiment.

We, the Peers of this Realm, being assembled with some of the Lords of the Privy Council, do hereby authorize and require you to pay one week's subsistence to the 7 Companies of Sir Charles Carney's Regiment of Foot.

Hallifax; Newport; P. Winchester; Hamilton; North and Grey; J. Trevor; T. Jermin; Ossulstone; T. Titus.

To the right honourable the Earl of Ranelagh, Paymaster-General of the Forces.

Also the following pass was granted to the Earl of Peterborough's servants.

A pass to Ezra Dodsworth and Henry Newman, servants to the Earl of Peterborough, to repair to Ramsgate, in Kent. Dated 14th December 1688.

Hallifax; Thomas Roffen.; Lawarr; Mulgrave; Vaughan Cherbury; Crew; Nottingham.

And a pass to Mr. Sayers, Vice-Chamberlain to the Queen Dowager, with his return, to attend the Prince of Orange from Her Majesty.

The following order was made to the Lord Lucas.

Artillery to be delivered to the Lord Lucas.

We, the Peers of this Realm, being assembled with some of the Privy Council, do hereby authorize and require you to issue out of the stores under your charge the artillery and ammunition, or other stores, that shall be demanded by the right honourable the Lord Lucas, Chief Governour of the Tower of London, with guns proportionable, and proper Officers to command them, who are to obey such orders as they receive from my Lord Lucas. Given at the Council Chamber, in Whitehall, the 14th day of December 1688.

Thomas Ebor.; Hallifax; Dorset; Sussex; Carlisle; Rochester; Newport; North and Grey; P. Winton.; Thomas Roffen.; Crew; Jermin.

To the Principal Officers of the Ordnance.

Mr. Packer, of the Exchequer, informing the Lords, that he could find Father Peter, they gave him the following order.

We, the Peers of the Realm, assembled with some of the Privy Council, do hereby will and require you forthwith to make diligent search for Edward Peter, *alias* called Father Peters, in all places whatsoever, where you have any reason to suspect him; and all Lieutenants, Deputy Lieutenants, Sheriffs, Justices of the Peace, Bayliffs, and all others His Majesty's Officers, civil and military, are to be aiding and assisting to you in the execution hereof. Given at the Council Chamber, in Whitehall, the 14th day of December 1688.

Thomas Ebor.; Hallifax; Dorset; Sussex; Carlisle; Nottingham; Rochester; Newport; N. Duresme; P. Winchester; Crew; Thomas Roffen.; North and Grey; T. Titus.

To Phillip Packer, Esquire.

Colonel Wacklin[100] acquainting the Lords that several of the soldiers of the Earl of Craven's Regiment say they are disbanded, and delivered in a list of those that went away. Whereupon the following order was made.

Lord Craven's Regiment to repair to their colours.

Whereas information hath been given by an Officer of the Regiment of Foot Guards, commanded by the Earl of Craven, that several soldiers of the Regiment being under a mistake, that they were disbanded, had withdrawn themselves from their Company; these are, therefore, to require all soldiers whatsoever, belonging to the said Regiment, forthwith to repair to their respective colours, there being no orders for the disbanding them. Given at the Council Chamber, at Whitehall, the 14th day of December 1688.

Thomas Ebor.; Hallifax; Dorset; Mulgrave; Rochester; Nottingham; Carlisle; Newport; P. Winchester; Crew; North and Grey; Ossulstone.

[The Peers' advertisement in *The London Gazette*, the official government newspaper, promising a reward for the recovery of Ronquillo's goods, had produced a sufficient response for them to employ the Clerk of the Green Cloth as their receiver. In the afternoon session they authorized the Parish Constables to conduct searches for the Ambassador's belongings. Meanwhile the Lord

Mayor committed a number of persons to prison charged with theft and the receiving of stolen goods from Weld House.]

Several persons bringing goods, which were taken from the Spanish Ambassador's, the following order was made.

Whereas complaint hath been made to us, the Peers of this Realm, and others the Lords of the Privy Council assembled in the Council Chamber, by the Spanish Ambassador, that his house was pulled down and plundered, we caused publick notice to be given in *The Gazette*, that whosoever should bring forth any of the said goods they should have a reward for the same.[101] We have, therefore, thought fit to appoint you, Sir Henry Firebrass,[102] Clerk of the Green Cloth, to receive into your charge all such goods of what sort soever, and the same to keep by inventory. And because other persons have carried their goods into the Spanish Ambassador's house, if the Spanish Ambassador, or any other person, shall make it appear unto you, that such and such goods, which have been brought unto you, is truly theirs, that then you shall demand of such persons the reward which you have given such persons who have brought in such goods. Which reward you are desired to give unto the first person bringing in the said goods, which reward is not to exceed the 20th part of the said goods, on your discretion; and that for your security you do not deliver such goods unto the owners, untill they have re-imbursed you of the reward by you paid unto the discoverer, we having promised to the discoverer a reward for the same. Council Chamber, December 14th, 1688.

Thomas Ebor.; Hamilton; Hallifax; Rochester; Newport; North and Grey; Crew; Carlisle; N. Duresme; Chandois; Lawarr; Jermin; P. Winchester; Thomas Roffen.; T. Titus.

Upon the motion of the Earl of Dorset the following letter was ordered to be writt to the Earl of Winchelsea.

Council Chamber,

December 14th, 1688.

My Lord,

The Earls (*sic*) assembled at Whitehall, having received information that the son of the Lord Arundel of Wardour,[103] his wife, and two children, are seized and stopt at Feversham, have commanded me to desire your Lordship to relieve them out of the danger of the rabble, and endeavour that they may proceed on their intended journey. This is what I have in command, and am, for my own part, with great respect, my Lord,

Your Lordship's most obedient, humble servant,

To the right honourable the Earl of Winchelsea. Francis Gwyn.

The following order was signed, with the addition of the words, *to receive his commands, and to protect his person from insolence*; which was delivered to the Earl of Feversham, and the former order cancelled.

Lord Feversham to attend the King with Guards.

We, the Peers of this Realm, being assembled with some of the Lords of the Privy Council, do hereby pray and authorize your Lordship to draw 40 men out of each

Troop of the Guards, and also 50 Grenadiers, and march with them with all speed to attend His Majesty, to receive his commands, and protect his person from insolence. Given at the Council Chamber, in Whitehall, the 14th December, 1688.

Thomas Ebor.; Newport; Jermin; Hallifax; Vaughan Cherbury; Godolphin; Mulgrave; P. Winchester.

Several gentlemen of Kent having given the Lords an account of what was done in that County, the following letter was ordered to be writt to them.

Gentlemen,

By the command of the Peers of the Realm, and others the Lords of the Council, I am to acquaint you, that their Lordships received a letter this morning, dated from Feversham, December 13th, signed by you (Bazil Dixwell,[104] William Honywood, James Oxenden,[105] Thomas Teyliand, Caleb Banks, Mark Dixwell, F. Kitchwell), and have given directions to the Earl of Feversham in all things necessary in this affair, which his Lordship will communicate unto you. I am, etc.,

F. Gwyn.

The Earl of Nottingham moves, that the warrant for the commitment of the Lord Jeffreys might be altered, and, in order thereunto, that he should be brought before them, and commit‹ted› again by another warrant. But it being objected that it was not safe to remove him out of the Tower, because of the rabble, who threaten violence to his person, there was nothing done at that time.

Duke of Hamilton moves, that some of the Lords of the Council and others may wait on the King.

One Foxcroft attended the Lords, and acquainted them he could discover that 12,000 guineas at least were carried by a coachman, who, not being paid sufficiently for his pains, had given the information. Whereupon he was ordered to bring the coachman in the afternoon.

Lieutenant-Colonel Warcop was complained of by some of the Officers of the Wardrobe, that he had opened Father Warner's lodgings,[106] and that some of the goods belonging to the King were wanting; and Colonel Warcop, attending, satisfyed their Lordships that, if any goods were lost, it was before he came into the room; that, being upon the guard, he found that lodging open, and had put his field bed in it, there being no furniture; which was all the use he made of it.

The Earl of Ranelagh, acquainting their Lordships that intimation was given him, that the Prince of Orange expected his attendance at Windsor, had a pass signed accordingly.

Lords adjourned untill 4 of the clock in the afternoon.

WHITEHALL, COUNCIL CHAMBER
FRIDAY AFTERNOON, DECEMBER 14TH, 1688

PRESENT

His Grace of York; Duke ‹of› Hamilton; Marquess ‹of› Hallifax; Earl of Thanet; Earl of Mulgrave; Earl of Anglesey; Earl of Nottingham; Lord Viscount Newport; Lord Viscount Preston; Lord Bishop ‹of› Winchester; Lord Bishop of Rochester; Lord Eure; Lord North and Grey; Lord Chandois; Lord Vaughan Cherbury; Lord Jermin; Lord Crew; Lord Godolphin; Sir John Trevor; Colonel Titus.

Sir Robert Sa‹w›yer and Mr. Finch attend.

[A report of an attempt on the life of the Duke of Grafton, but recently come to town from the Prince, put the Peers upon on a thorough examination of the incident, fearing some sinister motive in it. In the event it proved to be no more than a drunken affray, in which a trooper in drink quarrelled with a musketeer.]

Mr. John Hutchinson acquaints their Lordships, that coming through the Strand, just before Somerset House, he saw the Duke of Grafton on horseback at the head of his Regiment, and he saw another person on horseback riding apace after the Duke, and drew a pistol and levelled it, as he was told, at the Duke of Grafton. He saw the man fall off his horse, and heard a shott, by which, he was told, he fell, the shott being made by a musquetteer of that Regiment.

The Lords thereupon sent Captain Cholmley,[107] who was then on the guard, to enquire the particulars of that matter. And before he returned the Lord Falkland[108] came, and acquainted their Lordships from the Duke of Grafton, that his Grace, riding by Somerset House, met with one on horseback, who, pressing near him, was stopt by some of the soldiers, who apprehended he might have some evil intentions upon the Duke's person, but the Duke called to the men to let him go; which was no sooner done, but he rode up to the Duke with pistol cocked, and presented it to him, whereupon one of the soldiers shot him.

The Lords desired the Lord Falkland to write to the Duke of Grafton, that they had that matter then under examination, and would endeavour to find the bottom of it.

Captain Cholmley returns, and acquaints their Lordships, that the person shott was a trooper, who, being drunk, rode into the Battalion, as they marched, and, disturbing the ranks, was pushed out by one of the soldiers with a musquet, to go from among them; whereupon he drew his pistol and discharged it, and immediately one of the soldiers shot him.[109]

Captain Reddish informs their Lordships, that one Dyer, a joyner, had seized Father Warner on Wednesday, the 12th instant; and that he was a prisoner at *The Katherine Wheel*, in Gravesend; that Sir Robert Guildford[110] and 3, as they said, nephews of the Lord Shrewsbury were prisoners there likewise. The Lords thereupon made the following order.

Father Warner to be committed.

> We, the Lords of this Realm, assembled with some of the Lords of the Privy Council, do direct you to carry the body of ⟨John⟩ Warner, a Jesuit, before the next Justice of the Peace, in order to his being committed to the County Gaol. And for so doing, this shall be your warrant. Given at the Council Chamber, in Whitehall, the 14th day of December 1688.
>
> Hallifax; Nottingham; Chandois; Pembroke; Vaughan of Cherbury; Thomas Culpepper; Berkeley.
>
> To Captain John Reddish and Abraham Dyer, or either of them.

The Spanish Ambassador's Secretary, desiring a warrant to search for some goods belonging to the Spanish Ambassador, had this following warrant.

To search for goods taken from the Spanish Ambassador.

> We, the Peers of this Realm, being assembled with some of the Lords of the Privy Council, do hereby authorize you to make diligent search for goods, which were lately taken out of the Spanish Ambassador's house, in Wild Street, and to seize on all such goods; and to bring them to Sir Henry Firebrass's lodgings, in Whitehall, who hath orders to receive the same, and to give such proportionable reward, as he shall think you deserve. Given at the Council Chamber, in Whitehall, the 14th day of December 1688.
>
> Thomas Ebor.; Mulgrave; Thomas Roffen.; Chandois; Hallifax; Nottingham; R. Eure; Craven; Thanet; North and Grey; J. Trevor; Anglesey; P. Winchester; T. Titus.
>
> To all High Constables and Petty Constables, whom it may concern.

> We, the Peers of this Realm, with some of the Lords of the Privy Council, do hereby require and authorize you to pay one week's subsistence to Colonel John Hales's[111] Regiment of Foot. Given at the Council Chamber, the 14th day of December 1688.
>
> Thomas Ebor.; Hallifax; Mulgrave; Thanet; Anglesey; Nottingham; P. Winchester; Thomas Roffen.; R. Eure; North and Grey; Crew; T. Titus.
>
> To the right honourable the Earl of Ranelagh, Paymaster-General of the Forces.

A Groom of the King's Bedchamber and his Apothecary, desiring to attend His Majesty, had the following passes.

> A pass to Oliver Nicholas,[112] Esquire, Groom of His Majesty's Bedchamber, to repair to His Majesty. Dated 14th December 1688. Signed: Hamilton; Hallifax; Craven; Mulgrave; North and Grey; Weymouth; Thanet; J. Trevor.

> A pass to Mr. John Chase, [113]Apothecary to His Majesty, to repair to His Majesty. Dated 14th December 1688. Signed by: Hallifax; Thanet; Craven; Rochester; Weymouth; North and Grey; J. Trevor.

Lieutenant-Colonel Tuite delivered the following petition.

To the right honourable the Lords assembled in Council.

The humble petition of Lieutenant-Colonel Tuite and the disbanded Officers and soldiers of the Lord Forbes's[115] Regiment sheweth, that the said Regiment was disbanded and disarmed on Wednesday last in the evening, and the said Officers and soldiers for their own safety disperse themselves several ways, so that part of them came to this town; and, notwithstanding their civil deportment, are in continual danger of being massacred by the rabble, as they have reason to apprehend by last night's alarm. To prevent which, and to remove apprehensions on both sides, the said Officers and soldiers desire your Lordships' protection; and that you would propose some means for their security and subsistence, in case you will have them to continue here; or to give them a speedy licence to depart, either into their own country, or to the service of any Prince, that may be consistent with the interest of this Kingdom.
    And your petitioner‹s› shall ever pray.

Which being read, their Lordships made the following order, which they desired to be printed.

Irish soldiers to be quartered at Barnett.

Whereas all Irish Officers and soldiers are required to repair forthwith to their respective bodies, to which they do, or did lately belong, we, Peers of the Realm, assembled with some of the Lords of the Privy Council, do hereby appoint the town of Barnett, in the County of Hertford, where the Officers and soldiers late under the command of the Lord Forbes are to repair, and there to remain untill further order, without their arms, under the command of Colonel William Tuite; he taking care that they behave themselves peaceably and civilly; and all Justices of the Peace, Constables, and other officers are to be assisting to the said Officers and soldiers, as there shall be occasion. Given at the Council Chamber, Whitehall, the 14th day of December 1688.

Hallifax; Thanet; Anglesey; Nottingham; Rochester; North and Grey; J. Trevor.

The Lords being acquainted that the Earl of Seaforth[116] and his family were detained on board a yatch, the Lords spoke to Sir Henry Johnson to let them come on shore, and release them from any restraint.
    The Earl of Pembroke, Lord Viscount Weymouth, Lord Bishop of Ely, and Lord Culpepper, who attended the Prince of Orange with the Declaration from Guildhall, returned. The Earl of Pembroke acquainted their Lordships, that the Prince thanked them for their Declaration; that he intended to be in town within a few days, the City having invited him thither; that, God having pleased to prosper him so far, he intended to proceed in his care for the Protestant religion, and the laws, and properties of the subjects.[117]

[The following informations clearly indicate an element of planning in the London mobs' attack on private property in the polite residential quarter of Bloomsbury, an area of the town which had been developed since the Restoration.]

Mr. Price, of Great Russell Street, Bloomsbury, saith the rabble intended to visit (as they call it) that street, and had marked some houses there, which they intended to fall upon at night. Several other persons making the same complaints of other places, their Lordships desired my Lord Craven to acquaint them how the Forces were posted upon the guard.
    And his Lordship informed them, that there was one Company and half upon the guard at St. James's; two Companies at the Tilt Yard; two at the Scotland Yard; two at the Savoy; three at Somerset House; two at the Mews.

For the Horse: the Third Troop of Horse were at the Horse Guards, except 20, which are at Somerset House.

Their Lordships liked very well the posting of them where they were, but desired my Lord Craven, that an addition of three Troops of Colonel Slingsby's Regiment might be mounted at night: one of the Troops to be drawn up in Leicester Fields; another in St. James's Square, who were to send patroles towards Berkeley House;[118] and the third in Southampton Square, who were to send patroles into Great Russell Street.

[Day five. The two last sessions of the provisional government were mostly taken up with routine administration, civil and military: part of the continuing process of bringing the capital back to normality after earlier excesses. This was the most important and enduring of the Peers' achievements.]

28 Protestant propaganda: allegorical print portraying William of Orange, in the guise of warlike Hercules, coming to deliver an oppressed England. Note the priest (*left*), symbolic of the Catholic faith, being driven away from the bed of state. Dutch engraving by Gérard de Lairesse.

WHITEHALL, COUNCIL CHAMBER
SATURDAY MORNING, DECEMBER 15TH, 1688

His Grace of York; Marquess of Hallifax; Earl of Dorset; Earl of Mulgrave; Earl of Thanet; Earl of Berkeley; Earl of Craven; Earl of Nottingham; Earl of Rochester; Lord Viscount Newport; Lord Viscount Weymouth; Lord Bishop ‹of› Winchester; Lord Bishop ‹of› Rochester; Lord Bishop ‹of› Ely; Lord Eure; Lord Wharton; Lord North and Grey; Lord Crew; Lord Maynard; Lord Vaughan of Cherbury; Lord Culpepper; Lord Lucas; Lord Jermin; Lord Godolphin; Lord Ossulstone; Sir John Ernle; Sir John Trevor; Colonel Titus.

[Although Secretary Preston knew that James was in the Kingdom, he continued to defer to the Peers as the embodiment of authority in London. He referred to them the important offer of the surrender of Portsmouth, the last major stronghold held in the King's name, which the Catholic Duke of Berwick made to his cousin the Prince. He also forwarded to them the announcement by Sir Edward Vaudrey, one of Berwick's officers, of the resignation of his military commission. The Catholic Vaudrey, like the King and Berwick, judged 'resistance to the necessity of the times' to be 'useless', given the overwhelming Protestant interest which asserted itself in all parts of the nation.]

There was a letter sent from the Duke of Berwick, dated from Portsmouth, December 13th, 1688, directed to the Earl of Middleton, Principal Secretary of State; and, in his absence, was delivered by Sir George Berkeley[119] to the Lord Preston, who transmitted it to Mr. Gwyn the 14th of December at 10 o'clock at night.

Letter from ‹the› Duke of Berwick to the Earl of Middleton.

Portsmouth,

December 13th, 1688.

My Lord,

The King being gone, and the nation being desirous that all Roman Catholicks should lay down their arms, I desire you would acquaint the Prince of Orange, that I am ready to lay down my Government of Portsmouth, provided he will give passes and safe conduct to all those Officers and soldiers I have under my command to go to their respective countreys, or elsewhere. Sir George Berkley, Lieutenant-Colonel to Sir Edward Hales's Regiment, has instructions from me towards concluding this matter. I desire you will send me a speedy answer. In the mean time I am, my Lord,

Your Lordship's most humble, and obedient servant,

Berwick.

Which being laid before their Lordships at their first meeting in the morning, they writt the following letter, which was sent by Atterbury,[120] the Messenger; and Sir George Berkley was ordered to go with him to Windsor to attend the Prince's further pleasure.

> May it please Your Highness,
>
> The letter,[121] which will be tendered to Your Highness at the same time with this, being just now brought to us, we think it of that consequence, as that the account of it to Your Highness is not to be detained, that order may be taken for the security of such an important place as Portsmouth, in such manner as Your Highness shall judge to be most convenient. We remain, may it please Your Highness,
>
> > Your Highness's most obedient, and most humble servants,
>
> Thomas Ebor.; Hallifax; Dorset; Mulgrave; Craven; Berkeley; Thanet; Rochester; Nottingham; Vaughan Cherbury; North and Grey; R. Eure; Newport; Weymouth; F. Ely; P. Winchester; Thomas Roffen.; Maynard; Culpepper; Ossulstone; J. Trevor; T. Titus.

A letter was sent by Sir John Knatchbull to Lord Weymouth, in answer to their Lordships' letter of the 11th instant,[122] giving an account of the seizing of several persons in the County of Kent, etc., which original letter, together with that above to the Prince of Orange, were by their Lordships' order inclosed by Mr. Gwyn in a letter to Monsieur Benting, and sent as abovesaid.

The Lord Preston likewise transmitted the following letter sent to him by Sir Edward Vaudrey.[123]

29 Dr Peter Mews, Bishop of Winchester, one of the advocates of the King's return to London. He was known as 'Old Patch' on account of the patch (*left cheek*) which he wore to cover a wound received as a loyal Cavalier soldier in the Civil War. Plumbago portrait by David Loggan, *c.*1680. London, National Portrait Gallery.

Letter to Lord Preston from Portsmouth.

My Lord,

I have writt to your Lordship already by the post to acquaint you I had a design to surrender my commission into your hands, had I been so happy as to find you in town; failing of which, I am forced to trouble you with this, and beg the favour that, as I have reduced myself by quitting my employment to the private character of the Lord Duke of Berwick's Gentleman of Horse, so you will please to protect me from the inconveniencies, which may fall upon those, who, by an useless resistance to the necessity of the times, may act otherwise than I have done. In order to which let me humbly crave your Lordship's letter to assure me of your acceptance of my commission, and of the continuance of your protection towards,

Your Lordship's ever faithful, and obedient, humble servant,

Edward Vaudrey.

Which was read.

[Gwyn's order to the Sheriff of London shows how, by a system of public postings about the City, the Peers' decisions were relayed from the Council Chamber at Whitehall to the citizens at large.]

Council Chamber,

December 15th, 1688.

Sir,

The Lords having made an order concerning the Irish Forces, and having directed it to be made publick, I have by their Lordships' order sent some of them to you to be put up in some of the most publick places of the City,

To Sir Humphrey Edwyn, Knight,   F. Gwyn.
one of the Sheriffs of the City of London.

A pass to Benjamin Morris, servant to the Lord Dartmouth, to go to his Lordship to the Fleet, and to have a boat, if necessary. Dated 15th December 1688.

Hallifax; Mulgrave; Dorset; Craven; Clarendon; Nottingham; Rochester; Newport; Weymouth; ⟨P.⟩ Winchester; Vaughan Cherbury; North and Grey; Culpepper; Ossulstone; J. Trevor.

Lady Audley's coach and horses to be delivered.

We, Peers of the Realm, assembled with some of the Lords of the Privy Council, being informed that a coach and four horses, with two saddle horses, belonging to the Lady Audley, are seized and stopt at Dartford, do hereby will and require all persons concerned to permit John Langreth, the coachman, and Thomas Gossage, the groom, to bring the said coach and horses to London to the said Lady Audley. Dated at the Council Chamber, in Whitehall, the 15th December 1688.

Hallifax; Mulgrave; Nottingham; Rochester; Newport; Weymouth; T. Jermin; Ossulstone.

A pass to the Lord Carington[124] to go to Wootton, in Warwickshire. Dated 15th December 1688.

Lieutenant-General Worden[125] and Lord Dunmore's[126] Regiment. Subsistence.

We, the Peers of the Realm, assembled with some of the Lords of the Privy Council, do hereby authorize and require you to pay one week's subsistence unto Lieutenant-General Worden's Regiment of Horse, and to the Regiment of Scotts Dragoons under the command of the right honourable the Earl of Dunmore. Given at the Council Chamber, in Whitehall, the 15th day of December 1688.

Mulgrave; Clarendon; Nottingham; Newport; Weymouth; R. Eure; North and Grey; P. Winchester; Culpepper; Ossulstone; Vaughan Cherbury; J. Trevor; T. Titus.

To the right honourable the Earl of Ranelagh, Paymaster-General of the Forces.

Mr. Townley's pass.

A pass to Charles Townley and Richard Townley,[127] Esquires, with seven or eight servants, to go into Lancashire; and the persons who seized their horses to give an account to their Lordships. Dated 15th of December 1688.

Hallifax; Craven; Berkeley; Nottingham; Rochester; Newport; P. Winchester; Crew.

Their Lordships, being informed that several of the Officers of the Irish Guards were kept in custody about Blackwall, ⟨and⟩ that Lieutenant-Colonel Dorington[120] was amongst them, who is a dangerous person, made the following order.

Lieutenant-Colonel Dorington to be secured and others discharged.

We, Peers of the Realm, being assembled with some of the Lords of the Privy Council, being informed that Lieutenant-Colonel Dorington, Captain Arthur, and Captain Plunkett,[129] late Officers in the Irish Guards, are detained in or near Blackwall; these are to authorize and require you to secure the said Lieutenant-Colonel Dorington, untill further order; and to dismiss the said Captain Arthur and Captain Plunkett, letting them know that they and Lieutenant Lawless[130] are to attend us here at four of the clock this afternoon. Given at the Council Chamber, in Whitehall, the 15th December 1688.

Thomas Ebor.; Hallifax; Mulgrave; Clarendon; Berkeley; Rochester; Newport; Weymouth; North and Grey; Culpepper.

To Sir Henry Johnson.

The Earl of Nottingham moves, that the Lord Jeffreys may be brought down to be examined concerning the Great Seal, and that the persons who apprehended the Lord Jeffreys might attend in the afternoon to give an account in what manner he attempted to make his escape; and also Mr. Chiffinch might be sent for to give an account of what he knew of the Great Seal and the writts.

Council Chamber,

December 15th 1688.

Gentlemen,

I am commanded by the Peers of the Realm, and other the Lords of the Privy Council, to desire you to attend their Lordships this afternoon at the Council Chamber, at four of the clock, and to bring those persons with you, who were concerned in taking the Lord Chancellour. I am, etc.,

To Sir Henry Johnson, Sir John Friend,   F. Gwyn.
Champion Ashby, and Thomas Cooke, Esquires.

[In a matter of such importance as the Great Seal of England the Peers decided to obtain sworn testimonies from William Chiffinch and his servant.]

Mr. Chiffinch and his man, Joseph Huff, were sent for.

Mr. Bridgeman (being a Justice of the Peace)[131], by order of the Lords, gave them their oaths.

The information of William Chiffinch, Esquire, taken upon oath by order of the Peers of the Realm, assembled with some of the Lords of the Privy Council. 15th December 1688.

Mr. Chiffinch's deposition.

The deponent saith, that the Lord Chancellour on Monday night last, about nine of the clock, or before, sent a servant to the deponent to ask the King, whether he, the said Chancellour, might come to speak with His Majesty; which the deponent did, and the King said, bid him come. The deponent sent him this answer, and he, the Lord Chancellour, presently came to the King, with whom he staid a little while, and then came out, and, bidding the deponent, God b‹e› w‹ith› ye, went away. The deponent believes the Lord Chancellor had the Purse with him, and carried it back again. The deponent, after the Lord Chancellor's going, went up to the King's Lodgings.

Juratum die et anno praedicto coram me, William Bridgeman.

The information of Joseph Hough taken upon oath by order of the Peers of this Realm, assembled with some of the Privy Council, the 15th December 1688.

Joseph Hough's deposition.

This deponent saith, that a little before the King went to supper, about nine of the clock on Sunday night last, there came to him, the deponent, Mr. Gosseling,[132] a gentleman belonging to the Lord Chancellor, and asked him for his master, William Chiffinch, Esquire. He, the deponent, went up to the King's Lodgings, to let Mr. Chiffinch know it; which as soon as he did, he, this deponent, believes that Mr. Chiffinch went to the said Mr. Gosseling. This deponent did not see the said Mr. Gosseling any more that night. He says that Mr. Gosseling had a bag with him, but knows not of what colour the bag was, nor what was in it.

Joseph Hough.

Juratum die et anno praedicto coram me, William Bridgeman.

[Continuing their enquiries after the Great Seal and missing parliamentary writs, the Peers took occasion to ask Lord Jeffreys about the sealing of patents to new Sheriffs (they being the usual returning officers in parliamentary elections, James had 'pricked' a large number of Catholics to serve as Sheriffs), and whether he had the King's licence to go out of the country (the Peers evidently wished to know how so many of the grandees of James's Court had managed to make good their escape).]

Their Lordships thereupon, considering it would not be safe to bring the Lord Jeffreys from the Tower, made the following order.

Order to examine the Lord Jeffreys.

We, Peers of the Realm, assembled with some of the Lords of the Privy Council, do hereby desire the right honourable the Lord North and Grey, the Lord Chandois, and the Lord Ossulstone to go to the Tower of London, and examine the Lord Jeffreys upon such questions, as we have agreed upon; and Sir Robert Sa‹w›yer is to attend their Lordships. Dated 15th December 1688.

Questions to be asked Lord Jeffreys.
1. What he hath done with the Great Seal of England?
2. Whether he did seal all the writts for the Parliament, and what he hath done with them?
3. Whether he hath sealed the several patents for Sheriffs for the year ensuing?
4. Whether he had a licence to go out of the Kingdom?

[Lucas's information of a Catholic design on William's life reminds us that, despite a return to comparative calm in the capital, the 'dangerous times' were not yet over.[133] The Peers were quick to follow it up, and to commit the accused to Newgate Gaol, despite his denial of the charge.]

The Lord Lucas acquainted their Lordships, that an information was brought him of a design upon the Prince of Orange's life, and that the person who informed, as well as the person accused, were both without.

William Benning, *alias* Gozling, being sworn by Mr. Bridgeman by their Lordships' command, saith that one George Peters, a woollen-draper, at the sign of *The Lamb*, in the Strand, a Roman Catholick, came about a week agone to his house to clean a gun; and being asked by him, the said Gozling, whether he would sell it, the said Peters answered, no, for he intended to put a brace of bulletts in it, and shoot the Prince of Orange. Peters, being called in, denyed it; and was committed to Newgate by warrant of Mr. Bridgeman (being a Justice of the Peace) by their Lordships' order.

Foxcroft, who promised to bring a coachman that carried the 12,000 guineas, attended, and said the coachman had broke his word with him. But he brought one Mrs. Bulfen, who said the coachman told her there were six bags, full of gold, brought into his coach, as big as 100£ bags. The coachman was George Goose, who drove a hackney-coach for Finch, and lives in Cabbage Lane, Tothill Street.

WHITEHALL, COUNCIL CHAMBER
SATURDAY AFTERNOON, DECEMBER 15TH, 1688

PRESENT

His Grace of York; Duke of Somerset; Duke of Grafton; Marquess of Hallifax; Earl of Thanet; Earl of Clarendon; Earl of Anglesey; Earl of Berkeley; Earl of Craven; Earl of Nottingham; Earl of Rochester; Lord ‹Viscount› Newport; Lord ‹Viscount› Weymouth; Lord Bishop of Winton.; Lord Bishop of Ely; Lord Bishop of Rochester; Lord North and Grey; Lord Chandois; Lord Vaughan Cherbury; Lord Culpepper; Lord Maynard; Lord Jermin; Lord Lucas; Lord Crew; Lord Godolphin; Lord Ossulstone; Sir John Trevor; Colonel Titus.

[As a notorious Catholic, who had actively co-operated with the King in opening a 'mass-house' in Lime Street, in the City, Stanford was under Protestant disfavour.[134] His request to travel to Lancashire, the most Catholic of English counties and that nearest to Tyrconnell's Ireland, made the Peers suspect his motives in applying for a pass.]

Mr. Stamford, Envoy to the Elector Palatine, desired a pass to go into Lancashire, which was denied him.

[Secretary Middleton, back in his old post at the King's side, wrote to the Chairman of the provisional government announcing James's decision to return. After an overnight stay at Rochester, the King intended to be at Whitehall the next day. Middleton's letter was concerned with making the necessary practical arrangements: the appointment of fresh guards to await James at Dartford, and the preparation of the Royal Apartments at Whitehall.]

Thomas Lay[135] attended their Lordships about six of the clock in the evening, and brought a letter from the Earl of Middleton directed to the Marquess of Hallifax, as follows.

Feversham, December 15th.

Half an hour after 7 in the morning.

My Lords,

In obedience to your Lordships' commands I am to acquaint you, that at our arrival here we found His Majesty very well in his health, and the rabble appeased. And by his commands I am to tell you, that he sets out from hence this morning, and lyes at Rochester, and tomorrow will be at Whitehall; and that, therefore, you would take care to order his coaches and a fresh party of the Guards to go this night to Dartford, to wait for him there, and that his Lodging‹s› and all other things necessary for his reception be put in order. I am, my Lords,

Your Lordships' most obedient, humble servant,

Middleton.

This letter was docquetted: For the Peers assembled.

[Mulgrave, Lord Chamberlain of the King's Household, had, according to Ailesbury, 'thought fit' on James's leaving Whitehall, on 11 December, 'to break his white staff as the great officers do at the burial of the King', but on his return he 'took up his staff again'.[136] The Peers now called on him to discharge his office.]

Their Lordships hereupon desired the Earl of Mulgrave to prepare the King's Lodgings. They likewise ordered Colonel Villers to have the Guards ready, and made the following order.

Captain Morgan's pass, with Guards, to attend the King.

We, the Peers of this Realm, assembled with some of the Lords of the Privy Council, do hereby pray and require you to permit and suffer Captain Henry Morgan,[137] with 70 of the Horse Guards and 24 Grenadiers under his command, to pass freely without any lett, hindrance, or molestation. Dated 15th December 1688.

Somerset; Hallifax; Craven; Berkeley; Newport; Weymouth; J. Trevor; T. Titus.

To the Lord Mayor, Sheriffs, and all other Officers, civil and military, of the City of London, whom it may concern.

Their Lordships likewise ordered Sir William Villers to send the coaches, according to His Majesty's commands.

[The copies referred to here were of Middleton's letter announcing James's imminent return.]

The Duke of Grafton being then going to Windsor, their Lordships sent a copy of the said letter by him to His Highness the Prince of Orange.

They likewise ordered another copy to be sent to the Lord Mayor.

The Duke of Grafton acquaints them with the unfortunate accident he met with yesterday, in the afternoon, as he came by Somerset House. He said the man was drunk, and he was sorry he was shott, but, pressing in among the ranks, and discharging his pistol in the middle of them, he could not possibly prevent it, though he endeavoured it.

The Lords told him they were first informed the fellow had a design upon his life, and his behaviour in these dangerous times gave a just ground to suspect it, but they were very well satisfyed in the matter.

A complaint was made, that several of the landlords, where the soldiers quartered at this time, refused to admit them any longer into their quarters; and the Quartermaster of the Duke of Grafton's Regiment was called in, and the Lords told him they would bear him out, and made the following order.

Quarters for the First Regiment of Foot Guards.

You are to quarter the First Regiment of Foot Guards under your command in the Liberties of Westminster and places adjacent, the same quarters they were quartered in just before their march into the West; and your Officers are to see that the soldiers behave themselves civilly, and pay their landlords; and all magistrates, Justices of the Peace, High Constables, Petty Constables, and all other officers, whom these may concern, are hereby required to be aiding in the quartering of them, or otherwise, as there shall be occasion. Given under our hands at the Council Chamber, in Whitehall, the 15th day of December 1688.

Hallifax; Thanet; Berkeley; Anglesey; North and Grey; Rochester; Weymouth.

To His Grace, Henry, Duke of Grafton, Colonel of the First Regiment of Guards, or the Officer-in-Chief with the said Regiment.

An order was made for a week's subsistence for Lieutenant Craven's Company.

Lieutenant Craven's Independent Company. Subsistence money.

We, Peers of the Realm, assembled with some of the Privy Council, do hereby authorize and require you to pay one week's subsistence unto the Independent Company in Landguard Fort commanded by Lieutenant John Craven.[138] Given at the Council Chamber, Whitehall, 15 December 1688.

Somerset; Hallifax; Berkeley; Thanet; Rochester; North and Grey.

A complaint being made by Mr. Vaughan, Lieutenant-Colonel to the Earl of Salisbury's Regiment,[139] that many of the Troopers were gone away upon a mistake that they were disbanded, their Lordships give him the following order.

Order concerning the Earl of Salisbury's Regiment.

Whereas information hath been given unto us, Peers of the Realm, assembled with some of the Privy Council, that several Troopers in that Regiment, late commanded by the Earl of Salisbury, being under a mistake that they were disbanded, have withdrawn themselves from their Troops; these are, therefore, to require all Troopers, being Protestants, belonging to the said Regiment, forthwith to repair to their respective colours, there having been no order for disbanding them; and all such of the Protestant soldiers, as shall repair to their colours, with their horses and arms, shall have subsistence money paid them. Given at the Council Chamber, in Whitehall, the 15th day of December 1688.

Hallifax; Berkeley; Nottingham; Rochester; Newport; Weymouth; Culpepper; P. Winchester; Crew.

The Lord North and Grey, Lord Chandois, ⟨and⟩ Lord Ossulstone returned from the Tower, and acquainted their Lordships they had been with the Lord Jeffreys, according to their order, and brought his answer to their four questions in writing.

The answer of the right honourable the Lord Jeffreys to the questions proposed to him by the Lords, that were authorized by the Peers to interrogate him. Saturday, 15th December 1688.

Lord Jeffreys's answer.

To the first question his Lordship declareth, that on Saturday last in the afternoon, before the Cabinet Council sate, he was sent for to the King by Mr. Chiffinch; and that thereupon his Lordship did repair to the King with the Great Seal at Mr. Chiffinch's lodgings, and then did deliver to the King the Great Seal (no person being present), and from that time his Lordship never saw it, and that he returned with the Purse only.

To the second question his Lordship declareth, that the writts, as far as he understands, were all sealed; and that on Saturday last in the evening, or the next day, he sent the writts in a bag, sealed up, by his servant Gosling to the King; who brought back word that he had delivered them to the King in Mr. Chiffinch's chamber; and, according to the best of his remembrance, it was on Saturday in the evening ‹that› they were so delivered.

To the third question his Lordship declareth, that he did seal several patents of the new Sheriffs, which he directed to be delivered, according to course, but the particulars he cannot charge his memory with.[140]

To the fourth question his Lordship declareth, that he had several passes to go beyond the seas, which were all delivered to Sir John Friend, when he was brought before the Lord Mayor, as were all his other papers.

I affirm all this to be true upon my honour,

Jeffreys.

[The following additions to the Peers' warrant, committing Jeffreys to the Tower, were made to make good the failure to specify the cause of his committal.]

They likewise acquainted the Lords, that he returned them thanks for securing him from the rabble, who would probably have done him mischief, if he had not been sent to the Tower. Whereupon their Lordships resolved not to send for him, but ordered to be entered before the warrant the words following: *Whereas the Lord Jeffreys was seized, and brought to the house of the Lord Mayor, and was there in great danger by the insult of the people, to secure him from the said violence, and at his desire to the Lord Lucas to move him to the Tower, this following order was made.* And after the warrant the words following: *The Lords appointed to examine the Lord Jeffreys were desired by the Lord Jeffreys to return the Lords his humble thanks for their care in preserving him from violence.*

Sir Henry Johnson and Sir John Friend attended, according to order in the morning, and were called in.

[As a convinced loyalist, Sir John Friend had agreed to accept and conceal certain papers from Jeffreys at the time of his arrest. Lord Chandos's exposure of the subsequent cover-up reveals that Friend was motivated, not by any regard for Jeffreys, but by affection for the King's service: a pointer to his future, and sadly fatal, career as a Jacobite conspirator (he was executed in 1696).]

The Lord Chandois asked Sir John Friend what papers he received from the Lord Jeffreys; to which he answered, he had received none. He thereupon asked him, whether he did not tell my Lord Jeffreys, that, if he had any papers of consequence, such he had a mind to keep private, he would be true to him; which Sir John Friend owned he did, but he doth not know what papers he had. My Lord Chandois told him, that my Lord Jeffreys had discovered this to them in the Tower, and that, therefore, he thought he was discharged of his promise to the Lord Jeffreys, and might speak clearly.

Sir John Friend answered, that what papers he received from my Lord Jeffreys he put in his pocket, and when he came home he emptied his pocket, as he usually doth once a day, and put the papers into his closet. Being asked, whether he was desired by the Lord Jeffreys to have a particular care of a paper, to which the King's hand was, he answered in the affirmative; the Lord Jeffreys telling him it was a paper under the King's hand, and it was of great consequence to the King, that it should not be seen, which was the reason ‹that› made him endeavour to conceal it, and not any friendship to the Lord Jeffreys, which he never pretended to, being instrumental in seizing him. He owns he did read the paper, the contents of it was to certify whom it may concern, etc.

It was to the purpose that my Lord Jeffreys might go out of the land. It was writt all, as well as *James Rex* at the bottom, in the same hand. There was another paper, signed at the top, *J.R.*, and at the bottom, *Middleton*.

Mr. Musgrave, one of the Clerks of the Council, was ordered to go immediately with Sir John Friend to bring the papers. He went accordingly, and sealed them up in a paper with his own seal, and writt on the back of the outside paper what they were, and left them with Mr. Gwyn.

Captain Fowler acquaints the Lords that, searching according to their warrant, he had seized a vessel bound for Dunkirk with 500 barrells of powder.

Sir Charles Cotterell, attending according to order in the morning, acquaints the Lords with what he had said to the Spanish Ambassador, from their Lordships, upon the misfortune that happened unto him from the rabble, which their Lordships were very well satisfyed with.

[The letter, brought from the Deputy Lieutenants of Kent who had officiously appointed themselves the King's keepers, much to the anger of the local seamen, arrived curiously late at Whitehall. One of the bearers, Nappleton of Faversham, had already been in touch with the Prince, thinking that he had done great service by his intercepting the King. Such was the hectoring treatment that James received from Sir Basil Dixwell and Sir James Oxenden on this occasion, that, in 1692, King James excepted them by name from his general pardon, along with Nappleton 'and all others who offered personal indignity to us at Faversham'.[141]]

Two gentlemen that came out of Kent, with a letter to the Lords, were called in, and the letter is as follows.

> Feversham,
>
> December 13th, 1688.
>
> My Lords,
>
> We are now come into this place with one hundred and fifty Horse and three hundred Foot for the security of His Majesty's person, who was brought in hither on Munday last about ten of the clock. We know not what advice your Lordships might receive, and think it our duty to acquaint your Lordships thereof, begging your orders and directions in this weighty affair with all possible speed. We are, my Lords,
>
> Your Lordships' most obedient, humble servants,
>
> Bazill Dixwell; William Honywood; James Oxenden; Thomas Leyliard; Caleb Banks; Mark Dixwell; T. Kitchwell.

The gentlemen who brought the letter were Mr. Chadwick[142] and Mr. Nappleton.[143] They both gave an account of the seizing of the King by the rabble at Feversham. Mr. Nappleton likewise desires their Lordships' directions, concerning those who were secured in Kent. Whereupon the Lords made the following order.

> We do hereby pray and require the gentlemen of the County of Kent to take care, that all persons seized by them, or their order, be kept in safe custody, untill further order. And being informed that the Envoy Extra‹ordinary› from the Duke of Savoy[144] is stopt, we do direct that he, with such of his retinue as are foreigners, ‹are› to continue their intended journey to the seaside, and there embark, and pass beyond the seas without any hindrance or molestation; but that such of his retinue, as are the

> King's subjects, be detained, untill further direction. Council Chamber, December 15th, 1688.
>
> Somerset; Hallifax; Thanet; Craven; Clarendon; Berkeley; Newport; Weymouth; North and Grey.

Which was delivered to Mr. Nappleton to convey to the gentlemen who signed the letter.

> [Ireland being a separate Kingdom, and under the government of the Catholic Earl of Tyrconnell, James's Lord Deputy, the Peers were fearful what might happen if news of English events reached Dublin too quickly. On the advice of Samuel Pepys, Secretary at the Admiralty, they decided to close the English ports in a belated and unsuccessful attempt to stop outgoing news, and to prevent the return of disbanded Irish soldiers to Ireland.]

It being moved, that particular care should be taken that none of the Irish soldiers, who were broke, should go into Ireland, nor that any intelligence should go thither, least the Earl of Tyrconnell[145] might prepare himself to make a disturbance in that Kingdom. It being likewise thought convenient for diverse reasons, that the ports and foreign posts should be stopt, their Lordships sent for Mr. Pepys and Mr. Froude.

Mr. Pepys attended accordingly, and, being advised with by their Lordships which was the most effectual way to stop the ports, proposed their Lordships' signing a letter to the Chief Officers of the Customs in the respective ports; and, by their Lordships' order, he prepared the following letter.

Order for an embargo.

> We, Peers of the Realm, assembled with some of the Lords of the Privy Council, do hereby require that effectual care be by you taken, that an embargo be presently laid on all ships and vessels within the Port of Dover; that they presume not to put forth to sea from the said Port, or any member thereof, untill further order, without licence to that purpose, given under the hands and seals of five of the Peers; saving in the case of victuallers, or other vessels employed by the Officers of His Majesty's Navy and Ordnance for the use of the Fleet. Dated 15th December 1688.
>
> Somerset; Hallifax; Rochester; North and Grey; Culpepper; Craven; Berkeley; Weymouth; Lucas.
>
> To the Chief Officers of the Customs at the Port of Dover.

The like for Plymouth. Signed by: Somerset; Hallifax; Berkeley; Rochester; North and Grey; Weymouth; F. Ely; Culpepper.

The like for Lynn. Signed by: Hallifax; Berkeley; Newport; North and Grey; F. Ely; Lucas; Culpepper; Weymouth.

The like for Portsmouth. Signed by: Somerset; Hallifax; Berkeley; Rochester; Craven; North and Grey; Culpepper; Weymouth.

The like for Harwich. Signed by: Hallifax; Berkeley; North and Grey; Culpepper; Weymouth; Lucas; Francis Ely.

The like for Gravesend. Signed by: Somerset; Hallifax; Berkeley; Rochester; North and Grey; Weymouth; Vaughan of Cherbury; Lucas.

The like for Chester. Signed by: Hallifax; Berkeley; Newport; North and Grey; Weymouth; Francis Ely; Lucas.

The like for Falmouth. Signed by: Hallifax; Berkeley; Newport; North and Grey; Culpepper; Weymouth; Lucas.

The like for Carlisle. Signed by: Hallifax; Berkeley; Culpepper; North and Grey; Lucas; Weymouth; Francis Ely.

The like for Dartmouth. Signed by: Hallifax; Berkeley; Culpepper; North and Grey; Francis Ely; Weymouth; Lucas.

The like for Berwick. Signed by: Hallifax; Berkeley; Culpepper; North and Grey; Weymouth; Francis Ely; Lucas.

The like for Yarmouth. Signed by: Hallifax; Berkeley; North and Grey; Culpepper; Weymouth; Lucas.

The like for Holyhead. Signed by: Somerset; Hallifax; Berkeley; Craven; Rochester; North and Grey; Weymouth; Lucas.

And gave a list of the names of such persons, as were fit to be sent to.

Mr. Frowde had likewise the following letter delivered to him.

Stop to the foreign posts.

Council Chamber, Whitehall,

December 15th, 1688.

Sir,

The Peers of this Realm, assembled with some of the Privy Council, have commanded me to desire you to put a stop to all foreign posts out of England, not only to all foreign parts, but to Ireland and Scotland (to begin at Berwick for the Kingdom of Scotland), and to let no letters pass, untill further order. I am, etc.,

F. Gwyn.

Postscript.

I have sent you herewith orders of embargo on ships and vessels for several parts of the Kingdom, signed by their Lordships, and, by their command, addressed to you to be conveyed, according to their several directions.

F. Gwyn.

[The Peers' meetings, which began in the Queen's Presence Chamber at St. James's Palace on 21 December, and continued thereafter in the House of Lords at Westminster on 22, 24, 25, and 28 December, though recorded by Gwyn in the Journal, were not, strictly speaking, a part of the proceedings of the provisional government. That had very properly ceased to function on the afternoon of the 15th, on the morrow of James's announced return to the capital on the 16th. With the King back at Whitehall, the Peers deemed the emergency to be over, and saw no reason to continue their sessions. The loyalists returned to their role as courtiers, and the most conspicuous of the revolutionary Williamites either fled to Windsor, or retired out of the way. As for the Privy Councillors who had from the 12th attended the sessions of the provisional government, they also reverted to type and attended James's Privy Council meeting on the evening of the 16th. The far larger number of Peers who assembled at St. James's on the 21st, after the King's enforced removal, did so in response to the Prince's summons to meet him there, when he asked for their advice on how best to procure a free parliament. Though they included a greater proportion of his partisans than were present in the provisional government, they refrained from acknowledging his summons to meet, lest it infringe their 'birthright' as Peers of the Realm. (65 peers attended; 15 of those summoned did not attend, including Archbishop Sancroft, and 8 attended who had not been summoned.)]

His Highness the Prince of Orange was pleased to give the following summons.

Prince of Orange's summons.

We do hereby direct and require you to acquaint the Lords Spiritual and Temporal, whose names are here underwritten, and all others in or near the town, that we desire them to meet us in the Queen's Council Chamber, at St. James's, tomorrow, being Friday, at ten of the clock in the morning. Given at St. James's, the 20th of December 1688.

Prince of Orange.

Lord Archbishop of Canterbury; Lord Archbishop of York; Duke of Norfolk; Duke of Somerset; Duke of Grafton; Duke of Northumberland; Marquess of Hallifax; Earl of Oxford; Earl of Shrewsbury; Earl of Kent; Earl of Bedford; Earl of Pembroke; Earl of Suffolk; Earl of Dorset; Earl of Bridgwater; Earl of Leicester; Earl of Northampton; Earl of Devon‹shire›; Earl of Clare; Earl of Bolingbroke; Earl of Manchester; Earl of Mulgrave; Earl of Rivers (*sic*); Earl of Stamford; Earl of Thanet; Earl of Scarsdale; Earl of Clarendon; Earl of Anglesey; Earl of Carlisle; Earl of Craven; Earl of Aylesbury; Earl of Burlington; Earl of Sussex; Earl of Macclesfield; Earl of Radnor; Earl of Yarmouth; Earl of Berkeley; Earl of Nottingham; Earl of Rochester; Lord Viscount Fauconberg; Lord Viscount Mordant; Lord Viscount Newport; Lord Viscount Weymouth; Lord Bishop ‹of› London; Lord Bishop ‹of› Duresme; Lord Bishop ‹of› Winchester; Lord Bishop ‹of› St. Asaph; Lord Bishop ‹of› Ely; Lord Bishop ‹of› Rochester; Lord Bishop ‹of› Peterborough; Lord Delawar; Lord Grey ‹of› Ruthen; Lord Eure; Lord Wharton; Lord Paget; Lord North and Grey; Lord Chandois; Lord Mountague; Lord Lovelace; Lord Maynard; Lord Howard ‹of› Escrick; Lord Jermin; Lord Vaughan Cherbury; Lord Culpepper; Lord Lucas; Lord Berkeley; Lord Delamere; Lord Crew; Lord Lumley; Lord Ossulstone; Lord Godolphin; Lord Churchill.

To Thomas Atterbury, Clerk of the Cheque to the Messengers.

30 John Sheffield, Earl of Mulgrave, Lord Chamberlain to James II. Anonymous oil painting. University of Oxford, Examination Schools.

QUEEN'S ‹PRESENCE› CHAMBER, IN ST. JAMES'S
DECEMBER 21, 1688

The Queen's Council Chamber was found too little for the meeting of so many peers, and therefore the Queen's Presence Chamber, in St. James's, was the place they met in.

The former list was called over, and there appeared the Lords following, some of whom were in town, though not in the summons.

[The business of the first meeting was confined to thanking the Prince for his *Declaration* and his vigorous pursuit of it. This was all that the Peers were able to agree on. Although the Williamites were to the fore in the debates, they achieved little beyond obtaining a decision to meet the next day, Saturday, rather than after the weekend (though Halifax joined Clarendon in preferring a postponement until Monday, the 24th). Even the signing of the Exeter Association proved controversial.[146] It was read and tabled, but left to the discretion of individual Peers to sign, or not, as they pleased. Eleven signed. They included loyalists as well as Williamites. (65 peers attended.)]

31 The City of London's letter to William, Prince of Orange, 17 December 1688: the original document. London, Public Record Office. See appendix 17.

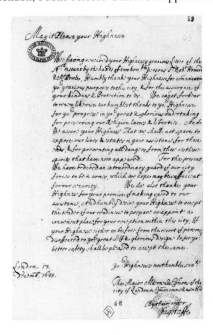

QUEEN'S PRESENCE CHAMBER, IN ST. JAMES'S
DECEMBER 21ST, 1688

PRESENT

Lord Archbishop of York; Duke of Norfolk; Duke of Somerset; Duke of Ormond; Duke of Beaufort; Marquess of Hallifax; Earl of Oxon.; Earl of Shrewsbury; Earl of Kent; Earl of Bedford; Earl of Pembroke; Earl of Dorset; Earl of Northampton; Earl of Devonshire; Earl of Bolingbroke; Earl of Westmoreland; Earl of Manchester; Earl of Mulgrave; Earl of Rivers (*sic*); Earl of Stamford; Earl of Winchelsea; Earl of Thanet; Earl of Scarsdale; Earl of Clarendon; Earl of Craven; Earl of Burlington; Earl of Sussex; Earl of Macclesfield; Earl of Radnor; Earl of Yarmouth; Earl of Berkeley; Earl of Nottingham; Earl of Rochester; Earl of Abingdon; Lord Viscount Falconberg; Lord Viscount Mordant; Lord Viscount Newport; Lord Viscount Hatton; Lord Bishop ‹of› London; Lord Bishop ‹of› Winchester; Lord Bishop ‹of› St. Asaph; Lord Bishop ‹of› Ely; Lord Bishop ‹of› Rochester; Lord Delawar; Lord Grey ‹of› Ruthin; Lord Eure; Lord Wharton; Lord Paget; Lord North and Grey; Lord Chandois; Lord Mountague; Lord Grey ‹of› Warke; Lord Maynard; Lord Howard ‹of› Escrick; Lord Jermin; Lord Vaughan Cherbury; Lord Culpepper; Lord Lucas; Lord Delamere; Lord Crew; Lord Lumley; Lord Carteret; Lord Ossulstone; Lord Godolphin; Lord Churchill.

As soon as the Peers were met His Highness the Prince of Orange came in, and spake to them, and left what he said to them in writing; which, after His Highness was pleased to withdraw, was read by their Lordships' order by Mr. Gwyn at the head of the table.

Prince of Orange's speech.

My Lords,

I have desired you to meet here to advise the best manner how to pursue the end of my *Declaration*, in calling a free parliament for the preservation of the Protestant religion, and returning the rights and liberties of the Kingdom, and settling the same, that they may not be in danger of being again subverted.

The Lords, considering that the Prince's speech referred to his *Declaration*, ordered it to be read; which was done by Mr. Gwyn at the end of the table, and is as follows.

PROTESTANT RELIGION AND LIBERTY

Loco sigilli.

Je maintiendray.

The Declaration of His Highness William Henry, by the Grace of God, Prince of Orange, etc., of the reasons inducing him to appear in arms in the Kingdom of England, and for preserving the Protestant religion, and for restoring the laws and liberties of England, Scotland, and Ireland.

It is both certain and evident to all men, that the publick peace and happiness of any state or kingdom cannot be preserved where the law, liberties, and customs, established by the lawful authority in it, are openly transgressed and annulled; more especially, where the alteration of religion is endeavoured, and that a religion, which is contrary ‹to› law, is endeavoured to be introduced; upon which those who are most immediately concerned in it are indispensibly bound to endeavour to preserve and maintain the established laws, liberties, and customs, and above all the religion and worship of God that is established among them, and to take such an effectual care, that the inhabitants of the said state or kingdom may neither be deprived of their religion, nor of their civil rights; which ‹is› so much the more necessary, being the greatness and security both of kings, royal families, and of all such as are in authority, as well as the happiness of the‹ir› subjects and people, depend in a most especial manner upon the exact observations and maintenance of these their laws, liberties, and customs.

Upon these grounds it is that we cannot any longer forbear to declare that, to our great regret, we see that those counsellors, who have now the chief credit with the King, have overturned the religion, laws, and liberties of these Realms, and subjected them in all things relating to their consciences, liberties, and properties to arbitrary government, and that not only by secret and indirect ways, but in an open and undisguised manner.

32 Dutch Protestant propaganda print, depicting Queen Mary Beatrice rocking the cradle of her infant son, the Prince of Wales. Behind her chair stands Fr Edward Petre, S.J., the reputed 'father' of the 'pretended Prince of Wales', who embraces her lasciviously. Mezzotint.

Those evil counsellors, for the advancing and colouring this with some plausible pretexts, did invent and set on foot the King's dispensing power, by virtue of which they pretend that, according to law, he can suspend and dispense with the execution of laws, that have been enacted by the authority of the King and Parliament for the security and happiness of the subjects, and so have rendered those laws of no effect; though there is nothing more certain than that as no laws can be made, but by the joint concurrence of King and Parliament, so likewise laws, so enacted, which secure the publick peace and safety of the nation, and the lives and liberties of every subject in it, cannot be repealed or suspended but by the same authority.

For ‹though› the King may pardon the punishment that a transgessor has incurred, and to which he is condemned, as in the cases of treason and felony, yet it cannot be with any colour of reason inferred from thence, that the King can intirely suspend the execution of those laws relating to treason or felony; unless it is pretended that he is clothed with a despotick and arbitrary power, and that the lives, liberties, honours, and estates of the subjects depend wholly on his goodwill and pleasure, and are intirely subject to him, which must infallibly follow on the King's having a power to suspend the execution of the laws and to dispense with them.

Those evil counsellors, in order to the giving some credit to this execrable maxim, have so conducted the matter, that they have obtained sentence from the Judges, declaring that this dispensing power is a right belonging to the Crown, as if it were in the power of the twelve Judges to offer up the laws, rights, and liberties of the whole nation to the King, to be disposed of by him arbitrarily and at his pleasure, and expressly contrary to laws enacted for the security of the subjects.[147] In order to the obtaining this judgment, these evil counsellors did beforehand examine secretly the opinion of the Judges, and procured such of them, as could not in conscience concurr in so pernicious a sentence, to be turned out, and others to be substituted in their room, till by the changes which were made in the courts of judicature they at last obtained that judgment. And they have raised some to those trusts who have made open profession of the Popish religion, though those are by law rendered incapable of such employments.[148]

It is also manifest and notorious, that as His Majesty was, ‹upon his› coming to the Crown, received and acknowledged by all the subjects of England, Scotland, and Ireland, as their King, without the least opposition,[149] though he then made open profession of the Popish religion,[150] so he did then promise, and solemnly swear at his coronation, that he would maintain his subjects in the free enjoyment of their laws and liberties, and, in particular, that he would maintain the Church of England as it was established by law.[151] It is likewise certain, that there hath been at diverse and sundry times several laws enacted for the preservation of those rights, and liberties, and of the Protestant religion; and among other securities it has been enacted, that all persons whatsoever that are advanced to any ecclesiastical dignity, or bear office in either University, and all others that should be put into any employment, civil or military, should declare that they were not Papists, but were of the Protestant religion, and that by their taking the Oaths of Allegiance and Supremacy and the Test, yet those evil counsellors have in effect annulled and abolished all those laws, both with relation to ecclesiastical and civil employments.

In order to ecclesiastical dignities and offices, they have not only without any colour of law, but against most expressive laws to the contrary, set up a Commission of a certain number of persons, to whom they have committed the cognizance and direction of all ecclesiastical matters;[152] in which Commission there hath been, and still is, one of His Majesty's Ministers of State who makes now publick profession of the Popish religion, and, at the time of his first professing of it, declared that for a great while before he had believed that to be the only true religion. By all which the deplorable state to which the Protestant religion is reduced is apparent, since the affairs of the Church of England are now put into the hands of persons, who have accepted of a commission that is manifestly illegal, and who have executed it contrary to all law; and that now one of their chief members has abjured the Protestant religion and declared himself a Papist, by which he is become incapable of holding any publick employment.[153]

The said Commissioners have hitherto given such proof of their submission to the directions given them, that there is no reason to doubt, but they will still continue to promote all such designs as will be most agreeable to them; and those evil counsellors take care to raise none to any ecclesiastical dignities, but persons who have no zeal for the Protestant religion, and that hide now their unconcernedness for it under the specious pretence of moderation.

The said Commissioners have suspended the Bishop of London,[154] only because he refused to obey an order that was sent him to suspend a worthy divine,[155] without so much as citing him before him to make his own defence, or observing the common form of process. They have turned out a President chosen by the Fellows of Magdalene College, and afterwards all the Fellows ‹of that Colledge›, without so much as citing them before any court that could take legal cognizance of that affair, or obtaining any sentence against them by a competent judge. And the only reason that was given for their turning them out was their refusing to choose for their President a person that was recommended to them by the instigation of those evil counsellors, though the right of a free election belonged undoubtedly to them.[156] But they were turned out of their freeholds, contrary to law, and to that express provision of *Magna Charta*, that no man shall lose his life, or goods, but by the law of the land.[157] And now those evil counsellors have put the said College wholly into the hands of Papists, though, as it is abovesaid, they are incapable of all such employments, both by the law of the land and the statutes of the College.

These Commissioners have also cited before them all the Chancellors and Archdeacons of England, requiring them to certify to them the names of all such clergymen, as have read the King's Declaration for Liberty of Conscience,[158] and of such as have not read it, without considering that the reading of it was ‹not› enjoined the clergy by the Bishops, who are their ordinaries.[159]

The illegality and incompetency of the said Court of Ecclesiastical Commissioners was so notoriously known, and it did so evidently appear that it tended to the subversion of the Protestant religion, that the most reverend Father in God, William, Archbishop of Canterbury, Primate and Metropolitan of All England, seeing that it was raised for no other end, but to oppress such persons as were of eminent virtue, learning, and piety, refused to sit or to concurr in it.[160]

And though there are many express laws against all churches and chappels for the exercise of the Popish religion, and also against all monasteries and convents, and, more particularly against the Order of the Jesuits, yet those evil counsellors have procured orders for the building of several churches and chappels for the exercise of that religion. They have also procured diverse monasteries to be erected, and, in contempt of the law, ‹they have› not only set up several colleges of Jesuits in diverse places, for the corrupting of youth, but have raised up one of the Order to be a Privy Counsellor and Minister of State.[161] By all which they do evidently shew that they are restrained by no rules ‹of› law whatsoever, but that they have subjected the honours and estates of the subjects and the established religion to a despotick power and arbitrary government: in all which they are served and seconded by these Ecclesiastical Commissioners.

They have also followed the same method in relation to civil affairs, for they have procured orders to examine all Lords Lieutenants, Deputy Lieutenants, Sheriffs,

Justices of ⟨the⟩ Peace, and all others that were in any publick employment, if they would concurr with the King in the repeal of the Test and penal laws; and all such, whose conscience did not suffer them to comply with their designs, were turned out, and others put in their places, who, they believed, would be more compliant to them in their designs of defeating the intent and execution of those laws, which have been made with so much care and caution for the security of the Protestant religion. And in many of these places they have put professed Papists, though the law has disabled them, and warranted the subjects not to have any regard to their orders.[162]

They have also invaded the priviledges and seized on the charters of most of those towns, that have a right to be represented by their Burgesses in Parliament, and have procured surrenders to be made of them, by which the magistrates in them have delivered up all their rights and priviledges to be disposed of at the pleasure of these evil counsellors, who have thereupon caused new magistrates in those towns, such as they can most entirely confide in; and in many of them they have ⟨put⟩ Popish magistrates, notwithstanding the incapacities under which the law has put them.

And whereas no nation whatsoever can subsist without the administration of good and impartial justice, upon which men's lives, liberties, honours, and estates do depend, those evil counsellors have subjected these to an arbitrary and despotick power. In the most important affairs they have endeavoured to discover beforehand the opinions of the Judges, and have turned out such as they have found would not conform themselves to their intentions, and have put others in their places, of whom they were more assured, without any regard to their abilities. And they have not stuck to raise ⟨even⟩ professed Papists to the courts of judicature, nothwithstanding their incapacity by law, and that no regard is ⟨due⟩ to any sentences flowing from them.

They have carried this so far, as to deprive such Judges, who, in the common administration of justice, shewed that they were governed by their consciences, and not by the directions which the others gave them. By which it is apparent that they design to render themselves the absolute masters of the lives, honours, and estates of the subjects, of what rank or dignity soever they may be, and that without having any regard ⟨either⟩ to the equity of the cause, or to the consciences of the Judges, whom they will have to submit in all things to their own will and pleasure: hoping by such means to intimidate those who are yet in employment, as also such others as they shall think fit to put in the room of those whom they have turned out; and to make them see what they must look for, if they should at any time act in the least contrary to their good liking, and that no failings of that kind are pardoned in any persons whatsoever. A great deal of blood has been shed in many parts of the Kingdom by Judges governed by those evil counsellors, against all the rules and forms of law, without so much as suffering the persons that were accused to plead in their own defence.

They have also, by putting the administration of justice into the hands of Papists, brought all the matters of civil justice unto great uncertainties, with how much exactness and justice soever that these sentences may have been given: for, since the laws of the land do not only exclude all Papists from all places of judicature, but have put them under an incapacity, none are bound to acknowledge or obey their judgments, and all sentences given by them are null and void of themselves; so that all such persons, as have been cast in trials before such Popish Judges, may justly look on their pretended sentences as having no more force and efficacy, than the sentences of any private and unauthorized person whatsoever; so deplorable is the case of the subjects, who are obliged to answer such Judges, that must in all things stick to the rules which are set them by those evil counsellors, who, as they raised them up to such employments, so can turn them out at pleasure; and who can never be esteemed lawful Judges, so that all their sentences are in the construction of the law of no force or efficacy.

33 James II surrounded by his leading courtiers. On the King's right are Lord Treasurer Rochester, holding his wand of office, and Lord Chancellor Jeffreys, holding the bag with the Great Seal in it; on his immediate left is Lord Chamberlain Mulgrave, with his wand of office, and the Earl of Sunderland, Lord President of the Council. Detail from *King James II Receiving the Mathematical Scholars of Christ's Hospital*, studio of Antonio Verrio. New Haven, Yale Center for British Art, Paul Mellon Collection.

34 The Protestant view of Church and State, with religion represented by Archbishop Sancroft (*left*), and law represented by Lord Chancellor Jeffreys (*right*), presided over by King James II, seated on the Throne of England. Frontispiece to Edward Chamberlayne, *The Present State of England* (London, 1687).

35 The Catholic view of Church and State, with James II's Ambassador, the Earl of Castlemaine, kneeling before Pope Innocent XI, seated on St Peter's Throne, while a medallion portrait of James II, supported by cherubs, appears over the Basilica of St Peter. Engraving by Arnoldo van Westerhout after Giovanni Baptista Lenardi. Frontispiece to John Michael Wright, *Ragguaglio Della Solenne Comparsa* (Rome, 1687).

36 James II, as Duke of York, with his first wife, Anne Hyde, and their two Protestant daughters, Mary and Anne. Oil painting by Sir Peter Lely and Benedetto Gennari. Royal Collection.

37 James II in exile, with his second wife, Queen Mary Beatrice of Modena, and their two Catholic children, James Francis Edward, Prince of Wales, and Princess Louisa Maria Theresa. Oil painting after Pierre Mignard. Royal Collection.

38 Queen Mary Beatrice of Modena, *c.* 1685. Oil painting by Willem Wissing. London, National Portrait Gallery.

39 James Francis Edward Stuart, the infant Prince of Wales. Engraving by John Smith, 1688, after a
painting by Sir Godfrey Kneller. Collection of Geoffrey Taylor, Esquire, M.V.O.

40 Lawrence Hyde, 1st Earl of Rochester, portrayed as Lord Treasurer of the Realm and wearing the robes and insignia of the Garter. Portrait by Sir Godfrey Kneller, *c.* 1685–7. Collection of the Rt. Hon. the Earl of Clarendon.

41 Henry Hyde, 2nd Earl of Clarendon. Oil painting by Willem Wissing. Collection of the Rt. Hon. the Earl of Clarendon.

42 Dr William Sancroft, Archbishop of Canterbury. Chalk drawing by Edward Luttrell, 1688. London, National Portrait Gallery.

43 Dr Francis Turner, Bishop of Ely. Oil painting attributed to Mary Beale, *c.* 1683–8. London, National Portrait Gallery.

44 Daniel Finch, 2nd Earl of Nottingham. Marble bust by Michael Rysbrack. London, Courtauld
Institute.

45 George Saville, 1st Marquess of Halifax, Chairman of the Provisional Government. Oil painting attributed to Mary Beale. London, National Portrait Gallery.

46 James II at prayer. Engraving by A. Trouvain, Paris 1694. Cambridge, Magdalene College, Pepys Library.

47 James Francis Edward Stuart, Prince of Wales (later James III, sometimes called the 'Old Pretender' by his enemies). Oil painting after Nicolas de Largillière. Edinburgh, National Galleries of Scotland.

48 Louis XIV. English engraving by P. Vandrebanc, 1685, after Sir Godfrey Kneller.

They have likewise disposed of all military employments in the same manner, for though the laws have not only excluded Papists from all such employments, but have, in particular, provided that they should be disarmed, yet they in contempt of these laws have not only armed the Papists, but have likewise raised them up to the greatest military trusts, both by sea and land, and that strangers as well as natives, and Irish as well as English; that so, by that means having rendered themselves masters both of the affairs of the Church, of the government of the nation, and of the course of justice, and subjected them all to a despotick and arbitrary power, they might be in a capacity to maintain and execute their wicked designs by the assistance of the Army, and thereby to enslave the nation.

The dismal effects of this subversion of the established religion, laws, and liberties in England appear more evidently to us by what we see done in Ireland; where the whole government is put in the hands of Papists, and where the Protestant inhabitants are under the daily fears of what may be justly apprehended from the arbitrary power which is set up there; which has made great numbers of them leave that Kingdom, and abandon their estates in it, remembering well that cruel and bloody massacre which fell out in that island in the year 1641.[164]

Those evil counsellors have also prevailed with the King to declare in Scotland that he is cloathed with absolute power, and that all the subjects are bound to obey him without reserve, upon which he has assumed an arbitrary power, both over the religion and laws of that Kingdom; from all which it is apparent what is to be looked for in England, as soon as matters are duly prepared for it.[165]

Those great and unsufferable oppressions, and the open contempt of all law, together with the apprehensions of the sad consequences that must certainly follow upon it, have put the subjects under great and just fears, and have made them look after such lawful remedies as have been allowed of in all nations, yet all has been without effect. And these evil counsellors have endeavoured to make all men apprehend the loss of their lives, liberties, honours, and estates, if they should go about to preserve themselves from this oppression by petitions, representations, or other means authorized by law. Thus did they proceed with the Archbishop of Canterbury, and the other Bishops, who, having offered a most humble petition to the King in terms full of respect, and not exceeding the number limited by law, in which they set forth in short the reasons for which they could not obey that order, which by the instigation of those evil counsellors was sent them, requiring them to appoint their clergy to read in their churches the Declaration for Liberty of Conscience, were sent to prison, and afterwards brought to a trial, as if they had been guilty of some enormous crime. They were not only obliged to defend themselves in that pursuit, but to appear before professed Papists, who had not taken the Test, and, by consequence, were men whose interest led them to condemn them; and the Judges who gave their opinions in their favours were thereupon turned out.

And yet it cannot be pretended that any kings, how great soever their power has been, and how arbitrary and despotick soever they have been in the exercise of it, have ever reckoned it a crime for their subjects to come in all submission and respect, and in a due number, not exceeding the limits of the law, and to represent to them the reasons that made it impossible for them to obey their orders. Those evil counsellors have also treated a Peer of the Realm as a criminal,[166] only because he said that the subjects were not bound to obey the orders of a Popish Justice of the Peace, though it is evident that they being by law rendered incapable of all such trusts, no regard is due to their orders; this being the security which the people have by law for their lives, liberties, honours, and estates, that they are not to be subjected to the arbitrary proceedings of Papists, that are, contrary to law, put into any employments, civil or military.

Both we ourselves, and our dearest and most entirely beloved Consort, the Princess, have endeavoured to signify, in terms full of respect to the King, the deep and just regret which all these proceedings have given us; and, in compliance with His Majesty's desires, signifyed unto us, we declared both by word of mouth to his Envoy, and in writing, what our thoughts were touching the repealing of the Test and penal laws; which we did in such a manner, that we hoped we had proposed an expedient, by which the peace of these Kingdoms, and an happy agreement amongst the subjects of all perswasions, might have been settled.[167] But those evil counsellors have put such ill constructions on those our good intentions, that they have endeavoured to alienate the King more and more from us, as if we had designed to disturb the quiet and happiness of this Kingdome.

The last and great remedy for all these evils is the calling of a Parliament for securing the nation against the evil practices of the wicked counsellors, but this could not be yet compassed, nor can it be easily brought about; for these men apprehending that a lawful Parliament, being once assembled, they would be brought to an account for all their open violations of law, and for their plots and conspiracies against the Protestant religion and the lives and liberties of the subjects, they have endeavoured under the specious pretence of liberty of conscience, first to sow divisions amongst Protestants, between those of the Church of England and the Dissenters: the design being laid to engage Protestants, that are equally concerned to preserve themselves from Popish oppression, into mutual quarrellings, that so, by these, some advantages might be given them to bring about their designs, and that both in the election of the Members of Parliament, and afterwards in the Parliament itself. For they see well that, if all Protestants could enter into a mutual good understanding, one with another, and concurr together in the preserving of their religion, it would not be possible for them to compass their wicked ends.

They have also required all persons in the several counties of England, that either were in any employment, or were in any considerable esteem, to declare beforehand that they would concurr in the repeal of the Test and penal laws; and that they would give their voices in the elections to Parliament only for such as would concurr in it. Such as would not thus pre-engage themselves were turned out of all employments, and others, who entered into those engagements, were put in their places, many of them being Papists; and contrary to the charters and priviledges of those burroughs, that have a right to send Burgesses to Parliament, they have ordered such regulations to be made, as they thought fit and necessary for assuring themselves of all the Members that are to be chosen by those corporations. And by this means they hope to avoid that punishment which they have deserved, though it is apparent that all acts made by Popish magistrates are null and void of themselves, so that no Parliament can be lawful for which the elections and returns are made by Popish Sheriffs and Mayors of towns; and, therefore, as long as the authority and magistracy is in such hands, it is not possible to have any lawful Parliament.

And though, according to the constitution of the English government and immemorial custom, all elections of Parliament men ought to be made with an entire liberty, without any sort of force, or requiring the electors to choose such persons as shall be named unto them, and the persons, thus freely elected, ought to give their opinions freely upon all matters that are brought before them, having the good of the nation ever before their eyes, and following in all things the dictates of their conscience; yet now the people of England cannot expect a remedy from a free Parliament, legally called and chosen, but perhaps they may see one called, in which all elections will be carried by fraud or force, and which will be composed of such persons, of whom those evil counsellors hold themselves well assured, in which all things will be carried on according to their direction and interest, without any regard to the good or happiness of the nation. Which may appear evidently from this, that the same persons tried the Members of the last Parliament,[168] to gain them to consent to the repeal of the Test and penal laws, and procured that Parliament to be dissolved when they found that they could not, neither by promises, or threatenings, prevail with the Members to comply with their wicked designs.[169]

But, to crown all, there are great and violent presumptions inducing us to believe that those evil counsellors, in order to their carrying on their ill designs, and to the gaining to themselves more time for effecting the same, for the encouraging of their accomplices, and for the discouraging all good subjects, have published that the Queen hath brought for⟨th⟩ a son: though there have appeared, both during the Queen's pretended bigness, and in the manner in which the birth was managed, so many just and visible grounds of suspicion, that not only we ourselves, but all the good subjects of these Kingdoms, do vehemently suspect that the pretended Prince of Wales was not born by the Queen. And it is notoriously known to all the world, that many both doubted of the Queen's bigness, and of the birth of the child, and yet there was not any one thing done to satisfy them, or put an end to their doubts.[170]

And since our dearest and most entirely beloved Consort, the Princess, and likewise we ourself, have so great an interest in this matter, and such a right, as all the world knows, to the sucession of the Crown; since also the English did in the year 1672, when the States General of the United Provinces were invaded in a most unjust war, use their utmost endeavours to put an end to that war, and that in opposition to those who were then in government, and, by their so doing, they ran the hazard of losing

49 St James's Palace, where William took up residence on 18 December 1688. Engraving from Leonard Knyff and Jan Kip, *Britannia Illustrata* (London, 1707).

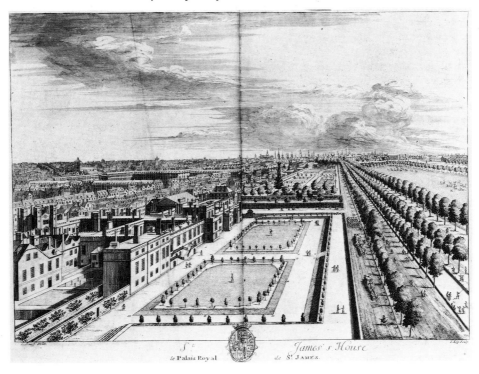

both the favour of the Court and their employments; and since the English nation has ever testifyed a most particular affection and esteem, both to our dearest Consort, the Princess, and to ourself, we cannot excuse ourself from espousing their interest in a matter of so high consequence, and from contributing all that lies in us for the maintaining both the Protestant religion and the laws and liberties of these Kingdoms, and for the securing to them the continual enjoyment of all their rights; to the doing of which we are most earnestly sollicited by a great many Lords, both Spiritual and Temporal, and by many gentlemen and other subjects of all ranks.[171]

Therefore it is, that we have thought fit to go over into England, and to carry over with us a force sufficient, by the blessing of God, to defend us from the violence of these evil counsellors. And we, being desirous that our intentions in this may be rightly understood, have for this end prepared this Declaration, in which as we have hitherto given a true account of the reasons inducing us to it, so we now think fit to declare, that this our expedition is intended for no other design, but to have a free and lawful Parliament assembled, as soon as is possible; and that, in order to this, all the late charters by which the election of Burgesses is limited, contrary to the antient custom, shall be considered as null and of no force; and likewise all magistrates, who have been unjustly turned out, shall forthwith re-assume their former employments, as well as the borroughs of England shall return again to their antient prescriptions and charters; and, more particularly, that the charter of the antient and famous City of London shall again be in force;[172] and that the writts for the Members of Parliament shall be addressed to the proper officers, according to custom; that also none be suffered to choose, or to be chosen, Members of Parliament, but such as are qualified by law; and that the Members of Parliament being thus lawfully chosen, they shall meet and sit in full freedom, that so the two Houses may concurr in the preparing ‹of› such laws, as they upon free and full debate shall judge necessary and convenient, both for confirming and executing the law concerning the Test, and such other laws as are necessary for the securing and maintenance of the Protestant religion; as likewise for making such laws as may establish a good assurance between the Church of England and the Protestant Dissenters,[173] as also for the covering and securing of all such, who will live peaceably under the government as becomes good subjects, from all persecution upon the account of their religion, even Papists themselves not excepted, and for the doing of all other things, which the two Houses of Parliament shall find necessary for the peace, honour, and safety of the nation, so that there may be no more danger of the nation's falling at any time hereafter under arbitrary government. To this Parliament we will also referr the enquiry into the birth of the pretended Prince of Wales, and of all things relating to it, and to the right of succession.

And we, for our part, will concurr in everything that may procure the peace and happiness of the nation, which a free and lawful Parliament shall determine, since we have nothing before our eyes, in this our undertaking, but the preservation of the Protestant religion, the covering of all men from persecution for the‹ir› consciences,[174] and the securing to the whole nation the free enjoyment of all their laws, rights, and liberties, under a just and legal government.

This is the design that we have proposed to ourselves in appearing upon this occasion in arms, in the conduct of which we will keep the Forces under our command under all the strictness of martial discipline, and take especial care, that the people of the countries through which we must march shall not suffer by their means: and as soon as the state of the nation will admit of it, we promise that we will send back all those foreign forces that we have brought along with us.

We do, therefore, hope that all people will judge rightly of us, and approve of these our proceedings; but we chiefly rely on the blessing of God for the success of this our undertaking, in which we place our whole and only confidence.

We do in the last place invite and require all persons whatsoever, all the Peers of the Realm, both Spiritual and Temporal, all Lords Lieutenants, Deputy Lieutenants, and all gentlemen, citizens, and other commons of all ranks to come and assist us, in order to the executing of this our design against all such as shall endeavour to oppose us; that so we may prevent all those miseries, which must needs follow upon the nation's being kept under arbitrary government and slavery, and that all the violences and disorders, which have overturned the whole constitution of the English government, may be fully redressed in a free and legal Parliament.

And we do likewise resolve, that, as soon as the nation is brought to a state of quiet, we will take care that a Parliament shall be called in Scotland for restoring the antient constitution of that Kingdom, and for bringing the matters of religion to such a settlement, that the people may live easy and happy, and for putting an end to all the unjust violences that have been in a course of so many years committed there.

We will also study to bring the Kingdom of Ireland to such a state, that the settlement there may be religiously observed, and that the Protestant and British interest there may be secured. And we will endeavour by all possible means to procure such an establishment in all the three Kingdoms, that they may all live in a happy union and correspondence together; and that the Protestant religion, and the peace, honour, and happiness of these nations may be established upon lasting foundations.

Given under our hand and seal, at our Court in The Hague, the 10th day of October in the year 1688.

William Henry, Prince of Orange.

By His Highness's special command,

C. Huygens.

His Highnesse's Additional Declaration.

After we had prepared and printed this our Declaration, we have understood that the subverters of the religion and laws of these Kingdoms, hearing of our preparations to assist the people against them, have begun to retract some of the arbitrary and despotick powers that they have assumed and vacate some of their unjust judgments and decrees. The sense of their guilt and the distrust of their force have induced them to offer unto the City of London some seeming relief from their great oppressions, hoping thereby to deceive the people and divert them from demanding a secure re-establishment of their religion and their laws under the shelter of our arms. They do also give out that we intend to conquer and enslave the nation, and therefore it is that we have thought fit to add a few words to our Declaration.

We are confident that no person can have so hard thoughts of us as to imagine that we have any other design in this undertaking than to procure a settlement of the religion and of the liberties and properties of the subjects upon so sure a foundation, that there may be no danger of the nation's relapsing into the like miseries at any time hereafter. And as the forces we have brought along with us are utterly disproportioned to that wicked design of conquering the nation, if we were capable of intending it, so the great numbers of the principal nobility and gentry that are men of eminent quality and estates, are persons of known integrity and zeal, both for the religion and government of England, many of them being also distinguished by their constant fidelity to the Crown, who do both accompany us in this expedition, and have earnestly sollicited us to it, will deliver us from all such malicious insinuations; for it is not to be imagined that either those who have invited us or those who are already come to assist us can join in a wicked attempt of conquest, to make void their own lawful titles to their honours, estates, and interests.

We are also confident that all men see how little weight there is to be laid on all promises and engagements that can now be made, since there can be so little regard had in times past to the most solemn promises, and as that imperfect redress, that is now offered, is a plain confession of those violations of the government that we have set forth, so the ‹defectiveness› of it is no less apparent, for they lay down nothing which they may not take up at pleasure, and they reserve entire, and not so much as mention, their claims and pretences to an arbitrary and despotick power, which has been the root of all their oppression, and of the total subversion of the government. And it is plain that there can be no redress, nor remedy offered, but in parliament by a declaration of the rights of the subject that have been invaded, and not by any pretended acts of grace to which the extremity of their affairs has driven them. Therefore it is that we have thought fit to declare that we will referr all to a free assembly of the nation in a lawfull parliament.

Given under our hand and seal, at our Court in The Hague, the 24th day of October 1688.

William Henry, Prince of Orange.

By His Highness's ‹special› command,

C. Huygens.

Printed at The Hague by Arnold Leers
by His Highness's order, 1688.

After which Lord Culpepper moves, that thanks be given to His Highness for his *Declaration*, and for calling the Peers together, and that, after that was done, they would adjourn till Monday.

Lord Wharton. That there is no room for delays, and that, therefore, their Lordships may meet tomorrow, but that thanks may be given with this addition, for pursuing the *Declaration*, as well as for the *Declaration*. His Lordship likewise moved, that Mr. Pollexfen[176] and Sir George Treby[177] might be two of the council learned in the law, with others of that profession, to attend their Lordships; and that the Lord Marquess of Hallifax, having performed the Chair so well, might be pleased to take it upon him again.

Earl of Craven seconds the latter.

Marquess of Hallifax agrees with thanks to His Highness for the *Declaration*, but desired tenderness might be used in thanks for calling the Peers together, since they had a birthright, which might be prejudiced; adds that their Lordships may meet in the House of Lords on Monday.

Lord Falconberg. That the affairs require their meeting sooner than Monday, and moves that they may meet tomorrow; but he doth not think the House of Lords proper, since they are not a House of Lords.

Lord Delamere moves, first, thanks for the *Declaration*, with an addition, that they will stand by His Highness with their lives and fortunes towards the attaining those ends.

Earl of Devonshire moves what the Lord Wharton did, thanks for pursuing the *Declaration*.

Earl of Clarendon ‹moves› thanks for the *Declaration*, but agrees with the Lord Hallifax, nothing ought to be mentioned in it for the meeting of the Peers; that they may adjourn untill Monday, but ‹is› against the meeting at the House of Lords.

Earl of Mulgrave ‹moves› for the House of Lords.

Marquess of Hallifax speaks to order; that they will not run into many debates, but keep to thanks to His Highness for his *Declaration*. Agreed on. But he did not like the words of *lives and fortunes*, ‹they› being so common and worn out, and that he thought them not fit for the dignity of that assembly; but that he agreed to any words to that effect, but more particularly that thanks may be given to His Highness for the resolution he hath shewn in pursuing the *Declaration*.

Lord Mordaunt agrees with what was formerly moved, that no notice should be taken in their return to the Prince for the meeting of the Peers, for they met of right; but desires that something to the same purpose with *lives and fortunes*; and proposes that to be the signing a declaration, which was formerly signed by all those that went to the Prince of Orange at Exeter, as those that attended him since in his journey. Moves likewise that the Roman Catholicks may be moved out of town.

Lord Wharton moves, that they would appoint a time and place to adjourn to, and that council may attend them, whereof Mr. Whitlock[178] be one.

To meet tomorrow morning at ten of the clock.

Lord Hallifax ‹moves› that it be in the House of Lords, it being more convenient for hearing than any other place.

Sir Thomas Duppa[179] called. Saith it will be ready by that time.

The council named to attend their Lordships tomorrow: Serjeant Maynard,[180] Serjeant Holt,[181] Mr. Pollexfen, Sir Robert Atkins,[182] Mr. Finch, Sir George Treby, Sir Francis Winnington,[183] Mr. Whitlock, Mr. Bradbury.[184]

Resolved, that the council learned in the law to attend their Lordships shall be five. Which were, after some debate, appointed: vizt. Serjeant Maynard, Serjeant Holt, Sir Robert Atkins, Mr. Pollexfen, and Mr. Bradbury.

Mr. Gwyn was thereupon ordered to write to them, and inclose a copy of His Highness's speech to the Peers, that they might be the better prepared to attend their Lordships at ten tomorrow morning at the House of Lords. And the following letter was thereupon writt.

Sir,

The Lords Spiritual and Temporal assembled here this day, and having appointed to meet again tomorrow morning at ten of the clock in the House of Lords, have commanded me to desire you would please to attend their Lordships at that time and place; and, that you may be the better prepared, I am commanded likewise to inclose the copy of what His Highness the Prince of Orange was this day pleased to say to the Peers. I am, etc.,

To Serjeant Maynard.   F. Gwyn.

Dated December 21, 1688.

The like to Mr. Serjeant Holt.

The like to Mr. Pollexfen.

The like to Sir Robert Atkins, senior.

The like to Mr. Bradbury.

The Association signed at Exeter was brought on the table, and ordered to be read.

Lord Nottingham gives several reasons against signing the Association, and that, at least, nobody ought to do it, but those who did it voluntarily.

Lord Delamere moves, that there may be no compulsion on any man to sign the Association, but that all may use their discretions; only desires it may be put to the question, whether it should be tendered to be signed, or no.

Lord Wharton. That he had in several times signed several declarations, but he never found any signify much; had forgot many he had signed; and perhaps the words of this may not be agreeable to all men; and that, therefore, their Lordships may consider of something that all may agree to, which their Lordships may sign to prevent a division.

Lord Delamere. That was a way to make a division, for several had signed this paper before.

The Association was laid on the table. Several signed it, vizt. Bedford, Dorset, Mulgrave, Norfolk, Thanet, Rochester, Berkeley, Devonshire, Grey ‹of› Ruthen, Radnor, Bolingbroke.

Lord Delamere moves again, as a matter that requires an immediate dispatch, the removing the Papists.

To be considered tomorrow, when the lawyers are present.

Their Lordships agree to an answer of thanks to His Highness the Prince of Orange for His Highness's *Declaration*, which hath been read to them, and for the vigour and conduct he hath shewn in the prosecution of the same.

Their Lordships desired the Duke of Norfolk to attend His Highness immediately to know his pleasure when the Peers should wait upon him.

His Highness was pleased in a short time after to come into the room, and the Lord Marquiss of Hallifax delivered their thanks as above, to which His Highness was pleased to return an answer.

Prince's answer.

I will do all I can for the good of the nation, which I think myself obliged to do, both in honour and conscience.

The words being taken short of what His Highness was pleased to say, Mr. Gwyn desires Monsieur Benting to move His Highness that he would be pleased to recollect what he said to the Peers, that it might be entered in his own words. But Monsieur Benting returned no answer, though he promised it several days.

[The second meeting of Peers, which had before it the consideration of the best ways to obtain a parliament and to rid London of Catholics, dealt only with the latter item. With the King still at Rochester it was difficult to broach the parliamentary question. The fear of Catholicism still persisting in the capital, the assembly under Halifax's chairmanship debated a new anti-Catholic measure, which had been called for the previous day by two Whig peers, Mordaunt and Delamer. The outcome was an order commanding all Catholics in town to depart to their homes within five days. Certain exceptions were allowed, on condition that those excepted should register their names and addresses with the City authorities within eight days. This was in line with previous practice under Charles II. (66 peers attended.)]

IN THE HOUSE OF LORDS
DECEMBER 22⟨N⟩D, 1688

Lord Archbishop of York; Duke of Norfolk; Duke of Somerset; Duke of Grafton; Duke of Ormond; Duke of Beaufort; Duke of Northumberland; Marquess of Hallifax; Earl of Oxford; Earl of Shrewsbury; Earl of Kent; Earl of Bedford; Earl of Pembroke; Earl of Dorset; Earl of Northampton; Earl of Devonshire; Earl of Bolingbroke; Earl of Manchester; Earl of Mulgrave; Earl of Rivers; Earl of Stamford; Earl of Winchelsea; Earl of Thanet; Earl of Scarsdale; Earl of Clarendon; Earl of Craven; Earl of Burlington; Earl of Sussex; Earl of Macclesfield; Earl of Radnor; Earl of Yarmouth; Earl of Berkeley; Earl of Nottingham; Earl of Rochester; Earl of Abingdon; Lord Viscount Fauconberg; Lord Viscount Mordaunt; Lord Viscount Newport; Lord Viscount Weymouth; Lord Viscount Hatton; Lord Bishop of London; Lord Bishop ⟨of⟩ Duresme; Lord Bishop ⟨of⟩ Winton.; Lord Bishop ⟨of⟩ St. Asaph; Lord Bishop ⟨of⟩ Ely; Lord Bishop ⟨of⟩ Peterborough (not there); Lord Delawarr; Lord Grey ⟨of⟩ Ruthen; Lord Eure; Lord Wharton; Lord Paget; Lord North and Grey; Lord Chandois; Lord Mountague; Lord Maynard; Lord Howard ⟨of⟩ Escrick; Lord Jermin; Lord Vaughan of Cherbury; Lord Culpepper; Lord Lucas; Lord Delamere; Lord Crew; Lord Lumley; Lord Carteret; Lord Ossulstone; Lord Godolphin; Lord Churchill.

The Lords met, according to order, in the House of Lords, at Westminster. The Lord Marquess of Hallifax, by desire of the Lords, took the Chair, sitting at the upper side of the table on the Woolsack.

Mr. Gwyn acquaints the Lords, that Sir Robert Atkins was gone out of town, and ⟨he⟩ had his letter returned back again. Whereupon the Lord Wharton moves that Mr. Whitlock, Earl of Macclesfield that Sir William Dolben,[185] Marquess of Hallifax that Mr. Finch, or Sir George Treby, might attend their Lordships in his room.

Lord Delamere moves, that the two last may not be named again, for, if they were, there would be reflections made on them.

The Lords resolved (Sir Robert Atkins being absent), ⟨that⟩ Serjeant Maynard, Serjeant Holt, Mr. Pollexfen, and Mr. Bradbury, should be the council learned in the law that should attend them.

They were called in accordingly.

The Lord Hallifax acquaints them, that the business of the day was principally to consider of a way to have a parliament, but desires first that the most ready and most effectual way to remove the Papists out of town be considered of, and desires that the council may be advised with about it.

Serjeant Maynard saith the way to remove convict Papists was easy.

Serjeant Holt acknowledgeth that, but saith such as are not convict cannot be judged so.

Mr. Bradbury thinks the act named Papists or reputed Papists.

Lord Hallifax saith, if they were so named in the act, there is no difficulty at all in it, for the order may go in the same terms, but he desires those Papists who have taken military commands may be distinguished from others.

The Bishop of London moves, that another sort of people may be likewise distinguished, which are those who have taken offices, and not taken the Oaths and Tests, such as he supposes to be in the same condition with Papists.

Mr. Pollexfen saith that those, that have done so, are by the statutes adjudged to be Papists convict.

Lord Mountague saith to the best of his memory the Proclamation *Caroli Secundi* used always to mention Papists and reputed Papists.[186]

Lord Hallifax proposes, that the Irish Officers may not be in the same condition with others, but that all other Papists and reputed Papists shall within three days leave the town, and repair to their own houses, from whence they are not to stirr above five miles.

Lord Newport said there was also an exception for tradesmen, and the exceptions that Ambassadors and Publick Ministers, with their domestick servants, being foreigners, etc., and except such as have been housekeepers or shopkeepers for three years last past (not including in this such as sell arms), they are to give an account to the Lord Mayor and Justices of the Peace.

The Earl of Clarendon moves, that all who are now actually on the service of the Queen Dowager may be likewise excepted.

Lord Hallifax moves, that all Popish Officers may be secured.

Lord Rochester ‹moves› that the Papists may be secured here to answer for what shall be done to the Protestants in Ireland, and that such as should give good security should not stand committed.

Lord Ossulstone moves, that directions be given the Justices of ‹the› Peace to enquire where they are, and that such as cannot give bail should be committed to some inns in the City, where they are to be under guard of the City Trained Bands.

It was said that many of the Irish soldiers, as well as Officers, were in a very ill condition, and therefore it was to be considered how they were to be provided for.

Lord Hallifax saith, that there is great care to be taken they should not have passes to go into Ireland, but that something should be done for them to keep them from starving.

The Duke of Ormond undertakes to speak to Lord Forbes to gather those that were of his Grace's Regiment.

Lord Churchill acquaints the Lords that care is taken of them already, and that they will have money to keep them from starving.

Lord Ossulstone complains, that there are 2 or 300 of them at his house, near Uxbridge; that he is told they are ready to give up their arms, and therefore desires somebody may be appointed to receive them.

Mr. Musgrave, an Officer of the Ordnance, being present as an assistant to Mr. Gwyn, promises he will give order to one of the Officers of the Ordnance to receive them.

The heads of an order for removing Papists out of town, upon this debate, was delivered to Mr. Serjeant Maynard and others the council learned ‹in the law›, who withdrew to make a draught of an order accordingly.

The Lord Delamere tells their Lordships, that he cannot but observe there is great alterations in men's opinions within these few days; that he cannot guess at any greater reason of that variety, than the frequent visits and the great concourse of people of all kinds to the Lord Jeffreys in the Tower. He, therefore, moves that the Lord Jeffreys may be under closer restraint; that he very well remembers what it is to be close prisoner in the Tower,[187] and that he supposes that the Lord Jeffreys doth not deserve more favour; that no man may speak with him without leave from their Lordships, or in the presence of a wardour; and that he be confined with one servant.

Lord Hallifax desires that the close confinement may be considered of; that he is a peer, and already committed without any cause shewn in the warrant. He, therefore, asks the council learned ‹in the law› what way they would propose to have this confinement, now mentioned, legal. It was proposed they might speak to my Lord Lucas, Chief Governour of the Tower, to do it; and his Lordship, coming in sometime after, was asked by my Lord Hallifax to do it; who answered that he was ready to obey any order their Lordships would give him, but he desired it might be in writing. Whereupon the Lord Hallifax proposed that Mr. Gwyn should sign an order, in their Lordships' names, to the Lord Lucas accordingly.

Mr. Gwyn desired that since there were more orders than this like to be signed by him by their Lordships' commands, that their Lordships would please to sign an order unto him, impowering him thereto. The following order was thereupon done accordingly, and ordered to be printed and published.

Mr. Gwyn to sign all orders.

We, the Lords Spiritual and Temporal, assembled in this extraordinary conjuncture, do appoint Francis Gwyn, Esquire, for us, and in our names, to sign and subscribe such orders, as shall be from time to time by us made. Dated at the House of Lords, in Westminster, the 22‹n›d day of December 1688.

Lord Archbishop of York; Duke of Norfolk; Duke of Somerset; Duke of Grafton; Duke of Ormond; Duke of Beaufort; Duke of Northumberland; Marquess of Hallifax; Earl of Oxford; Earl of Shrewsbury; Earl of Kent; Earl of Bedford; Earl of Pembroke; Earl of Dorset; Earl of Northampton; Earl of Devonshire; Earl of Bolingbroke; Earl of Manchester; Earl of Mulgrave; Earl of Rivers (*sic*); Earl of Stamford; Earl of Winchelsea; Earl of Scarsdale; Earl of Thanet; Earl of Clarendon; Earl of Craven; Earl of Burlington; Earl of Sussex; Earl of Macclesfield; Earl of Radnor; Earl of Yarmouth; Earl of Berkeley; Earl of Nottingham; Earl of Rochester; Earl of Abingdon; Lord Viscount Fauconberg; Lord Viscount Mordaunt; Lord Viscount Newport; Lord Viscount Weymouth; Lord Viscount Hatton; Lord Bishop ‹of› London; Lord Bishop ‹of› Duresme; Lord Bishop ‹of› Winchester; Lord Bishop ‹of› St. Asaph; Lord Bishop ‹of› Ely; Lord Bishop ‹of› Peterborough (not there); Lord Delawarr; Lord Grey ‹of› Ruthin; Lord Eure; Lord Wharton; Lord Paget; Lord North and Grey; Lord Chandois; Lord Mountague; Lord Grey ‹of› Warke; Lord Maynard; Lord Howard ‹of› Escrick; Lord Jermin; Lord Vaughan Cherbury; Lord Culpepper; Lord Lucas; Lord Delamere; Lord Crew; Lord Lumley; Lord Carteret; Lord Ossulstone; Lord Godolphin; Lord Churchill.

Whereas the Lords Spiritual and Temporal, assembled in this extraordinary conjuncture, have by an order under their hands, of the 22‹n›d instant, appointed me for them, in their names, to sign and subscribe such orders, as shall be from time to time by their Lordships made; their Lordships have ordered this day, that the Lord Jeffreys, being at this time prisoner in the Tower, shall not speak with any person, but in the presence of the Lord Lucas, Chief Governour of the Tower; and that the names of all such persons as shall speak with the said Lord Jeffreys shall be taken, and returned to their Lordships every morning when they meet. Signed by their Lordships' order,

To the right honourable Lord Lucas,   F. Gwyn.
Chief Governor of the Tower of London.

Lord Bishop of Ely complains of great disorders committed in his Diocese by the rabble, and desires that orders may be sent to the High Sheriff to take care that the peace may be kept, and to disperse the rabble.

The council learned ‹in the law› returned with the draught of an order for removing Papists out of town, which, being blotted, was first read by Mr. Bradbury, and afterwards by Mr. Gwyn at the table; which, being agreed to, was ordered to be printed, and is as follows.

Papists to go from the City of London

Orders of the Lords Spiritual and Temporal assembled at Westminster, December 22, 1688.

The Lords Spiritual and Temporal, assembled in this extraordinary conjuncture, considering the great mischiefs that have happened unto, and do still threaten, this Kingdom by the evil designs and practices of the Papists in great numbers resorting unto, and abiding in, the City of London and places adjacent to the said City; for the better preservation of the peace and common safety have thought fit, and do order and require, that all Papists and reputed Papists do, and shall, within five days after the date hereof, depart from the said City unto their respective habitations, from which they are not to stir above five miles' distance; except such as are now in the actual service of the Queen Dowager, and except all Ambassadors and Foreign Ministers, with their domestick servants, being foreigners, and all other foreigners, being merchants or factors, or who are come into or do reside in this Kingdom upon the account of trade only; except also all such persons as have been householders or have exercised any trade within the said City of London, or within ten miles of the same, by the space of three years last past (other than such as do sell arms), so as such householders shall within eight days from the date hereof leave an account in writing with my Lord Mayor, the Recorder, or some Alderman, being a Justice of the Peace within the said City, or other Justices of the Peace, of their respective names and places of their habitations; except also all such Parish Officers as shall, within six days of the date hereof, give good and sufficient bail before the Lord Mayor, the Recorder, or some Alderman, being a Justice of the Peace within the said City, for their appearance in the Court of King's Bench the first day of the next Term to answer such things as shall be there objected to them, who are in the mean time to keep the peace.

And it is hereby ordered that such Popish Officers, as shall not within the said eight days give such bail as aforesaid, shall be committed into custody, and be detained and kept in some publick inns by the Trained Bands or Militia of the said City, or Counties adjacent, respectively, untill further order. Signed by their Lordships' order,

F. Gwyn.[188]

It being proposed that several persons should be excepted by name in the said order, the Lord Hallifax moved that it would be much better, that particular licences should be given, signed by Mr. Gwyn. Which was agreed to, and accordingly the Dutchess of Mazarine,[189] Duchess of Bouillon,[190] Monsieur Sissack,[191] Monsieur Flamarine,[192] Monsieur St. Victor,[193] Monsieur Cauze, Monsieur St. Evremont, Monsieur Carmeline, and Madame Mirannion, with such as are now actually in their service, and Monsieur Boisset, may have such licences, when they call for them.

Monsieur Sissack and servants to remain in town.

The Lords Spiritual and Temporal, assembled in this extraordinary conjuncture, having by their order, dated this day, appointed me for them, and in their names, to sign and subscribe such orders as shall be from time to time by them made, do hereby licence and permit Monsieur le Marquis de Saissack; Francis Le Reverend and Anthony de la Bord, his *valet‹s› de chambre*; Francis de la Marre, Francis Courtee, and John Borrell, his servants, to dwell in his service, and remain in and about the City of

London, untill further order, without any lett or molestation for or by reason of their Lordships' order, requiring Papists or reputed Papists to depart from the said City within five days. Whereof all persons concerned are to take notice. Dated at the House of Lords, in Westminster, December 22⟨n⟩d, 1688. Signed by their Lordships' order,

F. Gwyn.

The like order to the Dutchess of Mazarine and her servants, vizt. Mr. Brunet, her steward; Mr. Richard, her secretary; Mr. Storton, her page; Monsieur Deny and Monsieur ———, her *valets de chambre*; Monsieur Romain and Monsieur Galais, her cooks; Monsieur Colo, her groom of the chambers; Villedrelin, her footman; Mademoiselle de Bragelone and her daughter; Mademoiselle Spencer, and Elizabeth Hood, her woman.

The like to Monsieur Flamerans and his servants, Monsieur Mozingvilla, Monsieur Charles Le Prince, and Monsieur Bolinge.

The like to Monsieur St. Evremont and his servants, Jasper Gerrerts and Adrian Swan.

The like to Monsieur Bossett.

Mr. Stafford and ⟨Mr.⟩ Mannock to be set at liberty.

The Lords Spiritual and Temporal, assembled in this extraordinary conjuncture, having by their order, dated this day, appointed me for them, and in their names, to sign and subscribe such orders as shall be from time to time by them made, do hereby desire the right honourable the Earl of Winchelsea to give directions, that Francis Stafford[194] and ⟨John⟩ Mannock,[195] Esquires, now detained in Kent, be forthwith set at liberty. Dated at the House of Lords, Westminster, 22⟨n⟩d December 1688. Signed by their Lordships' order,

F. Gwyn

The Lord Pagett moves, that on Monday morning they may consider of a free parliament.

Lord Delamere ⟨moves⟩, that on Monday morning the first business to be taken into consideration be the state of the government, in order to a free parliament.

Resolved, that on Monday at nine of the clock in the morning their Lordships will meet, and consider of the Prince's speech, in order to a free parliament, and that nothing else shall intervene.

Lord Devonshire moves, and it was agreed on, that none of the Peers should go out of town without leave, and that the Peers that were in town, and not present this day, should have particular summons to be present on Monday.

Mr. Churchill[196] was ordered to print such things as should be ordered by their Lordships to be printed.

[The Peers' third meeting, on the 24th, was very different from its predecessors. It was held in the aftermath of the King's departure for France, a fact which loosened the tongues of his opponents and produced a wide ranging, if far more contentious, debate than had taken place on the 21st and 22nd. After ordering the removal to London of the imprisoned fugitives from Kent, and their commitment to the Tower, Newgate, and the Gatehouse (one of the Peers' last executive actions in the present crisis), the assembly discussed what was to be done following James's final withdrawal. Again there was a notable division of opinion, chiefly between the loyalists, led by Clarendon, Rochester, Nottingham, Bishop Turner, Berkeley, Abingdon, Craven, and Ailesbury, and the Williamites, led by Devonshire, Montagu, Culpepper, Lumley, Wharton, and Cornwallis. (73 peers attended.)

AT THE HOUSE OF LORDS, WESTMINSTER
DECEMBER 24TH, 1688

Lord Archbishop of York; Duke of Norfolk; Duke of Somerset; Duke of Grafton; Duke of Ormond; Duke of Beaufort; Duke of Northumberland; Marquess of Hallifax; Earl of Lyndsey; Earl of Oxford; Earl of Shrewsbury; Earl of Kent; Earl of Bedford; Earl of Pembroke; Earl of Dorset; Earl of Northampton; Earl of Devonshire; Earl of Bolingbroke; Earl of Manchester; Earl of Mulgrave; Earl of Rivers (sic); Earl of Stamford; Earl of Winchelsea; Earl of Thanet; Earl of Scarsdale; Earl of Clarendon; Earl of Craven; Earl of Ailesbury; Earl of Burlington; Earl of Litchfield; Earl of Sussex; Earl of Macclesfield; Earl of Radnor; Earl of Yarmouth; Earl of Berkeley; Earl of Nottingham; Earl of Rochester; Earl of Abingdon; Lord Viscount Fauconberg; Lord Viscount Mordaunt; Lord Viscount Newport; Lord Viscount Weymouth; Lord Viscount Hatton; Lord Bishop ‹of› London; Lord Bishop ‹of› Winton.; Lord Bishop ‹of› St. Asaph; Lord Bishop ‹of› Ely; Lord Bishop ‹of› Chichester; Lord Bishop ‹of› Rochester; Lord Bishop ‹of› Bristol; Lord Delawarr; Lord Wharton; Lord Paget; Lord North and Grey; Lord Chandois; Lord Mountague; Lord Grey of Warke; Lord Lovelace; Lord Maynard; Lord Howard ‹of› Escrick; Lord Jermin; Lord Vaughan Cherbury; Lord Culpepper; Lord Astley; Lord Lucas; Lord Cornwallis; Lord Delamere; Lord Crew; Lord Lumley; Lord Carteret; Lord Ossulstone; Lord Godolphin; Lord Churchill.

Earl of Winchelsea acquaints the Lords, that there are several noblemen and gentlemen prisoners in Kent, and that the gentlemen of that County, who secured them, desire their Lordships' order for removing them.

Whereupon their Lordships directed Mr. Gwyn to sign warrants for the Earl of Salisbury, Earl of Peterborough, Sir Edward Hales, Charles Hales,[197] Obadiah Walker,[198] Sir Thomas Jenner,[199] Mr. Graham,[200] and Mr. Burton[201] to the Tower; the five first for treason.

And the other priests and Jesuits to Newgate or the Gatehouse, and the rest to be discharged. And the Earl of Winchelsea promised to bring in a list of their names to Mr. Gwyn.

Lord Culpepper informs, that one Warham Horsemanden,[202] in Essex, is committed, on pretence ‹of› his being a convert Catholick, whereas he was not so. An order for his discharge.

Mr. Horsemanden discharged.

The Lords Spiritual and Temporal, assembled in this extraordinary conjuncture, do hereby order, that Warham Horsemanden, who was committed into your custody by Sir Richard Everard,[203] be forthwith discharged and set at liberty. For which this shall be your warrant. Dated at the House of Lords, Westminster, 24th December 1688. Signed by their Lordships' order,

To the Keeper of the Gaol at Chelmsford.   F. Gwyn.

Duke of Norfolk informs, that five of his brother's children, with their maids, are in prison at Feversham. To be released.

Discharge for Lord Thomas Howard's children.

> The Lords Spiritual and Temporal, assembled in this extraordinary conjuncture, do hereby order, that you forthwith discharge and set at liberty the five children of the Lord Thomas Howard,[204] and three maid servants belonging to them. For which this shall be your warrant. Dated at the House of Lords, 24th December 1688. Signed by their Lordships' order,
>
> To the Keeper of the Gaol at Feversham;   F. Gwyn.
> to the Chief Marshall of the same;
> and all others whom it may concern.

Lord Devonshire moves, that the Lord Bellasis[205] may be excused from the severity of the order.

He is intended to be so, having been an housekeeper above these three years.

The Lords' names called. All absent sent to again.

The Prince's speech at St. James's ‹was› read again, as the ground of the debate, which was appointed to be today.

Serjeant Maynard, Serjeant Holt, Mr. Pollexfen, and Mr. Bradbury attend.

Earl of Berkeley moves to enquire what is become of the King. The Earl of Ailesbury came from him, and gave an account there was a letter writt by the King to the Earl of Middleton, which was not fit to be seen.

Earl of Clarendon desires the letter may be sent for. Earl of Lyndsey seconds the Earl of Clarendon for the letter.

Earl of Devonshire. That the letter would acquaint them with what they knew already, but it is to be considered how they may have the letter, it being only a private letter to the Earl of Middleton.

Lord Mordaunt. That the meeting here shews that the King is absent, either in power, or otherwise, and therefore not to be applied to.

Earl of Ailesbury. Knows only there was a letter, and heard he was gone.

Lord Mountague. That the letter or anything should not direct the business of the day. If the letter was of a publick nature, his Lordship would bring it to them.

Lord Mulgrave. If a private one, ‹it is› not fit to be enquired into.

Earl of Nottingham. That the letter may be desired, it being mentioned.

Lord Lumley. That if it had been a publick letter, it would have been communicated; otherwise, ‹it is› not to be sent for.

Lord Abingdon. He thinks Lord Ailesbury did not say he was gone.

Earl of Clarendon. That the letter may be seen, since it will be of great consequence to know whether the King is absolutely gone, which perhaps the letter shews, though the Earl of Ailesbury doth not speak positively.

Earl of Nottingham. The letter was writt to a Secretary of State, therefore proper to be communicated.

Lord Godolphin. That he hath not seen the letter, but he believes it not much of publick nature.

Earl of Rochester. That ‹the› Earl of Ailesbury thinks it necessary, Lord Godolphin not, therefore necessary to be judged by seeing.

Marquess of Hallifax. That may make a competition between two Lords.

Earl of Devonshire. That ‹the› Earl of Ailesbury may acquaint their Lordships with what he remembers.

Earl of Ailesbury excuses himself.

Earl of Lyndsey. That he may give an account of what is of publick concern, as he conceived.

Marquess of Hallifax. That he should not be put upon it.

Lord Lumley ‹moves to› let fall the debate, and go to the business of the day.

Lord Cornwallis. Not to lose time, there being necessity of immediate settlement of affairs by considering of a free parliament.

Lord Culpepper. The letter not to be called for; ‹moves› the business of the day.

Lord Paget. A great silence hath been long, and a great deal of time spent.

The question, for the King's letter to the Earl of Middleton to be sent for to be communicated.

Lord Culpepper ‹moves› the previous question, whether the Lords shall send to the Earl of Middleton for the letter, which was sent to him from the King.

Previous question, whether that shall be put, or no. Not-contents have it.

Lord Paget goes on. The business ‹is› now to consider of the calling a free parliament: to consider whether you are able to call, or what way is to be used for the calling one.

Lord North. Whether the King's going away is not a denial in law?

Lord Cornwallis. To advise with the council[206] what is fit to be done.

Earl of Devonshire. Whether the King's withdrawing himself from the government be not a demise in law?

Lord Mountague. Whether you will referr it to the advice of the lawyers, or determine it by your own prudence? That the Bill of Exclusion had methods in it, which might be considered.

Earl ‹of› Pembroke. That it is to be considered whether this is an abdication; that the Prince of Wales's right is to be considered into; and that all this cannot be better done than by ‹a› Convention. But there should be a power in the mean time, there being no officer.

Lord Wharton. That the Prince of Wales, as well as the King, is gone, and carryed away by him that had power. The council to advise, whether it is not to both.[207]

Lord Bishop of Ely. That there was particular examination of every circumstance in their own case as Bishops, therefore wishes this going away of the King may be as fully enquired into as possible.

Lord ‹Bishop of› London. That there is an absolute necessity of a government; that the council may be advised with on some questions; that, under the necessity we are, the question should be as if the King were not; that, not knowing where the King is, we are to look upon the government as dissolved.

Earl of Rochester. That the council shall have the question in writing, and that their answer should be in writing.

That the matter of fact should be first stated before the question, that is, matter of fact on what circumstances he is gone: whether he is gone, or no; to what place he is gone; whether he did it freely, or by constraint. These things ‹are› necessary to be known, and then the other part ‹is› easy.

Marquess of Hallifax ‹moves› to consider how to come to a free parliament.

Earl of Devonshire. Whether the King's absenting himself, and leaving all things in this confusion, be a demise in law?

Lord Paget. To know whether they can call a parliament, or no.

Earl of Abingdon ‹moves› to ask the council, whether the writts that be already gone out for the calling a Parliament may be proceeded upon.

Earl ‹of› Craven seconds the motion.

Lord Delamere desires to know whether all the writts are out. Answered, no, but sixteen writts.

Lord Culpepper. If the King be in the Kingdom, as to the government and protection of it, is the same thing as if he were out of the government. That there is no manner of government, no Sheriffs; the writts most returned.

That their meeting here is a certain sign there is no government, and therefore no need of any proof or enquiry by affidavits.

Earl of Devonshire reads a paper, signed by the Prince, summoning all of the Parliament of the late King's time. Moves that a way may be thought of for the cities, counties, and burroughs to choose their representatives.

Lord Hallifax ‹moves› that an address be made to the Prince, that circular letters be writt as above, and that an address be to him to take upon him the administration of the government till the free parliament hath settled it.

Earl of Clarendon ‹moves› that the Prince calls a legate, as well as a free parliament, which must therefore be considered, and therefore to be followed. Proposes, as an expedient only, that the 16 writts will choose 180 odd Members; that they may assemble, and they applying to this day or otherwise, as there is occasion, for the supplying the writts, may do so. Their Lordships having an hereditary right, ‹it is› less needful.

The Clerk of the Petty Bag to be examined, whether the writts were issued.

Lord Mordaunt. That the freedom of a parliament is the chief thing. That an Oath is to be taken, if they meet upon the King's writts, which would take off the freedom of a parliament.

Lord Delamere. That the Parliament is the thing desired. That the writts issued by the King cannot be, because of the Oaths of Allegiance and Supremacy. That there was never any precedent before to apply to the Prince of Orange for circular letters to the respective counties to choose two.

Earl ‹of› Nottingham. The obtaining a free parliament ‹is› the matter, which certainly cannot be. The nearest to a free parliament is what was before proposed, circular letters to the House of Lords, and to the Coroners, or High or Chief Constables; but that cannot be under three weeks.

In the mean time there was a case, in which Richard ‹the› First was taken prisoner, and his brother, King John, accepted the government of the Kingdom as Regent, and without commission from his brother. If there is a convention, no Oaths ‹are› to be taken; ‹if› a parliament, there are Oaths. In the mean time a Regency, but then a difficulty, if in the King's name. It is owning the King, who hath forsaken the Kingdom.

But there may be propositions sent to the King, the taking or refusing ‹of which› will be the doing the thing. Moves ‹an› address to the Prince to take upon him all other matters of the Regency.

Lord Mordaunt. That the Prince did all, that possibly he could, to act according to his *Declaration*, till the King rendered it impossible by withdrawing himself, and so there could not be that free parliament.

Lord Bishop of London ‹moves› that the Prince be addressed to send his circular letters to the Lords and Commons.

‹Resolved›, that an address be made to His Highness the Prince of Orange to desire him to cause circular letters to be written, subscribed by himself, to the several counties, cities, and burroughs; and to be directed to the Coroners, who are to give publick notice of the time, containing a direction to choose in all such counties, cities, and burroughs such persons, etc., and to be returned by the said Officer within five days after notice.

The gentlemen of the long robe being asked, in default of the Sheriffs, to whom the circular letters shall be directed, answered, to Coroners; in default of them, to the Clerk of the Peace.

For the Universities, to the Vice-chancellors.

Whether there should be one to a county, or every burrough one? ‹Answered›, ‹one› letter to a county, to direct the persons who receive them to issue out to the burroughs.

Lord Culpepper. That the most expeditious way is to the respective officers of the town.

The letters to be writt by the Prince to the respective burroughs and cities, as well as counties, and those to the cities and burroughs to the respective chief officers.

The Cinque Ports to be writt to, as the other particular burroughs.

Earl of Oxford. That all the Lords may sign the addresses, both with their own hands.

Lord Delamere. That such officers shall make proclamation on the Sunday after their receipt of the letters in the market towns.

The gentlemen of the long robe ‹are› to draw up the address upon the debate, the heads thereof being delivered to them in writing, and they withdrew accordingly.

Letters to the Lords Spiritual and Temporal.

Marquess ‹of› Hallifax. That Lord Nottingham, ‹the› Lord Bishop of London, Lord Delamere, Lord Culpepper, ‹the› Lord Bishop of Ely, ‹and› Lord Wharton do draw up an application to His Highness to take upon him the administration of affairs.

The Lords Committees bring in the draught, which was delivered by the Bishop of Ely, and read.

Earl of Stamford ‹moves› that *His Majesty's withdrawing himself* be left out.

Earl of Nottingham. It is the ground of desiring it.

Left out by general opinion.

Earl of Devonshire. England and Ireland to be in the address, and ‹the› disposal of the publick revenue.

A particular clause for Ireland.

Marquess ‹of› Hallifax ‹moves›, the word *legal* be left out.

Earl of Nottingham ‹moves› to keep the word, *legal*.

Earl of Devonshire. That none of the Peers, but Protestants, should be summoned.

The two addresses ‹are› to be writt, and signed tomorrow at two o'clock in the afternoon.

Earl of Shrewsbury. Will know the Prince's pleasure, when he will be attended.

The Earl of Winchelsea, according to his promise, brought in a list of such persons as were taken prisoners in Kent, with the places' names where they were detained.

Canterbury: Earl of Salisbury; Earl of Peterborough; Mr. Charles Hales; Captain Kingsley.

Feversham, at the Court House: Obadiah Walker; John Leybourn;[208] Ralph Clayton;[209] Thomas Rought;[210] Joseph Gifford;[211] Robert Jennison;[212] Charles Poulton;[213] Thomas Kingsley;[214] William Locker.[215]

Ralph Hardwick, a Spanish merchant,[216] with his wife and children. To be discharged.

Thomas Romain; Richard Challoner; Charles Edge, or Edwards,[217] Edward Sing,[218] servants.

Maidstone: Sir Edward Hales.

Feversham, at *The Ship* tavern: Mr. Thomas Arundell, his wife and children, and Mr. Henry Arundell.[219] Discharged by order.

Louis Goff; Henry Gibson, servants.

Feversham, at the Coffee House: Sir Thomas Jenner; Richard Graham; Phillip Burton.

Thomas Bennett; John Nowell, servants and Protestants. Discharged.

Cranbrook: Captain Stafford, of Lieutenant-General Worden's Regiment; Cornet Mannock, of Lord Oxford's Regiment.

Prisoners to be put in the Tower.

Earl of Salisbury; Earl of Peterborough; Sir Edward Hales; Sir Thomas Jenner; Mr. Charles Hales; Obadiah Walker; Richard Graham; Phillip Burton.

‹Ordered›, that the Lord Lucas take charge of those, who are to be brought to the Tower, and send down his Officers to bring them up, or otherwise, as their Lordships please to order.

‹Ordered›, that the priests and Jesuits be sent to Newgate, or the Gatehouse.

Question, what ‹is› to be done with their servants?

The Lord Tenham[220] to have a letter wrote to him, if their Lordships please, to return to his house at Upnor Castle, with his Lady and children, and to give security not to stir five miles from thence.

That Mr. Hardwick, the Spanish merchant, with his wife, children, and servants, may have his liberty to pursue his intended voyage beyond the seas.

Question, what ‹do› their Lordships please to order concerning Captain Stafford and Captain Mannock?

Sir Thomas Jenner, Richard Graham, and Phillip Burton, Esquires, to be brought to the Tower of London.

The Lords Spiritual and Temporal, assembled in this extraordinary conjuncture, having by their order of the 22‹n›d instant appointed me for them, and in their names, to sign and subscribe such orders as shall be from time to time by them made, do hereby order that the right honourable the Lord Lucas, Chief Governour of the Tower of London, do receive into his custody the persons of Sir Thomas Jenner, Knight, Richard Graham, and Phillip Burton, Esquires; and, in order thereunto, to appoint such person or persons as he shall think fit to receive, and bring them under a convenient guard to the Tower of London, there to be kept in safe custody till further order. And for so doing this shall be your warrant. Dated at the House of Lords, in Westminster, the 24th December 1688. Signed by their Lordships' order,

To the right honourable the Lord Lucas,   F. Gwyn.
the Chief Governor of the Tower of London.

Sir Thomas Jenner, Richard Graham, and Phillip Burton, Esquires, to be brought to the Tower of London.

The Lords Spiritual and Temporal, assembled in this extraordinary conjuncture, etc., do hereby order, that you forthwith deliver the persons of Sir Thomas Jenner, Knight, Richard Graham, and Phillip Burton, Esquires, to the right honourable the Lord Lucas, Chief Governour of the Tower of London. And for so doing this shall be your warrant. Dated at the House of Lords, in Westminster, the 24th day of December 1688. Signed by their Lordships' order,

To the Keeper of the Gaol at Feversham;   F. Gwyn.
to the Chief Magistrate there;
and all others whom it may concern.

The Lords Spiritual and Temporal, assembled in this extraordinary conjuncture, etc., do order the right honourable the Lord Lucas, Chief Governor of the Tower of London, to receive into his custody the persons of the right honourable James, Earl of Salisbury, and Henry, Earl of Peterborough, hereby committed for high treason in being reconciled to the Church of Rome; and the said Lord Lucas do, in order thereunto, send such person or persons as he shall think fit to receive, and bring them under a convenient guard to the Tower of London, there to be kept in safe custody untill they be discharged by due course of law. And for so doing this shall be his warrant. Dated at the House of Lords, at Westminster, 24th day of December 1688. Signed by their Lordships' order,

To the right honourable the Lord Lucas,   F. Gwyn.
Chief Governor of the Tower of London.

The Lords Spiritual and Temporal, assembled in this extraordinary conjuncture, etc., do hereby order, that you forthwith deliver the persons of the right honourable James, Earl of Salisbury, and Henry, Earl of Peterborough, to the right honourable the Lord Lucas, Chief Governor of the Tower of London, or to such as shall be appointed by him to receive them, in order to their commitment to the Tower of London. And for so doing this shall be your warrant. Dated at the House of Lords, in Westminster, the 24th day of December 1688. Signed by their Lordships' order,

To the Keeper of the Gaol at Canterbury;   F. Gwyn.
to the Chief Magistrates of the said City;
and all others whom it may concern.

The like order for Sir Edward Hales for high treason in being reconciled to the Church of Rome, and for diverse other dangerous practices, high crimes, and misdemeanours. One directed to Lord Lucas. The other to the Keeper of the Gaol at Maidstone; to the Chief Magistrate of the said town; and all others whom it may concern.

   The like order for Charles Hales and Obadiah Walker, gentlemen. One directed to Lord Lucas. The other to the Keeper of the Gaol at Maidstone; to the Keeper of the Gaol at Canterbury, or Feversham; and all others whom it may concern.

   The Lords Spiritual and Temporal, assembled in this extraordinary conjuncture, having by their order of the 22‹n›d instant appointed me for them, and in their names, to sign and subscribe such orders as shall be from time to time by them made, do order that Major Richardson, Keeper of Newgate Prison, in London, receive into his custody the persons of John Leybourne, Ralph Clayton, Thomas Rought, Joseph Gifford, Thomas Kingsly, Du Calamy, and William Locker, hereby committed for being Romish priests; and the said Mr. Richardson do, in order thereunto, send such person or persons as he shall think fit to receive, and bring them under a convenient guard to the said prison of Newgate, there to be kept in safe custody untill they be discharged by due course of law. And for so doing this shall be his warrant. Dated at the House of Lords, in Westminster, the 24th of December 1688. Signed by their Lordships' order,

   To Major Richardson,[221]   F. Gwyn.
   Keeper of Newgate Prison, in London.

   The Lords Spiritual and Temporal, assembled in this extraordinary conjuncture, having by their order of the 22‹n›d instant appointed me for them, and in their names, to sign and subscribe such orders as shall be from time to time by them made, do hereby order that you forthwith deliver the persons of John Leybourne, Ralph Clayton, Thomas Rought, Joseph Gifford, Robert Jennison, Charles Poulton, Thomas Kingsly, Du Calamy, and William Locker to Major Richardson, Keeper of Newgate Prison, in London, or to such as shall be appointed by him to receive them, in order to their commitment to the said prison of Newgate. And for so doing this shall be your warrant. Dated at the House of Lords, Westminster, the 24th day of December 1688. Signed by their Lordships' order,

   To the Keeper of the Gaol at Feversham,   F. Gwyn.
   and all others whom it may concern.

The Earl of Winchelsea brought up Du Calamy, whose name is interlined in the warrant with the rest of those mentioned in the list, and delivered him to Major Richardson, and acquainted Mr. Gwyn that he was a priest, though he was not in the list. Whereupon he was interlined.

   [The fourth of the Peers' meetings, held on the afternoon of Christmas Day, saw the signing of the two addresses to the Prince. That being done, they ordered Gwyn to sign three orders: one discharging from custody a harmless Catholic family, and two permitting Catholic ladies to remain in London on the grounds of health. (76 peers attended.)]

AT THE HOUSE OF LORDS, WESTMINSTER
DECEMBER 25, 1688
AT 2 OF THE CLOCK IN THE AFTERNOON

PRESENT

Archbishop ‹of› York; Duke of Norfolk; Duke of Somerset; Duke of Grafton; Duke of Ormond; Duke of Beaufort; Duke of Northumberland; Marquess of Hallifax; Earl of Lyndsey; Earl of Oxford; Earl of Shrewsbury; Earl of Kent; Earl of Bedford; Earl of Pembroke; Earl of Dorset; Earl of Northampton; Earl of Devon‹shire›; Earl of Bolingbroke; Earl of Manchester; Earl of Mulgrave; Earl of Rivers (sic); Earl of Stamford; Earl of Winchelsea; Earl of Thanet; Earl of Scarsdale; Earl of Clarendon; Earl of Anglesey; Earl of Craven; Earl of Ailesbury; Earl of Burlington; Earl of Litchfield; Earl of Sussex; Earl of Macclesfield; Earl of Radnor; Earl of Yarmouth; Earl of Berkeley; Earl of Nottingham; Earl of Rochester; Earl of Abingdon; Lord Viscount Fauconberg; Lord Viscount Mordaunt; Lord Viscount Newport; Lord Viscount Weymouth; Lord Viscount Hatton; Lord Bishop ‹of› London; Lord Bishop ‹of› Duresme; Lord Bishop ‹of› Winchester; Lord Bishop ‹of› St. Asaph; Lord Bishop ‹of› Ely; Lord Bishop ‹of› Chichester; Lord Bishop ‹of› Rochester; Lord Bishop ‹of› Bristol; Lord Grey ‹of› Ruthin; Lord Eure; Lord Wharton; Lord Paget; Lord North and Grey; Lord Chandois; Lord Mountague; Lord Grey ‹of› Wark; Lord Lovelace; Lord Maynard; Lord Howard ‹of› Escrick; Lord Jermin; Lord Vaughan Cherbury; Lord Culpepper; Lord Astley; Lord Lucas; Lord Cornwallis; Lord Delawarr; Lord Lumley; Lord Crew; Lord Carteret; Lord Ossulstone; Lord Godolphin; Lord Churchill.

The two addresses were writt fair in vellum, and brought to the House, according to order.
The names of the Lords were called over, according to the list.
The address for the Convention was read, approved, and signed, as follows.

> We, the Lords Spiritual and Temporal, assembled in this extraordinary conjuncture, do humbly desire Your Highness to cause letters to be written, subscribed by yourself, to the Lords Spiritual and Temporal, being Protestants, and to the several counties, Universities, cities, burroughs, and Cinque Ports of England, Wales, and Town of Berwick-upon-Tweed; the letters for the counties to be directed to the Coroners of the respective counties, or any one of them; and, in default of the Coroner, to the Clerk of the Peace of the respective counties; and the letters for the Universities to be directed to the respective Vice-chancellors; and the letters for the several cities, burroughs, and Cinque Ports to be directed to the Chief Magistrates of each respective city, burrough, and Cinque Port; containing directions for the choosing in all such counties, cities, Universities, burroughs, and Cinque Ports within ten days after the receipt of such respective letters such a number of persons to represent, as are of right to be sent to Parliament; of which elections, and the times and places thereof, the respective Officers shall give notice within the space of five days at the least. Notice of the intended elections for the counties to be published in the church, immediately

after the time of divine service, and within all market towns within the respective counties; and notice of the intended elections for the cities, Universities, burroughs, and Cinque Ports to be published within the said respective places. The said letters, and the execution thereof, to be returned by such Officer and Officers, who shall execute the same, to the Clerk of the Crown in the Court of Chancery, so as the persons, so to be chosen, may meet and sit at Westminster on the 22⟨n⟩d day of January next. Dated at the House of Lords, Westminster, December ⟨25th⟩, 1688.

Lord Archbishop of York; Duke of Norfolk; Duke of Somerset; Duke of Grafton; Duke of Ormond; Duke of Beaufort; Duke of Northumberland; Marquess of Hallifax; Earl of Lyndsey; Earl of Oxford; Earl of Shrewsbury; Earl of Kent; Earl of Bedford; Earl of Pembroke; Earl of Dorset; Earl of Northampton; Earl of Devonshire; Earl of Bolingbroke; Earl of Manchester; Earl of Mulgrave; Earl of Rivers; Earl of Stamford; Earl of Thanet; Earl of Winchelsea; Earl of Scarsdale; Earl of Clarendon; Earl of Anglesey; Earl of Craven; Earl of Ailesbury; Earl of Burlington; Earl of Litchfield; Earl of Sussex; Earl of Macclesfield; Earl of Radnor; Earl of Yarmouth; Earl of Berkeley; Earl of Nottingham; Earl of Rochester; Earl of Abingdon; Lord Viscount Fauconberg; Lord Viscount Mordaunt; Lord Viscount Newport; Lord Viscount Weymouth; Lord Viscount Hatton; Lord Bishop ⟨of⟩ London; Lord Bishop ⟨of⟩ Duresme; Lord Bishop ⟨of⟩ Winchester; Lord Bishop ⟨of⟩ St. Asaph; Lord Bishop ⟨of⟩ Ely; Lord Bishop ⟨of⟩ Chichester; Lord Bishop ⟨of⟩ Rochester; Lord Bishop ⟨of⟩ Bristol; Lord Delawarr; Lord Grey ⟨of⟩ Ruthin; Lord Eure; Lord Wharton; Lord Paget; Lord North and Grey; Lord Chandois; Lord Mountague; Lord Grey ⟨of⟩ Wark; Lord Lovelace; Lord Maynard; Lord Howard ⟨of⟩ Escrick; Lord Jermin; Lord Vaughan Cherbury; Lord Culpepper; Lord Astley; Lord Lucas; Lord Cornwallis; Lord Delamere; Lord Crew; Lord Lumley; Lord Carteret; Lord Ossulstone; Lord Godolphin; Lord Churchill.

The second address, concerning the Prince's taking upon him the administration of publick affairs, was read; and the word, *religion*, being omitted in the third line, it was ordered to be writt over again. Which, being read, was approved, and signed as follows.

Address to the Prince ⟨of⟩ Orange to take upon him the government untill the Convention.

We, the Lords Spiritual and Temporal assembled, do desire Your Highness to take upon you the administration of publick affairs, both civil and military, and the disposal of the publick revenue, for the preservation of our religion, rights, laws, liberties, and properties, and of the peace of the nation; and that Your Highness will take into your particular care the present condition of Ireland, and endeavour by the most speedy and effectual means to prevent the danger threatening that Kingdom. All which we make our requests to Your Highness to undertake and exercise untill the meeting of the intended Convention, the 22⟨n⟩d of January next. In which we doubt not such proper methods will be taken, as will conduce to the establishment of these things upon such sure and legal foundations, that they may not be in danger of being again subverted. Dated at the House of Lords, Westminster, December 25, 1688.

Lord Archbishop of York; Duke of Norfolk; Duke of Somerset; Duke of Grafton; Duke of Ormond; Duke of Beaufort; Duke of Northumberland; Marquess of Hallifax; Earl of Lyndsey; Earl of Oxford; Earl of Shrewsbury; Earl of Kent; Earl of Bedford; Earl of Pembroke; Earl of Dorset; Earl of Northampton; Earl of Devonshire; Earl of Bolingbroke; Earl of Manchester; Earl of Mulgrave; Earl of Rivers (*sic*); Earl of

Stamford; Earl of Winchelsea; Earl of Thanet; Earl of Scarsdale; Earl of Clarendon; Earl of Anglesey; Earl of Craven; Earl of Ailesbury; Earl of Burlington; Earl of Litchfield; Earl of Sussex; Earl of Macclesfield; Earl of Radnor; Earl of Yarmouth; Earl of Berkeley; Earl of Nottingham; Earl of Rochester; Earl of Abingdon; Lord Viscount Fauconberg; Lord Viscount Mordaunt; Lord Viscount Newport; Lord Viscount Weymouth; Lord Viscount Hatton; Lord Bishop ‹of› London; Lord Bishop ‹of› Duresme; Lord Bishop ‹of› Winchester; Lord Bishop ‹of› St. Asaph; Lord Bishop ‹of› Ely; Lord Bishop ‹of› Chichester; Lord Bishop ‹of› Rochester; Lord Bishop ‹of› Bristol; Lord Delawarr; Lord Grey ‹of› Ruthin; Lord Eure; Lord Wharton; Lord Paget; Lord North and Grey; Lord Chandois; Lord Mountague; Lord Grey ‹of› Wark; Lord Lovelace; Lord Maynard; Lord Howard ‹of› Escrick; Lord Jermin; Lord Vaughan Cherbury; Lord Culpepper; Lord Astley; Lord Lucas; Lord Cornwallis; Lord Delamere; Lord Crew; Lord Lumley; Lord Carteret; Lord Ossulstone; Lord Godolphin; Lord Churchill.

The Lords Spiritual and Temporal, assembled in this extraordinary conjuncture, etc., do hereby order, that you forthwith discharge and set at liberty Thomas Arundell, Esquire, and Margaret, his wife; Henry Arundell and Nathaniel Arundell, his sons; Elizabeth Green, Lewis Gough, Henry Gibson, and Thomas Read, his servants. And for so doing this shall be your warrent. Dated at the House of Lords, 25th December 1688. Signed by their Lordships' order,

To the Keeper of the Gaol at Feversham;   F. Gwyn.
to the Chief Magistrates of the same;
and all others whom it may concern.

The Lords Spiritual and Temporal, assembled in this extraordinary conjuncture, etc., do hereby licence and permit the Lady Bedingfield, wife to Sir Henry Bedingfield, Knight,[222] being great with child, and near the time of her delivery, as also the said ‹Sir› Henry Bedingfield, to dwell and reside in and about the City of London untill further order, without any lett or molestation for or by reason of their Lordships' late order, requiring Papists or reputed Papists to depart from the said City within five days. Whereof all persons concerned are to take notice. Dated at the House of Lords, Westminster, the 25th day of December 1688. Signed by their Lordships' order,

F. Gwyn.

The like order for the Lady Clanmalire,[223] being so indisposed in her health, that she cannot remove without danger.

[The fifth and final meeting of the Peers, on 28 December, was a mere formality. They were summoned on the 27th to St. James's Palace by William, who, in a speech delivered to them in the Queen's Presence Chamber, signified his acceptance of their addresses. (86 peers were summoned. The number of attendants is not recorded.)]

St. James's,
December 27th, 1688.

By the Prince of Orange's command you are hereby required to summon the Peers, hereunder named, and all other the Lords Spiritual and Temporal in or near the town, to attend His Highness at St. James's in the room where their Lordships attended him last in that place, at eleven of the clock tomorrow morning, being the 28th of December 1688.

To Thomas Atterbury, Clerk of the Cheque;   F. Gwyn.
or, in his absence, to George Brumwick, his Deputy Clerk
of the Cheque to the Messengers of the Chamber.

Lord Archbishop ‹of› Canterbury; Lord Archbishop ‹of› York; Duke of Norfolk; Duke
of Somerset; Duke of Grafton; Duke of Ormond; Duke of Beaufort; Duke of
Northumberland; Marquess of Hallifax; Earl of Lyndsey; Earl of Oxford; Earl of
Shrewsbury; Earl of Kent; Earl of Bedford; Earl of Pembroke; Earl of Suffolk; Earl
of Dorset; Earl of Bridgewater; Earl of Leicester; Earl of Northampton; Earl of
Devonshire; Earl of Clare; Earl of Bolingbroke; Earl of Westmoreland; Earl of
Manchester; Earl of Mulgrave; Earl of Rivers (sic); Earl of Stamford; Earl of
Winchelsea; Earl of Thanet; Earl of Scarsdale; Earl of Clarendon; Earl of Anglesey;
Earl of Carlisle; Earl of Craven; Earl of Ailesbury; Earl of Burlington; Earl of Litchfield;
Earl of Danby; Earl of Sussex; Earl of Macclesfield; Earl of Radnor; Earl of Yarmouth;
Earl of Berkeley; Earl of Nottingham; Earl of Rochester; Earl of Abingdon; Lord
Viscount Fauconberg; Lord Viscount Mordaunt; Lord Viscount Newport; Lord
Viscount Weymouth; Lord Viscount Hatton; Lord Bishop ‹of› London; Lord Bishop
‹of› Duresme; Lord Bishop ‹of› Winchester; Lord Bishop ‹of› St. Asaph; Lord Bishop
‹of› Ely; Lord Bishop ‹of› Chichester; Lord Bishop ‹of› Rochester; Lord Bishop ‹of›
Bristol; Lord Bishop ‹of› Peterborough (not summoned); Lord Delawarr; Lord Grey
‹of› Ruthin; Lord Eure; Lord Wharton; Lord Paget; Lord North and Grey; Lord
Chandois; Lord Mountague; Lord Grey of Wark; Lord Lovelace; Lord Maynard;
Lord Howard ‹of› Escrick; Lord Jermin; Lord Vaughan Cherbury; Lord Culpepper;
Lord Astley; Lord Lucas; Lord Cornwallis; Lord Delamere; Lord Crew; Lord Lumley;
Lord Carteret; Lord Ossulstone; Lord Godolphin; Lord Churchill.

The Lords being assembled in the Queen's Presence Chamber, at St. James's, the Prince of
Orange came in, and made the following speech.

My Lords,

I have considered of your advice, and as far as I am able I will endeavour to secure
the peace of the nation, untill the meeting of the Convention in January next; for the
election whereof I will forthwith issue out letters, according to your desire. I will also
take care to apply the publick revenue to the most proper uses that the present affairs
require, and likewise endeavour to put Ireland into such a condition as that the
Protestant religion and the English interest may be maintained in that Kingdom. And
I further assure you that, as I came hither for the preservation of the Protestant religion
and the laws and liberties of these Kingdoms, so I shall always be ready to expose
myself to any hazard for the defence of the same.

50 Allegorical print showing William III and Mary II enthroned as King and Queen of England. In the background (*left*) is the Banqueting House, Whitehall, where the Marquess of Halifax, as Speaker of the House of Lords in the Convention, formally tendered the crown to them on 13 February 1689.

APPENDIXES

1 Roger Morrice's account of James II's flight from Whitehall, 11 December, 1688[1]

About 2 a clock in the morning on Tuesday, the 11th, His Majestie carryed a wax candle in his hand to give him light to go down the stairs by. He went into a gentleman's coach at Whitehall Gate with three other persons besides himselfe.[2] They went to Westminster Bridge, and there entered into a boat that waited for them (not knowing it). The boat was hiered by Sir Edward Hales early in the evening. One of the three gentlemen came back in the coach from the Bridge, the other two entered into the boat with the King, one of which was Sir Edward Hales. The King and those two landed at Foxhall.[3] There they discharged the boat. The King carryed with him a pair of gamashas,[4] whence the watermen inferred they intended to take horse thence; and from Foxhall went by land to Shieldness, and thence down the River to the River's mouth, whether he came by daylight.

Amongst those very few he communicated his seacret thoughts to (which were but a very few) it abode a considerable debate. First, whether it was His Majestie's interest to depart the Kingdome; secondly, or to go to the Lords at Nottingham and Yorke, and by their advice treat with the Prince; thirdly; or entirely submitt himselfe and all his concernes to the Prince, and committ himselfe, the Queene, and the Prince of Wales to his trust and protection. Strong reasons for every opinion.

You see which he followed, probably upon such like reasons as these. If he fled, he should avoid the present vexation and dishonour the termes he must submitt to would bring upon him, etc. And again, he might reserve himselfe safe for a better juncture, which he might hope for, partly because the Prince possibly may not be the person he is thought to be, and, if he be so, it is impossible for him to satisfie the expectations of the generality of those that fall in with him, because those that do least service expect to engross all the considerable preferments to themselves, and the persons dissatisfied in course fall off to the King. And last of all, because it may be the interest of a great neighbour[5] by force to promote his restauration, and that great neighbour is now endeavouring a generall peace with all his neighbours, excepting Holland, and so may be at leasure to have an opportunity to espouse his interest.

1 Dr Williams's Library, London: MS Morrice Q, p. 346.

2 According to Lord Ailesbury, the King was attended by Sir Edward Hales, who was in charge of managing the first stage of James's flight to the Kentish coast; Ralph Sheldon, the King's trusted Equerry; James de la Badie (*alias* Labadie or Labady), Page of the Bedchamber in Ordinary or 'Back Stairs'; and Dick Smith, the King's Groom. *Memoirs*, p. 194. PRO, SP 44/336, p. 84.

3 Vauxhall, the popular pleasure gardens on the South Bank of the Thames.

4 Gamashes were leather leggings or gaiters worn as protection against mud and wet. Morrice later commented: 'They had gammashas with them to draw like bootes on their shoes and stockin‹g›s, whereupon it is inferred they tooke horse there, and rode a part or all of the way to E‹b›mley. MS Morrice Q, p. 361.

5 Louis XIV of France.

2 Proceedings of the Lord Mayor and Court of Aldermen of the City of London, Guildhall, London, 11 December 1688[1]

Martis, xi° die Decembris 1688, annoque regni Regis ‹Jacobi› Secundi Angliae, etc., quarto.

Chapman, *Maior*; Moore, Prichard, Tulse, Smith, Jeffery, Raymond, North, Daniel, Rich, Stamp, Dashwood, Thoroughgood, Kensey, Ashurst, Lethieulier, Gostlyn, Lane; *et* Fleet *ac* Edwyn, *Vice-comes.*
This day a great number of Lords, both Spirituall and Temporall, were pleased to come downe to this Court and here declare, that the King had this morning withdrawne himselfe, and, therefore, that they thought fitt to assemble in this place, that they might with better security consult and take the best meanes for the publique weale. After which their Lordships retired into the Gallery adjoyning to ·the Councell Chamber, and there they continued together untill towards the evening, and then did my Lord Maior the honour to dine with him at Grocers' Hall, having first bin pleased, by the Earles of Rochester and Weymouth and Bishops of Ely and Winchester,[2] to com‹m›unicat‹e› unto this Court a Declaration drawne up and signed by their Lordshipps, conteyning, in effect, their Lordshipps' resolution to assist the Prince of Orange in fully establishing the said nations in their religion, rights, and libertyes, which had bin evaded by Jesuiticall counsells.[3] And the said noble Lords declared they were by the rest of the Peeres, so assembled, deputed to carry the same to the Prince the next morning.

Whereupon this Court is deeply sencible of, and doth with all humble gratitude acknowledg‹e›, their Lordshipps' great favour vouchsafed to this Court and City therein.

And in this important occasion this Court did think fitt and order, that a Common Councell be duely called to advise what is requisit‹e› to be don‹e› in this conjuncture.[4]

It was also ordered, that Mr Serj‹e›ant Holt, Sir George Treby, and Mr Pollexfen, be im‹m›ediat‹e›ly sent for to this Court, to advise and assist this Court as there may be occasion.

It is likewise thought fit and ordered by this Court, that this evening, and hereafter constantly untill further order, all the City gates be shut, and the chaynes hung up crosse all the streets throughout this City, exactly at 10 of the clock at night, and so to continue untill 6 of the clock next morning. And that this order be forthwith printed and published, that all persons may take notice thereof.

1 Corporation of London Records Office, Guildhall, London: Repertory 94 (1688-1689), pp. 74–6.

2 *sic.* According to the Peers' Journal the second Bishop was Dr Thomas Sprat, Bishop of Rochester, not Dr Peter Mews, Bishop of Winchester. See above, p. 70.

3 For the Peers' Declaration, see above, pp. 71–2.

4 See Appendix 3.

3 Proceedings of the Common Council of the City of London, Guildhall, London, 11 December 1688[1]

Commune Concilium tentum in Camera Gui‹b›haldae Civitatis London' die Martis, undecimo die Decembris 1688, annoque regni Regis Jacobi Secundi, Angliae, etc., quarto, coram Johanne Chapman, milite, Maiore Civitatis London'; Johanne Moore, milite; Willielmo Pritchard, milite; Henrico Tulse, milite; Jacobo Smith, milite; Roberto Jeffery, milite; Dudleo North, milite; Petro Daniell, milite; Petro Rich, milite; Thoma Stam‹p›e, milite; Samu‹e›le Dashwood, milite; Benjamino Thoro‹w›good, milite; Thoma Kensey, milite; Willielmo Ashurst, milite; Christofero Lethieulier, armigero; Willielmo Gost‹l›in, milite; Thoma Lane, milite, Aldermannis, ac Johanne Fleete, milite, Aldermanno, ac uno Vice-‹Comitum› Civitatis praedictae, nec non maiori parte Communiae dictae Civitatis in Communi Concilio tunc et ibidem assemblat'.

Petition or address to the Prince of Orange.
This Court being informed that His Majestie hath this morning bin pleased to withdraw himselfe, and that severall of the Lords Spirituall and Temporall had made a Declaration or addresse to the Prince of Orange; this Court, upon the question put, did unanimously declare their resolution to make application alsoe to His Highnesse, and did agree that an addresse to His Highnesse should forthwith be prepared.

Whereupon Sir William Pritchard, Sir Samuell Dashwood, Sir Thomas Stampe, Sir William Ashurst, Knights and Aldermen; Sir Benjamin Newland, Mr John Morrice, Mr John H‹o›ublon, Mr James H‹o›ublon, Mr Leonard Robinson, Ralph Box, Esquire, Mr Deputy Langham and Mr John Ham‹m›ond, Commoners, togeather with Sir George Treby, Knight, and Mr Common Serjeant, were now by this Court nominated and appointed immediately to withdraw and prepare the said addresse; who, withdrawing, also accordingly after some time returned again, and brought in the draught of such addresse, the tenor whereof is as followeth: that is to say, *To His Highnesse, etc.* Which, being heare read, was very well liked and approved of by this Court *nemine contradicente*. And it is thereupon agreed and ordered by this Court, that the said Committee doe forthwith waite uppon the Prince of Orange, and humbly present to him the said addresse from this Court.[2]

Thanck⟨s⟩ to the Lords for their Declaration.
This Court doth returne their humble thankes to the Lords Spirituall and Temporall, this day assembled at Guildhall, for their Lordships' Declaration touching the present undertaking of His Highnesse the Prince of Orange, and their great favour in com⟨m⟩unicating the same to this Court.

1 Corporation of London Records Office, Guildhall, London: Journal 50, fos 363, 363v. Letter Book ZZ, fos 132v, 133v, which duplicates material from the Journal, but omits the name of Sir Peter Daniel from those present at the meeting.
2 See Appendix 4.

4 Address of the Lord Mayor and Corporation of the City of London to William, Prince of Orange, [Guildhall, 11 December 1688][1]

To His Highnesse the Prince of Orange.

The humble addresse of the Lord Maior, Aldermen, and Commons of the City of London in Common Councell assembled.

May it please Your Highnesse,

Wee taking into consideration Your Highnesse's fervent zeal for the Protestant religion, manifested to the world in your many and hazardous enterprizes, which it hath pleased Almighty God to blesse with miraculous successe, wee render our deepest thanks to the Divine Majesty for the same; and begg leave to present our most humble thankes to Your Highnesse, particulerly for your appearing in armes in this Kingdome, to carry on and perfect your glorious designe to rescue England, Scotland, and Ireland from slavery and Popery, and in a free parliament to establish the religion, the lawes, and the liberties of these Kingdomes upon a sure and lasting foundation.

We have hitherto lookt for some remedy for the oppressions and imminent dangers wee, togeather with our Protestant fellow subjects, laboured under, from His Majestie's concessions and concurrence with Your Highnesse's just and pious purposes expressed in your gracious Declarations; but, therein finding ourselves finally disappointed by His Majestie's withdrawing himselfe, we presume to make Your Highnesse our refuge, and so, in the name of this Capitall City, implore Your Highnesse's protection.

And most humbly beseech Your Highnesse to vouchsafe to repaire to this City, where Your Highnesse will be received with universall joy and satisfaction.

Wagstaffe.

1 PRO, SP 8/2, part 2, fo 97. It was later printed as *The Humble Address . . . of The City of London*, see Bodl., Ashmole G. 14 (cvii).

5 Address of the Lieutenancy of the City of London to William, Prince of Orange, 11 December 1688[1]

To His Highnesse the Prince of Orange.

The humble petition of the Lieutenancy of the Citty of London.

May it please Your Highnesse,

Wee can never sufficiently expresse the deep sence wee have conceived, and shall ever retaine in our hearts, that Your Highnesse hath exposed your person to soe many dangers, both by sea and land, for the preservation of the Protestant religion, and the lawes and liberties of this Kingdome; without which unparallel'd undertakeing, wee must probably have suffered all the miseries that Popery and slavery could have brought upon us.

Wee have beene greately concerned, that before this time wee have not had any seasonable opportunity to give Your Highnesse, and the world, a reall testimony, that it has beene our firme resolution to venture all that is deare to us to attaine those glorious ends, which Your Highynesse has proposed for restoreing and settleing these distracted nations.

Wee, therefore, now unanimously present to Your Highnesse our just and due acknowledgment for that happy releife you have brought to us; and, that wee may not bee wanting in this present conjuncture, wee have putt ourselves into such a posture, that (by the blessing of God) wee may bee capable to prevent all ill designes, and to preserve this Citty in peace and safety, till Your Highness's happy arrivall.

Wee, therefore, humbly desire, that Your Highnesse will please to repaire to this Citty, with what convenient speed you can, for the perfecting the greate worke which Your Highnesse has soe happily begun, to the generall joy and satisfaction of us all. December the 11th, 1688. By the Commissioners' command,

George Evans, Clerke to the Lieutenancy.

1 PRO, SP 8/2, part 2, fo 81. The Commissioners of the Lieutenancy appointed Sir Robert Clayton, Sir William Russell, Sir Basil Firebrace, and Charles Duncombe to carry their address to William on 12 Dec. Bodl., Ashmole H. 23 (iii).

6 Roger Morrice's account of the mob's attack on the Roman Catholic chapels of the metropolis, 11-12 December 1688[1]

The mobile was up in most parts of the town all Tuesday night and committed many tumulteous insolencies, and made the same invasion upon liberty and property, to the great grief of all wise men and to the great scandall of the City. They gathered togeather in the evening about most of the known Mass-houses in town (the Ambassadors' Chappells, that were open and publick, not escaping), and particularly about the Mass-house in Lyncoln's Inn Fields at the Arch, Weld House[2] (where the Spanish Ambassador's Residence is, who is now in town), St. John's, Bucklersbury, Lime Streete,[3] etc., and Seignieur Terese's[4] (the Florentine Resident's) Mass-Chappell, Barillion, the French Ambassador's Mass-Chappell, who is himselfe in town openly, but touched not his house, nor anything that was his, etc. They tooke out of these Mass-Chappells all the furniture, utensills, and combustable materialls, and brought them into the streete and there burnt them.

They have since pulled down, burnt, and carryed away all the timber in most of them, and particularly they have pulled down, burnt, and carryed away the summers,[5] girders, and almost all the joysts, etc., both in the Chappell and in the house in Lyncoln's Inn Fields. They were pulling up the ground joysts on Tuesday night about midnight, and multitudes carrying away bricks in baskets, so that they have left scarce anything but the bare walls.

I thinke few Popish Ambassadors' Chappells, that were open and publick, without their own closets, have escaped, but only Zurette,[6] the Venetian Resident, here, whose house is in Petty France. They have seized upon and exposed to rapine all the rich furniture and plate in the Spanish Ambassador's house, and the treasuries of severall Papists that were deposited with him.

It would have been thought a strange thing that the mobile should touch no goods in the French Ambassador's house, who is the great head of the opposite faction to that of the Prince, and spoile all the goods‹s› in the Spanish Ambassador's house, who is a great agent, under his master, for the Prince; but the reason thereof is plain, for the former Ambassador payes all tradesmen their bills immediat‹e›ly and owes not a penney, the latter contracts great debts and payes no man.

1 Dr Williams's Library, London: MS Morrice Q, pp. 351-2.

2 Weld (or Wild) House, named after Humphrey Weld, who built it in 1657 as an ambassadorial residence, was situated on the east side of Wild Street, an extension of the fashionable Great Queen Street, off Lincoln's Inn Fields. It was occupied after a number of ambassadors from different countries by the unpopular Spanish Ambassador, Don Pedro de Ronquillo. *Survey of London, v: St. Giles-in-the-Fields*, pt ii (London 1914), pp. 93–7, 99.

3 These attacks provided Francis Barlow with subject matter for no less than four playing-cards in his Revolution pack. They were the 3, 10, 4, and 2 of Diamonds respectively.

4 Francesco Terriesi, Resident of the Grand Duke of Tuscany, Ferdinando II. Leti, *Il Teatro Brittanico*, ii. 537-9.

5 Summer, a main beam, especially one supporting the girders or joists of a floor, or the rafters of a roof.

6 Paolo Zarotti (Sarotti), Resident of the Venetian Republic, was a relative new-comer to London's diplomatic community. *Ibid.*, ii 534-5. PRO, SP 44/336, p. 424: passport to land, 12 April 1686.

7 For his debts and an earlier attack on Weld House by the London rabble, who 'fell a-throwing great stones and firebrands at the windows, which they broke all to pieces', apparently being displeased at the news of the capture of Buda, see PRO, Adm. 77/3, no 58: newsletter, London, 15 Feb 1687; and SP 8/4, no 9: James II to William of Orange, Windsor, 10 Sept 1686.

7 William Henry, Prince of Orange, to [James, Duke of Ormonde, Chancellor of the University of Oxford], Abingdon, 12 December 1688[1]

My Lord,

Having receaved an account from His Majestie's Commissioners, dated from Colebrook,[2] at two of the clock in the afternoon yisterday, that His Majestie had quitted Whitehall, without anybodie's knowing whither he was gone, I have thought it absolutely necessary to make all the hast⟨e⟩ I could to London to settle matters there and to prevent the effusion of blood, which for want of my presence might happen, considering the heate people are in. And I hope your University[3] will accept of my good intentions towards them for the present, and I pray remember me very affectionately to them, and assure them of my protection and kindnesse on all occasions, and that I will take the first opportunity I can to come and see them. I am

Abbington,
the 12th December 1688.

Your most affectionate friend,
G. H., Prince d'Orange.

[Henry Gascoigne's endorsement] Prince of Orange. 12 December '88. Oxford.

1 Bodleian Library, Oxford: MS Carte 40, fos 502, 503v. The clerical text is signed by the Prince. Though the letter is unaddressed, the recipient is identified as Ormonde by the content of the letter, his secretary's autograph endorsement, and the presence of the letter among his surviving political papers.

2 i.e., Colnbrook, Bucks., four miles south-east of Slough, on the road to London.

3 For Ormonde's election as Chancellor of the University of Oxford on 23 July 1688, see Oxford University Archives, Convocation Register Bb 29, p. 204. He wrote from Windsor accepting the office on 13 Aug., and was installed at a specially summoned Convocation held in Northumberland House, off the Strand, on 23 Aug. 1688. *Ibid.*, pp. 204, 206–8.

8 James II to Heneage Finch, Earl of Winchilsea, Faversham, 12 December 1688[1]

Feversham,
December 12, 1688.

I am just now come in here, having been last night seased by some of this towne, who telling me you were to be here this day, I would not make myself known to them, thinking to have found you here. But, that not being, I desire you would come hether to me, and that as privat⟨e⟩ly as you could do, that I might advise with you concerning my saf⟨e⟩ty; hoping you have that true loyalty in you, as you will do what you can to secure me from my enemys, of which you shall find me as sensible as you can desire.

For the Earle of Winchilsea.

James R.

1 British Library, MS Additional 32,095 (Malet Collection), fos 298, 299v. Though an early eighteenth-century copy of an otherwise unknown original, its authenticity is beyond question. Its pedigree is avowed in an accompanying note added by the copyist: 'Exactly copied from the original lately in the possession of Heneage, the last Earl of Winchilsea, this 9th of January 1726/7 by J. Creyk'. He also noted that 'the seal' was 'a pheenix in flames on red wax'. The style and content of the letter are equally convincing.

9 Roger Morrice's account of the seizure of William Penn, and the Peers' debate thereon, 12 December 1688[1]

On Wednesday, the 12⟨th⟩ (I thinke it was when the Lords were met) Mr Pen⟨n⟩, as he has a long time done, went in course to Whitehall to the Secretary's Office, and thence to speake with the Lord Godolphin, one of the King's Commissioners, newly come from the Prince. A soldier, meeting Pen⟨n⟩ in the Gallery, said aloud, etc., *what doth this Jesuiticall fellow here*, etc? An Officer, coming by, immediat⟨e⟩ly said, *you must and shall come with me before the Peeres.* Pen⟨n⟩ answered, *if I must, I will*; and so did, etc.

The Officer sent in, and acquainted the Peeres that he had brought Pen⟨n⟩ thither, etc. The Earle of Thanet (it is thought without malice) spake much against him as a very dangerous person, for they knew very well that noble Peere understood him not. Then Sir Robert Sawyer spoak against him as the most dangerous person, and the great invader of lawes, liberties, and properties, and the great agitator for the Jesuits, etc. The Board gave him great discountenance by their lookes; notwithstanding Sawyer spoake a second and third time against him with great violence. Whereupon the Lord Brandon said, *of all men it worst becomes you, Sir Robert Sawyer, to speak against him. His faults, if he has any, are hidden, seacret, and invisible. Yours are open, notorious, committed in the face of the sun, and are upon record, and known to us, and all England, and can be proved, some of them by records, and others of them by multitudes on their own personall knowledge. His are not proved by any man, nor, for ought appeares, cannot ‹be›.* Whereupon Sir Robert held his tongue.

Many of the Lords said, *here is no particular matter charged on, much less proved against this gentleman.* The Marquesse of Hallifax and others said, *we know not how, nor why, this gentleman is brought hither. Those that brought him confess they can prove nothing against him.*

Then it was said, *you are under the ill opinion of the people, and they are in a great firmentation, etc. You would ease us, if you would give in bayle to appeare the first day of the next Terme in Westminster Hall.*

Pen‹n› replyed to this purpose, *my Lords, nothing is, nor can be proved against me, that is criminall. I confesse, I allwaies endeavoured an impartiall liberty of conscience to be established by law, so that the Papists might never be able to null it, and this is all that can be charged upon me, and I count it no crime. Consider, your Lordships are binding over a person neither charged, nor proved guilty, of any offence. Secondly, it is the first president that you have made, and it is a dangerous one, and you have alwaies condemned the committing of men to prison by the Counsell Board, or any other magistrate, without assigning some particular crime. But, seeing your Lordships move me to consent, I will consent.*

The Lord Wharton and the Lord Brandon offered to give bayle for him of 5,000*l.*, and so did severall other Lords. But two gentlemen of great estates in his neighbourhood were his bayle, and so he was bound over, etc., and went thence home.

1 Dr Williams's Library, London: MS Morrice Q, pp. 353–4. Morrice's account amplifies and explains Gwyn's summary treatment of this episode in the Journal, see above, pp. 76–77.

10 The seizure and confinement of George, Lord Jeffreys, 12 December 1688[1]

The Lord Chancellour, as such, though the Seale was taken from him on Saturday, continued dispatching busines‹s› and makeing Chancery orders, etc., for a colour at Whitehall long after it was dark on Monday night, and attempted not to fly till Wednesday morning; and then he went to Wapping, and had before or rather did agree with Mr Porter,[2] master of a ship bound for Newcastle, to carrey him thither, and so went on board to see the ship, and returned back with the master to an alehouse in Hope and Anchor Alley in Wapping.[3] Mr Burnham,[4] being accidentally there, told the master privat‹e›ly, *I know this man. You must not, nor shall not, carry him away.* The Chancellour was in a disguise (as to what cloathing he wears as Chancellour), but otherwise in habit very like to that he often weares at his house in the countrey, and alwaies when he goes a-hunting, save that he had added to it a long cloak, which was lost in the croud.

A person went to the Lord Mayor for a warrant to apprehend him. The Mayor would grant none, but with such limitations, as to time and place, as would certainly make it ineffectuall. The same person went thence to the Counsell at Whitehall, and had their warrant, and by vertue of it apprehended him at Wapping, and put him into a coach, three or four Constables sitting with him therein, and others on each side the coach with blunderbusses, drawn swords, or bagnetts.[5] Before he came to Aldgate a Justice was called in to conduct him, and by this time the croud was great, and growed beyond measure after he entered into the City, so that they altered their purposes of carrying him to the Counsell at Whitehall, and turned to the Lord Mayor's house, which is Grocers' Hall, to have him examined there.

The croud broke into his court and was very tumulteous, so the Mayour spoak to them out of a window or balconey, and told them the prisoner was safe, and should be kept so, and brought to justice, and sent to the Tower in their sight, etc. All this was before dinner. And as the Chancellour and the Lord Mayor sate at table, the Lord Mayor, considering that his oracle and patron was brought before him to be examined as a criminall, was overwhelmed hereby, so that he began to fall into all such distortions and motions of his hands, fingers, feet, face, and eyes, as are the certain presages of an immediate appoplectick, which issued into an appoplexie. Dr Lower[6] was sent for, and came very quickly, and found the Mayor dangerously ill, and left him so.

The Chancellour was forthwith in the sight of the croud carryed to the Tower, and to qualifie the mobile, and keepe them from violence, he put his head severall times out of the coach, that all might see it was he. He said, *it is I, it is I. I am in your custody and at your mercy.* It is reported ‹that› Mr Arnold,[7] the prisoner who has now liberty to go abro‹a›de, made the first discovery of him. Thus the Chancellour, that vomited out such rude, unmannerly, and brutall language (that was a reproach to the Bench on which he sate) against all men, is a sad subject of counter-passion, and the mobile pour out the same vomit upon him.

He was sent, without any commitment, under a guard of some Companies of the City Train Bands to the Tower of London, where the Lord Lucas received him upon a voluntary resignation, till quickly after a warrant came from the Lords assembled in Counsell for his commitment.[8]

The Lord Chancellour swears the King most faithfully promised him to give him notice when he fled, and that he should fly with him, but failed so to do, and that caused him to make no speedier preparations for his own flight any other way.

1 Dr Williams's Library, London: MS Morrice Q, pp. 355-6. The narrative augments and corrects that given in the standard biography, G. W. Keeton, *Lord Chancellor Jeffreys and the Stuart cause* (London 1965), pp. 452-4.

2 James Porter, master of *The Hope*, alias *Hopewell*, of London, then moored near Shadwell Dock, on the Middlesex Bank of the Thames.

3 *The Red Cow*, described by the Hon. Roger North as 'a little peddling alehouse . . . in Anchor and Hope Alley, near King Edward's Stairs', one of the busy landing-places of Wapping.

4 Presumably North's 'scrivener of Wapping', whom Jeffreys had previously abused in court as 'that monster', a Trimmer, and the unnamed person who had 'intimated' Jeffreys's whereabouts to the Peers.

5 i.e., bayonet.

6 Dr Richard Lower, FRS (1667), of King Street, Covent Garden, the eminent Oxford physiologist, who had built up a commanding reputation and lucrative practice in the capital.

7 Probably John Arnold, the former Whig MP for Monmouth (1680-1) and a rabid anti-Catholic, whose defamation of the Duke of Beaufort had resulted in imprisonment following an action of *scandalum magnatum* in 1683.

8 For the Peers' warrant and the Lord Nottingham's recurrent concern over the failure to specify the cause of Jeffreys's commitment, see above, pp. 79, 80, 104, 118, and the next item.

11 *Acknowledgement by Robert, Lord Lucas, of Lord Jeffreys's committal to the Tower of London, The Tower, 12 December 1688*[1]

I, Robert, Lord Lucas, Cheif Governour of the Tower of London, do hereby acknowledge to have had and received of and from Sir Henry Johnson and Sir John Freind, Knights, and Champion Ashby and Thomas Cook, Esquires, the body of George, Lord Jeffreys, committed to my custody by warrant from diverse of the Peers of this Realme and some of the Privy Councill. Dated at the Tower, this 12th day of December 1688.

Lucas.

1 British Library, MS Additional 22,183 (Johnson Papers), fo 140.

12 *Orders of the Council of War summoned and held by James II's Admiral of the Fleet, George, Lord Dartmouth, in response to the directives of the provisional government,* HMS Resolution, *Spithead, 13 December 1688*[1]

At a Council of Warr held on board
His Majesty's Ship Resolution
at Spithead, 13 December 1688
PRESENT

George, Lord Dartmouth, Admirall; Sir John Berry, Rear-Admirall; Lord Berkeley; Captain Davis; Sir William Jennens; Captain Akerman; Captain Ashby; Captain Delaval; Captain Skelton; Captain Carter; Captain Shovell; Captain Tyrrell; Captain Botham; Sir William Boothe; Captain Tennant; Captain Matthew Aylmer; Captain Wrenn; Captain St. Loe; Captain Hartings; Captain Nevill; Captain George Aylmer; Captain Ridley; Captain Coale; Captain Montgomery; Captain Beverly; Captain John Laten; Captain Cornwall; Captain Jenifer; Captain Leake; Captain Wivell.

The Admirall haveing received an order from the Lords Spirituall and Temporall, dated at Guildhall, the 11° of this instant December, the same, being read, was as follows, vizt: [a copy of the Peers' letter is here inserted][2]

Ordered:

That all acts of hostility cease.

That all acts of hostility with the Prince of Orange's Fleet doe from this time cease, and that all Roman Catholick Officers in the Fleete be im‹m›ediately removed out of their respective commands.

Each Captain to give an account of the Roman Catholic Officers on board him.

That every Captain give the Admirall an account of the said Roman Catholique Officers, soe quit‹t›ing and resigneing, and what vacancys of employments there are in their ships from this or any other occasion.

That the unanimous opinion of the Fleet be signifyed to the Prince for putting themselves under His Highnesse's protection.

That application be im‹m›ediately made to the Prince of Orange, signifying the unanimous resolution of the Fleete to putt themselves under His Highnesse's protection, in order to the King and Kyngdome's service and re-settlement; and that immediately Captain Matthew Aylmer and Captain Anthony Hartings be despatched to the Prince for His Highnesse's notice thereof.

1 National Maritime Museum Library, Greenwich: MS Dartmouth 16 (Order Book, 1688), pp. 164-5.

2 The text of the copy agrees, with many insignificant scribal variations, with that given above in the Journal, see pp. 68–9.

13 Roger Morrice's account of the 'Irish Night', or 'Great Fear' of a Popish massacre of Protestants in the capital and countryside, 13 December 1688.[1]

On Wednesday in the forenoon, pretty earley, the Lords (about 30 in number) mett in Counsell at Whitehall, and made at least a dozen orders about publick matters, and some of the best that could be framed for suppressing the mobile.[2] And for that end appointed some Regiments of Train Bands, and other soldiers, to stand upon the watch all over that end of the town all that night; and the City and Westminster count themselves very secure now under the protection either of the Militia, or of the soldiers that are received again into pay here, or of any other soldiers that are in or about the town (or, indeed, elsewhere in the Kingdome), and the town was very quiet on Wednesday night till about midnight.

And then a universall terrible alarme was taken all over London and Westminster with a fear and confident persuasion, that they should have their throats cut by the French and by the Papists; insomuch that almost all, but soldiers and footmen, kept in their houses, locked and bolted their doors. Luminaries were set up in all windowes in Great Lyncoln's Inn Fields[3] (and in other places), like as there is at lotteries; not a house excepted, Protestant, nor Papist, wherein any inhabitant resided. Some houses had a hundred lights, some fifty, some less, according to the number of candlesticks they had. It was grounded, no doubt, upon the proliphick phant‹a›sie of some hypocondraicall persons, who naturally believe all the dangers to be reall that their distempers can suggest to them, for, upon the most accurate enquiry that wise men can make, there was no kind of colour given. But at this time, and during this fermentation, the French and Papists are in ten thousand times more danger themselves. And to conclude this unaccountable consternation, the Lords at Counsell at Whitehall, who had sate at Counsell in the afternoon late, were[4] all called out of their beds at 12 a clock at night, and met in Counsell before one, and there sate till fair daylight, near 8 a clock on Thursday morning ...[5]

The like invisible feares possessed most part of the Kingdome, as London was possessed with in the beginning of this weeke, to wit upon the 10‹th›, 11‹th›, and 12‹th› instant. It circulated so generally throughout the Kingdome, that it is in vain to name particular countyes, but in none it was greater then in Buckinghamshire, Northamptonshire, Leicestershire, and especially Staffordshire, Derbyshire, and Nottinghamshire. In those three last countyes they sate up most of the nights in this weeke, and the universall cry was their throats should be cut. And the post-letters from London on Tuesday, the 11‹th›, and Thursday, the 13‹th›, increased their fears, if that were possible; and that which added thereunto in the close of this weeke was a universall report, that the disbanded Irish, who were thereby provoked, would joyne with the English Papists to cut all their throats.

In very many townes throughout the nation they staid up all night upon the watch, and the countrey came crouding in and sent all the horsemen and armed footmen they could raise, etc., into them.

1 Dr Williams's Library, London: MS Morrice Q, pp. 352, 359.

2 See above, pp. 75–6.

3 The grander, more northerly square, as opposed to the more irregularly shaped Little Lincoln's Inn Fields to the south of Portugal

Row. As one of the more recently built and classically inspired developments in London domestic architecture, it housed a rich clientele of noblemen, courtiers, and well-to-do citizens.

4 *MS* has *well.*

5 See above, p. 84.

14 *George, Lord Dartmouth, to the Peers, from on board* HMS Resolution, *at Spithead, 15 December 1688*[1]

My Lords,

Upon your Lordships' conveening at Guildhall the 11th instant, on His Majesty's private withdrawing himselfe, I have received from Mr Secretary Pepys the subscribed signiffication of your Lordships' pleasure at that great meeting, where you have resolved (for the preventing the effusion of bloud among us at this conjuncture, in consideration of the Prince of Orainge his Fleete being still on the English coast), that all acts of hostility should cease, and all Popish officers in the Fleete be removed out of theire respective commands.[2] On which weighty matters, as the only meanes, under God, to preserve the King, my master, and establish the laws, and proppertyes, and the Protestant religion, I had deliberated with myselfe (upon the surprizall and unfortunate newes of His Majesty's withdrawing himselfe) before the receipt of your Lordships', and was putting it in execution, and it is now actually done; and have likewise (withy the unanimous concurrence of the Fleete) addressed myselfe (as I see your Lordships have done) to the Prince of Orainge for the better effecting and set⟨t⟩ling all things that conduce to the King and Kingdome's safety and generall good, wherein I prommis⟨e⟩ to contribute as farr as is in my powre;[3] and, therefore, humbly reffering your Lordships, for all farther occurrances of the Fleete, to the particular account thereof I have with this sent to Mr Peppys, Secretary of the Admiralty, I subscribe myselfe Your Lordships' most humble servant,

Resolution, Spithead,

December 15th, 1688.   Dartmouth.

To the Lords Spirituall and Temporall, that were assembled at Guildhall, the 11th of December, 1688. London.

1 Bodleian Library, MS Rawlinson A. 186, fos 458, 459v.

2 See above, p. 68.

3 On 29 Nov. William of Orange had appealed to Dartmouth to join with him on the basis of 'the Protestant religion and the liberties of England'. Dartmouth had replied on 12 Dec 1688. *HMC Dartmouth*, pp. 219, 232.

15 *William Henry, Prince of Orange, to the Lord Mayor and City of London, Windsor, 16 December 1688*[1]

My Lord,

I have receaved just now a letter from the King, in which he intimates to me that he is coming backe to London, which is done without my approbation; nor doe I thinke it proper at this time, not knowing what it may produce, considering the present circumstances of affaires. I have, therefore, sent Monsieur Zeulesteyn to desire that he would stay his journey. This I thought fitt to acquaint you withall, an⟨d t⟩o desire you to keep yourself in that posture, that may be most for your safety and the security of the City; and I shall make all the speed I can to your assistance, and be with you on Tuesday next. You may give full creditt to what these two gentlemen shall further tell you upon this occasion. Assuring you of my kindnes⟨s⟩ and protection on all occasions, I am

                                              Your most affectionate friend,

Windesore,
16 December 1688.   W. H., Prince of Orange.

For my Lord Mayor, and the Court of Aldermen, and Common Councell, London.

1 Corporation of London Records Office, Guildhall, London: Small MSS Box 29, no. 15a: a clerical copy of the lost original, written on a single folded sheet of paper, which also contains a copy of 'the Common Councell's answear'. It is endorsed: 'Copy of the Prince of Orange's letter to the Common Councell, with their answear, 16 December '88'. The MS is torn with slight losses of text.

16 Roger Morrice's account of the adjourned meeting of the Lord Mayor and Court of Aldermen, Grocers' Hall, 16 December 1688, 4 p.m.[1]

At 4 a clock on ‹the› Lord's Day, the 16‹th›, the Court of Aldermen (to which hour it had been adjourned, as abovesaid) met at the Lord Mayor's house, to the makeing of which Court there must be above 12 Aldermen, etc. They debated of goeing to congratulate the King's comeing to Whitehall about an hour before that time (with some Troopes of Horse and, it is said, about a hundred of the rabble goeing bare headed before him, as they had used to do).

Some few murmured a little against this motion. At last the Court asked Sir George Treby, the Recorder, who was newly restored to his place, his opinion, who answered much to this purpose. First, the Court must consider what they had done. 2‹nd›, who they were. First, they must consider what they had done but a few dayes since, viz. the 11th instante ‹they had› made an address to the Prince, acknowledging how great a favour he had done them in taking up armes in defence of their religion, etc., and had also invited him to the town, and how utterly inconsistent this was with their congratulating the King's comeing to town, who must necessarily be come with a designe to oppose the Prince, and, if the Prince came, they must be forced to make another address to him with shame, or expose themselves to the maintaining of a war against him.

It is true the King had legall authority, but the Prince they had invited had power, etc. And there was another power, though it were very unwar‹r›antable, that the mobile had, and contradicting the invitation they had given the Prince, which quieted the rabble, they might give them a provocation to commit such forceable rapes upon their houses, as they had done upon others.

It is true they had used in ordinary cases to congratulate His Majestie upon his return to town, but this was an extraordinary case. The Peeres, whose account was uncontrolable, had assured them the King had left the Kingdome with an intent not to returne, and if he should come to Court with the same intention, by addressing to him they rather affronted him then obliged him, etc. And besides, when the Lords sent the Earle of Feversham to the King at Shildness or Feversham, he was as much in the Kingdom as when at Whitehall, and then they thought not fit to send any address to him, and this should be a president[2] to them, with much more to this purpose; so the Court was satisfied, and the debate fell, and so they did not go to congratulate the King, nor order publick bonfires, nor ringing of bells, as they had thought to have done.

Notwithstanding some of the Prince's Vauntguards came upon the said Saturday at night to town, yet many that had ventured for the Prince went out of London to him at Windsor that night for fear of being apprehended, for no men were sure which way the current would run.

1 Dr Williams's Library, London: MS Morrice Q, p. 365
2 i.e., precedent.

17 The City of London to William, Prince of Orange, The Guildhall, London, 17 December 1688[1]

May it please Your Highnesse,

Wee, having received Your Highnesse's gracious letter of the 16th instant[2] by the hands of two honourable persons, Sir Robert Howard and Mr Powle,[3] humbly thanke Your Highnesse for communicating your gracious purposes to this City, and for the assurance of your kindnes‹s› and protection to us. We cannot forbear to renew, likewise, our humblest thanks to Your Highnesse for your progresse in your great and glorious undertaking for preserving our religion, lawes, and liberties; and we assure Your Highnesse, that we shall not spare to expose our lives and estates in your assistance for those ends, and for preventing all dangers from those restlesse spirits that have now appeared.

For the present, we have ordered an extraordinary guard of our City Forces to be in armes,[4] which we hope may be sufficient for our security.

We doe also thanke Your Highnesse for your promise of making speed to our assistance, and humbly desire Your Highnesse to accept the tender of our readinesse to prepare or appoint a convenient place for your reception within this City, if Your Highnesse, either to be free from the resort of persons disaffected to your great self and glorious designe,[5] or for your better safety, shall be pleased to accept the same.

Your Highnesse's most humble servants,

The Maior, Aldermen,[6] and Commons of the City of London in Common Councell assembled.

London, 17 December 1688.

By their order, Wagstaffe.

1 PRO, SP 8/2, part 2, fo 89.

2 See previous item, Appendix 15.

3 The minutes of the Common Council record: 'Att this Court Sir Robert Howard and Henry Powle, Esquire, brought to this Court a letter from His Highnesse the Prince of Orange, which was here openly read'. They were also used by the City to return its answer, the Town Clerk being authorized, after signing and sealing it 'with the common seale', to deliver it to them 'to be by them humbly presented to His Highnesse the Prince of Orange from the Court'. Corporation of London Records Office: Journal 50, fos 364, 364v; Letter Book ZZ, fos 134, 134v.

4 'For the better security of this City in this present conjuncture this Court doth desire the Commissioners of Leiftenency for this City forthwith to cause the guards of Trained Bands to be for the present increased to the number of three Regiments'. Ibid., fo 134v; Journal 50, fo 364v.

5 The draft had originally read: 'free from the resort of those whoe are enemies to our religion and lawes', i.e., the Papists. See the 'Common Councell's answear to the Prince of Orange's letter, 17 December '88'. Small MSS Box 29, no 15b.

6 As Chapman was still ill, Sir John Moore deputized for him. Attending the Court were Aldermen Prichard, Tulse, Smith, Jeffreys, Treby (Recorder), Raymond, North, Rich, Stampe, Dashwood, Kinsey, Ashurst, Christopher Lethieullier, Gostlyn, Lane; Fleet and Edwyn (Sheriffs). Journal 50, fo 364.

18 Roger Morrice's account of James II's enforced removal from Whitehall, and of William of Orange's subsequent arrival at St. James's Palace, 18 December 1688[1]

On Monday, the 17‹th›, in the evening about 10 or 11 a clock the Earle of Cravon settled the Guards before the King went to bed, and about one a clock, after the King was in bed, Count Solmes (Colonell of the Prince's Guards, who in other countries is an executioner, like our Lieutenant of the Tower), the Marquesse of Hallifax, the Earle of Shrewsbury, and the Lord Delamere came with a message (I thinke not a letter) to the King from the Prince.[2] They desired admission to the King. They were admitted immediat‹e›ly, and the contents of their message was to this purpose. That His Majestie would remove from Whitehall, the concourse of Papists and other enemies to the Kingdome had been so very great at Whitehall on ‹the› Lord's Day in the evening, and on Monday, that the peace was thereby indangered, etc. That His Majestie, if he pleased, might go to Ham, a pleasant cituation, etc. But he chose rather to go to Rochester. Count Solmes immediat‹e›ly sent to Sion to know the Prince's pleasure, who concurred thereunto.

Then Count Solmes pressed the adding of some new Troopes of the Prince's, just then come to town, to the Guards at Whitehall. The King was unwilling of that. But Count Solmes said it was very necessary they should have shelter, and so, I thinke, they were added to the Guards, for Count Solmes was somewhat positive, and so the King concurred.

His Majestie said when these four first came in to the King in bed, and Count Solmes delivered the message, *must I rise now*? Count Solmes replyed, *you need not rise now, or till 8 a clock, or till your usuall levy*. The King said this was a force upon him, and he was driven hereby from London. Count Solmes saith, *force must be opposed by force*, and ‹that› the King raised the first force for the destroying of the subject, the religion, lawes, liberties, and lives, and had made a great progresse therein.

His Majestie went from Whitehall on Tuesday before noon. His three coaches and saddle naggs went through Cheapside about 11 a clock, and so over London Bridg‹e›. His Majestie went in his barge from Whitehall about 11 a clock towards the Bridge, and there attended him in the barge the Lord Ayl‹e›sbury, the Lord Ar‹r›an, the Lord Dunbarton, and Mr Griffin, and thence His Majestie went to Rochester.

The King's army was all sent on Monday, the 17‹th›, some miles out of London.

Ingressus. The Prince of Orange came from Sion on Tuesday, the 18‹th› instant, and came to St. James's betweene 12 and one a clock that day. He came through the Parke to it, so that he came not into the City at all, but severall of his Guards did come into the City, and some of his wearied and weakest horse that had much luggage with them. The universall joy and acclamation at his entrance was like that at the Restauration in all things, except in debaucheries, of which there was as little appearance as has been known upon such occasion and such a publick concourse. An orang‹e› woman without Ludgate gave divers baskets full of oranges to the Prince's officers and soldiers, as they marched by, to testifie her affection towards them. Divers ordinary women in Fleet Street shooke his soldiers by the hand, as they came by, and cryed, *welcome, welcome. God blesse you, you come to redeeme our religion, lawes, liberties, and lives. God reward you*, etc. I heard and saw these two passages myselfe.

1 Dr Williams's Library, London: MS Morrice Q, pp. 377-8.

2 For the message ordered to be delivered to James, see above, p. 58.

NOTES TO THE INTRODUCTION

ABBREVIATIONS

Akerman	*Moneys Received and Paid For Secret Services Of Charles II. And James II*, ed. J. Y. Akerman (Camden Society 1851).		*Society of Jesus ... in the sixteenth and seventeenth centuries* (7 vols, 1875–83).	Mulgrave	*The Works of John Sheffield, Earl of Mulgrave* (2 vols, 1753).

Akerman — *Moneys Received and Paid For Secret Services Of Charles II. And James II*, ed. J. Y. Akerman (Camden Society 1851).

Ailesbury — *Memoirs of Thomas, Earl of Ailesbury written by himself* (Roxburghe Club, 2 vols, Westminster 1890).

Bramston — *The Autobiography of Sir John Bramston*, ed. Braybrooke (Camden Society 1845).

Browning, *Danby* — A. Browning, *Thomas Osborne Earl of Danby, and Duke of Leeds, 1632–1712* (3 vols, Glasgow 1944–51).

Burnet — G. Burnet, *History of My Own Time*, ed. J. M. Routh (6 vols, Oxford 1833).

Cavelli — Marquise Campana di Cavelli, *Les Derniers Stuarts à Saint Germain en Laye* (2 vols, Paris 1871).

Clar. Corr. — *The Correspondence of Henry Hyde, Earl of Clarendon, And of his brother, Laurence Hyde*, ed. J. S. Clarke (2 vols, 1816).

Dalton — C. Dalton, *English Army Lists and Commission Registers, 1661–1714* (6 vols, 1892–1904).

Evelyn — *The Diary of John Evelyn*, ed. E. S. de Beer (6 vols, Oxford 1955).

Foley — H. Foley, *Records of the English Province of the* Society of Jesus ... in the sixteenth and seventeenth centuries (7 vols, 1875–83).

Foxcroft, *Halifax* — H. C. Foxcroft, *Life and letters of Sir George Savile, Bart, First Marquis of Halifax* (2 vols, 1898).

Hatton Corr. — *Correspondence of the Family of Hatton ... 1601–1704*, ed. E. M. Thompson (2 vols, Camden Society 1878).

Huygens, *Journaal* — 'Journaal van Constantijn Huygens, den zoon, van 21 October 1688 tot 2 September 1696', in *Werken Uitgegeven door het Historische Genootschaap, Gevestigdd te Utrecht*, new series, xxiii (Utrecht 1876).

Japikse — *Correspondentie van Willem III en van Hans Willem Bentinck, eersten Graaf van Portland*, ed. N. Japikse (Rijks geschiedkundige publ. 23, 24, 26–28 (5 vols, The Hague, 1927–37).

Luttrell — Narcissus Luttrell, *A Brief Historical Relation of State Affairs from September 1678 to April 1714* (6 vols, Oxford 1857).

Mazure, *Révolution* — F. A. J. Mazure, *Histoire de la Révolution de 1688 en Angleterre* (3 vols, Paris 1825).

Müller — P. L. Müller, *Wilhelm III von Oranien and Georg Friedrich von Waldeck* (2 vols, The Hague 1873–80).

Mulgrave — *The Works of John Sheffield, Earl of Mulgrave* (2 vols, 1753).

Powley — E. B. Powley, *The English Navy in the Revolution of 1688* (Cambridge 1928).

Steele — R. Steele, *Tudor and Stuart Proclamations 1485–1714* (2 vols, Oxford 1910).

Turner — F. C. Turner, *James II* (1948).

Verney Memoirs — *Memoirs Of the Verney Family*, ed. F. P. and M. M. Verney (2 vols, 1907).

Wood, *Life & Times* — *The Life and Times of Anthony Wood, antiquary of Oxford, 1632–1695, described by himself*, ed. A. Clark (5 vols, Oxford 1891–1900).

PRO — Public Record Office, London.
SP — State Paper
PC — Privy Council
Adm — Admiralty
BL — British Library, London
Bodl — Bodleian Library, Oxford
Ld Lt — Lord Lieutenant
Dep Lt — Deputy Lieutenant
Pr Cllr — Privy Councillor
succ. — Succeeded
cr. — Created
Kt — Knight
Bt — Baronet
HMC — Historical Manuscripts Commission (the name of the Report follows).
I — Ireland
S — Scotland
Add — Additional

1 'An Act for Safety and Preservation of His Majesties Person and Government against Treasonable and Seditious practices and attempts'. *The Statutes of the Realm*, v (1819), 304–5.

2 Evelyn, iv. 7.

3 On 15 June 1673 he resigned from being Lord High Admiral, Governor of Portsmouth, and Warden of the Cinque Ports. Turner, pp. 105–6.

4 Evelyn, iv. 87. Cavelli, i. 166–7.

5 *The Diaries and Papers of Sir Edward Dering, Second Baronet, 1644 to 1684*, ed.

M. F. Bond (1976), pp. 125, 126. On 10 Oct. 1678 Evelyn noted that the Catholics were 'exceeding bold, and busy every where, since the Duke forebore to go any longer to the Chapell'. Evelyn, iv. 154.

6 J. Bossy, *The English Catholic Community 1570-1850* (1975), pp. 182-94. A. Whiteman and M. Clapison, *The Compton Census of 1676: a critical edition* (Oxford 1986), appendix F.

7 R. A. Beddard, 'The Restoration Church', in *The Restored Monarchy 1660-1688*, ed. J. R. Jones (1973), pp. 156-9, 166-7.

I The Dynastic Context

1 *By the King, A Proclamation.* Whitehall, 20 Sept. See also James to Sophia, Electress of Hanover, 28 Sept., in *Memoirs of Mary, Queen of England 1689-1693*, ed. R. Doebner (London 1886), pp. 71-2.

2 N. Japikse, *Prins Willem III De Stadhouder-Koning* (2 vols, Amsterdam 1930-33). P. J. Blok, *History of the People of the Netherlands* (5 vols, 1898-1912) iv, 265, 421, 442, 466 ff. P. Geyl, *Orange and Stuart 1641-72 (1969)*, pp. 361-2, 420-1. *The Works of Sir William Temple, Bart.* (4 vols, 1814), i. 94 ff. S. Baxter, *William III* (New York, 1966), pp. 32-6, 111, 182, 185-6.

3 PRO, SP 8/2, pt 2, fos 188-9: French copy, translated in J. Dalrymple *Memoirs of Great Britain and Ireland* (3 vols, 1790), ii. 132-3.

4 Japikse, *Correspondentie*, I, ii. 242.

5 BL, MS Add. 34,512, fo 11v.

6 See below, pp. 146ff.

II Royal Catholicism

1 It was the result of a trade boom and better fiscal administration. C. D. Chandaman, *The English Public Revenue, 1660-88* (Oxford 1975), pp. 256-61.

2 Bodl., MS Tanner 28, fo 278; MS Don. c. 38, fos 341, 362. J. Childs, *The Army, James II, and the Glorious Revolution* (Manchester 1980), p. 184.

3 Dr. Williams's Library, MS Morrice Q, p. 375.

4 House of Commons' resolution of 28 Jan. 1689. *The Journal of the House of Commons*, x (1803), 14.

5 Dr. Williams's Library, MS Morrice Q, p. 375.

6 James, Duke of York, to Pope Innocent XI, Newmarket, 30 Mar. 1682: BL, MS. Add. 38,846, fo 37.

7 J. A. Williams, 'English Catholicism under Charles II', *Recusant History*, vii (1963), 139.

8 For James's sense of his inadequate achievement, which was 'poco a riguardo di quello che si conosceva in obbligo di dover fare', see BL, MS Add. 15,395, fo 390.

9 Bodl., MS Eng. misc. e. 4, fo 13: Hilkiah Bedford's report of Lauderdale's conversation with his chaplain, George Hickes.

10 Dr. Williams's Library, MS Morrice Q, p. 375: MS has 'loose', which I have corrected.

11 Reprinted in E. N. Williams, *The Eighteenth-Century Constitution, 1688-1815* (Cambridge 1960), p. 26.

12 R. A. Beddard, 'Vincent Alsop and the Emancipation of Restoration Dissent', *Journal of Ecclesiastical History*, xxiv (1973), pp. 181, 184.

13 Luttrell, i. 374. Bishop Compton's recommendation to his clergy, Fulham House, 2 Apr. 1686, 'in pursuance of His Majesties Commands'. R. G. Gwynn, *Huguenot heritage, the history and contribution of the Huguenots in Britain* (1985), pp. 130ff (though I cannot accept his view of James II).

14 House of Commons' resolution of 28 Jan. 1689. *The Journal of the House of Commons*, x. 14.

15 For Charles I, see K. Sharpe, 'Archbishop Laud', *History Today*, (August 1983), pp. 29-30; and for James I, see K. Fincham and P. Lake, 'The Ecclesiastical Policy of King James I', *Journal of British Studies*, xxiv (1985), 169-207.

16 PRO, PC 2/71, fo 6. *The London Gazette*, no. 2006. R. A. Beddard, 'The Church of Salisbury and the accession of James II', *Wilts. Archaeological Magazine*, lxvii (1972), 132ff.

17 James began his reign by going publicly and daily to Mass at Whitehall. PRO, SP 31/1, nos 34, 40.

18 J. Miller, *Popery and Politics in England 1660-1688*, pp. 239-40.

19 *The History of the King's Works*, ed. H. M. Colvin, v (1976), pp. 290-93. Evelyn, iv. 534-5. K. Downes, *English Baroque Architecture* (1966), pp. 22-3.

20 Akerman, pp. 162, 166, 172, 184ff. Luttrell, i. 405, 409, 420, 433. W. M. Brady, *The Episcopal Succession in England, Scotland, and Ireland A.D. 1400 to 1875* (Rome 1876-7), iii. 140-1.

21 Castlemain was to assure Pope Innocent XI 'of our filial obedience to him as Supreme Head of the Church upon earth and Christ's Vicar, and also of the particular value and great veneration we have for his person'. Bodl., MS Rawlinson A. 257, fo 243. PRO, SP 44/56, pp. 320, 363; 337, pp. 11, 90ff, 267; Adm. 77/3, nos

31, 54. J. M. Wright, *Ragguaglio Della Solenne Comparsa, Fatta in Roma . . . MDCLXXXVII, Dall'Illustrissimo... Conte Di Castelmaine, Ambasciadore Straordinario... Di Giacomo Secundo* (Rome 1687).

22 Bramston, p. 280. *The Diary of Dr. Thomas Cartwright, Bishop of Chester*, ed. J. Hunter (Camden Society, xxii, 1843), pp. 52, 53. Ailesbury, i. 152-3, 165. Luttrell, i. 399, 402, 408.

23 In Jan. the Franciscans converted a house, which had been 'lately the countess of Bathe's', and the Dominicans opened their chapel on 2 Feb. 1688. Luttrell, i. 427, 430.

24 Philipp Hoffmann to Leopold I, London, 23 Apr. 1688. *Cavelli*, ii. 185.

25 With the fleeting exception of Bishop Smith under Charles I. D. Mathew, *Catholicism in England* (2nd edn, 1948), p. 78 and Dom Basil Hemphill, *The Early Vicars Apostolic of England 1685-1750* (1954), pp. 9, 16. Akerman, pp. 208-9.

26 Brady, *The Episcopal Succession in England*, iii. 145-6, 147, 203, 243, 281.

27 *A Pastoral Letter From The Four Catholic Bishops To The Lay-Catholics of England* (London: Printed by Henry Hills, Printer to the King's most Excellent Majesty for his House-hold and Chappel; and are to be sold at his Printing-house on the Ditchside of Black-Friers. 1688), pp. 2, 5.

28 BL, MS Add. 34,503, fo 12v.

29 Bodl., MS Tanner 28, fos 147ff: draft answer to the *Pastoral Letter* of the Catholic Bishops, written by Dr. Henry Maurice, chaplain to Archbishop Sancroft of Canterbury. See also N. Sykes, *William Wake* (2 vols, Cambridge 1960), i. 20-8.

III The Tories' King

1 R. A. Beddard, 'William Sancroft, as Archbishop of Canterbury, 1677-1691' (Oxford D.Phil. thesis), chapters 1 and 2.

2 PRO, SP 31/1, no.40: R. L. to the Mayor of Bridgewater, 24 Feb. 1685.

3 R. A. Beddard, 'A relic of Stuart Popery: Prayers for Queen Mary Beatrice, anno 1688', *The Bodleian Library Record*, viii (1971), 274.

4 Burnet, iii. 244-5, 246-9, 250-9, 275, 318-23.

5 *Ibid.*, iii. 241. Besides such backing being useful to William in coming to England, it was an argument for winning over the States General, who, in the end, adopted 'the entreaty of the English gentry' as 'the cause of their furnishing' William with ships and money. Bodl., Rawlinson Letters 109, fo 11. BL, MS Sloane 972, fo 29.

6 Reprinted in Williams, *The Eighteenth-Century Constitution*, pp. 8-10.

IV The Dutch Invasion

1 Powley, pp. 35-6.

2 'Tot maintien van de Protestantse religie ende de Vryheyt van het Coninckrijk van Groot Brittagne'. Japikse, *Correspondentie*, I, ii. 610-613.

3 In Mar. 1686 Vice-Admiral Herbert 'was turned out of all his places', on refusing to agree to the repeal of the Test Acts. Though at first forbidden to leave England, he stole over to Holland. Luttrell, i. 396, 397, 398, 450, 451. PRO, SP 44/337, pp. 231, 245; 69, p. 194; 164, pp. 387-8. For William's expectation that the English seaman would give 'an entire credit to everything' Herbert would say to them in his name, see BL, MS. Egerton, 2,621, fo 13: William to the officers and men of the English Fleet, Dieren, 29 Sept. 1688. *Admiral Herbert's Letter To All Commanders of Ships of Sea-men In His Majesties Fleet*, despatched from 'Aboard the Leyden in the Goree', n.d.

4 Powley, pp. 43-4: Hellevoetsluys, 17/27 Oct. 1688.

5 *Ibid.*, pp. 45, 70-2. William to Waldeck, 2 Nov. 1688. P. L. Müller, *Wilhelm III von Oranien und Georg Friedrich von Waldeck* (2 vols, The Hague, 1873-1880), ii. 116. BL, MS Add. 34,503, fo 14: 'Journal du Voyage d'Angleterre commencé le 28e Octobre 1688, N. Stile'. *HMC Dartmouth*, p. 178. Burnet, iii. 313-14. Huygens, *Journaal*, pp. 11-12: 9 Nov. N.S. *Archives ou Correspondance Inédite de la Maison d'Orange-Nassau*, ed. G. Groen van Prinsterer, 2nd ser., v (Utrecht 1861), 592-3.

6 BL, MS Egerton 2,621, fo 49: G. Burnet to Arthur Herbert, 2 Nov. 1688. Burnet, iii. 324-5.

7 Japikse, *Correspondentie*, I, ii. 618-19. Burnet, iii. 284, 325-6. Browning, *Danby*, i. 387-88 Powley, pp. 45, 79-80.

8 'Instructie by Sijne Hoogheit gegeven aen den Heer Arthur Herbert, sijnen aengestelden Lieutenant Admiral-General', 27 Oct. 1688 (N.S.), in Japikse, *Correspondentie*, I, ii. 613-16.

9 BL, MS Egerton 2,621, fo 29: William to Hans Willem Bentinck, *The Brill*, [2 Nov. 1688], 'a un ⟨h⟩eure'.

10 J. P. Kenyon, *The Nobility in the Revolution of 1688*, p. 12.

11 BL, MS Add. 34,503, fo 14. Powley, pp. 81ff.

12 As it sailed by, the fleet provided 'la piu bella vista del mondo'. BL, MS Add. 34,503, fo 14. *The London Gazette* no. 2396 (1-5 Nov). P. Rapin de Thoyras, *Histoire d'Angleterre* (12 vols, The Hague 1749), x. 683.

13 Cavelli, ii. 315-16.

14 'La France trembla à sa vue, et l'Angleterre, voyant son libérateur venir à pleines voiles à son aide, tressaillit de joie'. *Mémoires inédits de Dumont de Bostaquet gentilhomme Normand, sur les temps qui ont précédé et suivi la révocation de l'Edit de Nantes*, ed. C. Read and F. Waddington (Paris 1864), p. 214.

15 John Whittle, *An Exact Diary Of The Late Expedition Of ... The Prince of Orange* (1689), pp. 30-34. J. A. de Mesmes, Comte d'Avaux, *Négociations du Comte d'Avaux en Hollande, depuis 1685, jusqu'en 1688*, ed. E. Mallett (6 vols, Paris, 1752-53), vi. 283, 310: 8 Oct. 1688.

16 BL, MS Egerton 2,621, fos 35, 37: Edward Russell and William to Admiral Herbert, *The Brill*, 4/14 Nov; MS Add. 33,970, fo 1v.

17 BL, MS Egerton 2,621, fos 39, 40: William to Admiral Herbert, 'Au Camp de Torbay', 6/16 Nov. 1688; MS Add. 33,970, fos 1v-2.

18 Though received 'avec grande acclamation du peuple', William noted 'mais point de gentils hommes me sont encore venu trouve, n'y le clerge, n'y le Maire de cette ville'. BL, MS Egerton 2,621, fo 41: William to Admiral Herbert, Exeter, 10/20 Nov. 1688. Burnet, iii. 330. Huygens, *Journaal*, p. 21.

19 James nominated Lamplugh to York on 15 Nov. The royal assent to the Dean and Chapter of York's election was given on 2 Dec. PRO, SP 44/150, pp. 1-3. Bodl., MS Rawlinson Letters 109, fo 113. *Clar. Corr.*, ii. 204. Luttrell, i. 476, 484.

20 William took over the Bishop's Palace as his lodging. *Seker ende omstandigh Verhael Van het gepasseerde, sedert het overgaen van Syne Hoogheydt naer Engeland* (1688).

21 BL, MS Egerton 2,621, fos 41, 42. Burnet, iii. 331, note 'c'.

22 The best account of William's army is in Carswell, *The Descent on England* (1969), pp. 169-170.

23 *A True and Exact Relation of the Prince of Orange His Publick Entrance into Exeter.*

24 Childs, *The Army, James II and the Glorious Revolution*, chapter v. J. Mackay, *The Life of Lt-General Hugh Mackay, Commander-in-Chief of the Forces in Scotland, 1689 and 1690* (Edinburgh 1836), pp. 1-14.

25 William of Orange's *Second Declaration* was read at Plymouth. *The English Currant*, no. 1 (12 Dec.).

26 Müller, *Wilhelm III von Oranien und Georg Friedrich von Waldeck*, ii. 118: Exeter. 16/26 Nov.

27 PRO, SP 31/4, fos 228-31: William's autograph notes, headed 'Preventions necessaires pour le dessin de Juillet'. He was

so keen to pay his debts, as he incurred them, that before leaving Exeter he felt the need to raise more funds. Burnet, iii. 331.

28 In his *Additional Declaration*, issued from The Hague, 24 Oct., William explicitly stated that his forces were 'utterly disproportioned to that wicked Design of Conquering the Nation'. Bodl., Wood 529 (2), p.16. See above, p.149.

V William's Supporters

1 J. Walker, 'The English exiles in Holland during the reigns of Charles II and James II', *Transactions of the Royal Historical Society*, 3rd series, xii (1947), 111-25.

2 A detailed account was sent to London from The Hague by Ignatius White, Marquis d'Albeville, who was not always the 'sad tool of an Embassador', that he was held to be by his critics. It gives the fullest 'List of officers and others coming with the Prince of Orange', BL, MS Add. 41,822, fo 230. For 'A List of what Scotsmen ar⟨e⟩ at The Hague', see *ibid.*, fo 231. Fletcher, Wildman, Ferguson, Burnet, Peyton, and Gwynne were excepted by name from James's General Pardons of 27 Sept. and 2 Oct. Steele, nos 3875, 3879. Huygens, *Journaal*, pp. 2, 4, 5, 7, 9, 10, 12, 14, 21, 23, 36. Bodl., MS Don. c. 38, fos 352v, 361. D'Avaux. *Négociations*, vi. 248, 250, 269, 275ff.

3 T. E. S. Clarke and H. C. Foxcroft, *A Life of Gilbert Burnet* (Cambridge 1907), pp. 219ff. Burnet, iii. 274-8.

4 Bodl., MS Rawlinson C. 983, fo 103: Dr. William Stanley, Mary's Anglican chaplain, to Bishop Compton of London, The Hague, 21/31 Dec. 1686. Stanley deliberately held aloof from Burnet, Gwynne, and Forrester, knowing them to be 'ill affected to our Church, as well as displeasing to the King'.

5 *Clar. Corr.*, ii. 204-5. On 17 Nov. William 'with a great number of English and forreigne noblemen and gentlemen' went to view Cornbury's Dragoons at Ottery St. Mary. BL, 'Viscount Preston's Papers. 1688. Letters from England', fo 79: 'Letter from Exon., dated 17th November 1688'. Bodl., MS Rawlinson Letters 109, fo 115; MS Don. c. 38, fos 361, 362; MS Carte 130, fo 313. BL, MS Add. 28,053, fo 367. Dr. Williams's Library, MS Morrice Q, p. 326. Huygens, *Journaal*, pp. 19-20. Burnet, iii. 331-2.

6 'Mr. S⟨e⟩ymour, sometimes Speaker of the House of Commons, Sir William Portman, with sev⟨e⟩rall gentlemen of Wiltshire, Dorset, and Sumerset, came hither to the Prince on Sauterday night'. BL, 'Viscount Preston's Papers. 1688. Letters from England', fo 83: Alexander Sampson to P. Frowde, Exeter Post Office, 19 Nov. Huygens, *Journaal*, p. 22. Bodl., MS Carte 130, fo 305.

7 BL, MS Egerton 2,621, fos 45, 47: Bentinck and Edward Russell to Admiral Herbert, Exeter, 12 and 13 Nov. Bodl., MS Rawlinson Letters 109, fo 115. Huygens, *Journaal*, p.17.

8 Huygens, *Journaal*, p. 16. *HMC Dartmouth*, p. 188: Samuel Pepys to Dartmouth, Admiralty, 8 Nov.

9 BL, Egerton 2,621, fos 51, 55: G. Burnet and Bentinck to Admiral Herbert, Exeter, 16 and 17 Nov. *Plymouth Memoirs ... by Dr. James Yonge*, ed. J. J. Beckerlegge (1951), pp. 44, 44n. Huygens, *Journaal*, p. 24. Bodl., MS Ballard 45, fo 65.

10 Dr. Williams's Library, MS Morrice Q, p. 335. They carried William's letter to the Mayor 'to require him to deliver up the City', and 'to give the same credit to that Earl, that they would to himself'. Huygens, *Journaal*, pp. 29, 31, 34. *Letters of John Pinney 1679-1699*, ed. G. F. Nuttall (1939), p. 60.

11 BL, 'Viscount Preston's Papers. 1688. Letters from England', fo 79; MS Egerton 2,717, fo 412. *Clar. Corr.* ii. 217, 218. Luttrell, i. 477.

12 Burnet also read William's manifesto 'in de groote Kerck', i.e., the Cathedral, whereupon the clergy and part of the congregation left. *Seker ende omstandigh Verhael Van het gepasseerde ... Van den 11 November tot den 23 dito* (1688). Huygens, *Journaal*, pp.17, 18. Clarke and Foxcroft, *A Life of Gilbert Burnet*, pp. 252-3.

13 *An Account Of The Proceedings and Transactions that have happened in the Kingdom of England, Since the Arrival of the Dutch Fleet* (London, Printed for P. B. in the Year 1688), p. 2.

14 Müller, *Wilhelm III von Oranien und Georg Friedrich von Waldeck*, ii. 118: Exeter, 16/26 Nov.

15 Two of Admiral Herbert's letters, both dated 6 Nov. from *The Leyden*, one addressed to Andrew Tucker at Lyme Regis, the other to Colonel Thomas Strangways, were delivered unopened, with William's *Declaration*, to the Mayor, who forwarded them to Secretary Preston on 7 Nov. BL, 'Viscount Preston's Papers. 1688. Letters from England', fos 32, 33v; 34, 35v; 44, 45. BL, MS Add. 36,707, fo 46: 10 Nov.

16 Huygens, *Journaal*, p. 22.

17 Burnet, iii. 337. Bodl., MS Don. c. 39, fos 6, 41: newsletters, 24 Nov. and 4 Dec.

18 For the text of the Exeter Association, see *The General Association, Of the Gentlemen of Devon, to his Highness The Prince of Orange* (Exon, Printed in the Year, 1688). On 28 Nov. it was expected to 'goe throˈughˈ all countys, as it has already throˈughˈ Dorset, Devon, and Somerset'. Bodl., MS Ballard 45, fo.19; MS Rawlinson D. 691, pp. 46-7; MS Don. c. 38, fo 350.

19 Burnet, iii. 337.

20 See below, p. 32.

21 'The Prince of Orange has brought over a printing presse and makes use of it in printing severall papers by way of remonstrance, as also by way of gazettes, which comprehend the particulars of their proceedings'. Bodl., MS Rawlinson Letters 109, fo 110; MS Don. c. 38, fo 359: newsletter, 20 Nov.

22 *A True and Exact Relation of the Prince of Orange His Publick Entrance into Exeter* (no imprint).

23 BL, 'Viscount Preston's Papers, 1688. Letters from England', fo 85.

24 'The Prince has put forth a *Second Declaration*, and printed it at Exeter, which takes notice of the reflections made upon his first', affirming 'the private league betweene us and France', that he forbore to insert 'into the first purely out of deference to the King'. Dr. Williams's Library, MS Morrice Q, p. 324.

25 *The Speech Of the Prince of Orange, To Some Principle Gentlemen of Somersetshire and Dorsetshire, on their coming to Joyn his Highness at Exeter the 15th of Nov: 1688* (Exeter, Printed by J. B. 1688)

26 BL, MS Egerton 2,717, fo 412: newsletter, London, 22 Nov., reporting that 'Dr. Burnet's Form for the Prince' was 'used by some' at Exeter. Bodl., MS Rawlinson Letters 109, fo 113. Luttrell, i. 477.

27 This would appear to be a reprint of the celebrated publication of the same name. *A Memorial From The English Protestants, For Their Highnesses The Prince And Princess Of Orange* (no imprint). D'Avaux, *Négociations*, vi. 313.

28 BL, 'Viscount Preston's Papers, 1688. Letters from England', fo 138: unsigned letter to Secretary Preston, [Exeter], 5 Dec. William compiled a list of those whom he regarded as the chief offenders against the laws, see PRO, SP 8/2, pt 2. fos 135-6 (undated).

29 BL, 'Viscount Preston's Papers, 1688. Letters from England', fo 87.

30 Burnet, iii. 259-60, 275, 300. For Mary's attitude, which was based on Princess Anne's malicious reports, see *Lettres et Mémoires de Marie Reine d'Angleterre*, ed. Mechtild, Countess Bentinck (The Hague 1880), pp. 3, 45-8, 73-6, 91.

31 Burnet 'understood' the petitions for a free parliament 'to be a declaring for us'. Clarke and Foxcroft, *A Life of Gilbert Burnet*, p. 253.

32 BL, 'Viscount Preston's Papers. 1688. Letters from England', fo 85: 'Extract of letters taken in the maile from Exeter to London, all dated 21 November 1688, intercepted at Salisbury the 22th November 1688'. For lists of those who had joined William at Exeter, see *ibid.*, fo 89; E. Green, *The March of William of Orange Through Somerset* (1892), pp. 56-8.

VI James's Advance and Retreat

1 PRO, SP 44/97, p. 15: Secretary Middleton to the Duke of Beaufort, 12 Nov. Cf. *ibid.*, p. 13 and SP 31/4, fo 182. BL, MS Egerton 2,717, fo 413: 29 Nov.

2 BL, MS Add. 36,707, fo 47. Dr. Williams's Library, MS Morrice Q, pp. 310, 311, 317. Bramston, p. 332. R. A. Beddard, 'Anti-Popery and the London Mob in the Revolution of 1688', *History Today* (July 1988), p. 38.

3 Bodl., MS Tanner 28, fo 249a: Sancroft's autograph text of 'The humble Petition of the Lords Spiritual and Temporal'. It was later printed, see PRO, SP 31/4, fo 195. Bodl., MS Carte 130, fo 313; MS Don. c. 38, fo 348.

4 BL, MS Add. 36,707, fo 48: 17 Nov. James had already authorised 'Praiers ... during this time of publick danger'. See Sancroft's draft: Bodl., MS Tanner 28, fos 192-3.

5 *Clar. Corr.*, ii. 204-5. Clarke, *Life of James II*, ii. 217-19. Burnet, iii. 331-2.

6 BL, MS Add. 36,707, fo 48: 17 Nov. Bodl., MS Carte 130, fo 303: [Robert Price] to the Duke of Beaufort, 15 Nov.

7 *Ibid.*, fo 313: [17 Nov.].

8 BL, MS Add. 36,707, fo 48: 17 Nov. Bodl., MS Don. c. 38, fo 359: newsletter, 20 Nov.

9 Steele, nos 2302, 2305, 2306.

10 Bodl., MS Rawlinson Letters 109, fo 110.

11 James ordered the Lord Mayor and Aldermen of London 'to take care of the citty in his absence, and that if he should fall in battle, to proclaim the prince of Wales successor to the crown'. Luttrell, i. 473. Bodl., MS Rawlinson B. 217, fos 12-14: Roger North's draft of James's will. What appears to be an earlier sketch by William Bridgeman precedes it. *Ibid.*, fos 8-10. *HMC Stuart*, p. 34. Clarke, *Life of James II*, ii. 243.

12 Feversham had to re-assure his troops at Warminster, who feared that, if James overcame William, 'he intended to destroy the protestant Religion, and especially the Church of England', telling them the King 'had as much kindness for them as they could desire, and that he would establish the Church of England as much as any Protestant Prince ever could'. 'Mr. Francis Gwyn's Journal', ed. C. T. Gatty, *The Fortnightly Review*, xlvi (1886), p. 363.

13 It began on 15 Nov. Bodl., MS Ballard

45, fo 18; MS Carte 130, fo 307; MS Rawlinson Letters 109, fo 114. Burnet, iii. 333. Cavelli, ii. 338. D. H. Hosford, *Nottingham, Nobles, and the North*, pp. 85-95. Browning, *Danby*, i. 397. *An Account Of The Proceedings and Transactions ... Since the Arrival of the Dutch Fleet.*

14 Gatty, 'Mr. Francis Gwyn's Journal', pp. 362, 363, 364. Cavelli, ii. 336. Bodl., MS Carte 130, fo 305; MS Ballard 45, fo 18.

15 Dr. Williams's Library, MS Morrice Q, p. 327: *circa* 21 Nov. Cavelli, ii. 331-33, 344.

16 *HMC F. W. Leyborne-Popham* (1899), p. 267. Burnet, iii. 333.

17 Cavelli, ii. 343. Turner, p. 430. BL, MS Add. 28,053, fo 357: W. Blathwait to [Danby], Salisbury, 23 Nov.

18 BL, 'Viscount Preston's Papers. 1688. Letters from England', fos 104, 108: Middleton to Preston, 24 and 25 Nov. Bodl., MS Carte 130, fo 309.

19 Cavelli, ii. 344-46. The Earl of Litchfield commented: 'Poor man (meaning the King) they will leave him so fast they will not give him time to make terms'. *HMC Leyborne-Popham*, p. 267: Dr. George Clarke's autobiography.

20 Bodl., MS Ballard 45, fo 19. BL, MS Add. 28,053, fo 367. Cavelli, ii. 338-39. Browning, *Danby*, i. 400ff. Hosford, *Nottingham, Nobles, and the North*, pp. 103-4, 107-9.

21 BL, MS Add. 19,253, fo 56: the Earl of Chesterfield's account of the Revolution.

22 E. Carpenter, *The Protestant Bishop* (1956), pp. 132ff. Cavelli, ii. 348-9, 351. D. Hosford, 'Bishop Compton and the Revolution of 1688', *Journal of Ecclesiastical History*, xxiii (1972), 209-18.

23 Clarke, *Life of James ii*, ii. 222-5.

24 BL, MS 36,707, fo 49: 27 Nov.

VII The Hungerford Negotiations

1 BL, MS Egerton 2,717, fo 413: newsletter, 29 Nov.

2 Bodl., MS Rawlinson Letters 109, fo 116: [27 Nov.]; MS Don. c. 39, fo 16: 27 Nov. Dr. Williams's Library, MS Morrice Q, pp. 329-30. *Clar. Corr.*, ii. 208-11. BL, MS Sloane 3,929, fo 113.

3 James issued his proclamation on 30 Nov. Steele, nos 3909-12. For the holding of elections William's co-operation was needed. 'It is not known how elections can be made in very many countyes at this time, if the Prince etc., concur not hereunto'. 'Many writts', authorizing elections, subsequently 'passed the Seale', but few were 'issued out' of Chancery. Dr. Williams's Library, MS Morrice Q, pp.

333, 338. Bodl., MS Don. c. 39, fo 46: newsletter, 8 Dec.

4 *Clar. Corr.*, ii. 212. Foxcroft, *Halifax*, ii. 17-18.

5 BL, MS Add. 28,053, fo 367: James Cranston to the Marquess of Douglas, London, 1 Dec. Bodl., MS Ballard 45, fo 19. Cavelli, ii. 355, 359.

6 All Souls College, Oxford, MS 273, item i.

7 *Ibid.*, item iii: Whitehall, 4 Dec. William was expected to do the same, and both were to have 'an equall number' of guards.

8 *Ibid.*, items viii, ii: William to Feversham, 2 Dec., enclosing his 'blanck passeports', dated Hindon, 3 Dec. Huygens, *Journaal*, p. 34.

9 *Clar. Corr.*, ii. 215. William was so impressed with the 'seer notabele schilderijen van van Dijck', that he sent Huygens back to see them. Huygens, *Journaal*, pp. 35, 36.

10 *Ibid.*, pp. 37-38. *Clar. Corr.*, ii. 213-18.

11 All Souls College, Oxford, MS 273, items xvii, xiv: King's Commissioners to Middleton, Andover, 7 p.m., 5 Dec., and Owen Wynne to Dumbarton, Andover, 6 Dec.

12 Bodl., MS Rawlinson A. 139[b]: King's Commissioners to Secretary Middleton, Ramsbury House, 8 Dec. Huygens, *Journaal*, pp. 38-9.

13 *Clar. Corr.*, ii. 219-20.

14 'Pour adjuster avec vous les points necessaires touchant l'assemblé du Parlament que j'ay convoqué, et pour lever tous les obstacles qui pourroient empecher un accommodement', and affirming 'ma disposition sincere à l'establissement d'une paix ferme et solide'. All Souls College, Oxford, MS 273, item vii: James 'a mon fils et neveu Le Prince d'Orange', Whitehall, 1 Dec.

15 Bodl., MS Rawlinson A. 139[b]: King's Commissioners to Secretary Middleton, Ramsbury House, 8 Dec.

16 *Clar. Corr.*, ii. 220.

17 Bodl., MS Rawlinson A. 139[b], fo 278v.

18 Burnet, iii. 340-1.

19 *Clar. Corr.*, ii. 220. All Souls College, Oxford, MS 273, item xix. Huygens recorded that the inn was 'soo vol menschen, dat men sigh niet roeren konde'. *Journaal*, p. 38.

20 *Clar. Corr.*, ii. 221.

21 *Commons*, ii. 8-10.

22 *Ibid.*, ii. 585-86; 484-87.

23 Hotham supported Henry Powle's move for an address to Charles ii, on 20 Oct. 1673, 'that the intended match of the Duke of York with the Princesse of

Modena might not be consummated'. Sir Robert Howard also supported the motion. Bond, *The Diaries and Papers of Sir Edward Dering*, p. 56.

24 *Commons*, ii. 486.

25 *Clar. Corr.*, ii. 219: 7 Dec.

26 *Ibid.*, ii. 221-3: 8-9 Dec. On 4 Dec. the Earl of Abingdon had told Clarendon 'he feared we should be disappointed in our expectations; that he was resolved to keep to his principles, and not join with what, he saw, was aiming at'. He 'did not like Wildman's and Ferguson's being in the Prince's train; nor several other persons, who, he found, were of their principles, whatever they pretended'. *Ibid.*, ii. 216.

27 Bodl., MS Rawlinson A. 139[b], fo 279.

28 Bodl., MS. Don. c. 39, fo 40: newsletter, London, 4 Dec.

29 Burnet said that the Londoners ('het volck te Londen') ridiculed the idea of calling a free parliament while any Papist remained in England or any Irish troops, i.e., Catholics, in the armies of the three Kingdoms. He evidently corresponded with like-minded Whigs in the capital. Huygens, *Journaal*, p. 35. *Clar. Corr.*, ii. 218.

30 Huygens, *Journaal*, p. 31.

31 Bentinck said 'dat wij met die dingen niet te doen hadden, dat alle de saken bij een Parlament mosten geexamineert werden en dat S. H. sich maer bij sijne declaratie moste houden'. Huygens, *Ibid.*, p. 34. *Clar. Corr.*, ii. 215.

32 On 1 Dec. Zuylestein had laughingly remarked that, by sending his Commissioners to William, James was seeking to capitulate. Huygens, *Journaal*, p. 33.

33 All Souls College, Oxford, MS 273, item xx: Littlecote, 9 Dec. *Clar. Corr.*, ii. 222-23. Huygens, *Journaal*, pp. 39-40.

34 BL, MS Egerton 2,621, fo 77: Edward Russell to Admiral Herbert, Newbury, 10 Dec.

35 James's Commissioners 'seemed to be very well satisfied'. Burnet, iii. 341-2. See Bishop Mews's opinion below, p. 93. Others considered them 'fair proposals', *HMC Dartmouth*, p. 230. Huygens, *Journaal*, p.41.

36 BL, MS Add. 28,103, fo 72: King's Commissioners to [Secretary Middleton], Littlecote, 10 Dec. All Souls College, Oxford, MS 273, items xxi and xii: Owen Wynne to Middleton, 12 o'clock, Littlecote, 10 Dec.

VIII The Third Declaration

1 The promotion was later noticed in James's warrant granting Chetwood's

Archdeaconry to John Robinson, 10 Dec. PRO, SP 44/57, p. 219. Dr. Williams's Library, MS Morrice Q, p. 362.

2 PRO, SP 44/150, p.5: James's warrant, 8 Dec. It did not pass the Seals, and therefore remained ineffectual, BL, MS Add. 36,707, fo 52: 22 Dec. See also, Bodl., MS Tanner 28, fo 306: K. Chetwood to William Needham, no date.

3 All Souls College, Oxford, MS 273, items viii and xiii: William to Feversham, 2 Dec., and James's passport, signed by Secretary Preston, Whitehall, 4 Dec. Cf. PRO, SP 44/339, pp. 35-6: 3 Dec. BL, 'Viscount Preston's Papers. Royal Letters', fos 29v-30: James's passport for Capt. Ernst Zühm. Cf. Huygens, *Journaal*, p.41.

4 PRO, SP 44/338, p. 156: passport to Connor O'Brien, Michael Studholme, and other servants of Prince George. Bodl., MS Don. c. 39, fo 52: newsletter, 8 Dec.

5 BL, MS Loan 57/71 (Bathurst Papers), fo 19: Anne to Sir Benjamin Bathurst, Nottingham, 6 Dec.

6 Dr. Williams's Library, MS Morrice Q, pp. 320, 331, 347. 'Thank God there‹e› is like to be noe fighting, al‹l› people being of a mind'. BL, MS Loan 29/184 (Harley Papers), fo 118: 13 Dec.

7 Bodl., MS Ballard 45, fo 19: 4 Dec; MS Don. c. 39, fo 43v: 6 Dec. BL, MS Add. 36,707, fo 50: 4 Dec. Cavelli, ii. 363: Hoffmann to Leopold I, London, 13 Dec: 'welche gar Nichts Gutes vor die Catholische prädiciret'. Cf. *ibid.*, p. 370: Rizzini to the Duke of Modena, London, 16 Dec., which speaks of the 'minaccia severamente' against Catholics.

8 *By His Highness William Henry, Prince of Orange, A Third Declaration* is reprinted in [H. Speke], *The Secret History Of The Revolution, in 1688* (London 1715), pp. 34-9. PRO, SP 31/4, fos 198-9. Speke later claimed to be its author. [H. Speke], *Some Memoirs Of the most Remarkable Passages And Transactions On the Late Happy Revolution in 1688* (Dublin 1709) pp. 59-62, 65-71. See also Bodl., Wood 529 (v).

9 Burnet, iii. 338. Cf. *The London Courant*, no. 2 (12-15 Dec.): where it is described as being 'the invention of some restless Brain'.

10 Luttrell subsequently noted that it 'did the prince of Orange no little service here in this town, tho I am well informed it was really none of his'. Luttrell, i. 485. Evelyn, iv. 609. When it was known 'that the Prince absolutely disownes the *Third Declaration*' there was 'a great consternation' in the City. Dr. Williams's Library, MS Morrice Q, p. 362.

11 Bodl., MS Ballard 45, fo 55a, verso: [R. Sare] to A. Charlett. Post marked 6 Dec.

12 'Anderseits seint alle Catholische, schuldig oder unschuldig in äussersten

Angustiis undt werdten von Glück zu sagen haben, wann sie dem Bluthbad entgehen; so gross ihre Desolation ist, so gross ist hingegen der Protestanten Frohlockung'. Hoffmann to Leopold I, London, 9/19 Dec. Cavelli, ii., 373.

13 Evelyn, iv. 609.

14 E.g., 'Divers Protestant officers, especially all in the Irish Regiment under a Popish Colonel, layd down their commissions last night'. Bodl., MS Ballard, 45, fo 20: 8 Dec. BL, MS Add. 36,707, fo 50: 4 Dec.

15 Bodl., MS Ballard 45, fo 20. Dr. Williams's Library, MS Morrice Q, pp. 341, 343. It took Craven's 'powerfull mediations and persuasions' to let the presentment against the King's soldiers drop.

16 *Ibid.*, pp. 317, 323. Bodl., MS Carte 130, fo 313v: [17 Nov.]. Beddard, 'Anti-Popery and the London Mob in the Revolution of 1688', *History Today* (July 1988), p. 38.

17 BL, MS Egerton 2,717, fo 414: 6 Dec. Luttrell, i. 472, 483. Bodl., MS Don. c. 39, fo 43: newsletter, 6 Dec.

18 'All the Romish chappells in this town are shutt up except their majesties, queen dowagers, and those of foreign ambassadors'. Bishop Crew of Durham had on 15 Nov. petitioned James to withdraw his protection from the mass-houses. Luttrell, i. 475. Bodl., MS Carte 239, fo 338v; MS Don. c. 38, fo 346: newsletter, 15 Nov.

19 Evelyn, iv, 609. Dr. Williams's Library, MS Morrice Q, pp. 338, 339, 347. Luttrell, i. 482. *Verney Memoirs* ii. 469. BL, MS Add. 28,053, fo 368.

20 Dr. Williams's Library, MS Morrice Q, p. 340. His remark was occasioned by the flight of the Earl of Melfort, 'a principall man in laying down and promoting the late methods, both in Scotland and England'.

21 Luttrell, i, 469, 470, 471. The process was incomplete when it was overtaken by the Revolution, see L. K. J. Glassey, *Politics and the Appointment of Justices of the Peace 1675-1720* (Oxford 1979), pp. 98-99.

22 BL, MS Egerton 2,717, fo 414. Luttrell, i. 482, 484. Bodl., MS Tanner 28, fo 283; MS Don. c. 39, fos 40, 49: newsletter, 4 and 6 Dec. Dr. Williams's Library, MS Morrice Q, p. 338.

23 Luttrell, i. 484. Bodl., MS Tanner 28, fo 283; MS Carte, 239, fo 339. Wood, *Life and Times*, iii. 283ff.

24 Bodl., MS Ballard 45, fo 20; MS Don. c. 39, fo 43: newsletter, 6 Dec. BL, MS Add. 28,053, fo 371: 8 Dec. Burnet, iii. 339.

25 *The Advice of divers Trades-men, Apprentices, and others, To the Right*

Honourable Sir John Chapman, Kt. Lord Mayor of the City of London (no date).

26 Dr. Williams's Library, MS Morrice Q, p. 341. For the citizens involved, see J. R. Woodhead, *The Rulers of London, 1660-1689* (London and Middlesex Archaeological Society 1965), pp. 103, 93-4, 42. Luttrell, i. 485.

27 Corporation of London Records Office, Journal of the Common Council 50, fo 358: Chapman's precept of 6 Dec., signed by William Wagstaffe, the Town Clerk. Bodl., MS Don. c. 39, fo 52: newsletter, 8 Dec.

28 'The Prince‹'s› 3‹r›d Declaration has put all people upon a resolution of disarmeing Papist‹s›'. Bodl., MS Ballard 45, fo 20: 8 Dec. BL, MS Add. 4,194, fo 430; MS Add. 29,563, fo 364: 11 Dec.

IX James's First Flight

1 *HMC Dartmouth*, p. 224: James to Admiral Dartmouth, Whitehall, 9 a.m., 5 Dec.

2 Burnet, iii. 339. That others of his co-religionists felt equally desperate, see Bodl., MS Tanner 28, fo 283: 'Ecco finite tutte le belle speranze del progresso della santa religione in questo paese'. London, 10 Dec.

3 'Abundance of Roman Catholeks are gon‹e› away, it is soposed into France'. Bodl., MS Carte 239, fo 338: 11 Dec. Clarke, *Life of James II*, ii. 242. Cavelli, ii. 341, 342, 350, 351-2, 358-9, 360, 366, 367, 369ff.

4 ''Tis my sonne they aime at and 'tis my sonne I must endeavour to preserve, what so ever becom‹e› of me'. *HMC Dartmouth*, pp. 219-20, 224: James to Dartmouth, Whitehall, 29 Nov., 1 and 5 Dec. Sir Richard Beach feared that the Prince would, by being sent abroad, prove a second Perkin Warbeck. *Ibid.*, p. 224: Portsmouth Dockyard, 5 Dec. Cavelli, ii. 367ff. Clarke, *Life of James II*, ii. 241.

5 See below, p. 118. Dr. Williams's Library, MS Morrice Q, p. 346. Mazure, *Histoire de la Révolution de 1688, en Angleterre*, iii. 264

6 Dover Castle was seized by '30 of the inhabitants' of the town, who believed that 'some Irish forces were on the road, comeing hither, as also that a considerable force of French were designed to be landed in these parts'. They claimed that they acted 'for their own safety'. BL, 'Viscount Preston's Papers. 1688. Letters from England', fo 150: William Stokes to Secretary Preston, Dover, 9 Dec. Mazure, *Révolution*, iii. 264.

7 Bodl., MS Rawlinson A. 139[b], fo 279v: King's Commissioners to James, Ramsbury House, 8 Dec. Clarke, *Life of James II*, ii. 241, 249. For the signing of the Association in Cornwall, Devon, Dorset, and Somerset, see Bodl., MS Ballard 45, fo 19; MS Don. c. 39, fo 53.

8 *HMC Dartmouth*, p. 228: Samuel Pepys to Dartmouth, 10 Dec. Cavelli, ii. 365. *An Account of Last Sundays Engagement Between His Majesty's, and the Prince of Orange's Forces, in the Road between Reading and Maidenhead* (London, Printed for W. D. 1688); *A Short Account of a Second Engagement, That happened on Monday and Tuesday Morning, between the King and Prince of Oranges Army near Windsor* (London, Printed for W. D. 1688). Burnet, iii. 351. Huygens, *Journaal*, p.41. Clarke, *Life of James II*, ii. 249.

9 BL, MS Egerton 1,677, fos 30-5, 36–41v: Francesco Riva's account of the retreat of the Queen and Prince of Wales. Dr. Williams's Library, MS Morrice Q, p. 345. BL, MS Add. 15,397, fo 495: D'Adda to the Cardinal Secretary of State, London, 7/17 Dec. *HMC Stuart*, i. 34-5: James and Mary to Innocent XI and Cardinal Cibo (n.d.). Clarke, *Life of James II*, ii. 244-9. Mulgrave, ii. 72-73.

10 Clarke, *Life of James II*, ii. 242-3. Cavelli, iii. 377: Terriesi to the Grand Duke of Tuscany, London, 10 Dec.

11 Staffordshire County Record Office, D(W) 1778/Ii/1655a. Dartmouth's endorsement makes it clear, from the Duke of Berwick himself (James's intended messenger concerning the fleet), that 'the King neither sent any orders by him, nor so much as told him at his comming away what he would have me do'.

12 All Souls College, MS 273, item xxi, note.

13 Barillon to Louis XIV, 17/27 Dec. Mazure, *Révolution*, iii. 233.

14 See Appendix 1.

15 Ailesbury, ii. 192.

16 Staffordshire County Record Office, D(W) 1778/Ii/1655b. Dartmouth's endorsement indicates that the letter was slow in reaching him: 'Received the 14th by the common post. Mr. Peppys or whom this was committed to should be answerable for the delay, for this letter came not till after the Councell of Warr that sent too the Prince upon the letter from the Lords at Yealdhall (sic) and the quitting of the Roman Catholick officers'. The wording of the letter is echoed in Clarke, *Life of James II*, ii. 241. See Bodl., MS Rawlinson A. 186, fos 222, 222v.

17 Dr. Williams's Library, MS Morrice Q, p. 345.

18 Ailesbury, ii. 195-6. That James thought seriously of retreating to the North, see Browning, *Danby*, i. 412, and Appendix 1.

19 Mulgrave, ii. 71.

20 Dr. Williams's Library, MS Morrice Q, p. 346.

21 *The King's Letter to the General of his Army: With the General's Letter to the Prince of Orange*. Clarke, *Life of James II*, ii. 249-50: James to Feversham, 10 Dec. Dr. Williams's Library, MS Morrice Q, pp. 347, 349. For Feversham's submission to William, Uxbridge, 11 Dec., see PRO, SP 8/2, pt 2 fos 79-80.

22 Mulgrave, ii. 73.

23 See Appendix 1.

24 On the fate of the Great Seal, see H. Jenkinson, 'What happened to the Great Seal of James II?', *The Antiquaries Journal*, xxiii (1943), pp. 1-13; and E. S. de Beer, 'The great seal of James II', *ibid.*, xlii (1962), pp. 81-90.

X William's Regal Ambition

1 *Clar. Corr.*, ii. 215. Cf. Huygens, *Journaal*, p. 34.

2 PRO, SP 8/2, pt 2, fos 95-6: [Sir Robert Howard] to William, [2 Dec.]. For the identity of the anonymous writer of this letter, see Foxcroft, *Halifax*, ii. 20, note 3.

3 Bodl., MS. Don. c. 39, fo 54v: newsletter, London, 11 Dec. *The London Courant*, no. 1 (12 Dec.).

4 Burnet, iii. 350. Huygens, *Journaal*, p. 43.

5 Bodl., MS Carte 40, fos 502, 503v: William to Chancellor Ormonde, Abingdon, 12 Dec. See below, Appendix 7.

6 Burnet, iii. 351-2.

7 J. H. Plumb and Alan Simpson, 'A letter of William, Prince of Orange, to Danby on the Flight of James II', *Cambridge Historical Journal*, v (1937), pp. 107-8.

8 *Clar. Corr.*, ii. 224.

XI James's 'Old Friends'

1 *Ibid.*, ii. 189. Browning, *Danby*, ii. 143.

2 For their part in building up the 'Yorkist' reversionary interest under Charles II, see R. A. Beddard, 'The Commission for Ecclesiastical Promotions, 1681-84: an instrument of Tory Reaction', *The Historical Journal*, x (1967), 11-40.

3 Beddard, 'William Sancroft', pp. 160-72.

4 Bodl., MS Rawlinson D. 836, fos 113-116v, published in Beddard, 'The Loyalist Opposition in the Interregnum: a Letter of Dr. Francis Turner, Bishop of Ely, on the Revolution of 1688', *Bulletin of the Institute of Historical Research*, xl (1967), 101-9.

5 For an edited text of the Journal, see below, pp. 66-121.

XII The Provisional Government

1 Mulgrave, ii. 74. See below, Appendix 2.

2 See below, pp. 38, 67. For Gwyn, see *Commons*, ii. 455. Mulgrave, ii. 74. *An Account of the Proceedings at White-Hall, Guild-Hall, In the City of London, And At The Tower* (no imprint).

3 Ailesbury, ii. 197-8. On the political composition of the first session, see R. A. Beddard, 'The Guildhall Declaration of 11 December 1688 and the counter-revolution of the loyalists', *The Historical Journal*, xi (1968), 411.

4 Mulgrave, ii. 74.

5 PRO, SP 44/339, p. 32; 97, p. 20. BL, 'Viscount Preston's Papers. 1688. Letters from England', fo 98: Middleton to Preston, Salisbury, 22 Nov. Cavelli, ii. 362.

6 It was Skelton's 'misfortune in that conjuncture that the Citty was jealous of him in that post'. His absence was soon misconstrued: 'Skilton is fled and the City has seased the Tower'. In fact, he had gone to Whitehall to confirm the news of the King's flight. Bodl., MS Rawlinson D. 1064, fo 11. Dr. Williams's Library, MS Morrice Q, pp. 347, 349. Cavelli, ii. 362. Ailesbury, ii. 198. *Verney Memoirs*, ii. 469.

7 See below, p. 69. It was another false alarm, the truth was very different. 'The Papists forces are disbanded, and are drawing up an address or pettition to His Highness, laying downe theire armes ‹that› they may have free leave to depart to theire countryes and habittations, and accordingly they are drawing towards Houndsley Heath, where they are to lay them downe'. Bodl., MS Don. c. 39, fo 54v.

8 For concern over the Channel Islands, see BL, MS Add. 29,563 (Hatton-Finch Papers), fo 360: P. Bonamy to Lord Hatton, Guernsey, 10 Dec: 'we did never more earnestly wish your return to this your Government then we doe now, and indeed it was never more necessary, especially if the reports we heare of our neighbours' preparations and designs are well grounded'. See also *ibid.*, fos 364, 383, 385.

9 See below, pp. 70-71. Mulgrave, ii. 74. *The London Gazette*, no. 2409 (10-13 Dec.). Browning, *Danby*, ii. 153: Danby to the Countess of Danby, York, 14 Dec.

10 Ailesbury, ii. 198-99. Skelton was displaced despite his having taken the Anglican sacrament and 'subscribed to the Prince's *Declaration*'. Bodl., MS Don. c. 39, fo 54v.

11 For a detailed discussion of this theme, see R. A. Beddard, "The violent party':

the Guildhall revolutionaries and the growth of opposition to James II', *The Guildhall Miscellany*, iii (1970), 120-136.

12 Beddard, 'The Guildhall Declaration', pp. 412-13.

13 Bodl., MS Rawlinson D. 836, fo 110. [H. Bedford], *A Vindication of the Late Archbishop Sancroft, And of his Brethren, The rest of the Depriv'd Bishops, From the Reflections of Mr. Marshal In His Defence of Our Constitution in Church and State* (London 1717), pp. 29-30.

14 Burnet, iii. 349, 354. Others misconstrued the political import of the Guildhall Declaration, see BL, MS Egerton 3,361, p. 2; MS Add. 29,563, fo 364; Bodl., MS Eng. hist. d. 307, fo 4; MS Don. c. 39, fos 54v, 56, 60; and Cambridge University Library, MS Eee 12¹⁵.

15 Bodl., MS Rawlinson D. 836, fo 103. [Bedford], *A Vindication of the Late Archbishop Sancroft*, p. 27.

16 Bodl. MS Don. c. 39, fo 54v: newsletter, 11 Dec.

17 Bodl., MS Rawlinson D. 836, fo 108.

18 See Appendix 3, which gives the names of the committee members. They were advised by 'the City counsell', Treby, Holt, and Pollexfen, who were 'immediately sent for', and 'all appeared'. Dr. Williams's Library, MS Morrice Q, p. 349.

19 See Appendix 4. Cavelli, ii. 421. *An Account of the Proceedings at White-Hall, Guild-Hall, In the City of London, And At The Tower*. Bodl., MS Don. c. 39, fo 54v: newsletter, London, 4 Dec.

20 BL, MS Sloane 3,929, fo 113v: newsletter, London, 1 Dec.

21 See Appendix 5. Dr Williams's Library, MS Morrice Q, p. 350.

22 *Clar. Corr.*, ii. 224-5. Beddard, 'The Guildhall Declaration', p. 419.

23 See below, p. 107. Huygens, *Journaal*, p. 45.

24 BL, MS 32,096, fo 334: the Non-juror George Harbin's transcript of Bishop Turner's fragmentary 'Memoirs Civil and Ecclesiastical from the time in which the landing of the Prince of Orange was apprehended to the time of King James's going away. December 1688'. Cf. *Clar. Corr.*, ii. 225.

25 Bodl., MS Eng. hist. d. 307, fo 7v. During the Guildhall session the Peers 'often sent for the Lord Mayor, who received all their orders as submissively, as if they had been the most legal commands'. Mulgrave, ii. 74, 75. For the Tory Lord Mayor, Chapman, see Woodhead, *The Rulers of the London 1668-1689*, p. 45.

26 See below, p. 74.

27 This 'happened to be the cause of all

his favour with the Prince of Orange ... tho' before, he had always forbidden his agents ever to trust him with their design of coming into England'. Mulgrave, ii. 76.

XIII The Eruption of Anti-Popery

1 *The English Currant*, no. 2 (12-14 Dec.). *Memoirs of Sir John Reresby*, ed. A. Browning (Glasgow 1936), p. 537.

2 Dr. Williams's Library, MS Morrice Q, p. 350.

3 *The London Courant*, no. 1 (12 Dec.). Dr. Williams's Library, MS Morrice Q, p. 348.

4 *The English Currant*, no. 1 (12 Dec.). *The London Courant*, no. 1 (12 Dec.). Though the firing of Rochester was widely reported, the report turned out to be bogus.

5 BL, MS Egerton 1,703, fo 65: 'In questi due giorni d'assenza del Rè la plebe non riconoscendo più governo, delle negl' eccessi noti contro i Cattolici, rovinando case, bruciando chiese, rubando, senza una gociola di sangue'. Cavelli, ii. 421.

6 Dr. Williams's Library, MS Morrice Q, p. 350.

7 *The Universall Intelligence*, no. 2 (11-15 Dec.). Dr. Williams's Library, MS Morrice Q, p. 350. Cf. Cavelli, ii. 369.

8 *The English Currant*, no. 1 (12 Dec.). *The London Courant*, no. 1 (12 Dec.). See also Appendix 6.

9 BL, MS Add. 4,194, fo 430: 11 Dec. *Universal Intelligence*, no. 2 (11-15 Dec.).

10 *The London Courant*, no. 1 (12 Dec.).

11 James had earlier ordered the Lord Mayor to provide Hills's premises with a sufficient guard after it had been 'attempted' three times by a thousand-strong mob in Nov. PRO, SP 44/97, p. 15. The 'enraged' mob not only destroyed Hills's workshop, but 'spoil'd his Forms, Letter, &c. and burnt 2 or 300 Reams of Paper, printed and unprinted'. *The English Currant*, no. 2 (12-14 Dec.). Cavelli, ii. 430: Terriesi to the Grand Duke of Tuscany, London, 17/27 Dec.

12 At Weld House the mob 'ransackt, destroy'd and burnt all the Ornamental and Inside Part of the Chappel; some Cartloads of choice Books, Manuscripts, &c. And not content here, some villanous Thieves and Common Rogues, no doubt, that took this opportunity to mix with the Youth, and they plunder'd the Ambassadors House of Plate, Jewels, Money, rich foods, &c.' BL, MS Add. 4,194, fo 432: London, 13 Dec. *The London Mercury*, no. 1 (15 Dec.). *The London Courant*, no. 2 (12-15 Dec.). *The London Gazette*, no. 2409 (10-13 Dec.). Dr.

Williams's Library, MS Morrice Q, p. 351. Cavelli, ii. 421-2, 430.

13 Many Catholics had carried their goods to Ronquillo's embassy, as into 'a franchise', thinking that diplomatic immunity, resting on the established principle of extraterritoriality, would preserve them safe and sound. *Verney Memoirs*, ii. 470. Clarke, *Life of James II*, ii. 257. BL, MS Add. 29,563, fo 374.

14 Ronquillo reported to Madrid: 'Sirviendole solo de consuelo el haber tenido prevencion de poder consumir El Santisimo'. Macaulay, *The History of England*, ed. C. H. Firth (6 vols, 1914). iii. 1208, note 1. Cavelli, ii. 421-22.

15 Dr. Williams's Library, MS Morrice Q, p. 348.

16 *Verney Memoirs*, ii. 469: Dr. William Denton to Sir Ralph Verney, [12 Dec.]. Browning, *Memoirs of Sir John Reresby*, p. 537.

17 See below, p. 75. BL, MS Add. 4,194, fo 432.

18 BL, MS Add. 2,560, fo 234.

19 See below, pp. 78, 89, 92. Beddard, 'The Loyalist Opposition in the Interregnum', p. 106. Ailesbury, *Memoirs*, ii. 200.

20 On the 12th, 'the Rabble made an assault on the Chappel at St. James's ... but were forcibly repelled by some of the Guards, and so that Chappel remains standing'. *The London Courant*, no. 2 (12-15 Dec.). The previous night, there was concern for the Chapel at Whitehall, though it had been 'shut up'. BL, MS Egerton 2,717, fo 415: 11 Dec. Cavelli, ii. 430. Mazure, *Révolution*, iii. 245. See below, pp. 79-81.

21 Cavelli, ii. 422: Hoffmann to Leopold I, London, 14/24 Dec.

22 *Ibid.*, ii. 430.

23 *The English Currant*, no. 2 (12-14 Dec.). *The London Mercury*, no. 1 (15 Dec.). BL, MS Add. 28,053, fo 378; MS Add. 4,194, fo 432v: 13 Dec.

24 *The London Mercury*, no. 1 (15 Dec.) Cavelli, ii. 430. BL, MS Add. 25,377, fos 202-4; MS Add. 34,510, fos 198-9. Dr. Williams's Library, MS Morrice Q, p. 352.

XIV The Irish Fear

1 See below, p. 84. For the 'disorders' committed by the Irish at Uxbridge, which occasioned the Fear, see Bodl., MS Carte 239, fo 336v, and G. H. Jones, 'The Irish Fright', *Bulletin of the Institute of Historical Research*, lv (1982), p. 149.

2 BL, MSS Add. 4,194, fo 433; Add. 25,377, fo 217; MS Loan 29/184 (Harley Papers), fo 118; MS Egerton 2,717, fo 416:

13 Dec. Ailesbury, ii. 200. Luttrell, i. 487. HMC Portland, iii. 420-1. Hatton Corr., ii. 124, 125. See Appendix 13.

3 BL, MS Add. 36,707, fo 51: 13 Dec.

4 BL, MS Add. 512, fo 1. The popular 'terrours' were dispelled, in part, 'upon notice that the Prince of Orange's Advance Guard was near town'. BL, MS Add. 4,194, fo 433.

5 Corporation of London Records Office, L.M.B. 1685-88: 13 Dec.

6 Loc. cit: 15, 17, 19, 24 Dec. Dr. Williams's Library, MS Morrice Q, p. 361.

7 Ailesbury, ii. 209. Mulgrave, ii. 74. Beddard, 'The Loyalist Opposition in the Interregnum', p. 106.

XV Military and Civilian Administration

1 PRO, SP 31/4, fo 203: Earl of Craven, six Colonels, and three Captains to William of Orange, London, 11 Dec. Feversham, Northumberland, etc., 'declared to their Lordships they would in their respective spheres and places obey their commands'. Dr. Williams's Library, MS Morrice Q, p. 347. Mazure, Révolution, iii. 242.

2 See below, p. 75.

3 See below, pp. 86-7, 89, 100-1, 102, 107, 117.

4 See below, p. 85.

5 See below, pp. 87, 100, 101, 106, 112, 117.

6 See below, pp. 100-1. The Irish forces also submitted to Williams's authority. See PRO, SP 8/2, pt 2, fos 75-6: Feversham and eight commanders to William of Orange, Uxbridge, 11 Dec.

7 See below, pp. 106-7.

8 See below, pp. 88-9.

9 William of Orange's proclamation for keeping military discipline, Henley, 13 Dec. Steele, nos 3923-26. Dr. Williams's Library, MS Morrice Q, p. 347.

10 See below, pp. 120-1.

11 The London Courant, no. 2 (12-15 Dec.).

12 PRO, SP 44/56, pp. 163-4; SP 31/1, nos 2-3.

13 See below, pp. 72-3.

14 Dr. Williams's Library, MS Morris Q. pp. 355, 356, 357. BL, MS Add. 36,707, fo 51: 13 Dec. See below, pp. 78, 99, 119, 156, 158, 162ff.

15 Verney Memoirs, ii. 469.

16 See below, pp. 76, 78, 94, 97, 101, 103, 111, 112.

17 For James Stamford, see Bodl., MS Rawlinson A. 266, fo 103. G. Macdonald,

'The Lime Street Chapel', The Dublin Review, nos 361 (1927), pp. 253-65; and 362, pp. 1-16. See below, p. 115.

18 See below, pp. 77-8, 79 and Appendix 10. The English Currant, no. 2 (12-14 Dec.). The London Courant, no. 2 (12-15 Dec.).

19 As he was one of the earliest to flee the country, it is probable that the information related to his brother, Fr. Charles Petre, S.J., Rector of the Jesuit college in Lime Street. Cavelli, ii. 341, 350. Bodl., MS Carte 130, fo 303. MS Don. 39, fos 44v, 54. Foley, v. 282. Dr. Williams's Library, MS Morrice Q, p. 362. See below, p. 102.

20 See below, p. 72.

21 See below, pp. 81, 98. Luttrell, i. 487. BL, MS Add. 28,053, fo 379: 13 Dec.

22 Dr. Williams's Library, MS Morrice Q, p. 359.

23 See below, pp. 109-11. For Lord Dartmouth's concern for the garrison at Portsmouth and the Duke of Berwick, see National Maritime Museum, Greenwich, Dar/17, pp. 48-9, 50-2.

24 See below, p. 71.

25 See below, pp. 87-8, 113-14, 117-18; cf. p. 100.

XVI Bringing the King Back

1 Beddard, 'The Guildhall Declaration', pp. 417, 419.

2 Turner, pp. 445-7. Miller, James II, pp. 206-7.

3 See below, pp. 90-91. Mews had attended James at Salisbury, and 'pressed him with all imaginable arguments to call Parliament ... to put a stop to those confusions that threat〈e〉ned the gover〈n〉ment'. Bodl., MS Tanner 28, fo 262.

4 Mulgrave, ii. 77-8.

5 See below, p. 91 and Appendix 8.

6 Ailesbury, ii. 201.

7 Mulgrave, ii. 78. The Whig Morrice thought 'few matters in this age have been of greater difficulty' to determine. Dr. Williams's Library, MS Morrice Q, p. 356.

8 Foxcroft, Halifax, ii. 50. Dr. Williams's Library, MS Morrice Q, p. 356. Mulgrave, ii. 77.

9 The Journal vindicates the truth of Ailesbury's hitherto rejected account of Sancroft's being present, as against the usually accepted view, expressed in Mulgrave, that the Archbishop refused 'to come any more among those Lords who met at Whitehall'. Ailesbury, ii. 200-1. Mulgrave, ii. 76.

10 Dr. Williams's Library, MS Morrice Q, p. 359.

11 See below, pp. 92-3.

12 Dr. Williams's Library, MS Morrice Q, p. 360.

13 See below, pp. 93-5, 103-4, 106.

14 Ailesbury, ii. 202. Feversham was 'commonly reported to have told the King, when he was at Feversham, 〈that〉 he would dye in his quarrel, or would conduct him safe to sea, or to London, or whether ever he pleased'. His attachment to James's cause was his 'Capital-Verbrechen', according to Hoffman. Cavelli, ii. 437-8. Dr. Williams's Library, MS Morrice Q, p. 363. BL, MS Add. 36,707, fo 51: 13 Dec.

15 Clarke, Life of James II, ii. 261-62. Ailesbury, ii. 203-12. Dr. Williams's Library, MS Morrice Q, p. 363. Mulgrave, ii. 79. Bramston, p. 340. BL, MS Egerton 2,717, fo 417: 18 Dec. Bodl., MS Tanner 28, fo 286.

16 The London Gazette, no. 2410 (13-17 Dec.). Dr. Williams's Library, MS Morrice Q, p. 365.

XVII William and the City of London

1 Clar. Corr., ii. 226-7. Hatton Corr., ii. 127. Dr. Williams's Library, MS Morrice Q, p. 363. Huygens, Journaal, pp. 47-8. Mulgrave, ii. 79.

2 Mulgrave correctly concluded that Feversham's arrest was in accordance with William's 'design of forcing' James 'away by the despair of any accommodation'. Ibid., ii. 80. That William thought the Lords of the provisional government 'had not used him well' in making 'this step without consulting him', see Burnet, iii. 354.

3 Clarke, Life of James II, ii. 262. Clar. Corr., ii. 226 and note. Dr. Williams's Library, MS Morrice Q, p. 363.

4 Clar. Corr., ii. 228.

5 Bond, The Diaries and Papers of Sir Edward Dering, p. 55. Clarke, Life of James II, i. 485.

6 PRO, SP 8/2, pt 2, fos 95-6: [Sir Robert Howard] to William, [2 Dec.].

7 PRO, SP 44/338, pp. 205-6: warrant to Attorney General, 5 Oct., to prepare a bill to pass the Great Seal for constituting Sir John Chapman, Lord Mayor of London, and empowering William Wagstaffe, the Town Clerk, to administer the oaths to the Mayor, Aldermen, and other civic officers. Sir William Pritchard had declined to execute the Mayoralty. Clar. Corr., ii. 192-3.

8 Corporation of London Records Office, Repertory 94; fo 69. BL, MS Sloane 3,929, fo 113v. R. R. Sharpe, London and the Kingdom (3 vols, 1895), ii. 532.

9 See Appendix 15. Dr. Williams's Library, MS Morrice Q, p. 374.

10 Dr. Williams's Library, MS Morrice Q, p. 365. BL, MS Sloane 3,929, fo 119v.

11 Treby, who had previously refused to be re-instated, though he had 'multiplyed sollicitations from the City', changed his mind and accepted the Recordership on 15 Dec., 'on purpose to serve the Church, the State, and the City in this juncture', i.e., the Protestant cause of William of Orange. Dr. Williams's Library, MS Morrice Q, p. 364.

12 M. Landon, *The Triumph of the Lawyers*, pp. 94-5. *Commons*, iii. 581-3.

13 See Appendix 16.

14 Treby was later esteemed 'the greatest instrument under God's providence in preparing the way for the Prince's entrance into the City ... no man could influence the City to such good purposes as he, and that it was very like to recoile, for all they had done was by the force of fear and necessity against their own inclinations'. Dr. Williams's Library, MS Morrice Q, p. 388.

15 See below, p. 179.

16 Mulgrave, ii. 80.

17 Clarke, *Life of James II*, ii. 262-3. Dr. Williams's Library, MS Morrice Q. p. 363.

18 Woodhead, *The Rulers of London 1660-1689*, pp. 108-9, 155.

19 Clarke, *Life of James II*, ii. 271-2.

20 Dr. Williams's Library, MS Morrice Q, pp. 365, 377, 379, 382. For Sir Robert Howard's view of 'the mistaken notion of an accom‹m›odation', see PRO, SP 8/2, pt 2, fo 95.

XVIII James's Return

1 *Clar. Corr.*, ii. 211.

2 P. C. Vellacott, 'The Diary of a Country Gentleman in 1688', *Cambridge Historical Journal*, ii (1926), pp. 59, 61. BL, MS Add. 27,989, fos 4, 4v. MS Harleian 6,582, fo 402.

3 Ailesbury, ii. 210, 213-15. *Clar. Corr.*, ii. 230. Bodl., MS Ballard 45, fo 63: 16 Dec. Cavelli, ii. 431. Mazure, *Révolution*, iii. 264.

4 PRO, PC 2/72, fos 356-8. *The London Gazette*, no. 2410 (13-17 Dec.).

5 Dr. Williams's Library, MS Morrice Q, pp. 375-6. *Calendar of Treasury Books, 1685-1689*, ed. W. A. Shaw (London 1923), p. 2140.

6 Dr. Williams's Library, MS Morrice Q, pp. 363, 377. BL, MS Add. 15,062, fo 99. It was reported that there were 'five Papists to one Protestant' at Court. Bramston, p. 340.

7 PRO, SP 8/2, pt 2, fos 91, 92v: Dr. William Lloyd, Bishop of St. Asaph, to Hans Willem Bentinck, 'now with the Prince at Sion House', [London] 17 Dec.

8 William 'having intelligence' of the 'unexpected confluence of Papists, insomuch that it was difficult to come near' the King's person, he sent the English Lords 'with a very sharp letter to His Majestie'. BL, MS Egerton 2,717, fo 417: London, 18 Dec. P. Rapin de Thoyras, *Histoire d'Angleterre*, x. 702-4.

9 The negotiations were instantly seen as a conspiracy against William by the Whig Morrice: 'This conspiracy many of the Lords Spirituall and Temporall and Commoners promote with all their might. They first combined and knit together for enabling themselves behind the King, as their back, when he returned to Whitehall on Lord's Day in the evening, the 16‹th›'. Dr. Williams's Library, MS Morrice Q, p. 378; also *ibid.*, pp. 380-91.

10 Beddard, 'The Commission for Ecclesiastical Promotions', pp. 25-30.

11 Dr. Williams's Library, MS Morrice Q, p. 381.

12 PRO, SP 8/2, pt 2, fo 91.

13 For the 'very signall letter' which the City addressed to William of Orange 'with very great deference and veneration', see Appendix 17. Dr. Williams's Library, MS Morrice Q, p. 363.

14 In noting the 'throng of Papists' about the King, it was also noted that 'Monsieur Barillon' was 'in the head of them'. PRO, SP 8/2, pt 2, fo 91. BL, MS Add. 15,920, fo 67.

15 Dr. Williams's Library, MS Morrice Q, pp. 363, 381.

16 Corporation of London Records Office, Journal 50, fo 60.

17 See Appendix 17. Dr. Williams's Library, MS Morrice Q, p. 363. There had been talk of preparing Southampton House for the Prince. BL, MS Egerton 2,717, fo 416.

XIX The Windsor Consultations

1 *Hatton Corr.*, ii. 200. Burnet, iii. 354.

2 Clarke, *Life of James II*, ii. 263-4.

3 *Clar. Corr.*, ii. 228.

4 BL, Althorp MSS: Halifax's Papers, item f: Halifax's notes on the Windsor meeting. His endorsement reads: 'Concerning the message to the King'.

5 *Clar. Corr.*, ii. 229.

6 See above, p. 50. Bodl., MS Wood D. 18, fo 61.

7 *Clar. Corr*, ii. 229.

8 Mulgrave, ii. 76, 77. Foxcroft, *Halifax*, ii. 39.

9 *Clar. Corr.*, ii. 229-30. P. Rapin de Thoyras, *Histoire d'Angleterre*, x. 703.

10 BL, MS Add. 32,096, fo 334.

11 *Clar. Corr.*, ii. 230.

XX William the King-Breaker

1 BL, Althorp MSS: Halifax Papers, item g/i: the text is written in a clerical hand, but signed by William. Halifax has endorsed it: 'The Prince's message to the King'.

2 Clarke, *Life of James II*, ii. 264-5. Mulgrave, ii. 81. P. Rapin de Thoyras, *Histoire d'Angleterre*, x. 703-4.

3 BL, Althorp MSS: Halifax papers, item g/ii: Halifax, Shrewsbury, and Delamer to Secretary Middleton, with Halifax's endorsement: 'Copy of the letter to the Earle of Middleton'. William's three Commissioners met at Delamer's lodgings to concert tactics before going to Whitehall.

4 Mulgrave, ii. 80.

5 BL, Althorp MSS: Halifax Papers, item g/iii: an autograph unsigned copy, endorsed by Halifax: 'Copy of the letters sent from Whitehall' (no date).

6 BL, *ibid.*, g/iv: Hans Willem Bentinck to Halifax, 'Sion, ce 28 Decembre, a 5 heures du matin' (N.S.). Halifax's endorsement reads: 'Monsieur Bentinck. December 18, '88'.

7 Mulgrave, ii. 77. Evelyn, iv. 49.

8 See Appendix 18.

9 Burnet, iii. 356.

10 Mulgrave, ii. 81.

11 In resolving to return to London from Faversham, James had remarked to Lord Feversham: 'My father there suffered martyrdome for the Church of England, and I can be content to suffer martyrdom there for the Church of Rome by the Church of England.' Dr. Williams's Library, MS Morrice Q, p. 363. Bodl., MS Smith 145, fo 60. *Clar. Corr.*, ii. 230. Mulgrave, ii. 81. Ailesbury, ii. 218.

12 Mazure, *Révolution*, iii. 270. Evelyn, iv. 72.

13 Clarke, *Life of James II*, ii. 267. Ailesbury, ii. 217-18. Foxcroft, *Halifax*, ii. 43. Mazure, *Révolution*, iii. 269.

14 Ailesbury, ii. 218.

XXI William's Arrival

1 Dr. Williams's Library, MS Morrice Q, pp. 366, 377. BL, MS Egerton 2,717, fo 417: 18 Dec. *A True Account Of his Highness the Prince of Orange's Coming to St. James's, on Tuesday the 18th of December 1688* (Printed in the Year 1688).

2 BL, MS Egerton 2,717, fo 417: 18 Dec.

3 See Appendix 18.

4 *Clar. Corr.*, ii. 231. Dr. Williams's Library, MS Morrice Q, p. 366. Evelyn iv. 50.

5 Foxcroft, *Halifax*, ii. 203-4: Halifax's account of his conversation with William on 30 Dec.

6 *Clar. Corr.*, ii. 231.

7 Burnet, iii. 359.

8 Dr. Williams's Library, MS Morrice Q, p. 379.

9 BL, MS Egerton, 2,621, fo 83: G. Burnet to Admiral Herbert, St. James's, 25 Dec.

10 Burnet, iii. 359. Catholics were amazed at William's peaceful and unopposed progress: 'con una armata straniera senza una minima oppositione, una cosa non più vista, ni udita, ni mentionata nell' historia, un Re pacifico possessore del suo regno con una armata di trenta mila conbatenti huomini, e quaranta vascelli di guerra uscir del suo regno senza tirar un culpo di pistola'. Bodl., MS Tanner 28, fo 278.

11 Burnet, iii. 359. Clarke, *Life of James II*, ii. 241.

12 *Clar. Corr.*, ii. 238: 1 Jan. 1689. Browning, *Memoirs of Sir John Reresby*, p. 541.

13 See above, pp. 54-5. Dr. Williams's Library, MS Morrice Q, p. 379.

14 *Ibid.*, pp. 378, 382, 393, 395. The most outspoken advocate was Henry Pollexfen, who declared 'that the Prince of Orange had nothing to do, but in the head of his army to declare himself King'. *Clar. Corr.*, ii. 225: 15 Dec.

15 See below, pp. 153-4.

XXII James's Second Flight

1 Clarke, *Life of James II*, ii. 270. Dr. Williams's Library, MS Morrice Q, pp. 382, 385.

2 J. G. A. Pococke, 'Dr. Robert Brady', *Cambridge Historical Journal*, ii (1948), 101-3.

3 *Clar. Corr.*, ii. 232-3, 234. James appointed Clarendon's messenger Belson to speak to him on the morning of the 23rd, but his flight unwisely prevented their meeting.

4 Dr. Williams's Library, MS Morrice Q, p. 413.

5 Clarke, *Life of James II*, ii. 271.

6 Dr. Williams's Library, MS Morrice Q, p. 391. *Clar. Corr*, ii. 233.

7 Clarke, *Life of James II*, ii. 270, 272.

8 Dr. Williams's Library, MS Morrice Q, p. 390. Ailesbury, ii. 222.

9 Dr. Williams's Library, MS Morrice Q, p. 387. *Clar. Corr.*, ii. 233. Clarke, *Life of James II*, ii. 272.

10 Ailesbury, ii. 222-3, 224. Dr. Williams's Library, MS Morrice Q, p. 390.

11 *Loc. cit.* Clarke, *Life of James II*, ii. 275-7. *Clar. Corr.*, ii. 234.

12 See below, pp. 149-51, 153.

13 William of Orange's letter of summons, St. James's Palace, 23 Dec. Bodl., MS Rawlinson D. 691, pp. 36-37.

14 William thereby cast 'an aspersion on his Majesty's government, as if nothing had been regular in his days', just as the Whigs wished to maintain against the Tories. Clarke, *Life of James II*, ii. 285.

15 See below, pp. 159-161.

16 BL, MS Add. 28,053, fo 380: anon. to the Duke of Queensberry, 25 Dec.

17 See below, pp. 161-2, 165-6, 166-7.

18 Bodl., MS Rawlinson D. 691, pp. 49-52. *HMC Dartmouth*, p. 241: Barbara, Lady Dartmouth to Dartmouth, 26 Dec.

19 See below, p. 168. Bodl., MS Rawlinson D. 691, pp. 56-7; MS Eng. hist. d. 307, fos 23-4.

20 Foxcroft, *Halifax*, ii. 203-4: Halifax's note of a conversation with William on 30 Dec.

NOTES TO THE JOURNAL

1 Col. Bevill Skelton, soldier and diplomatist. Envoy in Holland (1685), where he acquired a reputation for intrigue and incompetence, he was removed to France (1686). He was recalled in Sept. 1688 'for haveing exceeded his commission at that court', where he countenanced Louis XIV's attempt to hinder Orange's invasion plans. Committed to the Tower 'for high misdemeanours' (18 Sept.), he was released (5 Oct.), commissioned as Col. (9 Oct.), and appointed Lieutenant of the Tower in place of Hales (27 Nov. 1688). Later he went into exile as a Jacobite, and became a Catholic. PRO, SP 44/338, pp. 100, 205;

165, p. 105; 339, pp. 31, 32, 39. *Clar. Corr.* i. 163, 166-7, 208. Luttrell, i. 462, 467, 520, 543; ii. 175. Dalton, i. 71, 82, 100, 123; ii. 187, 189. P. S. Lachs, *The Diplomatic Corps under Charles II and James II* (Rutgers 1965), pp. 21, 28, 30, 51, 60, 191-6.

2 Sir John Chapman, Kt (28 Oct. 1678), of St. Lawrence Jewry, London. Master, Mercers' Company (1678). Alderman, Tower Ward (1680-2 Aug. 1687), restored 3 Oct. Lord Mayor of London (29 Oct. 1688). Sharpe, *London and the Kingdom*, ii. 530, 533, 537, 546. Woodhead, *Rulers of London*, p. 45. *The London Gazette*, no. 2395. Luttrell, i. 83, 410, 472, 512, 513.

Bodl., MS Don. c. 38, fo 328: newsletter, London, 30 Oct.

3 William Mann, and his son Daniel, had been granted the office of Sword-Bearer and Keeper of the Sessions House belonging to the City, 8 Aug. 1686. PRO, SP 44/337, pp. 87-8.

4 William Blathwait, of Scotland Yard, Whitehall, and Dyrham Park, Glos. Secretary at War (1683-Feb 1689, May 1689-1704). MP for Newtown, Isle of Wight (1685). Clerk of the PC in Extraordinary (1676-86), and in Ordinary (1686). *Ibid.*, p. 121. SP 44/56, p. 437. G. A. Jacobsen, *William Blathwait, A Late*

Seventeenth Century Administrator (Newhaven, 1932), pp. 227ff.

5 Samuel Pepys, of Winchester Lane, London, and Derby House, Cannon Row, Westminster. Secretary of the Admiralty (1673-9, 1684-9). President, Royal Society (1684-6). A close associate and admirer of James at the Admiralty, he stayed at his post throughout the Revolution, but was dismissed in Mar. 1689. For Gwyn's summons to Pepys to attend the Peers at the Guildhall 'immediately', see Bodl., MS Rawlinson A. 186, fo 210. He was defeated at Harwich 'after a long debate and sharpe words' in the parliamentary election (16 Jan. 1689). Non-juror. Bodl., MS. Rawlinson A. 179, fos 140-175, 177, 225. A. Bryant, *Pepys and the Revolution* (London, 1979), chaps vi and vii.

6 Col. the Hon. Sackville Tufton, 5th son of John, 2nd Earl of Thanet. MP for Appleby (1681, 1685). Tory. His commission as Lt.-Governor of the fort of West Tilbury and of the town and fort of Gravesend was renewed on 20 July 1688. PRO, SP 44/165, p. 57. BL., MS Add. 33,924, fos 68, 70, 72. Dalton, i. 175, 292, 315, 325; ii. 19, 37, 101, 145.

7 Sir Robert Sawyer, Kt (17 Oct. 1677), of Highclere, Hants. MP for Chipping Wycombe (1673-8), Cambridge University (1689). High Church Tory. Attorney General (1681), he was dismissed in 1687 for opposing royal dispensations to Catholics. He defended the Seven Bishops (1688). Dr. Williams's Library, Morrice MS. Q, pp. 360, 397-8. Evelyn, iv. 320, 327, 529, 546, 587. Wood, *Life and Times*, iii. 76, 121, 189, 245, 397. Luttrell, i. 67, 368, 424, 444, 446. *Commons*, ii. 399-403.

8 Perhaps the informer mentioned in PRO, SP 8/2, pt 2, fos 83-4. The 'backs and breasts' referred to were pieces of armour.

9 Salisbury House, south of the Strand and west of Worcester House, was built by Simon Basil for Robert, 1st Earl of Salisbury. The garden gave access to the Thames. *Survey of London*, xviii: *The Strand* (1937), pp. 91, 121-3. For the 'searching for armes at the Lord Salisbury's and other great Romanist houses', see Bodl., MS Don. c. 39, fo 54v: newsletter, London, 11 Dec.

10 The Sheriffs of London were: Sir Humphrey Edwyn, Kt (18 Nov. 1687). Master, Barber-Surgeons' Company (1688). Alderman, Tower Ward (6 Aug. 1687-3 Oct. 1688), superseded; Cheap Ward (25 Oct. 1688). Whig Dissenter. Sir John Fleet, Kt (11 Oct. 1688). Master, Coopers' Company (1689). Alderman, Langborn (9 Oct. 1688). Sharpe, *London and the Kingdom*, ii. 530, 554, 570, 598, 607, 609, 613, 642. Luttrell, i. 411, 457, 468, 469, 523, 556, 582, 595. Woodhead *Rulers of London*, pp. 64-5, 70. W. Foster, 'Sir

John Fleet', *English Historical Review*, li (1936), 681-5. *Middlesex County Records*, old series, iv (1667-1689), ed. J. C. Jeaffreson (1892), p. 326.

11 Henry Crisp, of the Inner Temple. Common Serjeant of the City of London (22 Oct. 1678-11 Dec. 1700). Corporation of London Records Office, Guildhall, London: Journal 48, fo 415.

12 For the original signed Declaration forwarded to William, see PRO, SP 8/2, pt 2, fos 85-6.

13 For the minutes of their proceedings sent to William, see *ibid.*, fos 83-4.

14 Sir John Knatchbull, 2nd Bt (succ. 5 Feb. 1685), of Mersham Hatch, Kent. MP for New Romney (1660), Kent (1685, 1689). Though a Dep. Lt. until Feb., he refused in Oct. 1688 to serve under Lord Teynham, the Catholic Ld Lt. He supported William, sanctioned the reading of his *Declaration* at Faversham, and signed the 'Association'. PRO, SP 31/4, fo 101. Sir Hughe Knatchbull-Hugessen, *Kentish Family* (1960), pp. 56ff. BL., MS Add. 33,923, fo 456. G.E.C., ii. 118. *Commons*, iii. 691-2.

15 Sir William Thomas, 1st Bt (cr. 23 July 1660), of Folkington, Sussex. MP for Seaford (1661, Mar. and Oct. 1679), Sussex (1681), Seaford (1685), Sussex (1689). Moderate Tory. JP (1668), he was dismissed in July 1688 for opposing the repeal of the Test and Penal laws, restored Nov. 1688; Dep. Lt. for Sussex (1670-May 1688), restored Oct. 1688. G.E.C., iii. 95-6. R. A. Beddard, 'The Sussex General Election of 1695', *Sussex Archaeological Society*, cvi (1968), 149-50, 153.

16 Sir Thomas Dyke, 1st Bt (cr. 3 Mar. 1677), of Horeham, Waldron, Sussex. MP for Sussex (1685), East Grinstead (1689). High church Tory, he was upset by James's 'closetting' campaign. JP (1680-July 1688), restored Nov. 1688; Dep. Lt. (1685-May 1688), restored Oct. 1688. *Ibid.*, p. 155. Bramston, pp. 198, 269. MS Morrice Q, p. 52. G.E.C., iv. 80.

17 Thomas Hearne was appointed one of James's twenty Messengers, 25 May 1686. PRO, SP 44/56, p. 334; 44/337, p. 44. Luttrell, i. 521.

18 Philip Frowde, Postmaster-General. PRO, SP 44/56, pp. 164, 177, 287, 333; 63/340, p. 231; 31/4, fo 84; 8/1, pt 2, fo 23. *HMC Dartmouth*, pp. 184, 192, 193, 230, 249.

19 Heneage Finch, of Albury, Surrey, younger son of Heneage, 1st Earl, and brother of Daniel, 2nd Earl of Nottingham. KC (1677). Solicitor-General (1679-86). MP for Oxford University (Mar. 1679, 1689) and Guildford (1685). Tory. He advocated a Regency for James. PRO, SP 44/56, pp. 191, 194. Evelyn, iv. 500. Burnet, iii. 96-7. *Commons*, ii. 323.

20 Sir John Ernle, Kt (4 Apr. 1664), of Burytown, Blunsdon, Wilts. Chancellor of the Exchequer (1676-89), Pr. Cllr (10 May 1676-Dec. 1688), Lord of the Treasury (1687-9). MP for Wilts. (1660), Cricklade (1661), New Windsor (Feb.-Apr. 1679), Great Bedwyn (1681), Marlborough (1685, 1689). Tory. PRO, Adm. 77/2, no. 134; SP 44/337, p. 170; 31/3, fos 258-9. *Clar. Corr.*, ii. 231. *Commons*, ii. 271-4.

21 Sir John Trevor, Kt (29 Jan. 1671), of Clement's Lane, Westminster, and Pulford, Denbys. Speaker of the House of Commons and Master of the Rolls (1685); Pr. Cllr (6 July-16 Dec. 1688). Cousin of Lord Chancellor Jeffreys. MP for Castle Rising (1673), Bere Alston (Mar. and Oct. 1679), Denbighshire (1681), Denbigh (1685), PRO, PC 2/72, p. 138; SP 8/1, pt 2, fo 234; 44/56, pp. 435, 440. Luttrell, i. 343, 449-50, 529.

22 Col. Silas Titus, of Bushey, Herts. Parliamentarian turned Royalist. Groom of the Bedchamber to Charles II (1660). MP for Ludgershall (1660), Lostwithiel (1670), Herts. (Mar. 1679), Hunts. (Oct. 1679, 1681). A Whig, 'of the Presbyterian and Independent party', like Christopher Vane, he was sworn Pr. Cllr (6 July 1688), 'hoping thereby to divert that party from going over to the Bishops and Church of England, which they now began to do'. Bramston, pp. 311-12. Cavelli, ii. 239. PRO, PC 2/72, p. 138; SP 8/1, pt 2, fos 234-7.

23 Sir Charles Cotterell, Kt (18 Feb. 1687), Master of Ceremonies in succession to his father of the same name (27 Dec. 1686). SP 44/337 p. 167. Wood, *Fasti*, ii. 324-5.

24 Don Pedro de Ronquillo, Spanish Ambassador successively to Charles II, James II, and William and Mary. He was a considerable connoisseur, collector and bibliophile, being a 'vero Padre, e Mecenate de' Letterati'. G. Leti, *Il Teatro Brittanico*, ii. 506-13. Ailesbury, i. 152, 224, 235, 455. PRO, SP 44/56, pp. 381-2. Luttrell, i. 58, 133, 561.

25 The mob had wreaked his residence, Weld (or Wild) House, leaving it 'a ruinated place'. It stood on the east side of Wild Street, an extension of John Webb's Great Queen Street, and was named after its builder, Humphrey Weld. *Survey of London*, v: *St Giles-in-the-Fields*, pt ii (1914), pp. 93-7. Bramston, pp. 339-400.

26 Captain Thomas King, of the Earl of Huntingdon's Regiment of Foot, son of Thomas King, Gentleman of the Privy Chamber (1671-85). Later MP for Queenborough (1696). PRO, SP 44/165, pp. 69ff. Dalton, i. 221, 297; ii. 26, 106, 134, 167.

27 Lt.-Col. Ferdinando Hastings, of the Earl of Huntingdon's Regiment of Foot (21 Apr. 1686). Government parliamentary candidate for Scarborough

(Sept. 1688). He helped to arrest his cousin, Theophilus, Earl of Huntingdon, at Plymouth, and received a commission from William *via* the Earl of Bath (Nov. 1688). PRO, SP 44/164, p. 310; 56, p. 435; 8/2, pt 2, fo 198. *HMC Hastings*, ii. 195-9. *Hatton Corr.*, ii. 108-9. Dalton, i. 59, 170, 281, 294, 319; ii. 19, 72, 143.

28 Perhaps Charles O'Hara (Hare, Haira, Harah). Later Lt.-Col. of the First Foot Guards (16 Mar. 1689). Dalton, ii. 71, 114, 129.

29 Titus Oates, a renegade Catholic and Anglican clergyman, currently a prisoner in King's Bench. As the notorious originator of the Popish Plot, and a convicted perjuror, he had been condemned to stand in the pillory and be whipped 'yearly duringe his life'. *State Trials*, x. 1316. PRO, Adm. 77/3, nos 1, 23, 24; SP 44/54, p. 353. He and Johnson, it was reported on 20 Dec., 'have libertie to goe abroade and will suddenly be discharged from theire imprisonments'. Bodl., MS Don. c. 39, fo 74. Bramston, pp. 178, 194, 318. J. P. Kenyon, *The Popish Plot* (1972), pp. 51ff.

30 Samuel Johnson, Whig clergyman, who had been deprived of his orders (20 Nov. 1686), sentenced to stand twice in the pillory, be whipped from Newgate to Tyburn, and fined 500 marks, for having committed 'high misdemeanours' in publishing 'two scandalous and seditious pamphlets and libels' defaming the King's government. The Londoners showed their strongly Protestant sympathies by 'being very kind to him' by not throwing anything at him, and in cheering when he was taken down from the pillory. Bramston, pp. 232, 248, 319. PRO, SP 44/336, p. 401; 337, p. 35; Adm. 77/3, nos 4, 10, 41. Bodl., MS Tanner 30, fo 146. J. Wickham Legg, 'The Degradation in 1686 of the Rev. Samuel Johnson', *English Historical Review*, xxix (1914), pp. 723-42.

31 For Sigismund Stydolph, Sheriff of Surrey, see *The London Gazette*, no. 2397 (5-8 Nov.).

32 Edward Jones, of the Savoy. Later King William's Printer in London and Dublin (1689). R. R. Plomer, *A Dictionary of the Printers and Booksellers who were at work in England . . . from 1668 to 1728*, ed. A. Esdale (The Bibliographical Society, Oxford, 1968), p. 174.

33 See Appendix 9.

34 William Penn, the Quaker friend of James II, who had supported the King's policy of religious toleration in England, and had attempted to persuade William and Mary to agree to the repeal of the penal laws and Test Act. James had freed him from Anglican prosecution (9 Mar. 1686). PRO, SP 44/336, pp. 385-6. *The Speech of William Penn To His Majesty, Upon His Delivering the Quakers Address.*

35 Shere to Dartmouth, Whitehall, 13 Dec. *HMC Dartmouth*, p. 223.

36 Philip Musgrave, of Westminster. Son of Sir Christopher Musgrave, 4th Bt, and husband of Mary Legge, daughter of George, 1st Lord Dartmouth. Clerk of the Deliveries, Ordnance Office (1685). Tory MP for Appleby (1685, 1689). Having refused Hales's request for mortars with which to overawe the City, he advised his father-in-law not to oppose the declaration from the Fleet in favour of William during 'this unhappy revolution'. *HMC Downshire*, i. 64. *HMC Dartmouth*, pp. 211, 216-17, 231, 235, 245.

37 Sir Henry Shere, Kt (?20 July 1685), military engineer. He was knighted for his services in Monmouth's Rebellion. Master Surveyor of the Ordnance in succ. to Sir Bernard de Gomme (25 Nov. 1685). As Ld Lt of the Ordnance and Comptroller of the Train of Artillery, he had been appointed to attend James's army to Salisbury (15 Oct. 1688). *Ibid.*, pp. 202-3, 233, 236. PRO, SP 44/70, p. 175; 164, pp. 149, 277, 279, 280; 165, p. 129. Dalton, ii. 44. C. Dalton, 'Sir Henry Shere, Kt', *Proceedings of the Royal Artillery Institution*, xix, no. 9.

38 For *The Hope*, alias *Hopewell*, of London, see PRO, SP 44/336, p. 49; 71, p. 293.

39 For James Porter, see Appendix 10.

40 Sir Henry Johnson, Kt (Mar. 1685), shipbuilder, of Blackwall, Middx., and Friston, Suffolk. Dep. Master, Shipwrights' Company, of Rotherhithe, Surrey (31 Jan. 1686). Col. of Militia Foot, Tower Hamlets (by Aug. 1688). JP, Middx (1685-7, 1689). Tory MP for Aldeburgh (1689), he voted against the vacancy of the throne. PRO, SP 44/337, p. 41. BL, Add. MSS 22,185, fo 140; 22,183, fo 140. Shaw, ii. 260. *Commons*, ii. 654

41 Sir John Friend, Kt (3 Aug. 1685), of Hackney, Middx. Member, Hon. Artillery Company (1667-90). Lt.-Col. of Militia Foot (1680), JP for Middx. (1685-Feb. 1688, Sept. 1688-9). High Church Tory. MP for Great Yarmouth (1685), and recommended as Court candidate for the same, being 'a person of approved loyalty and known affections to the peace and welfare' of James's government (Sept. 1688). Later Non-juror and Jacobite, executed (3 Apr. 1696). *Ibid.*, ii. 369-70. Shaw, ii. 261. PRO, SP 44/164, p. 416; 166, p. 2; 56, p. 430. *HMC Dartmouth*, p. 157. *True Copy of Papers Delivered by Sir John Friend* (London, 1696). J. H. Overton, *The Nonjurors* (London, 1902), pp. 124, 217. J. Garrett, *The Triumphs of Providence: the Assassination Plot, 1696*, (Cambridge 1980), pp. 22-3, 45-6, 48, 65, 108ff.

42 Champion Ashby, Assistant of the remodelled Salters' Company (22 Feb. 1685). PRO, SP 44/70, pp. 134-5.

43 Jane (née Lows), 2nd wife of the Irish peer, Charles Calvert, 3rd Baron Baltimore, the well-known Governor of Maryland, who had been commissioned by the King as Capt. of an independent troop of horse on William's invasion (10 Oct. 1688). Lord Baltimore was reported to have been 'taken' into custody, along with Jeffreys, by Johnson. Bodl., MS Don. c. 39, fo 62: newsletter, 13 Dec.; Don. c. 38, fo 339v: newsletter, London, 10 Nov. PRO, SP 44/165, pp. 108ff.

44 The original order reads *daughters*, not *daughter*, and *also*, not *already*. BL, MS Add. 22,183 (Sir Henry Johnson's Papers), fo 139.

45 Capt. John Reddish, of Col. John Carne's Regiment of Foot. *Ibid.*, pp. 125, 153ff.

46 Capt. William Selwyn, of the First Regiment of Foot Guards. One of the military officers who upheld the peace of London, and submitted to William (11 Dec. 1688). PRO, SP 31/4, fo 203. Dalton, i. 287, 315; ii. 19, 114, 129.

47 Lt.-Col. Richard Bagot, Capt. of a Company in the Hereditary Prince of Denmark's Regiment of Foot (20 Nov. 1688). PRO, SP 44/166, p. 10. Dalton, i. 64, 91, 127, 306, 321; ii. 26, 90, 133, 201.

48 Capt. Thomas Symmonds (Symms), veteran Royalist officer, who had raised forces for Charles I and II. PRO, SP 44/71, p. 235; 31/3, fos 185, 186-8; 31/4, fo 34; 63/351, fos 324-5.

49 Lt.-Col. the Hon. Sir Edward Villiers, Kt (7 Apr. 1680), 4th son of Edward, Viscount Grandison. Knight Marshall. Brigadier of Horse (12 Nov. 1688). He too submitted to William's authority (11 Dec. 1688). SP 44/165, p. 136; 31/4, fo 203. Dalton, i. 14, 73, 80, 126, 134, 210, 234, 311; ii. 15, 38, 66.

50 Dr. Williams's Library, MS Morrice Q, p. 354.

51 Queen Catherine of Braganza, widow of King Charles II, had removed from Whitehall Palace to her dower house, Somerset House, off the Strand, on 7 Apr. 1685. *Grande Enciclopédia Portuguesa e Brasileira* (Lisbon, n.d.), vi. 286 ff.

52 Sir Francis Wheeler, Capt. of a Company in the First Regiment of Foot Guards, in the King's service at sea. PRO, SP 44/165, p. 67; Adm. 77/2, no. 140; SP 44/56, p. 209. Dalton, ii. 114, 129.

53 William Herbert, 1st Marquess of Powis (cr. 24 Mar. 1687), premier Roman Catholic peer of England, and leader of the moderate Catholic group at Court. Pr. Cllr (17 July 1686). Ld Lt of Cheshire (15 Feb. 1688). Later a Jacobite exile, cr. Duke of Powis (12 Jan. 1689). Luttrell, i. 301, 383, 396, 421, 428ff. PRO, SP 44/337, p. 229; 44/165, pp. 9, 18.

54 *The London Mercury*, no. 1 (15 Dec.). It was also spared 'because it was guarded'. Bodl., MS Don. c. 39, fo 62: newsletter, London, 13 Dec.

55 *The London Courant*, no. 2 (12-15 Dec.).

56 Powis House, 'in the corner of Lyncoln's Inn's Fields next to Queen Street', designed by Capt. William Winde, and begun in 1684, following the fire which destroyed its predecessor. From 1705 it was known as Newcastle House. *Survey of London*, iii: *St Giles-in-the-Fields*, pt 1 (1912), 110-18.

57 Sir Thomas Rowe, of Muswell Hill, Middx, and Swarford, Oxon, Lt.-Col. of Sir Henry Johnson's Regiment. BL, MS Add. 22,187, fo 116.

58 BL, MS Loan 29/184, fo 118: A. Pye to Mrs Abigail Harley, [London], 13 Dec.

59 Ailesbury, ii. 200-1.

60 Richard Jones, 1st Earl of Ranelagh (cr. 11 Dec. 1677), of St. James's Square, Westminster. Former Chancellor of the Exchequer (I), 1668-74; Pr. Cllr (I), 1668-85; Tory MP for Plymouth (1685). Paymaster-General of the Forces in England (16 Dec. 1685-1702). He was reported to have been sent to William of Orange on 11 Dec., 'for his commands about paying the army'. *HMC Dartmouth*, p. 230. PRO, SP 44/334, p. 442; 63/340, p. 51; SO 1/12, pp. 41, 152, 301-3; SP 31/3, fo 348.

61 Major Thomas Soper, Commander of a Company in the Royal Regiment Fuziliers. PRO, SP 44/165, p. 112. *HMC Dartmouth*, p. 224. Dalton, ii. 28, 74, 92, 137.

62 Lt.-Gen. Lord James Douglas, son of James, 2nd Marquess of Douglas. He was deserted by a battalion of the Scotch Guards at Reading Fight on 9 Dec. 1688. PRO, SP 44/165, p. 135. *HMC Dartmouth*, p. 228: Pepys to Dartmouth, Admiralty, 10 Dec. Luttrell, i. 485. Dalton, ii. 210.

63 Colnbrook, Bucks., 4 miles south-east of Slough.

64 Col. John Wachop (Warcop), who had been charged by James II with making arrangements for the return of the Six Regiments from Holland. Commander of one of the six Scottish Regiments ordered into England by James II on 1 Nov. His regiment was mostly officered by Catholics who had quitted Dutch service to return to the King. Luttrell, i. 429, 432-3; BL, MS Add. 41,815, fos 157-8. PRO, SP 44/165, p. 157; 44/69, pp. 215-18, 220, 223-24.

65 Col. Thomas Bochan, Col. of a Scottish Regiment of Foot. He remained loyal to King James, and was therefore removed from his command by William. Later the celebrated Jacobite commander. *Ibid.*, pp. 200, 210, 218.

66 Luttrell, i. 529. Evelyn, iv. 616.

67 William Chiffinch (Chiffing), of Whitehall, and Philberts, Bray, Berks. Page of the Backstairs to Queen Catherine of Braganza (1662), and of the Bedchamber and Keeper of the Closet (1666-85). Keeper of Hyde Park (1681-91). Tory MP for New Windsor (1685). Master, Cutlass Co. (1685). D. Allen, 'The Political Function of Charles II's Chiffinch', *Huntington Library Quarterly*, xxxix (1976), 277-90.

68 The Earl of Mulgrave, as Ld Chamberlain, provided the Spanish Ambassador, who had been lucky to 'escape at a back doore' from his embassy, with temporary lodgings in the Palace of Whitehall, for which courtesy he was later thanked both by King James and the Prince of Orange. Mulgrave, ii. 76. Bramston, p. 340.

69 Sir Stephen Fox, Kt (1 July 1665), of Farley, Wilts, and Whitehall. Royalist. Eldest Clerk of the Green Cloth (1661-78, 1679-89), Ld Commissioner of the Treasury (1679-85, 1687-9). He was one of the last officials to be interviewed by the King on the evening of 10 Dec. PRO, SP 44/335, p. 472; 44/337, p. 170; 44/56, p. 429. Ailesbury, i. 194. C. Clay, *Public Finance and Private Wealth. The Career of Sir Stephen Fox, 1627-1716* (Oxford, 1978), p. 227.

70 The Board of the Green Cloth supervised the running of the Royal Household below stairs, and was responsible, *inter alia*, for lodging and diet in the Palace of Whitehall.

71 Col. Henry Slingsby, of Whitehall, and Portsmouth, Hants., 2nd son of Sir Henry Slingsby, 1st Bt. Lt.-Governor of Portsmouth (1682-9), Groom of the Bedchamber to James, as Duke of York (1682-5), and as King (1685-Dec. 1688). Tory MP for Portsmouth (1685, 1689). PRO, SP 44/165, p.25; 44/69, p. 230; 44/56, p. 435. Dalton, ii. 149, 185.

72 *The English Currant*, no. 2: 12-14 Dec., *The London Mercury*, no. 1: 15 Dec.

73 Major Michael Arnold, of Great Peter Street, Westminster, Major of the Middx Militia and JP of Westminster (1680-89). Tory MP for Westminster (1685), Brewer to the King until July 1688. Juryman in the Seven Bishops' Trial (June 1688). PRO, SP 44/165, p. 12. Luttrell, i. 446, 448.

74 John Whitfield, gentleman, of the parish of St. Mary Magdalene, Burgate, Canterbury, 'Largus Pauperum Patronus' (died 1691). I owe this information to Miss A. M. Oakley, Archivist of the Cathedral, City, and Diocesan Record Office, Canterbury.

75 Sir Henry Palmer, 3rd Bt (succ. 1656), of Wingham, Kent. Former Dep. Lt of Kent, he had refused to be deputed by the

Catholic Ld Lt, Lord Teynham, in Oct. 1688. PRO, SP 44/164, p. 178; SP 31/4, fo 101. Bodl., Tanner MS. 124, fo 112. Dr. Williams's Library, MS Morrice Q, p. 356. G.E.C., i. 164.

76 Sir William Honeywood, 2nd Bt (succ. 1670), of Evington Place, Elmsted, and Canterbury, Kent. JP (1675-Feb. 1688, Oct. 1688), and Dep. Lt (1679-Feb. 1688, Oct. 1688) of Kent. MP for Canterbury (1689). Bodl., MS Tanner 41, fo 93. PRO, SP 44/164, p. 178. BL, MS Stowe 746, fo 7. G.E.C., iii. 90.

77 Sir Anthony Aucher, 1st Bt (cr. 4 July 1666), of Bishopsbourne, Kent. Royalist. JP (1660-92) and Dep. Lt (1660-89) for Kent. MP for Canterbury (1660); High Steward of St. Augustine's Court (1663-92). Bodl., MS Tanner 41, fo 83; MS Wood F. 4, p. 147. PRO, SP 44/164, p. 178; 44/165, p. 13; 44/338, p. 28.

78 Dr. John Lee, nephew, heir, and executor of Dr. John Warner, Bishop of Rochester. Rector of Milton (29 Apr. 1642) and of South Fleet (inducted 4 May 1660); Archdeacon and Canon of Rochester Cathedral (9 Aug. 1660). Though he refused, out of fear of the rabble, to aid James's escape from Faversham, he did his best to alieviate his sufferings, and, 'with some other gentry and clergy', collected about £100 'to serve his present wants'. BL, MS Add. 32,095, fo 305. Kent County Record Office, D Rc/R9, fos 96, 101v, 103, 112. E. Lee-Warner, *The Life of John Warner . . . with some account . . . of the Lee-Warner Family* (London 1901), pp. 63, 64, 67, 79, 80.

79 Col. Sir Edward Hales, 3rd Bt, of Paulersbury, Northants., and of Hackington, *alias* St. Stephen's, Kent. Catholic convert (formally reconciled 11 Nov. 1685). JP (1675-85, 1687-Nov. 1688) and Dep. Lt (Feb.-Oct. 1688). Ld of the Admiralty (1679-84). Col. of Regiment of Foot (1685-Oct. 1688). Lt.-Governor of Dover Castle (1686-Nov. 1688); Judge of the Admiralty, Cinque Ports (1686-Dec. 1688); Lt of the Tower of London (1687-Nov. 1688). Later imprisoned in the Tower and charged (26 Oct. 1689) with high treason 'in being reconciled to Rome' and 'other high crimes'. He was excepted from the Williamite Act of Pardon and fled to James II in France, where he was created Earl of Tenterden. PRO, SP 29/359, pp. 211-13, 217-18; 8/1, pt 2, fos 74-5; 44/56, p. 365; 44/69, p. 198; 44/70, p. 246; 44/337, pp. 87-9, 299-305. Wood, *Life and Times*, iii. 190, 212, 233, 238, 287-9, 313, 323-4, 331, 493. Dalton, ii. 35, 144.

80 Heneage Finch, 2nd Earl of Winchelsea, had been replaced as Ld Lt of the County of Kent by the Catholic Lord Teynham (9 Dec. 1687). James II re-appointed him to the Lord Lieutenancy before returning to London on 16 Dec. 1688 in place of the Earl of Feversham.

PRO, SP 44/165, p. 3; 44/69, p. 151. *The London Gazette*, no. 2392.

81 Henry Mordaunt, 2nd Earl of Peterborough (succ. 19 June 1643). Catholic convert. Groom of the Stole and First Gentleman of the Bedchamber (1685); Ld Lt of Northants (1685) and Rutland (9 Dec. 1687). He had received a warrant for a royal pardon in Oct. 1688, and a passport for himself and his servants on 8 Dec. 1688. PRO, Adm. 77/2, no. 132; 44/70, p. 265; 44/56, p. 165; 44/164, p. 142; 44/165, p. 2; 44/338, pp. 112, 114, 158. Wood, *Life and Times*, ii. 462; iii. 18, 46, 54. Luttrell, i. 336, 338-9, 345, 348 ff; ii. 113, 123, 376, 425, 551; iii. 254, 256.

82 Nicholas Chounce (Chowne), Dep. Lt of the Borough of Southwark and Major of the Regiment of the Trained Bands of Southwark. PRO, SP 44/165, p. 12.

83 Halifax's incomplete notes, endorsed 'Concerning King James his being taken', appear to have been jotted down from Clinton's report: 'The gentlemen bid them stop Jesuites, and perhaps they might take somebody else. Mr. Marsh knew the King and fell upon his knees. The King wept, and said hee hoped hee was fallen into good hands, and that they would do him no hurt. The gentlemen said they would not detaine him. The seamen said they would not let him go. Wee were afraid hee was coming to some of his forces to kill us. The seamen said they would let him go, if the City of London was willing to it'. BL, Althorp MSS: Halifax Papers, (e).

84 i.e., the King.

85 Richard Marsh, 'a brewer, first discovered the King', i.e., recognized him, as he was 'passing along the street to The Queens Arms', in Faversham, with his captors. Bodl., MS Wood D. 18, fo 59. E. Jacob, *The History Of The Town and Port of Faversham* (London 1774), Appendix x.

86 But James had received the Commissioners' letter with William's proposals. See above, p. 32.

87 George Douglas, 1st Earl of Dumbarton (cr. 9 Mar. 1675). Scottish Catholic peer with a title, but no lands. Col. of the Royal Regiment of Foot. Gentleman of the Bedchamber (adm. 9 July 1688). James had contributed towards paying off his debts. He was reluctant to submit to William. Akerman, pp. 159, 160, 161, 163. Dalton, ii. 52, 62, 89, 91, 131.

88 Ailesbury, iii. 202.

89 James Grahme, of Bagshot, Surrey, and Levens, Westmorland. Keeper of the Privy Purse (1685–Dec. 1685), Master of the Buckhounds (1685-9). MP for Carlisle (1685). Tory. Later Jacobite. J. V. Beckett, 'The Finances of a former Jacobite: James Grahme of Levens Hall', *Trans. of the*

Cumberland and Westmorland Antiquarian and Archaeological Society, lxxxv (1985), 131–42. J. Bagot, *Col. James Grahme of Levens*. PRO, SP 44/336, p. 51; Adm. 77/2, no. 132.

90 Thomas Heywood, Page of the Bedchamber in Ordinary (adm. 14 May 1685). SP 44/336, p. 84.

91 Thomas Fraser, one of the King's Barbers in Ordinary (adm. 30 May 1685). *Ibid.*, pp. 131, 229.

92 Hans Willem Bentinck, Gentleman of the Bedchamber to William of Orange and his intimate friend. He had conducted the negotiations with Friedrich III, Elector of Brandenburg, on the eve of the invasion. He often acted as William's secretary. Later 1st Earl of Portland (cr. 9 Apr. 1689). Japikse, *Correspondentie*, I, ii. 626-34. For the Peers' original letter to William, see PRO, SP 8/2, pt. 2, fo 87. It was also signed by T. Jermyn.

93 Perhaps John Wroth, of Loughton Hall, Essex, who had aided the escape of Princess Anne and Bishop Compton from London. Later MP for Essex (1689). Ailesbury i. 191. Bramston, pp. 317-18, 346. *VCH Essex*, iv. 118.

94 Capt. Richard Fowler commanded a Company in the Royal Regiment of Fusiliers. PRO, SP 44/165, p. 124; 164, p. 242; 71, p. 222. Dalton, ii. 28, 137.

95 See Appendix 8. Dr. Williams's Library, MS Morrice Q, pp. 359-60.

96 Sir Robert Filmer, 2nd Bt (succ. 22 Mar. 1676), of East Sutton. Sheriff of Kent (1688-9). *The London Gazette*, no. 2397 (5- 8 Nov.).

97 George Bromwich was sworn Messenger on 25 May 1686. PRO, SP 44/56, p. 334; 337, p. 44.

98 Col. Sir Charles Carney, Kt, appointed Col. of the Earl of Bath's Regiment of Foot (8 Dec. 1688). He had been commissioned as Lt.-Governor of the town and garrison of Portsmouth in the absence or indisposition of Sir Edward Scott (30 Nov. 1688). Catholic loyalist. SP 44/164, pp. 410-11; 165, pp. 146, 151, 155, 156-7; 336, pp. 280-4. Dalton, ii. 31, 91, 107, 140.

99 Fr. Edward Petre (Peter, Peters), S.J., 2nd son of Sir Francis Petre, 1st Bt, of Granham Hall, Essex, and grandson of the 1st Baron Petre. He succ. to the Baronetcy on the death of his brother, Sir Francis, the 2nd Bt (1679). Clerk of the Closet (1685). Pr. Cllr (11 Nov. 1687). He was maligned by Protestant propagandists as the real father of the 'supposed' Prince of Wales. Foley, v. 272-77. J. Gillow, *A Literary and Biographical History . . . of the English Catholics* (5 vols., n.d.), v. 290-1. G.E.C., ii. 247.

100 Lt.-Col. William Wakelin (Wakelyn,

Wacklin), Capt. in the Earl of Craven's Regiment of Foot Guards (12 Feb. 1685). PRO, SP 44/164, p. 408; 44/165, pp. 70ff. Dalton, ii. 21, 130.

101 'December 12. Whereas several disorderly. Persons did, in a Tumultuous and Riotous manner, last Night insult the House of his Excellency the Spanish Ambassador, Plundering, Rifling, and Defacing the same, and carrying away Plate, Goods, Books, and Papers, to a great Value: These are to give Notice, by particular Command from the Peers Assembled, That if any Person shall discover any of the said Plate, Goods, Books, or Papers, and bring the same to the Council-Chamber in Whitehall, or give such Information that they may be recovered, they shall be very well rewarded in proportion to what shall be so recovered'. *The London Gazette*, no. 2409 (10-13 Dec.).

102 Sir Henry Firebrace (Firebrass), Clerk Comptroller of the Green Cloth. PRO, SP 44/336, p. 31; 53, p. 471. G.E.C., iv. 175. Shaw, ii. 263. Akerman, p. 114.

103 Henry Arundell, 3rd Baron Arundell of Wardour (succ. 1643). Catholic, and veteran Royalist. Pr. Cllr (17 July 1686); Lord Privy Seal (12 Mar. 1687); Ld Lieutenant of Dorset (7 July 1688). PRO, SP 44/336, pp. 84, 97, 99, 412-7; 337, pp. 238, 274, 299; 165, p. 55. Akerman, p. 156.

104 Sir Basil Dixwell, 2nd Bt (succ. 7 May 1668), of Broom House, Barham, Kent. Col. of the Kent Militia Horse (1688). Whig. Great nephew of the regicide, John Dixwell. James complained of his 'rude and rebellious carriage' towards him while he was a prisoner. Dixwell and Oxenden had brought their troops to Faversham 'under pretence of securing the King from the rabble, but indeed to secure him for themselves and to make their peace with the Prince of Orange'. Later MP for Dover (1689). Hasted, *Kent*, vi. 350-1. Ailesbury, ii. 210-12. BL, MS Add. 28,037, fo 50. G.E.C., iii. 44. Wood, *Life and Times*, ii. 370; iii. 388.

105 Sir James Oxenden, 2nd Bt (succ. Aug. 1686), of Deane, Wingham, Kent. Capt. of the Kent Militia Horse (1688). Whig Exclusionist. MP for Sandwich (Mar. and Oct. 1679, 1681, 1689). An avid Williamite, he denounced the King on 28 Jan. 1689 for chosing 'to go away and stir up foreign princes to bring in a foreign power to destroy us'. PRO, SP 44/70, p. 133. G.E.C., iv. 99. Grey, *Debates*, ix. 21.

106 Fr. John Warner, S.J., the King's Confessor, whom the King had lodged at Whitehall and paid a stipend of £200 *per annum*. Akerman, pp. 182, 186, 188, 199, 210. Dr. Williams's Library, MS Morrice P, pp. 532, 628; Q, p. 210. Cavelli, i. 33. Luttrell, i. 339; ii. 606. Wood, *Life and Times*, iii. 406.

107 Capt. George Cholmondley (Cholmley), Capt. of a Troop in the Queen Consort's Regiment of Horse (1 June 1686). PRO, SP 44/164, p. 261. Dalton, ii. 15, 17, 56, 77, 121.

108 Anthony Carey, 5th Viscount Falkland (succ. 2 Apr. 1663), of Great Tew, Oxon. Treasurer of the Navy (1681–89). Groom of the Stole to George of Denmark (1687–90). MP for Oxfordshire (1685, 1689). He spoke in favour of James's 'abdication'. PRO, SP 31/1, no. 51.

109 For Morton, the drunken 'Scotchman', and his having no 'malitious purpose to kill the Duke', see Dr. Williams's Library, MS Morrice Q, pp. 361-2.

110 Sir Robert Guildford (Guilford, Guldeford), 1st Bt (cr. 4 Feb. 1686), of Hempstead Place, Benenden, Kent. Catholic. Dep. Lt of Kent (4 Feb. 1688), and Cornet to Capt. Sir Robert Throckmorton in Col. George Holman's Regiment of Horse. PRO, SP 44/336, pp. 271-3; 165, pp. 13ff; 338, p. 28; 69, pp. 233-4. G.E.C., iv, 139. Dalton, ii. 191.

111 Col. John Hales, Col. of a Regiment of Foot (Mar. 1688), had submitted to William on 11 Dec. PRO, SP 31/4, fo 203; cf. SP 44/165, p. 34.

112 Col. Oliver Nicholas, of Aldbourne, Wilts. Groom of the Bedchamber in Ordinary (adm. 2 May 1685), and later to James III at St. Germain-en-Laye (1702). MP for Wilton (1685). Tory. Later Jacobite. PRO, SP 44/336, p. 80; 56, p. 438; 165, pp. 100, 128. Akerman, p. 101.

113 John Chase was Apothecary to Charles and James II. PRO, SP 44/71, p. 310; 336, p. 252.

114 Lt.-Col. William Tuite, of Lord Forbes's Regiment of Foot. Catholic. PRO, SP 44/336, pp. 314-22. Dalton, ii. 179, 185.

115 Col. Arthur Forbes, Viscount Forbes, son of Arthur, 1st Earl of Granard, Lord President of the Council in Ireland. Protestant. He commanded one of the five Irish Regiments ordered into England by King James on the invasion. PRO, SP 44/169, pp. 156-7; SP 63/340, pp. 151-64; SO 1/12, p. 85. HMC Dartmouth, p. 158: James II to Dartmouth, Whitehall, 14 Oct. Dalton, ii. 209, 221.

116 Kenneth Mackenzie, 4th Earl of Seaforth, Scottish Pr. Cllr (1686), KT (1687). Catholic loyalist. Husband of Frances Herbert, daughter of William, 1st Marquess of Powis. Later Jacobite. PRO, SP 44/336, pp. 412-17. For the original of the Peers' order to take off 'the restraint laid upon the Earle … and his family', see BL, MS Add. 22,183, fo 140: Whitehall, 14 Dec. (signed by Halifax, Mulgrave, Thanet, Anglesey, Rochester, and Hamilton).

117 William's reply was: 'My Lords, as it has pleased God, by His Spirit, to bring on and prosper this undertaking for the preservation of the Protestant religion, and of your laws and liberties, so I trust the same Spirit will lead us till the work be perfected.' BL, MS Add. 32,096, fo 334.

118 Berkeley House, St. James's (Piccadilly), had been 'made a priorie for Benedictines and was consecrated for that use' in the presence of Queen Mary Beatrice on 30 Apr. 1686. Wood, Life and Times, iii. 266.

119 Lt.-Col. Sir George Berkeley (Barclay), of Sir Edward Hales's Regiment of Foot. Catholic. PRO, SP 44/337, pp. 299-305. Dalton, ii. 62, 85, 144. Later an active Jacobite conspirator. Garrett, The Triumphs of Providence, pp. 45, 88-9, 92ff.

120 Thomas Atterbury, one of the twenty Messengers in Ordinary (25 May 1686), and Clerk of the Cheque. PRO, SP 44/56, p. 334; 72, p. 219; 338, p.131.

121 See above, p. 109.

122 See above, pp. 72-3.

123 Lt.-Col. Sir Edward Vaudrey, Kt (28 May 1687), Lt.-Col. of the Queen Dowager's Regiment of Horse (21 Dec. 1687). Former tutor and companion of James, Duke of Berwick, whom he attended to the siege of Buda (1686). Catholic. PRO, SP, 44/165, pp. 5, 147-8; 336, p. 152. Shaw, ii. 263. Dalton, ii. 113, 125. Akerman, pp. 187, 194, 198, 208. Luttrell, i. 405.

124 Francis Smith, 2nd Viscount Carrington of Burford, (I), and Baron Carrington of Wootton (succ. 1665), of Wootton Wawen, Worcs. Catholic loyalist. Ld Lt of Worcs. (1687-89). Husband of Anne Herbert, daughter of William, 1st Marquess of Powis. Later Jacobite. PRO, SP 44/336, pp. 412-17; 164, p. 429; 56, pp. 425, 431.

125 Lt.-Gen. Robert Werden, Lt.-Gen. over all the King's Forces (8 Nov. 1688), and Col. of a Regiment of Horse. He submitted to William's orders on 11 Dec. 1688. PRO, SP 44/165, pp. 53, 134-7; 69, p. 222; SP 31/4, fo 203. Dalton, ii. 3, 46, 52, 58, 89, 113, 123, 198.

126 Charles Murray, 1st Earl of Dunmore (S), cr. 16 Aug. 1686. Second son of John, 1st Marquess of Atholl. Col. of the Royal Regiment of Dragoons (1685). He was ordered into England from Scotland by King James at the invasion. Master of Horse to Queen Mary Beatrice (1685-88). Tory MP for Wigan (1685). He requested William's permission to withdraw his troops to Scotland from Watford, Herts., on 11 Dec. 1688. PRO, SP 44/336, p. 212; SP 31/1, no. 81; SP 8/2, pt 2, fos 77-8. Dalton, ii. 210.

127 Capt. Charles Townley, of Townley, Lancs. Capt. of Col. George Holman's

Regiment of Horse, to whom Richard Townley was Cornet. PRO, SP 44/69, pp. 233-4: 10 Oct. 1688. Dalton, ii. 191.

128 Lt.-Col. Andrew Dorrington, of the Earl of Ossory's Regiment of Foot (Irish Guards). HMC Dartmouth, p. 158: James II to Dartmouth, Whitehall, 14 Oct. He was granted a pass to Dover on 10 Dec. 1688. PRO, SP 63/340, pp. 151-64, 209-12, 269; 44/339, p. 41.

129 Capt. John Plunkett, of the Earl of Ossory's Regiment of Foot (Irish Guards), PRO, SP 63/340, p. 283.

130 Richard Lawless, Lt. to Capt. Arthur Macmahen in Maj.-General Justin Maccarty's Regiment of Foot. Ibid., pp. 251-4.

131 William Bridgeman, of Pall Mall, Westminster, and Combs Hall, Suffolk. Under-Secretary of State (1667-81, 1683-9), Clerk of the Privy Council (1685-Dec. 1688), Registrar of the Court of Ecclesiastical Commission (1687-Oct. 1688). Tory MP for Bramber (1685). JP for Middx (1677-89) and Westminster (1677-89). PRO, SP 44/337, p. 392; 56, p. 440; 337, p. 121. HMC Dartmouth, pp. 183, 201.

132 Joseph Gosling, an old and trusted servant, to whom Lord Jeffreys left an annuity of £40. G. W. Keeton, Lord Chancellor Jeffreys and the Stuart Cause, p. 464.

133 For another Catholic threat against William's life by Peters, 'prentice to Mr. Manock of the City, both Papists', see Dr. Williams's Library, MS Morrice Q, p. 399.

134 James Stanford (Stamford), Envoy of Philipp Wilhelm von Neuburg, the Elector Palatine of the Rhine (1685-90). Catholic. He was unpopular because he had used his diplomatic status as a means of opening a Catholic Chapel in Lime Street in the City. The Lord Mayor was commanded to appoint a sufficient guard for his servants and goods on their removal from the City in Nov. 1688. PRO, SP 44/97, p. 16. Dr. Williams's Library, MS Morrice Q, pp. 530, 570, 623.

135 Thomas Lee (Lea, Lay), one of the twenty Messengers in Ordinary (25 May 1685). PRO, SP 44/56, p. 334; 337, p. 44.

136 Ailesbury, ii. 202.

137 Capt. Henry Morgan, Quartermaster of the 4th Troop of Horse Guards (23 May 1686). PRO, SP 44/164, p. 324. Dalton, ii. 193.

138 Lt. John Craven, of Capt. William Gibbons's Independent Company of Foot (3 Oct. 1688). PRO, SP 44/165, pp. 95ff.

139 Lt.-Col. John Vaughan, of the Earl of Salisbury's Regiment of Horse (5 Nov. 1688). Ibid., p. 133.

140 For the patents of new Sheriffs sealed

by Lord Chancellor Jeffreys since 6 Nov. 1688, see *The London Gazette*, nos. 2397-2401, 2403, 2405-7. It was reported that, though the parliamentary writs were sealed, 'yet but few ‹were› given out, for that the new Sheriffs doe not come to take out their patents'. Bodl., MS Don. c. 39, fo 46: newsletter, London, 8 Dec.

141 Burnet, iii. 352. Wood, *Life and Times*, iii. 388.

142 James Chadwick, son-in-law of Dr. John Tillotson, Dean of Canterbury. Ailesbury, ii. 207. T. Birch, *The Life Of... Dr. John Tillotson* (London 1752), pp. 134, 273, 366, 369.

143 Thomas Nappleton, 'an inferior sort of lawyer', who 'very unworthily' read William's *Declaration* under James's window during his detention at Faversham, and had been the first who 'ventur'd to kneel doune and beg the favour of His Majesty's hand'. Bodl., MS Wood D. 18, fo 59. Ailesbury, ii. 201, 207, 208. E. Jacob, *The History Of the Town and Port of Faversham* (London 1774), p. 206.

144 Count Rovero, Envoy Extraordinary to James II from Victor Amadeus II, Duke of Savoy. He had a pass to go beyond seas. PRO, SP 44/338, p. 150: 30 Nov. 1688.

145 Richard Talbot, 1st Earl of Tyrconnell (cr. 20 June 1685), Lt.-General of the Army in Ireland (1 Mar. 1686), executed James's instruction to re-model the army in favour of Catholics. Pr. Cllr (1686), and Ld Lt of Ireland (11 Feb. 1687) in succession to Henry, 2nd Earl of Clarendon. Catholic. Later cr. Duke of Tyrconnell (30 Mar. 1689) by James acting as *de facto*, as well as *de jure*, King of Ireland. HMC *Stuart*, i. 39. G.E.C., i, appendix F. PRO, SP 63/430, p. 188; 44/337, p. 173; SO 1/12, p. 148.

146 For the importance of the Association, see above, pp. 22, 32.

147 For the test case of Godden *versus* Hales (1686), see J. R. Tanner, *English Constitutional Conflicts of the Seventeenth Century 1603-1689* (Cambridge 1962), pp. 253-4, 289-91.

148 The Catholic Judges were Sir Christopher Milton, brother of the poet (1686); Sir Richard Allibone (1687); and Sir Charles Ingelby (1688). Luttrell, i. 375; 387, 388, 402, 456; 449, 450, 482.

149 For James's being joyously owned by his subjects in 1685, see Beddard, 'The Church of Salisbury and the Accession of James II', *Wiltshire Archaeological Magazine*, lxvii (1972), pp. 132-35.

150 As King, James went openly to daily Mass. PRO, SP 31/1, nos 34, 40.

151 For James's accession declaration, see *The London Gazette*, no. 2006 (5-9 Feb. 1685).

152 The Ecclesiastical Commission was

created on 8 July 1686 (Archbishop Sancroft of Canterbury (who declined to sit), Jeffreys, Rochester, Sunderland, Bishop Crew of Durham, Bishop Sprat of Rochester, and Lord Chief Justice Sir Edward Herbert). It was renewed on 19 Nov. 1686 (when Sancroft was omitted and Mulgrave inserted), and re-created on 9 Jan. 1687 (with the addition of Theophilus Hastings, 7th Earl of Huntingdon). PRO, SP 44/337, pp. 68-74, 136, 173-4.

153 i.e., Robert Spencer, 2nd Earl of Sunderland.

154 For Dr. Henry Compton's suspension from the See of London (6 Sept. 1686-30 Sept. 1688), see E. Carpenter, *The Protestant Bishop*, pp. 93-100, 125. PRO, Adm. 77/3; no. 31: 11 Sept. 1686.

155 Dr. John Sharpe, Rector of St. Giles-in-the-Fields (1675) and Dean of Norwich (1681). Bramston, pp. 233, 234, 266.

156 For the case of Magdalen College, Oxford, see J. R. Bloxam, *Magdalen College and King James 1686-1688*, Oxford Historical Society, vi (Oxford 1886).

157 H. Stubbs, *Select Charters* (9th edn, 1910), pp. 292ff.

158 For the text of James's Second Declaration of Indulgence of April 1688, see PRO, PC 2/72, fos 115-16v; SP 44/337, p. 427.

159 Dr. Thomas Sprat, Bishop of Rochester, resigned from the ranks of the Ecclesiastical Commissioners 'as by no meanes approving of their prosecution of the Cleargy who refus'd to reade his Majesties declaration for liberty of Conscience'. Evelyn, iv. 596., *The Lord Bishop of Rochester's Letter*.

160 For the importance of the Archbishop of Canterbury's declining to sit, see Beddard, 'Sancroft', pp. 143-8.

161 Fr. Edward Petre, S.J., Pr. Cllr (11 Nov. 1687). PRO, PC 2/72, fo 49v.

162 The best account of the 'closetting' campaign is in J. R. Jones, *The Revolution of 1688 in England*, chapter 6.

163 See A. F. Havighurst, 'James II and the Twelve Men in Scarlet', *Law Quarterly Review*, lxix (1953), pp. 522-46.

164 For Tyrconnell and the Catholic revival in Ireland, see J. G. Simms, *Jacobite Ireland 1685-91*, pp. 19-43.

165 Bodl., MS Tanner 28, fo 217: Sir George Mackenzie, Lord Advocate of Scotland, to Archbishop Sancroft, no date.

166 John Lovelace, 1st Baron Lovelace. In Feb. 1688 he was summoned before the Council 'for telling some constables they need not obey the Roman catholick justices of the peace, haveing not qualified themselves; and an information is ordered against them for it'. Luttrell, i. 432.

167 See 'A Letter, Writ by Mijn Heer Fagel, Pensioner of Holland, To Mr. James Stewart, Advocate; Giving an Account of the Prince and Princess Of Orange's Thoughts concerning the Repeal of the Test, and the Penal Laws' in *Literae Illustr: Domini Fagel, Hollandiae Pensionarii* (1688). There was a Dutch version: *Een Brief Gescherven door den Heer Pensionaris Fagel, Aen Mr. James Steward Advocaet*.

168 The 'Loyal Parliament' of 19 May to 20 Nov. 1685, so denominated in contrast to the three factious Parliaments of the Exclusion period, 1679-81.

169 James dissolved his only parliament on 2 July 1687.

170 Despite the partisan claim that 'not one in a thousand here believes' the Prince of Wales 'to be the Queen's' son, his birth was widely celebrated. James took firm steps to authenticate the birth, notably in collecting the sworn testimonies of the witnesses before an extraordinary meeting of the Council on 22 Oct. 1688. R. A. Beddard, 'Two letters from the Tower, 1688', *Notes and Queries*, xxxi (1984), p. 350. PRO, SP 31/4, fos 160-78.

171 For the 'invitation' to William, see E. N. Williams, *The Eighteenth-Century Constitution*, pp. 8-10.

172 See J. Levin, *The Charter Controversy in the City of London, 1660-1688, and its Consequences* (1969), pp. 50ff.

173 Such as was called for in the Seven Bishops' petition of 18 May 1688, see J. P. Kenyon, *The Stuart Constitution 1603-1688* (1966), pp. 441-2.

174 Including Catholics, see above, p. 12.

175 The text has a number of scribal variants from the printed text of *The Declaration*, with which it has been collated.

176 Henry Pollexfen, of Woodbury, Devon, and Lincoln's Inn Fields, London. Bencher (1674) and Reader (1683) of Inner Temple. Whig. He had acted for the prosecution in the Western Assize (1685) and as defence counsel for the Seven Bishops (1688). A zealous Williamite. Later Attorney-General (4 Mar. 1689). M. Landon, *The Triumph of the Lawyers: their Role in English Politics, 1678-1689* pp. 43ff.

177 Sir George Treby, Kt (20 Jan. 1681). Recorder of London (1680-3, 15 Dec. 1688-92). MP for Plympton Erle (1677, Mar. and Oct. 1679, 1681, 1689). Whig. An enthusiastic and diligent Williamite, especially in the City of London. Later Solicitor-General (Feb.-May 1689) and Attorney-General (May 1689). *Ibid.*, pp. 43ff.

178 William Whitelock, of Phyllis Court, Henley, Oxon. Bencher (1671), Reader (1676), and Treasurer (1680) of Middle Temple. MP for West Looe (1659), and

later for Great Marlow (14 Dec. 1689).
Whig. He entertained William on his
march to London.

179 Sir Thomas Duppa, Kt (6 May 1683),
Gentleman Usher of the Black Rod. Shaw,
ii. 258. Luttrell, i. 253; iii. 300.

180 Sir John Maynard, Kt (16 Nov. 1660),
of Gunnersbury and Lincoln's Inn Fields,
London. Protector's (1658-9) and King's
Serjeant (1660). MP for Plymouth (Mar.
and Oct. 1679, 1681, 1689) and Bere Alston
(1685). Keen Williamite. Later a
Commissioner for the Great Seal (1689).
Commons, iii. 38-45.

181 Sir John Holt, Kt (9 Feb. 1686), of
Bedford Row, Middx, and Redgrave,
Suffolk. King's Serjeant (1686-9).
Recorder of London (1686), but dismissed
for refusing to pronounce the death
penalty on a deserter. Dr. Williams's
Library, MS Morrice Q, p. 384. BL, MS
Add. 36,707, fo 45. Luttrell, i. 375, 522ff.
Bramston, pp. 245, 276, 393. Shaw, ii. 261.
Landon, *The Triumph of the Lawyers*,
pp. 44, 128, 158ff.

182 Sir Robert Atkyns, KB (23 Apr.
1661), of Lincoln's Inn, and Sapperton,
Glos. KC (1671), Justice of the Common
Pleas (1672-80). MP for East Looe (1661-
72) and Middx (1681). He was presented
to William by Lord Macclesfield (17
Dec.). Being 'out of town' he 'had no
summons' to attend the Peers. Later Chief
Baron of the Exchequer (1689). *Clar. Corr.*,
ii. 228. Luttrell, i. 233ff. Dr. Williams's
Library, MS Morrice Q, p. 384. Shaw, i.
166.

183 Sir Francis Winningham, Kt (17 Dec.
1672), of Middle Temple, and Stanford
Court, Stanford-on-Teme, Worcs. KC
(1673), Solicitor-General (1674-9). MP for
New Windsor (1677), Worcester (Mar.
and Oct. 1679, 1681). Convert to
Exclusion. Luttrell, i. 80, 85, 195ff. Shaw,
ii. 247.

184 George Bradbury was 'named by the
Lord Dorset, for he does the busines⟨s⟩ of
that family'. Dr. Williams's Library, MS
Morrice Q, p. 384. PRO, SP 44/338,
p. 155.

185 Sir William Dolben, Kt (3 Feb. 1677).
Bencher, Inner Temple (1672), Recorder
of London (1676). Puisne Judge of the
King's Bench (1678-83, 1689-94). Luttrell,
i. 509, 527.

186 'A Proclamation commanding all
persons being popish recusants, or so
reputed, to depart from the Citties of
London and Westminster, and all other
places within ten miles of the same'.
Whitehall, 30 Oct. 1678. PRO, PC 2/66,
pp. 430-1.

187 Delamer had been kept a close
prisoner when in the Tower on a charge
of high treason in 1685-6. PRO, SP 31/1,
no. 139; 44/336, pp. 180, 297, 298; 56, pp.
272, 280, 283, 307, 313, 315.

188 For the printed version, see PRO, SP
31/4, fo 213.

189 Hortense Mancini, Duchesse de
Mazarin, niece of Cardinal Mazarin, and
a distant cousin of Queen Mary Beatrice.
A former mistress of Charles ii. PRO, SP
8/2, pt 2, fos 166-7; 44/56, p. 175. C. H.
Hartmann, *The Vagabond Duchess* (1926).

190 For the Duchesse de Bouillon, see
PRO, SP 44/56, p. 375.

191 For the Marquis de Sessac, see PRO,
SP 44/336, p. 172.

192 François de Grossolles, Marquis de
Flamarens, 'the little French gamster', who,
though 'a Papist, supped' with William on
19 Dec., 'for his table must be free to all'.
PRO, SP 44/336, pp. 131-3. Dr. Williams's
Library, MS Morrice Q, p. 382.

193 Monsieur St. Victor, gentleman of
Avignon, took part in the escape of Queen
Mary Beatrice and the Prince of Wales.
Cavelli, ii. 381-413. Clarke, *Life of James
ii*, ii. 246.

194 Capt. Francis Stafford, of Major-
General Werden's Regiment of Horse.
Catholic. PRO, SP 44/337, pp. 299ff:
dispensation from oaths, Windsor, 3 July
1687. Dalton, ii. 98, 123.

195 John Mannock, Cornet of Capt.
David Lloyd's Troop in the Royal
Regiment of Horse. PRO, SP 44/165,
p. 25. Dalton, i. 149.

196 Perhaps Awnsham Churchill, of
Paternoster Row, near Amen Corner, St.
Paul's Churchyard (1681-1728), a major
bookseller and stationer of London. There
are other booksellers of the same surname,
e.g., Joshua Churchill, who printed the
broadside, *A Paper delivered to His Highness
the Prince of Orange*, 1688 (BL: T.100★
(199)).

197 Charles Hales, of St. James-in-the-
Fields, Catholic, was granted a pardon for
all treasons on 4 Dec. 1688. PRO, SP
44/338, p. 156; cf. 44/336, p. 40.

198 Dr. Obadiah Walker, Master of
University College, Oxford (1679-88).
The leading Catholic convert at Oxford,
nicknamed 'Ave-Maria' Walker by the
Protestant scholars and townees. PRO, SP
44/336, pp. 417-20; 337, pp. 22-6. Wood,
Life and Times, iii. 176, 177, 182-3, 184,
192, 202, 214ff.

199 Sir Thomas Jenner, Kt (4 Oct. 1683),
of Petersham, Surrey. Bencher of the Inner
Temple (1682). Recorder of London
(1683-6). Baron of the Exchequer (1686-
July 1688). Ecclesiastical Commissioner
(1687-Oct. 1688). Justice of the Common
Pleas (July 1688-Dec. 1688). He was
granted a pardon of all treasons on 9 Oct.
1688. He was so unpopular that his
lodgings in Serjeants' Inn were broken
into, 'and the unmerciful rogues, not
content to carry off 400*l*., have robbed

him also of his pardon'. BL, MS Add.
36,707, fo 50: 4 Dec. William objected to
his carriage. PRO, SP 44/338, p. 108; SP
8/2, pt 2, fo 135. Evelyn, iv. 342.
Bramston, pp. 118, 221, 286, 302, 311.

200 Richard Graham, Treasury Solicitor,
received a pardon of all treasons on 10
Oct. 1688. PRO, SP 44/338, pp. 108-9.
BL, MS Add. 36,707, fo 51.

201 Philip Burton, Treasury Solicitor, had
acted against the Seven Bishops. He was
objected to by William for his 'indue
proceedings'. PRO, SP 8/2, pt 2, fos 135-
6. Bodl., MS Don. c. 39, fo 73.

202 Warham Horsemanden, Dep. Lt. of
Essex. PRO, SP 44/165, p. 49. Bramston,
p. 304.

203 Sir Richard Everard, 2nd Bt (succ.
1680), of Westminster, and Langleys,
Much Waltham, Essex. JP for Essex (Oct.
1688). Former MP for Westminster
(1661). G.E.C., ii. 68.

204 Lord Thomas Howard of Worksop
(sometimes styled of Norfolk), brother
and heir of Henry, 7th Duke of Norfolk,
and nephew of Cardinal Philip Howard.
Catholic. Lt. of the Yeoman of the Guard,
and Capt. of a Volunteer Troop of Horse
(1685), Envoy Extraordinary to Pope
Innocent xi (1687). Master of the Robes
(1687), Ld Lt of the West Riding of Yorks.
(1688). He was granted a pardon for all
treasons on 8 Dec. 1688. Again William
objected to his 'indue' actions. Later a
Jacobite exile. PRO, SP 44/335, p. 494;
337, pp. 299-305; 165, pp. 27, 48; 338,
pp. 3, 160; SP 8/2, pt 2, fos 135-6. Dalton,
ii. 16.

205 John Belasyse, 1st Baron Bellasis of
Worlaby (cr. 27 Jan. 1645), 2nd son of
Thomas, 1st Viscount Fauconberg.
Catholic Royalist. Ld Lt of the East
Riding of Yorks. (1660-73), Governor of
Hull (1661-73), Pr. Cllr (17 July 1686-89),
First Lord Commissioner of the Treasury
(1687-88). PRO, SP 44/336, pp. 97, 99,
412-17; 337, p. 170.

206 i.e., legal counsel.

207 For Wharton's outburst against 'that
child, who was called the Prince of Wales',
see *Clar. Corr.*, ii. 235. Bodl., MS
Rawlinson D. 836, fo 110; MS Carte 130,
fo 320v.

208 John Leyburn, Bishop of Adrumetum
(consecrated 9 Sept. 1685), Vicar
Apostolic of England (1685-88), and Vicar
Apostolic of the London District (1688).
T. B. Trappes-Lomax, 'Bishop Leyburn's
Visitation in 1687', *Newsletter for Students
of Recusant History*, iv (1962). Bodl., MS
Don. c. 39, fo 73: newsletter, London, 18
Dec. D. A. Bellenger, *English and Welsh
Priests 1558-1800* (Downside 1984), pp. 82,
209.

209 Ralph Clayton, secular priest of the
London District. Chaplain to Bishop

Giffard. *Ibid.*, pp. 48, 229. G. Anstruther, *The Seminary Priests, A Dictionary of the Secular Clergy of England and Wales 1558-1850* (4 vols, Great Wakering 1968-77), iii. 28, 35-6, 110, 117, 194.

210 Perhaps Walter (not Thomas) Rought, secular priest of the London District. Bellenger, *England and Welsh Priests 1558-1800*, pp. 103, 236.

211 Bonaventure Giffard, Bishop of Madaura (consecrated 22 Apr./2 May 1687), Vicar Apostolic of the Midland District (1688-1703). President of Magdalen College, Oxford (nominated 28 Mar. 1688). *Ibid.*, pp. 64, 207, 231. Anstruther, *The Seminary Priests*, iii. 67-75.

212 Perhaps Ralph (not Robert) Jenison, S.J., of the Northern District, described at the time as 'tutor to the lord Howard's children'. Jacob, *The History Of... Faversham*, p. 212. Bellenger, *English and Welsh Priests 1558-1800*, pp. 76, 232.

213 Charles Poulton (alias Roberts), S.J., schoolmaster of the Jesuit School at the Savoy in London. *Ibid.*, pp. 98, 235. Foley, v. 307-9.

214 Thomas Kingsley (alias DeBois), S.J., of the London District, and chaplain to Lord Teynham. Bellenger, *English and Welsh Priests 1558-1800*, pp. 78, 233. BL, MS Add. 5,842, fo 241. Foley, v. 309.

215 William of St. Francis Lockier, O.F.M. (Recollect), 'Colonel Finch's priest'. Bellenger, *English and Welsh Priests 1558-1800*, p. 83. Jacob, *The History Of ... Faversham*, p. 212.

216 Ralph Hardwicke, Catholic merchant dealing in the Spanish trade. A stay of recusancy prosecutions against him was ordered by James on 18 Apr. 1685. PRO, SP 44/336, pp. 66-8. Bodl., MS Don. c. 39, fo 73.

217 Charles Edge (*alias* Edwards), perhaps Ensign in the Earl of Granard's Regiment

of Foot. PRO, SP 63/340, p. 54.

218 Edward Syng (Sing), Quartermaster of Sir Edward Hales's Regiment of Foot. PRO, SP 44/336, pp. 314-22; 337, pp. 299-305; 164, p. 313-14. Jacob, *The History Of ... Faversham*, pp. 206, 213. Dalton, ii. 35, 144.

219 Thomas and Henry Arundell, Dep. Lts of Wilts. (9 June 1688). PRO, SP 44/165, p. 49. Bodl., MS Don. c. 39, fo 73.

220 Christopher Roper, 5th Baron Teynham (succ. 1673). Catholic. Ld Lt of Kent (9 Dec. 1687-Oct. 1688). PRO, SP 44/165, p. 3; 338, p. 28; SP 31/4, fo 101. Luttrell, i. 563.

221 Major William Richardson, Keeper of Newgate Prison. PRO, SP 44/154, pp. 306, 307, 308, 318; 56, p. 190; 336, p. 352.

222 Anne (née Bermingham), wife of Maximilian O'Dempsey, 3rd Viscount Clanmalier.

SELECT BIBLIOGRAPHY

Ashley, M. *The Glorious Revolution of 1688* (1966).

Baxter, S. B. *William III* (1966).

Beer, E. S. de, 'The Marquis of Albeville and his Brothers', *English Historical Review*, xlv (1930), pp. 397-408.

Beddard, R. A. 'Observations of a London clergyman on the Revolution of 1688-9: being an excerpt from the autobiography of Dr. William Wake', *The Guildhall Miscellany*, ii (1967), pp. 406-17.

—— 'The loyalist opposition in the interregnum: a letter of Dr. Francis Turner, Bishop of Ely, on the Revolution of 1688', *Bulletin of the Institute of Historical Research*, xl (1967), pp. 101-9.

—— 'The Guildhall Declaration of 11 December 1688 and the Counter-Revolution of the Loyalists', *Historical Journal*, xi (1968), pp. 403-20.

—— 'The Violent Party': the Guildhall revolutionaries and the growth of opposition to James II', *The Guildhall Miscellany*, iii (1970), pp. 120-36.

—— 'Vincent Alsop and the emancipation of Restoration Dissent', *Journal of Ecclesiastical History*, xxiv (1973), pp. 161-84.

Browning, A. *Thomas Osborne, Earl of Danby and Duke of Leeds, 1632-1712*, (3 vols, Glasgow 1944-51).

Carswell, J. *The Descent on England* (1969).

Chandaman, C. D. *The English Public Revenue, 1660-88* (Oxford 1975).

Cherry, G. L. 'The Legal and Philosophical Position of the Jacobites, 1688-9', *Journal of Modern History*, xii (1950), pp. 309-21.

—— The Convention Parliament, 1689 (New York 1966).

Childs, J. *The Army, James II and the Glorious Revolution* (Manchester 1980).

Cruickshanks, E., Hayton, D., Jones, C., 'Divisions in the House of Lords on the Transfer of the Crown and Other Issues, 1688-94', *Bulletin of the Institute of Historical Research*, liii (1980), pp. 56-87.

Evans, A. M. 'Yorkshire and the Revolution of 1688', *Yorkshire Archaeological Journal*, xxix (1929), pp. 258-85.

Feiling, K. G. *History of the Tory Party, 1640-1714* (Oxford 1924).

Foxcroft, H. C. *The Life and Letters of Sir George Savile, Marquis of Halifax* (2 vols, 1898).

Green, E. *The March of William of Orange through Somerset* (1892).

Haley, K. H. D. 'A List of the English Peers, *c.* May 1687', *English Historical Review*, lxix (1954), pp. 302-6.

Havighurst, A. F. 'James II and the Twelve Men in Scarlet', *Law Quarterly Review*, lxix (1953), pp. 522-46.

Hemphill, Dom Basil. *The Early Vicars Apostolic of England 1685-1750* (1954).

Henning, B. D. *The House of Commons 1660-1690* (3 vols, 1983).

Horwitz, H. *Revolution Politicks: The Career of Daniel Finch, Second Earl of Nottingham* (Cambridge 1968).

—— 'Parliament and the Glorious Revolution', *Bulletin of the Institute of Historical Research*, xlvii (1974), pp. 36-49.

Hosford, D. H. *Nottingham, Nobles and the North* (Hamden, Conn., 1976).

—— 'The Peerage and the Test Act: a List, *c.* November 1687', *Bulletin of the Institute of Historical Research*, xlii (1969), pp. 116-20.

Jones, G. H. *Charles Middleton* (Chicago 1967).

Jones, J. R. *The Revolution of 1688 in England* (1972).

Keeton, G. W. *Lord Chancellor Jeffreys and the Stuart Cause* (1965).

Kenyon, J. P. *The Nobility in the Revolution of 1688* (Inaugural Lecture, Hull 1963).

Landon, M. *The Triumph of the Lawyers: their Role in English Politics, 1678-1689* (Alabama 1970).

Lart, C. E. 'The Huguenot Regiments', *Proceedings of the Huguenot Society of London*, ix (1911), pp. 476-529.

Macaulay, T. B. *History of England from the Accession of James II* (ed. C. H. Firth, 6 vols, 1913).

Mackintosh, J. *History of the Revolution of 1688* (1834).

Miller, J. *Popery and Politics in England* (Cambridge, 1973).

—— *James II: A Study in Kingship* (1978).

Milne, D. J. 'The Results of the Rye House Plot and Their Influence upon the Revolution of 1688', *Transactions of the Royal Historical Society*, 5th series, i (1951), pp. 81-108.

Muilenburg, J. 'The Embassy of Everaard van Weede, Lord of Dykvelt, to England in 1687', *The University Studies of the University of Nebraska*, xx (1920), pp. 85-161.

Oliver, H. J. *Sir Robert Howard, 1626-1698* (Durham, North Carolina, 1963).

Pinkham, L. B. *William III and the Respectable Revolution* (Cambridge, Mass., 1954).

Plumb, J. H. *The Growth of Political Stability in England, 1675-1725* (1967)

—— 'The elections to the Convention Parliament of 1689', *Cambridge Historical Journal*, v (1937), pp. 235-54.

Powley, E. B. *The English Navy in the Revolution of 1688* (Cambridge 1928).

Prall, S. E. *The Bloodless Revolution in England* (New York 1972).

Ranke, L. von. *A History of England, Principally in the Seventeenth Century* (6 vols, Oxford 1875).

Sachse, W. L. 'The Mob and the Revolution of 1688', *Journal of British Studies*, iv (1964), pp. 23-40.

Simms, J. G. *Jacobite Ireland, 1685-91* (1969).

Straka, G. M. *The Revolution of 1688: Whig Triumph or Palace Revolution?* (Boston, Mass., 1963).

Turner, F. C. *James II* (1948).

Walker, J. 'The English Exiles in Holland during the Reigns of Charles II and James II', *Transactions of the Royal Historical Society*, 4th series, xxx (1948), pp. 111-125.

Western, J. R. *Monarchy and Revolution: The English State in the Sixteen Eighties* (1972).

Wood, A. C. 'The Revolution of 1688 in the North of England', *Transactions of the Thoroton Society of Nottinghamshire*, xliv (1940), pp. 72-104.

Woodhead, J. R. *The Rulers of London 1660-1689* (1965).

GAZETTEER OF PEERS

A: The Spirituality

Canterbury. Dr. William Sancroft, Archbishop of (1677). The pivot of the former 'Yorkist' reversionary interest, he had led the opposition to James's Catholic policies from Lambeth. He refused to attend the Convention. His 'strange obstinate passiveness' considerably weakened the loyalists' efforts to obtain a Regency. Loyalist. Later a Non-juror. Deprived of the Primacy by William.

York. Dr. Thomas Lamplugh, Archbishop of (nominated 15 Nov. 1688). A diligent diocesan and supporter of Sancroft's stand against Catholicism. He fled from Exeter on William's landing. Along with Turner, he tried to cement a better understanding with James at Whitehall on 17 Dec. 1688. Loyalist.

London. Dr. Henry Compton, rebel Bishop of (1675). Son of Spencer, 2nd Earl of Northampton. Suspended from his diocese (1686-88), he invited William over, and superintended Anne's flight to Nottingham. His assumption of arms against James caused grave scandal. He voted for declaring William and Mary king and queen on 31 Jan., against abdication on 4 Feb., and for abdication on 6 Feb. 1689. His initial preference was for recognizing Mary as sole sovereign.

Winchester. Dr. Peter Mews, Bishop of (1684). A former Royalist soldier, he was one of the most active Tories on the episcopal bench. The last prelate to see the King, whom he visited at Rochester between 18 and 22 Dec. 1688. Loyalist.

Durham. Dr. Nathaniel Crew, Bishop of (1674). The younger brother of Thomas, 2nd Baron Crew. A complete creature of James, when Duke of York, he was the most powerful of the Court's episcopal collaborators. Ecclesiastical Commissioner (1686-88). Absent from earlier divisions, he voted for abdication on 6 Feb. 1689.

Ely. Dr. Francis Turner, Bishop of (1684). A *protégé* of Sancroft and the Hyde brothers, he was the most politically adept of the loyalist bishops. Later a Non-juror and active Jacobite. Deprived of his See by William.

Rochester. Dr. Thomas Sprat, Bishop of (1684). Tory propagandist. Ecclesiastical Commissioner (1686-88), but latterly he repented his collaboration with the Court. Loyalist.

St. Asaph. Dr. William Lloyd, Bishop of (1680). A client of Henry, Earl of Clarendon. A former chaplain to Princess Mary. He admired William, and was only with difficulty brought to vote against abdication on 6 Feb. 1689. He was absent from the earlier votes.

Peterborough. Dr. Thomas White, Bishop of (1685). Basically a pastor, he was a gifted administrator and a supporter of Sancroft's drive for Anglican renewal in the dioceses. Loyalist. Later a Non-juror. Deprived of his See by William.

Chichester. Dr. John Lake, Bishop of (1685). Pastorally minded, he was one of Sancroft's ablest diocesans. Loyalist. Later a Non-juror. He was suspended from his See, but died on 30 Aug. 1689 before he could be deprived by William.

Bristol. Dr. Jonathan Trelawny, Bishop of (1685). Like Lloyd of St. Asaph, he was drawn into supporting William, but conformed to the loyalist line followed by all the bishops, save Compton, in the Convention.

B: The Temporalty

Abingdon. James Bertie, 1st Earl of (cr. 30 Nov. 1682). Ld Lt of Oxon (1674-87). High Steward of Oxford (16 Sept. 1687). Patron of the ejected Fellows of Magdalen College. The first peer to join William, to whose expedition he contributed £30,000. High church Tory, he rapidly became disillusioned with the Prince's Whig entourage. Loyalist.

Ailesbury. Thomas Bruce, 2nd Earl of (succ. 20 Oct. 1685). Ld Lt of Beds. and Hunts. (1685-89). Gentleman of the Bedchamber (23 Oct. 1688). He offered his sword to the King against William. High church Tory. Active loyalist. Later a Jacobite exile and Catholic convert.

Anglesey. James Annesley, 2nd Earl of (succ. 6 Apr. 1686). Former Whig MP for Winchester. He voted against abdication on 4 Feb. 1689, but was absent from other votes concerning the crown.

Astley. Jacob Astley, 3rd Baron Astley of Reading (succ. 1662). Absent from earlier votes, he voted for abdication on 6 Feb. 1689.

Bath. John Granville, 1st Earl of (cr. 20 Apr. 1661). Royalist. Ld Lt of Cornwall and Plymouth (1660-96) and Devon (1685-96). Tory magnate and electoral manager for the Court in the South-West. He corresponded with William before the invasion, and secured Plymouth, Devon, and Cornwall for him. Williamite.

Beaufort. Henry Somerset, 1st Duke of (cr. 2 Dec. 1682). Ld Lt of Glos., Herefs., and Mons. (1660-89) and Bristol (1673-89). Ld President of the Council in the Marches of Wales (1672-89). Gentleman of the Bedchamber. Tory magnate. Having briefly held Bristol against William, he retired with James's permission. He waited on William at Windsor (16 Dec. 1688), but was coldly received. Loyalist. Absent from earlier votes, he voted against abdication on 6 Feb. 1689.

Bedford. William Russell, 5th Earl of (succ. 1641). Parliamentarian. KG (1672). An ultra-Protestant, he was a leading patron of nonconformist clergy. Whig. His son, William, Lord Russell, a vehement Exclusionist and anti-Romanist, was executed for high treason in 1683. Staunch Williamite.

Berkeley. George Berkeley, 1st Earl of (cr. 11 Sept. 1679). Custos Rotulorum of Glos. (1660-89). Governor of the Levant Company (1673-96). Pr. Cllr (1685-Feb. 1689). Loyalist.

Berwick. James FitzJames, 1st Duke of (cr. 19 Mar. 1687), the elder of James II's two illegitimate sons by Arabella, sister of John, Lord Churchill. Professional soldier. Catholic. Ld Lt of Hants., and Governor of Portsmouth (1687-88). He left England with his father on 23 Dec. 1688. Later a Jacobite General.

Bolingbroke. Paulet St. John, 3rd Earl of (succ. 18 Mar. 1688). Former Whig MP for Bedford. Williamite.

Bridgwater. John Egerton, 3rd Earl of (succ. 26 Oct. 1686). Ld Lt of Bucks. (1686-87). Williamite.

Bristol. John Digby, 3rd Earl of (succ. 20 Mar. 1677). Williamite.

Burlington. Richard Boyle, 1st Earl of (cr. 20 Mar. 1664). Royalist. Ld Treasure of Ireland (1660-95). Ld Lt of West Riding, Yorks. (1679-Mar. 1688). Recorder of York (1685-88). Tory. Voted against declaring William and Mary king and queen on 31 Jan. 1689, after which he absented himself from the Lords.

Carlisle. Edward Howard, 2nd Earl of (succ. 24 Feb. 1685). Opposed to James's policies, he offered his service to William on 10 July 1688. An active Williamite.

Cartaret. George Cartaret, 1st Baron Cartaret of Hawnes (cr. 19 Oct. 1681). The son-in-law of John, Earl of Bath. Williamite.

Chandos. James Brydges, 8th Baron Chandos of Sudeley (succ. Aug. 1676). Diplomatist. A strong Tory. Loyalist.

Churchill. John Churchill, 1st Baron Churchill of Sandridge (cr. 14 May 1685). Gentleman of the Bedchamber (1685-Nov. 1688). Lt.-General (Nov. 1688). He deserted to William on 24 Nov. 1688. After opposing the declaration of William and Mary as king and queen on 31 Jan. 1689, he voted for abdication. He and his wife, Sarah, persuaded Princess Anne to accept William as King regnant.

Clare. John Holles, 4th Earl of (succ. 16 Jan. 1689). He was sounded out by Dijckveld in 1687. Whig MP for Notts. (1689). Williamite.

Clarendon. Henry Hyde, 2nd Earl of (succ. 19 Dec. 1674). A leading high church Tory. The former Anglican brother-in-law of the King. Ld Privy Seal (Feb.-Sept. 1685), Ld Lt of Ireland (Sept. 1685-Feb. 1687), Pr. Cllr (1680-89). His son, Edward, Lord Cornbury, was one of the first of James's officers to desert to William, who was his cousin. He joined William near Hindon on 3 Dec. 1688. Loyalist. Later a Jacobite and Non-juror, 'he did not close in the least with the Revolution, but stood firm to the last, though he almost wanted bread to eat'.

Cornwallis. John Cornwallis, 3rd Baron Cornwallis of Eye (succ. 1673). A former son-in-law of Sir Stephen Fox, he had on 6 May 1688 married Anne, *suo jure* Duchess of Buccleuch, widow of the executed rebel, James, Duke of Monmouth. Williamite.

Craven. William Craven, 1st Earl of (cr. 16 Mar. 1665). Royalist. Professional soldier. Colonel of the Coldstream Guards (1670-89). Ld Lt of Middx and Southwark. Lt.-General of James's army (1678-89). He submitted to William's orders on 11 Dec. 1688, and mobilized the Militia of Middx, Westminster, and Southwark to stem disorders in and about the capital. James refused his offer to resist William's forces in their take-over of the posts at Whitehall on 17 Dec. 1688.

Crew. Thomas Crew, 2nd Baron Crew of Stene (succ. 12 Dec. 1679). Elder brother of Dr. Nathaniel Crew, Bishop of Durham. Whig Exclusionist. He favoured a Regency, and voted against abdication on 4 and 6 Feb. 1689.

Culpepper (Colepeper). Thomas Colepeper, 2nd Baron Colepeper of Thoresway (succ. 11 July 1660). He disgraced himself by his unauthorised return from the Governorship of Virginia in 1682. A determined opponent of James at the Guildhall on 11 Dec. 1688. He died

on 27 Jan. 1689, and was succeeded by his Whig brother, John, 3rd Baron Colepeper, also a Williamite.

Danby. Thomas Osborne, 1st Earl of (cr. 27 June 1674). Former Ld High Treasurer (1673-79). Tory. He invited William over (30 June), and raised the North in support of his enterprise (Nov. 1688). Initially the chief advocate of Mary's independent claims to the crown following James's final flight, he switched to the support of William and Mary.

Dartmouth. George Legge, 1st Baron Dartmouth (cr. 2 Dec. 1682). Active Tory. Master General of the Ordnance and Armouries (24 Mar. 1685), Master of the Horse (31 Mar. 1685). Pr. Cllr (1682-89). Constable of the Tower of London (1685-89). Admiral of the Fleet (Oct. 1688), it was his misfortune not to command the loyalty of the Fleet. He submitted to William on 13 Dec. 1688. Loyalist. Later a suspected Jacobite.

Delamer. Henry Booth, 2nd Baron Delamer of Dunham Massey (succ. 8 Aug. 1684). Ultra-Protestant. Former Whig MP for Cheshire, he was implicated in Monmouth's Rebellion, but was acquitted in a trial for high treason by his peers (1686). He raised his tenants on 16 Nov., and with his cousin, the Earl of Stamford, joined forces with William at Hungerford on 7 Dec. 1688. Avid Williamite.

Delawarr. John West, 6th Baron Delawarr (succ. 22 Dec. 1687). Tory. Loyalist.

Devonshire. William Cavendish, 4th Earl of (succ. 23 Nov. 1684). Whig convert. He invited William over, and took up arms in his cause. A convinced Williamite.

Dorset. Charles Sackville, 6th Earl of Dorset (succ. 1677) and 1st Earl of Middlesex (cr. 4 Apr. 1675). Poet. He escorted Anne to Nottingham. Williamite.

Essex. Algernon Capel, 2nd Earl of (succ. 13 July 1683). He was absent from the debates on the crown..

Eure. Ralph Eure, 7th Baron Eure (succ. Oct. 1672). Whig. Williamite.

Fauconberg. Thomas Belasyse, 2nd Viscount Fauconberg (succ. 18 Apr. 1653). Son-in-law of Oliver Cromwell. Ld Lt of the North Riding of Yorks. (1660-87). One of William's correspondents in 1687. Staunch Williamite.

Feversham. Louis de Duras (De Durfort), 2nd Earl of Feversham (succ. 16 Apr. 1677). Nephew of Marshal Turenne. Naturalized Frenchman. Ld Chamberlain to Queen Catherine (1680-1705). Colonel of the Third Troop of Horse Guards (1685-89). Gentleman of the Bedchamber (1685-88). Lt.-General (1685), he commanded against Monmouth's rebels at Sedgemoor, and under the King at

Salisbury (Nov. 1688). Ld Lt of Kent (1688). In compliance with James's order he disbanded the royal forces, submitted to William, and requested permission for the safe withdrawal of the Irish forces on 11 Dec. 1688. At Faversham he again offered his sword to King James. Tory. Loyalist.

Godolphin. Sidney Godolphin, 1st Baron Godolphin of Rialton (cr. 28 Sept. 1684). He had advised Charles II to pass the Bill of Exclusion. Ld of the Treasury (1686-88). Pr. Cllr (1680-89). Ld Chamberlain to Queen Mary Beatrice (1685-88). One of James's Commissioners at Hungerford. Loyalist.

Grafton. Henry FitzRoy, 1st Duke of Grafton (cr. 11 Sept. 1675), the 2nd of Charles II's three illegitimate sons by Barbara Palmer, Duchess of Cleveland. Professional soldier. KG (1680). Colonel of the First Regiment of Foot Guards (1681-88). Brig.-General of Foot (1688). Governor of the Isle of Wight (1684-90). Ld Lt of Suffolk (1685-89). He deserted to William on 24 Nov. 1688, but, even so, in the Convention favoured a Regency.

Grey of Ruthin. Henry Yelverton, 15th Baron Grey of Ruthin (succ. 28 Jan. 1676). Tory. He took part in the Northern Rebellion. Williamite.

Grey of Warke. Ford Grey, 3rd Baron Grey of Warke (succ. 15 June 1675). Violent Whig Exclusionist. Implicated in the Rye House Conspiracy of 1683, he joined Monmouth's Rebellion in 1685, turned King's evidence, was pardoned, and restored in honours and blood by James. Active Williamite.

Halifax. George Savile, 1st Marquess of Halifax (cr. 22 Aug. 1682). A leading opponent of Exclusion. Ld President of the Council (Feb.-Dec. 1685). He opposed James's Catholic policies and wrote anonymously against them. He refused to join in inviting William over. He accepted with misgiving the role of chief Commissioner in the Hungerford embassy to William, and transferred his support to the Prince following James's first flight. Williamite chairman of the provisional government (12-15 Dec.), and of the assembly of Peers (22-25 Dec. 1688).

Hamilton. William Douglas, 1st Duke of (cr. 20 Sept. 1660) in the Scottish peerage. Pr. Cllr (Scotland, 1685-89; England, 14 Oct. 1687-Feb. 1689). KG (1682). Later President of the Scottish Convention at Edinburgh (14 Mar. 1689), which declared the throne vacant.

Hatton. Christopher Hatton, 1st Viscount Hatton of Gretton (cr. 17 Jan. 1683). Tory. Governor of Guernsey (1670-1706). Custos Rotulorum of Northants. (1681-89). He voted against declaring William and Mary king and queen on 31 Jan., and against abdication on 4 Feb., but absented himself at the final vote on 6 Feb. 1689.

Howard of Escrick. William Howard, 3rd Baron Howard of Escrick. Former Anabaptist preacher. Fomenter of the Popish Plot and Whig Exclusionist, he was Dryden's 'canting Nadab'. Rye House plotter who turned informer against John Hampden, William Lord Russell, and Algernon Sidney, he was pardoned. Absent from earlier votes, he voted for abdication on 6 Feb. 1689.

Jeffreys. George Jeffreys, 1st Baron Jeffreys of Wem (cr. 16 May 1685). Tory. Former Recorder of London (1678-80). Pr. Cllr (1683-1689). Ld Chancellor (28 Sept. 1685-Dec. 1688). Ld Lt Bucks. and Salop (1687-1689). He presided as Ld High Steward at Lord Delamere's trial for high treason (1686). Ecclesiastical Commissioner (1686-88). The most hated of James's Protestant collaborators.

Jermyn. Thomas Jermyn, 2nd Baron Jermyn of St. Edmundsbury (succ. 2 Jan. 1684). Elder brother of the Catholic Henry, 1st Baron Dover. Tory. Governor of Jersey (1685-1703). Loyalist.

Kent. Anthony Grey, 11th Earl of (succ. 1651). Having opposed declaring William and Mary king and queen on 31 Jan., and abdication on 4 Feb., he switched to supporting abdication on 6 Feb. 1689.

Lichfield. Edward Henry Lee, 1st Earl of (cr. 5 June 1674), husband of Charlotte FitzRoy, illegitimate daughter of Charles II by Barbara Palmer, Duchess of Cleveland. Gentleman of the Bedchamber (1685-88). Colonel of the First Regiment of Foot Guards (Nov. 1688). Ld Lt of Oxon (1687-88). High Tory. Loyalist. Later a Non-juror, and suspected Jacobite.

Lindsey. Robert Bertie, 3rd Earl of (succ. 1666). Ld Lt of Lincs. (1666-1700). Tory. Ld Great Chamberlain (1685-89). He favoured declaring William and Mary king and queen on 31 Jan., opposed abdication on 4 Feb., but switched his vote on 6 Feb. 1689.

Lovelace. John Lovelace, 3rd Baron Lovelace of Hurley (succ. 24 Sept. 1670). A violent Whig, he was implicated in the Rye House Conspiracy. He visited Holland in Sept. 1688. On 11 Nov. he was taken prisoner, when conducting 70 horse to William. He was rescued from Gloucester Goal and made Governor of the town. On 5 Dec. he occupied Oxford for William, whose *Declaration* 'was read openly to the multitude' on 6 Dec. 1688. Williamite.

Lucas. Robert Lucas, 3rd Baron Lucas of Shenfield (succ. *circa* 28 Nov. 1688), 'late a captain of foot in Ireland'. Williamite.

Lumley. Richard Lumley, 2nd Viscount Lumley of Waterford in the Irish peerage, and 1st Baron Lumley of Lumley Castle (cr. 31 May 1681). A Protestant convert from the Church of Rome. Professional soldier. Colonel of the Queen Dowager's

Regiment of Horse (1685-87). He helped to capture Monmouth in 1685. He invited William over (30 June). He eluded arrest in Oct. and Nov., and secured Newcastle for William in Dec. 1688. Active Williamite.

Macclesfield. Charles Gerard, 1st Earl of (cr. 21 July 1679). Royalist. Professional soldier. Whig. An intimate of Monmouth, he fled abroad in 1685. He returned with William and commanded his bodyguard at the landing (5 Nov.). Williamite. His son, Charles, Viscount Brandon, submitted to William on 11 Dec. 1688.

Manchester. Charles Montagu, 4th Earl of (succ. 14 Mar. 1683). Williamite.

Maynard. William Maynard, 2nd Baron Maynard of Estaines (succ. 17 Dec. 1640). Comptroller of the Household (1685-87). Tory. Loyalist.

Middleton. Charles Middleton, 2nd Earl of (succ. 3 July 1673) in the Scottish peerage. Principal Secretary of State (1684-89). Pr. Cllr (1684-89). Tory. His wife Catherine (née Brudenell), daughter of Robert, 2nd Earl of Cardigan, was a Catholic. Loyalist. Later a Jacobite exile.

Montagu. Ralph Montagu, 3rd Baron Montagu of Boughton (succ. 10 Jan. 1684). Former Master of the Great Wardrobe and Charles II's Ambassador to Louis XIV. Vehement Whig. His attempts to regain Court favour under James completely failed. Active Williamite.

Mordaunt. Charles Mordaunt, 2nd Viscount Mordaunt of Avalon (succ. 5 June 1675). Williamite.

Mulgrave. John Sheffield, 3rd Earl of (succ. 24 Aug. 1658). KG (1674). Tory. Pr. Cllr (24 July 1685-89). Ld Chamberlain of the Household (23 Oct. 1685-Dec. 88). Ecclesiastical Commissioner (1686-88). Ld Lt of the East Riding of Yorkshire (1687-88). James refused his request for a marquisate on 16 Dec. 1688, which he desired for his service in standing up for the King at Whitehall on the 13th. Thereafter he became a Williamite.

Newport. Francis Newport, 1st Viscount Newport of Bradford (cr. 11 Mar. 1675). Royalist. Ld Lt of Salop (1660-87), and Treasurer of the Household (1672-87). Tory. After his dismissal from office he became one of James's fiercest opponents. Williamite.

Norfolk. Henry Howard, 7th Duke of (succ. 1684). Protestant convert from the Church of Rome. Tory. Ld Lt of Berks., and Surrey (1682), and of Norfolk (1683-1701). KG (1685). Having voted against declaring William and Mary king and queen on 31 Jan., he voted for abdication on 4 and 6 Feb. 1689.

North and Grey. Charles North, 5th Baron North (succ. 24 June 1677) and Baron Grey of Rolleston (writ of summons 24 Oct. 1673). Whig. Williamite.

Northampton. George Compton, 4th Earl of (succ. 15 Dec. 1681). Nephew of Bishop Compton of London. Williamite.

Northumberland. George FitzRoy, 1st Duke of (cr. 6 Apr. 1683), 3rd of Charles II's illegitimate sons by Barbara Palmer, Duchess of Cleveland. KG (1684). Professional soldier. Gentleman of the Bedchamber (28 Nov. 1688), he was on duty the night of James's first flight. Though approached by his brother Grafton and Churchill, he had refused to join William. Loyalist.

Nottingham. Daniel Finch, 2nd Earl of (succ. 18 Dec. 1682). Tory. Pr. Cllr (1680-96), though he never sat in Council after the introduction of Fr. Edward Petre in 1687. Though it was expected that he would have joined in inviting William over, he declined on last minute scruples of conscience. A foremost advocate of a Regency. Loyalist.

Ormonde. James Butler, 2nd Duke of (succ. 21 July 1688). Tory. Gentleman of the Bedchamber (1685-29 Nov. 1688). He deserted to William (24 Nov.), but retained his allegiance. Successively son-in-law of Lawrence, 1st Earl of Rochester, and Henry, 1st Duke of Beaufort. Loyalist. After at first accepting the Revolution he later became a Jacobite.

Ossulston. John Bennet, 1st Baron Ossulston (cr. 24 Nov. 1682). A minor courtier who owed everything to his younger brother, Henry, 1st Earl of Arlington. He absented himself from all votes concerning the crown.

Oxford. Aubrey de Vere, 20th Earl of (succ. 1632). KG (1661). Professional soldier. An impoverished Tory. Pr. Cllr (1681). Colonel of the Royal Regiment of Horse, 'Oxford's Blues' (1661-88). Ld Lt of Essex (1685-1703). He joined William on 5 Dec. 1688. Williamite.

Paget. William Paget, 7th Baron Paget of Beaudesert (succ. 19 Oct. 1678). Whig. He seems to have favoured declaring Mary queen after James's withdrawal on 23 Dec. 1688, but voted for William and Mary in the Convention.

Pembroke. Thomas Herbert, 8th Earl of Pembroke and Montgomery (succ. 29 Aug. 1683). Tory. Ld Lt of Wilts. (1683-87). Though one of William's correspondents, he offered his services to James on the Prince's landing. An advocate of a Regency. Loyalist.

Preston. Richard Grahme, 1st Viscount Preston (cr. 12 May 1681) in the Scottish peerage. Tory. Pr. Cllr (21 Oct. 1685-17 Dec. 1688). Master of the Great Wardrobe

(1685-88). Ld Lt of Cumberland and Westmorland (29 Aug. 1687-88). Principal Secretary of State (28 Oct. 1688-89). Cr. 1st Viscount Preston in the English peerage at St. Germain-en-Laye (21 Jan. 1689), but the House of Lords subsequently held James's patent to be void. Later a Jacobite.

Radnor. Charles Robartes, 2nd Earl of (succ. 17 July 1685). Probably he was opposed to Exclusion like his father, but sided with William in 1688. Williamite.

Ranelagh. Richard Jones, 1st Earl of (cr. 11 Dec. 1677) in the Irish peerage. Tory. Paymaster-General of the Army (1685-1702).

Rivers. Thomas Savage, 3rd Earl Rivers (succ. 10 Oct. 1654). Whig. Father of Richard Savage, Viscount Colchester, Whig MP for Wigan (1681) and an army plotter, who joined William at Exeter. Williamite.

Rochester. Lawrence Hyde, 1st Earl of Rochester (cr. 29 Nov. 1682). High church Tory. Younger brother of Henry, 2nd Earl of Clarendon, and former brother-in-law of James. Ld High Treasurer (1685-87). KG (1685). Ecclesiastical Commissioner (1686-88). Ld Lt of Herts. (1687-89). He was slighted by William at Windsor (16 Dec. 1688). A major advocate of a Regency. Unlike his brother, he accepted the Revolution, and took the oaths to William and Mary, his nephew and niece.

Salisbury. James Cecil, 4th Earl of (succ. May 1683). High Steward of Hertford (9 Aug. 1688). Colonel of a Regiment of Horse (5 Nov.). Gentleman of the Bedchamber (29 Nov. 1688). Catholic convert from the Church of England.

Saye and Sele. William Fiennes, 3rd Viscount (succ. 1674). He was absent from all the votes concerning the crown.

Scarsdale. Robert Leke, 3rd Earl of (succ. 27 Jan. 1681). Ld Lt of Derbys., and Colonel of Princess Anne's Regiment of Horse (1685-87). Groom of the Stole to Prince George of Denmark. He joined William, but opposed his interest in the crown. Loyalist. Later a suspected Jacobite.

Shrewsbury. Charles Talbot, 12th Earl of (succ. 1668). Protestant convert from the Church of Rome. Ld Lt of Staffs. (1681-87). Colonel of the 7th Regiment of Horse (1685-87). He invited William over (30 June), took money into Holland (Sept.), and returned with William (5 Nov.). He occupied Bristol for William (1 Dec. 1688). Williamite.

Somerset. Charles Seymour, 6th Duke of (succ. 20 April 1678). Tory. Ld Lt of the East Riding of Yorks. (1682-87) and

Somerset (1683-87). Gentleman of the Bedchamber (1685-87). Though he joined William, he opposed his interest in the Convention. Loyalist.

Stamford. Thomas Grey, 2nd Earl of (succ. 1673). Whig. Imprisoned in the Tower for suspected complicity in the Rye House Conspiracy (1683) and Monmouth's Rebellion (1685), he was pardoned by James (27 Mar. 1686). Close collaborator with his cousin, Henry, 2nd Baron Delamer. Williamite.

Suffolk. James Howard, 3rd Earl of (succ. 3 June 1640). Whig. He died on 7 Jan. 1689.

Sussex. Thomas Lennard, 1st Earl of (cr. 5 Oct. 1674). An ultra-Protestant. Estranged husband of Anne FitzRoy, Charles II's illegitimate daughter by Barbara Palmer, Duchess of Cleveland. Williamite.

Thanet. Thomas Tufton, 6th Earl of (succ. 8 Mar. 1684). High church Tory. Ld Lt of Westmorland and Cumberland (1685-87). Son-in-law of Henry Cavendish, 2nd Duke of Newcastle. He voted against declaring William and Mary king and queen on 31 Jan., and against abdication on 4 Feb., but voted for it on 6 Feb. 1689.

Vaughan (Carbery). John Vaughan, 2nd Baron Vaughan of Emlyn (succ. 3 Dec. 1686), and 3rd Earl of Carbery (succ. 3 Dec. 1686) in the Irish peerage. Whig. Son-in-law of George, 1st Marquess of Halifax. Williamite.

Westmorland. Charles Fane, 3rd Earl of (succ. 12 Feb. 1666). Tory. Loyalist.

Weymouth. Thomas Thynne, 1st Viscount Weymouth (cr. 11 Dec. 1682). High church Tory. He favoured a Regency. He voted against declaring William and Mary king and queen on 31 Jan., and against abdication on 4 Feb., but was absent on 6 Feb. 1689. Later a patron of the Non-juring clergy.

Wharton. Philip Wharton, 4th Baron Wharton (succ. 1625). Veteran puritan and Parliamentarian. Whig. A patron of nonconformist clergy. Williamite.

Winchilsea. Heneage Finch, 3rd Earl of. Tory. Ld Lt of Kent (1673-87). On 12 Dec. 1688 James sent from Faversham for him, and re-appointed him to his Lieutenancy. Williamite.

Yarmouth. William Paston, 2nd Earl of (succ. 8 Mar. 1683). Strong Tory. Treasurer of the Household (1687-89). Joint Ld Lt of Wilts. (20 Feb. 1688-89). Later a Non-juror and Jacobite sympathizer.

INDEX

This index does not include references to peers acting as signatories to the orders of the provisional government and assembly of peers. Variant spellings of personal names in the manuscript of the Journal are given in brackets. Numbers in *italic* refer to the illustrations.